Mac OS X Tiger for Unix Geeks

Brian Jepson and Ernest E. Rothman

O'REILLY®

Beijing · Cambridge · Farnham · Köln · Paris · Sebastopol · Taipei · Tokyo

Mac OS X Tiger for Unix Geeks
by Brian Jepson and Ernest E. Rothman

Printed in the United States of America.

Published by O'Reilly Media, Inc., 1005 Gravenstein Highway North, Sebastopol, CA 95472.

O'Reilly books may be purchased for educational, business, or sales promotional use. Online editions are also available for most titles (*safari.oreilly.com*). For more information, contact our corporate/institutional sales department: (800) 998-9938 or *corporate@oreilly.com*.

Editor: Chuck Toporek

Production Editor: Mary Brady

Cover Designer: Ellie Volckhausen

Interior Designer: David Futato

Printing History:

October 2002:	First Edition. Originally published under the title *Mac OS X for Unix Geeks*.
February 2004:	Second Edition. Originally published under the title *Mac OS X Panther for Unix Geeks*.
May 2005:	Third Edition.

This book uses RepKover™, a durable and flexible lay-flat binding.

ISBN: 0-596-00912-7
[M]

Table of Contents

Part II. Building Applications

Part III. Working with Packages

Part IV. Serving and System Management

Part V. Appendixes

Preface

Once upon a time, Unix came with only a few standard utilities and, if you were lucky, included a C compiler. When setting up a new Unix system, you'd have to crawl the Net looking for important software: Perl, *gcc*, *bison*, *flex*, *less*, Emacs, and other utilities and languages. That was a lot of software to download through a 28.8-Kbps modem. These days, Unix distributions come with much more, and it seems like more and more users are gaining access to a wide-open pipe.

Free Linux distributions pack most of the GNU tools onto a CD-ROM, and now commercial Unix systems are catching up. IRIX includes a big selection of GNU utilities, Solaris comes with a companion CD of free software, and just about every flavor of Unix (including Mac OS X) now includes Perl. Mac OS X comes with many tools, most of which are open source and complement the tools associated with Unix.

This book serves as a bridge for Unix developers and system administrators who've been lured to Mac OS X because of its Unix roots. When you first launch the Terminal application, you'll find yourself at home in a Unix shell, but like Apple's credo, "Think Different," you'll soon find yourself doing things a little differently. Some of the standard Unix utilities you've grown accustomed to may not be there, */etc/passwd* and */etc/group* have been supplanted with something called NetInfo, and when it comes to developing applications, you'll find that things like library linking and compiling have a few new twists to them.

Despite all the beauty of Mac OS X's Aqua interface, you'll find that some things are different on the Unix side. But rest assured, they're easy to deal with if you know what to do. This book is your survival guide for taming the Unix side of Mac OS X.

Audience for This Book

This book is aimed at Unix developers, a category that includes programmers who switched to Linux from a non-Unix platform, web developers who spend most of their time in *~/public_html* over an *ssh* connection, and experienced Unix hackers. In catering to such a broad audience, we chose to include some material that advanced users might consider basic. However, this choice makes the book accessible to all Unix programmers who switch to Mac OS X as their operating system of choice, whether they have been using Unix for one year or ten. If you are coming to Mac OS X with no Unix background, we suggest that you start with *Learning Unix for Mac OS X Tiger* by Dave Taylor (O'Reilly) to get up to speed with the basics.

Organization of This Book

This book is divided into five parts. *Part I* helps you map your current Unix knowledge to the world of Mac OS X. *Part II* discusses compiling and linking applications. *Part III* takes you into the world of Fink and covers packaging. *Part IV* discusses using Mac OS X as a server and provides some basic system management information. *Part V* provides useful reference information.

Here's a brief overview of what's in the book:

Part I, *Getting Around*
: This part of the book orients you to Mac OS X's unique way of expressing its Unix personality.

  Chapter 1, *Inside the Terminal*
  : This chapter provides you with an overview of the Terminal application, including a discussion of the differences between the Terminal and the standard Unix *xterm*.

  Chapter 2, *Searching and Metadata*
  : Mac OS X Tiger introduces Spotlight, a new subsystem for searching your Mac. In this chapter, you'll learn how to access this powerful metadata store from the command line.

  Chapter 3, *The Mac OS X Filesystem*
  : Here you'll learn about the layout of the Mac OS X filesystem, as well as descriptions of key directories and files.

  Chapter 4, *Startup*
  : This chapter describes the Mac OS X boot process, from when the Apple icon first appears on your display to when the system is up and running.

Chapter 5, *Directory Services*
: Use this chapter to get started with Mac OS X's powerful system for Directory Services, which replaces or complements the standard Unix flat files in the */etc* directory.

Chapter 6, *Printing*
: This chapter explains how to set up a printer under Mac OS X and shows you around CUPS, the open source printing engine under Mac OS X's hood.

Chapter 7, *The X Window System*
: In this chapter, you'll learn how to install and work with the X Window System on Mac OS X.

Chapter 8, *Multimedia*
: This chapter discusses working with multimedia, including burning CDs, displaying video, and manipulating images.

Chapter 9, *Third-Party Tools and Applications*
: This chapter introduces some third-party applications that put a new spin on Unix features, such as virtual desktops, SSH frontends, and TeX applications.

Chapter 10, *Dual-Boot and Beyond*
: Mac OS X isn't the only operating system you can run on your Mac. In this chapter, you'll learn how you can run many operating systems on your Mac, perhaps even two or three at a time.

Part II, *Building Applications*
: Although Apple's C compiler is based on the GNU Compiler Collection (GCC), there are important differences between compiling and linking on Mac OS X and on other platforms. This part of the book describes these differences.

Chapter 11, *Compiling Source Code*
: This chapter describes the peculiarities of the Apple C compiler, including using macros that are specific to Mac OS X, working with precompiled headers, and configuring a source tree for Mac OS X.

Chapter 12, *Libraries, Headers, and Frameworks*
: Here we'll discuss building libraries, linking, and miscellaneous porting issues you may encounter with Mac OS X.

Part III, *Working with Packages*
: There are a good number of packaging options for software that you compile, as well as software you obtain from third parties. This part of the book covers software packaging on Mac OS X.

Chapter 13, *Fink*

In this chapter, you'll learn all about Fink, a package management system and porting effort that brings many open source applications to Mac OS X.

Chapter 14, *DarwinPorts*

DarwinPorts offers another way to install lots of open source software on your Mac. You'll learn all about it in this chapter.

Chapter 15, *Creating and Installing Packages*

This chapter describes the native package formats used by Mac OS X, as well as packaging options you can use to distribute applications.

Part IV, *Serving and System Management*

This part of the book talks about using Mac OS X as a server, as well as system administration.

Chapter 16, *Using Mac OS X as a Server*

In this chapter, you'll learn about setting up your Macintosh to act as a server, selectively letting traffic in (even through a Small Office/Home Office firewall such as the one found in the AirPort base station), and setting up Postfix.

Chapter 17, *System Management Tools*

This chapter describes commands for monitoring system status and configuring the operating system.

Chapter 18, *Free Databases*

This chapter explains how to set up and configure MySQL and PostgreSQL, and how to work with SQLite, the embeddable lightweight SQL system that comes with Mac OS X.

Chapter 19, *Perl and Python*

This chapter describes the versions of Perl and Python that ship with Mac OS X, as well as optional modules that can make your experience that much richer.

Part V, *Appendixes*

The final part of the book includes miscellaneous reference information.

Appendix A, *Mac OS X GUI Primer*

If you are totally new to Mac OS X, this appendix will get you up to speed with the basics of its user interface and introduce terminology that we'll use throughout the book.

Appendix B, *Mac OS X's Unix Development Tools*

This appendix provides a list of various development tools, along with brief descriptions.

Xcode Tools

This book assumes that you have installed the Xcode Tools, which includes the latest version of *gcc*, ported by Apple. If you bought the boxed version of Mac OS X, Xcode should be included on a separate CD-ROM. If you bought a boxed version of Mac OS X Tiger, you can find the installer for Xcode in the Xcode folder on the same DVD that you used to install Tiger. Failing either of those, or if you'd like to get the latest version of the tools, they are available to Apple Developer Connection (ADC) members at *http://connect.apple.com*.

Where to Go for More Information

Although this book will get you started with the Unix underpinnings of Mac OS X, there are many online resources that can help you get a better understanding of Unix for Mac OS X:

Apple's Open Source Mailing Lists
: This site leads to all the Apple-hosted Darwin mailing lists, and includes links to list archives.

  http://developer.apple.com/darwin/mail.html

The Darwin Project
: Darwin is a complete Unix operating system for x86 and PowerPC processors. Mac OS X is based on the Darwin project. Spend some time at the project's web page to peek as deep under Mac OS X's hood as is possible.

  http://developer.apple.com/darwin/

Open Darwin
: The Open Darwin project was founded in 2002 by Apple Computer and the Internet Software Consortium, Inc. (ISC). It is an independent project with a CVS repository that is separate from Apple's Darwin project, but it aims for full binary compatibility with Mac OS X.

  http://www.opendarwin.org/

Fink
: Fink is a collection of open source Unix software that has been ported to Mac OS X. It is based on the Debian package management system, and includes utilities to easily mix precompiled binaries and software built from source. Fink also includes complete GNOME and KDE desktop distributions.

  http://fink.sourceforge.net/

DarwinPorts
DarwinPorts is a project of OpenDarwin that provides a unified porting system for Darwin, Mac OS X, FreeBSD, and Linux. At the time of this writing, it includes thousands of ports, including the GNOME desktop system.

http://darwinports.opendarwin.org/

GNU-Darwin
Like Fink, GNU-Darwin brings many free Unix applications to Darwin and Mac OS X. GNU-Darwin uses the FreeBSD ports system, which automates source code and patch distribution, as well as compilation, installation, and resolution of dependencies.

http://gnu-darwin.sourceforge.net/

Mac OS X Hints
Mac OS X Hints presents a collection of reader-contributed tips, along with commentary from people who have tried the tips. It includes an extensive array of Unix tips.

http://www.macosxhints.com/

Stepwise
Before Mac OS X, Stepwise was the definitive destination for OpenStep and WebObjects programmers. Now Stepwise provides news, articles, and tutorials for Cocoa and WebObjects programmers.

http://www.stepwise.com/

VersionTracker
VersionTracker keeps track of software releases for Mac OS X and other operating systems.

http://www.versiontracker.com/

MacUpdate
MacUpdate also tracks software releases for Mac OS X.

http://www.macupdate.com/

FreshMeat's Mac OS X Section
FreshMeat catalogs and tracks the project history of thousands of mostly open source applications.

http://osx.freshmeat.net/

Conventions Used in This Book

The following typographical conventions are used in this book:

Italic
: Used to indicate new terms, example URLs, filenames, file extensions, directories, commands and options, Unix utilities, and to highlight comments in examples. For example, a path in the filesystem will appear in the text as */Applications/Utilities*.

`Constant width`
: Used to show functions, variables, keys, attributes, the contents of files, or the output from commands.

`Constant width bold`
: Used in examples and tables to show commands or other text that should be typed literally by the user.

`Constant width italic`
: Used in examples and tables to show text that should be replaced with user-supplied values.

Menus/Navigation
: Menus and their options are referred to in the text as File → Open, Edit → Copy, etc. Arrows are also used to signify a navigation path when using window options; for example: System Preferences → Accounts → *`username`* → Password means that you would launch System Preferences, click the icon for the Accounts preference panel, select the appropriate *`username`*, and then click on the Password pane within that panel.

Pathnames
: Pathnames are used to show the location of a file or application in the filesystem. Directories (or *folders* for Mac and Windows users) are separated by a forward slash. For example, if you're told to "...launch the Terminal application (*/Applications/Utilities*)," it means you can find the Terminal application in the Utilities subfolder of the Application folder.

$, #
: The dollar sign ($) is used in some examples to show the user prompt for the *bash* shell; the hash mark (#) is the prompt for the *root* user.

↵
: Used in place of a carriage return.

These icons signify a tip, suggestion, or a general note.

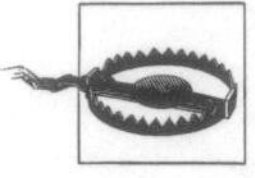

These icons indicate a warning or caution.

Menu symbols

When looking at the menus for any application, you will see some symbols associated with keyboard shortcuts for a particular command. For example, to open a document in Microsoft Word, you could go to the File menu and select Open (File → Open), or you could issue the keyboard shortcut, ⌘-O.

Figure P-1 shows the symbols used in the various menus to denote a keyboard shortcut.

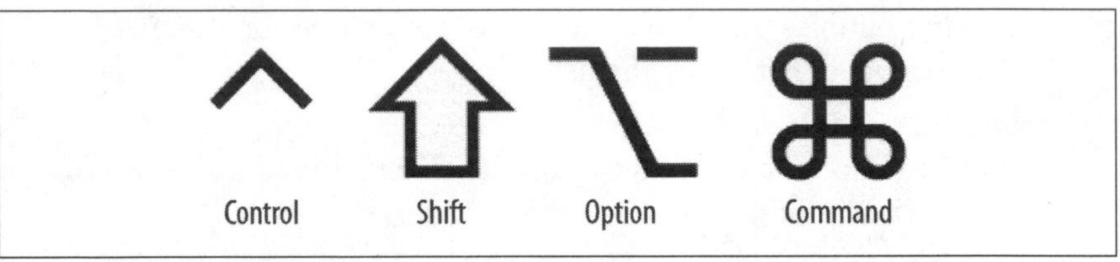

Figure P-1. These symbols, used in Mac OS X's menus, are used for issuing keyboard shortcuts so you can quickly work with an application without having to use the mouse.

Rarely will you see the Control symbol used as a menu command option; it's more often used in association with mouse clicks to emulate a right click on a two-button mouse or for working with the bash shell.

Comments and Questions

Please address comments and questions concerning this book to the publisher:

O'Reilly Media, Inc.
1005 Gravenstein Highway North
Sebastopol, CA 95472
(800) 998-9938 (in the United States or Canada)
(707) 829-0515 (international/local)
(707) 829-0104 (fax)

To comment or ask technical questions about this book, send email to:

bookquestions@oreilly.com

We have a web site for the book, where we list examples, errata, and any plans for future editions. The site also includes a link to a forum where you can discuss the book with the author and other readers. You can access this site at:

http://www.oreilly.com/catalog/macxtigerunix/

For more information about books, conferences, Resource Centers, and the O'Reilly Network, see the O'Reilly web site at:

http://www.oreilly.com

Safari Enabled

When you see a Safari® Enabled icon on the cover of your favorite technology book, it means the book is available online through the O'Reilly Network Safari Bookshelf.

Safari offers a solution that's better than e-books. It's a virtual library that lets you easily search thousands of top technology books, cut and paste code samples, download chapters, and find quick answers when you need the most accurate, current information. Try it for free at *http://safari.oreilly.com*.

Acknowledgments from the Previous Editions

This book builds on *Mac OS X for Unix Geeks*, for which we had help from a number of folks:

- The folks at the ADC, for technical review and handholding in so many tough spots!
- Erik Ray, for some early feedback and pointers to areas of library linking pain.
- Simon St.Laurent for feedback on early drafts, and prodding us towards more Fink coverage.
- Chris Stone, for tech review and helpful comments on the Terminal application.
- Tim O'Reilly, for deep technical and editorial help.
- Brett McLaughlin, for lots of great technical comments as well as helpful editorial ones.
- Brian Aker, for detailed technical review and feedback on Unixy details.

- Chuck Toporek, for editing, tech review, and cracking the whip when we needed it.
- Elaine Ashton and Jarkko Hietaniemi, for deeply detailed technical review, and help steering the book in a great direction.
- Steven Champeon, for detailed technical review and help on Open Firmware and the boot process.
- Simon Cozens, for technical review and pushing us toward including an example of how to build a Fink package.
- Wilfredo Sanchez, for an immense amount of detail on everything, and showing us the right way to do a startup script under Jaguar. His feedback touched nearly every aspect of the book, without which there would have been gaping holes and major errors.
- Andy Lester, Chris Stone, and James Duncan Davidson for reviewing parts of the book and pointing out spots that needed touching up.

Acknowledgments from Brian Jepson

Thanks to Nathan Torkington, Rael Dornfest, and Chuck Toporek for helping shape and launch this book, and to Ernie Rothman for joining in to make it a reality. Thanks also to Jason Deraleau who started out assisting Chuck with some editing tasks, but then left to go write a book of his own. I'd especially like to thank my wife, Joan, and my stepsons, Seiji and Yeuhi, for their support and encouragement through my late night and weekend writing sessions, my zealous rants about the virtues of Mac OS X, and the slow but steady conversion of our household computers to Macintoshes.

Acknowledgments from Ernest E. Rothman

I would first like to thank Brian Jepson, who conceived the book and was generous enough to invite me to participate in its development. I would like to express my gratitude to both Brian and Chuck Toporek for their encouragement, patience, stimulating discussions, and kindness. I am also grateful to reviewers for useful suggestions and insights, to visionary folks at Apple Computer for producing and constantly improving Mac OS X, and to developers who spend a great deal of time writing applications and posting helpful insights on newsgroups, mailing lists, and web sites. Finally, I am very grateful to my lovely wife, Kim, for her love, patience, and encouragement, and to my Newfoundland dogs, Max and Joe, for their love, and patience.

PART I

Getting Around

This part of the book orients you to Mac OS X's unique way of expressing its Unix personality. You'll start out with a quick overview of the Terminal application—Mac OS X's Unix interface—and then go on to learn more about Spotlight and searching, the filesystem, startup processes, and more. You'll also see how to run Linux on your Mac, as well as how to run Mac OS X on x86 PCs.

Chapters in this part of the book include:

CHAPTER 1

Inside the Terminal

The Terminal application (*/Applications/Utilities*) is Mac OS X's graphical terminal emulator. Inside the Terminal, Unix users will find a familiar command-line environment. In this chapter we describe Terminal's capabilities and compare them to the corresponding *xterm* functionality when appropriate. We also highlight key features of another Aqua-native terminal application, iTerm. The chapter concludes with a synopsis of the *open* command, which you can use to launch Aqua applications from the Terminal.

Mac OS X Shells

Mac OS X comes with the Bourne-Again shell (*bash*) as the default user shell and also includes the TENEX C shell (*tcsh*), the Korn shell (*ksh*), and the Z shell (*zsh*). The *bash, ksh,* and *zsh* are *sh*-compatible. When *tcsh* is invoked through the *csh* link, it behaves much like *csh*. Similarly, */bin/sh* is a hard link to *bash*, which also reverts to traditional behavior when invoked through this link (see the *bash* manpage for more information).

The version of *bash* that ships with Tiger has improved POSIX support over *bash* implementations that shipped with earlier releases of Mac OS X. Invoking *bash* with the *-posix* command-line option changes the default behavior of *bash* to comply with the POSIX 1003.2 standard in cases where the default behavior differs from this standard.

If you install additional shells, you should add them to */etc/shells*. To change the Terminal's default shell, see "Customizing the Terminal," later in this chapter. To change a user's default shell (used for both the Terminal and remote console logins), see "Modifying a User" in Chapter 5.

The Terminal and xterm Compared

There are several differences between Mac OS X's Terminal application and the *xterm* and *xterm*-like applications common to Unix systems running X Windows:

- You cannot customize the characteristics of the Terminal with command-line switches such as *–fn*, *–fg*, and *–bg*. Instead, you must use the Terminal Inspector.
- Unlike *xterm*, in which each window corresponds to a separate process, a single master process controls ⌘the Terminal. However, each shell session is run as a separate child process of the Terminal.
- The Terminal selection is not automatically put into the clipboard. Use ⌘-C to copy, and ⌘-V to paste. Even before you press ⌘-C, the current text selection is contained in a selection called the *pasteboard*. One similarity between Terminal and *xterm* is that selected text can be pasted in the same window with the middle button of a three-button mouse. If you want to paste selected text into another window, you must drag and drop it with the mouse or use copy and paste. The operations described in "The Services Menu section of this chapter also use the pasteboard.
- The value of `$TERM` is `xterm-color` when running under Terminal (it's set to `xterm` under *xterm* by default).
- Pressing ⌘-Page Up or ⌘-Page Down scrolls the Terminal window, rather than letting the running program handle it.
- On compatible systems (generally, a system with at least an ATI Radeon or NVidia GeForce AGP graphics adapter), the Terminal (and all of the Aqua user interface) uses Quartz Extreme acceleration to make everything faster and smoother.

If you need an *xterm*, you can have it; however, you must first install Apple's X11 package, which is bundled with Mac OS X Tiger as an optional installation. See Chapter 7 for more information about the X Window System.

There are also Aqua-native applications that offer an alternative to Apple's Terminal, such as the freeware iTerm. We'll have more to say about iTerm later in this chapter.

Using the Terminal

The first order of business when exploring a new flavor of Unix is to find the command prompt. In Mac OS X, you won't find the command prompt in the Dock or on a Finder menu. Instead, you'll need to use the Terminal

Enabling the root User

By default, the Mac OS X *root* user account is disabled, so you have to use *sudo* to perform administrative tasks. Even the most advanced Mac OS X users should be able to get by with *sudo*, and we suggest that you do *not* enable the *root* user account. However, if you must enable the *root* user account, start NetInfo Manager (*/Applications/Utilities*), click the lock to authenticate yourself, and select Security → Enable Root User.

application, located in */Applications/Utilities*. Don't open it just yet, though. First, drag Terminal's application icon to the Dock so you'll have quick access to it when you need to access the command line. To launch the Terminal, click its icon in the Dock once, or double-click on its icon in the Finder.

The full path to the Terminal is */Applications/Utilities/Terminal.app*, although the Finder hides the *.app* extension. *Terminal.app* is not a binary file. Instead, it's a Mac OS X *bundle*, which contains a collection of files, including the binary and support files for the Terminal's user interface.

You can Control-click (or right-click) on the Terminal in the Finder and select Show Package Contents to see what's inside. You can also use the Unix commands *ls* and *cd* to explore the directory */Applications/Utilities/Terminal.app*.

After the Terminal starts, you are greeted by the banner message from */etc/motd* and a *bash* prompt, as shown in Figure 1-1.

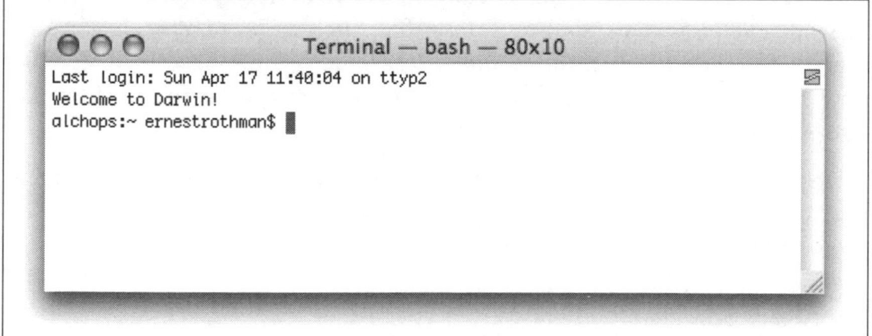

Terminal — bash — 80x10
Last login: Sun Apr 17 11:40:04 on ttyp2
Welcome to Darwin!
alchops:~ ernestrothman$

Figure 1-1. The Terminal window

Launching Terminals

One difference *xterm* users will notice is that there is no obvious way to launch a new Terminal window from the command line. For example, the Mac OS X Terminal has no equivalent to the following commands:

```
xterm &
xterm -e -fg green -bg black -e pine -name pine -title pine &
```

Instead, you create a new Terminal window by pressing ⌘-N or selecting File → New Shell from the menu bar.

To cycle between open Terminal windows, you can use the same keystroke that most other Mac OS X applications use: ⌘-`. You can also switch between windows by pressing ⌘-Right Arrow or ⌘-Left Arrow, using the Window menu, or by using the Terminal's Dock menu. You can also jump to a particular Terminal window with ⌘-*number* (see the Window menu for a list of numbers).

You can customize startup options for new Terminal windows by creating *.term* and *.command* files.

.term files

You can launch a customized Terminal window from the command line by saving some prototypical Terminal settings to a *.term* file and then using the *open* command to launch the *.term* file. (For more information on *open*, see "The open Command section, later in this chapter.) To create a *.term* file, open a new Terminal window, and then open the Terminal Inspector (File → Show Info or ⌘-I) and set the desired attributes, such as window size, fonts, and colors. When the Terminal's attributes have been set, save the Terminal session (File → Save or ⌘-S) to a *.term* file, such as *proto.term*. If you save this file to *~/Library/Application Support/Terminal*, you'll be able to launch a new Terminal window with the *proto.term* file's special attributes from the File → Library menu.

Alternatively, you can launch such a Terminal window from the command line by issuing the following command (depending on where you saved *proto.term*):

```
open ~/Library/Application\ Support/Terminal/proto.term
open ~/Documents/proto.term
```

You can also double-click on *proto.term* in the Finder to launch a Terminal window.

The *.term* file is an XML property list (*plist*) that you can edit with a text editor like *vim* (it can be invoked with *vi*, which is a symbolic link to *vim*) or with the *Property List Editor* application (*/Developer/Applications/Utilities*).* By default, opening the *.term* file creates a new Terminal window. You can configure the window so it executes a command by adding an *execution string* to the *.term* file. When you launch the Terminal, this string is echoed to standard output before it is executed. Example 1-1 shows an execution string that connects to a remote host via *ssh* and exits when you log out.

Example 1-1. An execution string to connect to a remote host

```
<key>ExecutionString</key>
<string>ssh xyzzy.oreilly.com; exit</string>
```

.command files

Adding the *.command* extension to any executable shell script turns it into a double-clickable executable. The effect is similar to that of a *.term* file, except that you can't control the Terminal's characteristics in the same way. (A *.command* file uses the Terminal's default settings.) However, you can stuff the shell script full of *osascript* commands to set the Terminal characteristics after it launches. The *osascript* utility lets you run AppleScript from the command line.† Example 1-2 is a shell script that sets the size and title of the Terminal, and then launches the *pico* editor.

Example 1-2. Launching the pico editor

```
#!/bin/sh
# Script RunPico.command
osascript  <<EOF
tell app "Terminal"
  set number of rows of first window to 34
  set number of columns of first window to 96
  set custom title of first window to "PICO Editor"
end tell
EOF
pico $@
```

If you don't want to give the shell a *.command* extension, you could also use the Finder's Get Info option (File → Get Info or ⌘-I) to choose which application opens the executable. To do this, perform the following steps:

1. Highlight the script's icon in the Finder.

* For more information on XML, see *Learning XML* (O'Reilly) or *XML in a Nutshell* (O'Reilly).

† More details on Scripting are covered in this book in Chapter 19. To learn more about AppleScript, see *AppleScript: The Definitive Guide* (O'Reilly).

2. Choose Get Info from the File menu (⌘-I).
3. In the Get Info dialog, choose "Open with."
4. Click the drop-down menu and choose Other.
5. In the Choose Other Application dialog, select All Applications rather than Recommended Applications.
6. Find and choose the Terminal (*/Applications/Utilities*) application.
7. Click Add.
8. Close the Get Info window (⌘-W).

You can assign a custom-made icon to your shell scripts, and place them in the right section of the Dock. You can also drag the executable's icon to the lower section of the Finder's Sidebar, although this section of the Finder is intended primarily for quick access to frequently visited folders. To change an icon, use the following procedure:

1. Copy the desired icon to the clipboard.
2. Select your script in the Finder and open the Get Info window (⌘-I). The file's icon appears in the upper-left corner.
3. Click the current icon, and use the Paste option (Edit → Paste or ⌘-V) to paste the new icon over it.
4. Close the Get Info window (⌘-W) to save the icon to the application.

To add the shell script application to the Dock, locate the application in the Finder and drag its icon to the Dock. Now you can click on the script's Dock icon to invoke the script.

Split Screen Terminal Feature

You can split a Terminal window (see Figure 1-2) into upper and lower sessions by clicking on the small broken rectangle located just above the Terminal's scroll bar. This feature is useful, for example, if you need to edit a file and copy and paste output from earlier in the Terminal session. The upper window contains the buffer (i.e., what you would see if you scrolled up in a non-split window), while the lower window contains your current Terminal section.

Contextual Menu

Users familiar with the X Window System know that right-clicking an *xterm* window opens a terminal-related contextual menu. Mac OS X's Terminal also has a contextual menu that can be accessed with Control-clicking (or

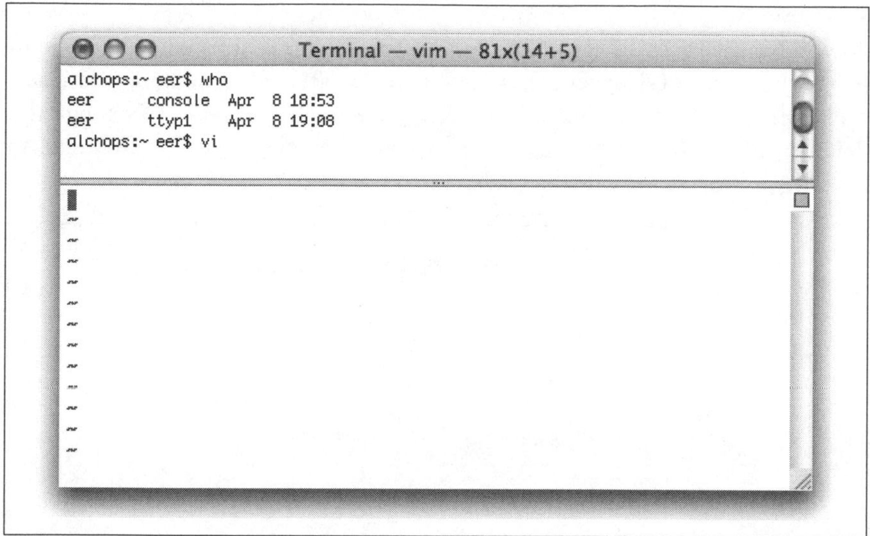

Figure 1-2. The Terminal's split screen

right-clicking if you have a two- or three-button mouse). The Terminal contextual menu includes the following choices: Copy, Paste, Paste Selection, Paste Escaped Text, Select All, Clear Scrollback, Send Break (equivalent to Control-C), Send Hard Reset, Send Reset, and Windows Settings. Each of these items also has a keyboard shortcut.

Customizing the Terminal

To customize the shell used by the Terminal, start by changing the Terminal's Preferences (Terminal → Preferences). In the Preferences pane, you can tell the Terminal to execute the default shell or a specific command (such as an alternative shell) at startup.* You can also declare the terminal type (`$TERM`), which is set as *xterm-color* by default. The other choices for the environment variable TERM are *ansi*, *dtterm*, *rxvt*, *vt52*, *vt100*, *vt102*, and *xterm*. Among other things, the default setting for TERM allows you to take advantage of the support for color output in *ls* (via the *-G* option) and color syntax highlighting in the *vim* editor. Although color is enabled by the default *xterm-color, dtterm* provides some additional capabilities. For example, the visual bell in *vi* works with *dtterm*, but not with *xterm-color.*

* You can change the default shell in the Terminal preferences, but it will not affect the login shell used for remote or console logins. Changing a user's default shell is covered later in this chapter.

You can also adjust the Terminal's characteristics using Terminal → Window Settings (or ⌘-I), which brings up the Terminal Inspector, shown in Figure 1-3. Table 1-1 lists the available window settings. Changing these settings affects only the topmost Terminal window. If you want to change the default settings for all future Terminal windows, click the Use Settings As Defaults button at the bottom of the Terminal Inspector window.

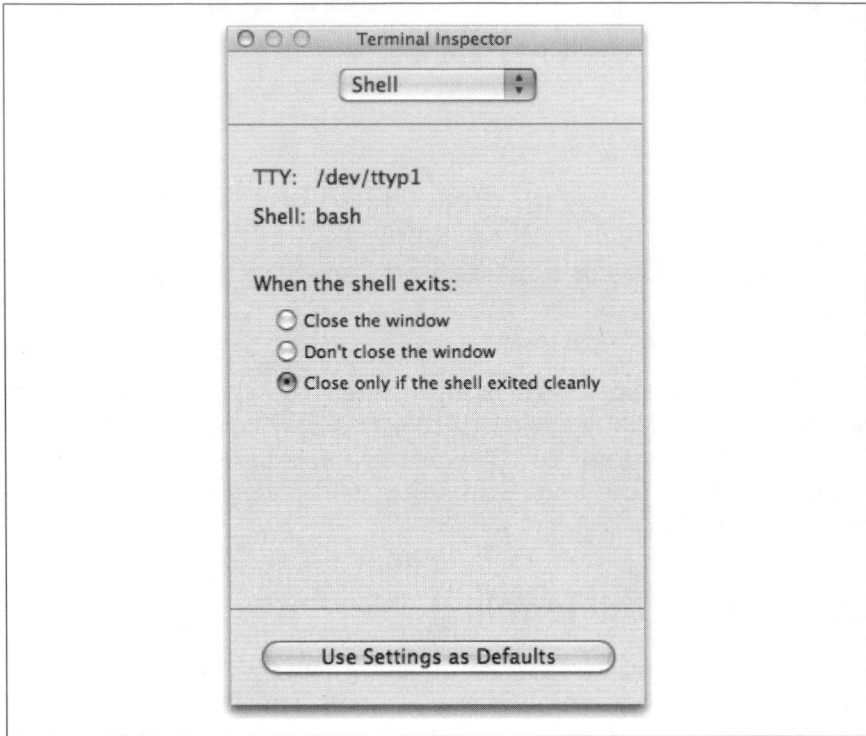

Figure 1-3. The Terminal Inspector

Table 1-1. Window settings

Pane	Description
Shell	Displays the shell used by the Terminal and lets you choose whether to close the Terminal window when the shell exits.
Processes	Displays the processes running under the frontmost window. You can also control whether Terminal will warn you if you try to close the window while you are running a program. You can disable this by choosing Never under "Prompt before closing window." You can also supply a list of commands that should be ignored, so if you're running a program (such as *vi* or *Emacs*) that's not in the list, the Terminal will warn you before closing the window.
Emulation	Controls the Terminal emulation properties.
Buffer	Sets the size and properties of the scrollback buffer.

Table 1-1. Window settings (continued)

Pane	Description
Display	Changes the character set encoding, cursor style, font, and other attributes.
Color	Changes colors and transparency of the Terminal window.
Window	Controls window dimensions, title, and other settings.
Keyboard	Controls key mappings.

One useful option available in the Emulation tab is "Option click to position cursor". If you enable this feature, you will be able to Option-click with the mouse to position the cursor in Terminal applications such as *vim* or *Emacs* (this could save you many keystrokes when you need to move the insertion point). This option also works over a remote login session, assuming that this is supported by the remote host's terminal capabilities.

Customizing the Terminal on the Fly

You can customize the Terminal in shell scripts using escape sequences or AppleScript commands. *xterm* users may be familiar with the following command to set the *xterm* window's title when using the *bash* shell:

```
echo -n -e "\033]0;My-Window-Title\007"
```

or the equivalent when using *tcsh*:

```
echo '^[]2;My-Window-Title^G'
```

Mac OS X's Terminal accepts these sequences as well.

`^[` is the ASCII ESC character, and `^G` is the ASCII BEL character. (The BEL character is used to ring the terminal bell, but in this context, it terminates an escape sequence.) The escape sequences described here are ANSI escape sequences, which differ from the shell escape sequences described earlier. ANSI escape sequences are used to manipulate a Terminal window (such as by moving the cursor or setting the title). Shell escape sequences are used to tell the shell to treat a metacharacter, such as `|`, as a literal character rather than an instruction to pipe standard output somewhere else.

To type the `^[` characters in *bash*, use the key sequence Control-V, Escape (press Control-V and release, then press the Escape key). To type `^G`, use Control-V, Control-G. The *vim* editor supports the same key sequence; *Emacs* uses Control-Q instead of Control-V.

You can capture the *bash* escape sequence in a function that you can include in your *.bash_profile* script:

```
function set_title ( )
{
    case $TERM in
        *term | xterm-color | rxvt | vt100 | gnome* )
            echo -n -e "\033]0;$*\007" ;;
        *) ;;
    esac
}
```

Then you can change the title by issuing the following command:

```
set_title your fancy title here
```

You may want to package this as a shell script and make it available to everyone who uses your system, as shown in Example 1-3.

Example 1-3. Setting the Terminal title in a shell script

```
#!/bin/bash
#
# Script settitle
# Usage:  settitle title
#
if [ $# == 0 ]; then
  echo "Usage:  settitle title"
else
   echo -n -e "\033]0;$*\007"
fi
```

You can also use *osascript* to execute AppleScript commands that accomplish the same thing:

```
osascript -e \
  'tell app "Terminal" to set custom title of first window to "Title"'
```

Working with File and Directory Names

Traditionally, Unix users tend to avoid spaces in file and directory names, sometimes by inserting hyphens and underscores where spaces are implied, as follows:

```
textFile.txt
text-file.txt
text_file.txt
```

However, most Mac users tend to insert spaces into file and directory names and, in a lot of cases, these names tend to be long and descriptive. While this practice is okay if you're going to work in the GUI all the time, it creates a small hurdle to jump over when you're working on the command line.

To get around these spaces, you have two choices: escape them, or quote the file or directory name.

To escape a space on the command line, simply insert a backslash (\) before the space. This also works with other special characters, such as a parenthesis. Because they have meaning to the shell, special characters that must be escaped are: `* # ` " ' \ $ | & ? ; ~ ( ) < > ! ^`. Here is an example of how to use a backslash to escape a space character in a file or directory name:

```
cd ~/Documents/My\ Shell\ Scripts
```

Or you can use quotation marks around the file or directory name that contains the space, as follows:

```
cd ~/Documents/"My Shell Scripts"
```

There is one other way to get around this problem, but it involves using the Finder in combination with the Terminal application. To launch a Classic (Mac OS 9 and earlier) application such as Word 2001, which probably lives on the Mac OS 9 partition of your hard drive, you could enter the path as follows, using escape characters:

```
open -a /Volumes/Mac\ OS\ 9/Applications\ \(Mac\ OS\ 9\)/Microsoft\ Office\ ↵
2001/Microsoft\ Word
```

Or you can enter the path using quotes:

```
open -a /Volumes/"Mac OS 9"/"Applications (Mac OS 9)"/"Microsoft Office ↵
2001"/"Microsoft Word"
```

As you can see, neither way is very pretty, and both require you to know a lot of detail about the path. Now for the easy way:

1. Type *open –a*, followed by a space on the command line (don't press Return yet).
2. Locate Microsoft Word in the Finder and then drag its icon to the Terminal window to insert the path after the space. When you do this, the spaces and any other special characters will be escaped with backslashes automatically:

   ```
   open -a /Volumes/Mac\ OS\ 9/Applications\ \(Mac\ OS\ 9\)/Microsoft\ ↵
   Office\ 2001/Microsoft\ Word
   ```

3. Press Return to invoke the command and launch Word 2001. (If Classic isn't already running, Classic starts, too.)

You can also drag and drop URLs from a web browser. For example, to use *curl* to download files from the command line:

1. Open a new Terminal window and type *curl -O*, with a space after the switch.
2. Bring up your web browser and navigate to *http://www.oreilly.com*.

3. Drag the image at the top of the page to the Terminal window. You should now see the following in the Terminal window:

```
curl -O http://www.oreilly.com/graphics_new/header_main.gif
```

4. Press Enter in the Terminal window to download *header_main.gif* to your computer.

Tab completion

If you want to type a long pathname, you can cut down on the number of keystrokes needed to type it by using tab completion. For example, to type */Library/StartupItems*, you could type */Li<Tab>*, which gives you */Library/*. Next, type *S<Tab>*. This time, instead of completing the path, you're given a choice of completions: *Screen Savers, Scripts*, and *StartupItems*. Type a little bit more of the desired item, followed by a tab, as in *t<Tab>*. The full key sequence for */Library/StartupItems* is */Li<Tab>St<Tab>*.

If you have multiple completions where a space is involved, you can type a literal space with *<Space>*. So, to get a completion for */System Folder* (the Mac OS 9 system folder), you should use */Sy<Tab>\ <Space><Tab>*. It stops just before the space because */System* (Mac OS X's System folder) is a valid completion for the first three characters.

Changing Your Shell

Although other shells are available in Mac OS X, as we noted earlier, the default shell in Mac OS X Tiger is *bash*. Earlier versions of Mac OS X shipped with *tcsh* as the default shell. Although you can change the default shell in the Terminal preferences, this does not affect the login shell used for remote or console logins. To change your default shell in a more pervasive manner, see "Modifying a User" in Chapter 5. If you install additional shells on the system, you'll need to add them to the */etc/shells* file to make Mac OS X aware that they are legitimate shells.

The Services Menu

Mac OS X's Services menu (Terminal → Services) exposes a collection of services that can work with the currently running application. In the case of the Terminal, the services operate on text that you have selected (the pasteboard). To use a service, select a region of text in the Terminal and choose one of the following items from the Services menu:

ChineseTextConverter
: This service can be used to convert selected text either to simplified Chinese or Traditional Chinese.

Disk Utility
: This service invokes Disk Utility to calculate either a CRC-32 or an MD-5 image checksum of a selected disk.

Finder
: The Finder Services menu allows you to open a file (Finder → Open), show its enclosing directory (Finder → Reveal), or show its information (Finder → Show Info).

Font Book
: This can be used either to create a font collection or a font library from text.

Grab
: Not supported by the Terminal.

Import Image
: Not supported by the Terminal.

Mail
: The Mail → Send To service allows you to compose a new message to an email address, once you have selected that address in the Terminal. You can also select a region of text and choose Mail → Send Selection to send a message containing the selected text.

Make New Sticky Note (Shift-⌘-Y)
: This service creates a new Sticky (*/Applications/Stickies*) containing the selected text.

Open URL
: This service opens the URL specified by the selected text in your default web browser.

Script Editor
: This service gets the result of an AppleScript, makes a new AppleScript (in the Script Editor), or runs the selected text as an AppleScript.

Search with Google (Shift-⌘-L)
: This service searches for the selected text using *google.com* in your default web browser.

Send File To Bluetooth Device (Shift-⌘-B)
: This service sends the file specified by the selected text to a Bluetooth device.

Speech
: The Speech service is used to start speaking the selected text. (Use Speech → Stop Speaking to interrupt.)

Spotlight (Shift-⌘-F)
: This service invokes Tiger's system-wide search technology Spotlight to search for selected text. (Tiger provides command-line utilities for working with Spotlight. See Chapter 2.)

Summarize
: This service condenses the selected text into a summary document. The summary service analyzes English text and makes it as small as possible while retaining the original meaning.

TextEdit
: The TextEdit service can open a filename or open a new file containing the selected text.

View in JavaBrowser (Shift-⌘-J)
: This service browses Java documentation for the selected class name. This is available whether the selected text is a real Java class name or not. (Garbage In, Garbage Out applies here.)

Third-party applications may install additional services of their own. When you use a service that requires a filename, you should select a fully qualified pathname, not just the filename, because the service does not know the shell's current working directory. (As far as the service is concerned, you are invoking it upon a string of text.)

Bonjour

Bonjour (*http://developer.apple.com/networking/bonjour*), formerly known as Rendezvous, is a networking technology that allows Bonjour-enabled devices on a local network to automatically discover each other. As are many Mac OS X applications, Terminal is Bonjour-enabled. For example, you can select File → Connect to Server to make an SSH connection to any other Mac OS X system on the LAN, provided it allows such connections. The other Macs on the LAN are identified by their computer names, as specified in their Sharing System Preferences.

Announced in 2002 as Rendezvous, Bonjour is Apple's implementation of the Zero Configuration Networking open source project, also known as Zeroconf (*http://www.zeroconf.org*), which was initiated by the Internet Engineering Task Force (*http://www.ietf.org*) in 1999.

You can learn more about Rendezvous by reading Apple's Rendezvous Technology Brief at *http://images.apple.com/macosx/pdf/Panther_Rendezvous_TB_10232003.pdf*.

Alternative Terminal Applications

As noted earlier, other Aqua-native terminal applications are available, and the freeware iTerm (*http://iterm.sourceforge.net*), developed by Fabian and Ujwal S. Sathyam, is a particularly attractive one. Although Mac OS X's Terminal is rich with useful features, iTerm offers some interesting extras that make it worthy of consideration. We won't cover iTerm in great detail, but will touch on a few of its more attractive aspects.

Before getting into what makes iTerm distinct, here are some similarities between iTerm and Terminal:

- One feature that each of these terminal applications share is that they use the same Services menu.
- Both iTerm and Terminal support transparency, language encodings, and AppleScript, and have contextual menus that can be accessed by Control-clicking or right-clicking (if you have a two- or three-button mouse) in a window.

iTerm supports several language encodings, vt100/ANSI/xterm/xterm-color/rxvt emulations, and many GUI features. Particularly interesting features of iTerm include support for multiple tabbed terminal sessions within each window, bookmarks that allow you to open new iTerm sessions with preset terminal settings, and bookmarks for launching non-shell commands. The default value for `TERM` is `vt100`, but this can be changed either on the fly with a *bash* shell command, such as *TERM=xterm-color*, in the Configure menu, or, if you want a global change, in iTerm's Preferences dialog. Like the Terminal application, iTerm is also Bonjour-enabled.

iTerm's tabbed view should be familiar to GNOME users, since the *gnome-terminal* also supports this feature. Tabs in iTerm are designed to make efficient use of desktop space, much as they do in Safari and other popular web browsers. Figure 1-4 shows an iTerm window with two tabs.

The same *bash* (or *tcsh*) shell commands that can be used to customize the Terminal's titlebar work just as well with iTerm's titlebar. When used in iTerm, these commands also set the tab labels as shown in Figure 1-5.

iTerm's support for bookmarks should be familiar to KDE users, as the KDE Konsole terminal emulator offers a similar feature. Bookmarks are used to define iTerm sessions with preset terminal settings. For example, you can define the color or typeface to use for text.

The default bookmarks are Default, which specifies the default login shell, and Bonjour, which includes *ssh* and *sftp* connections to SSH- and Bonjour-enabled computers on the LAN. To define a new bookmark, select iTerm → Preferences and click the Bookmarks tab in the Preferences window. Then,

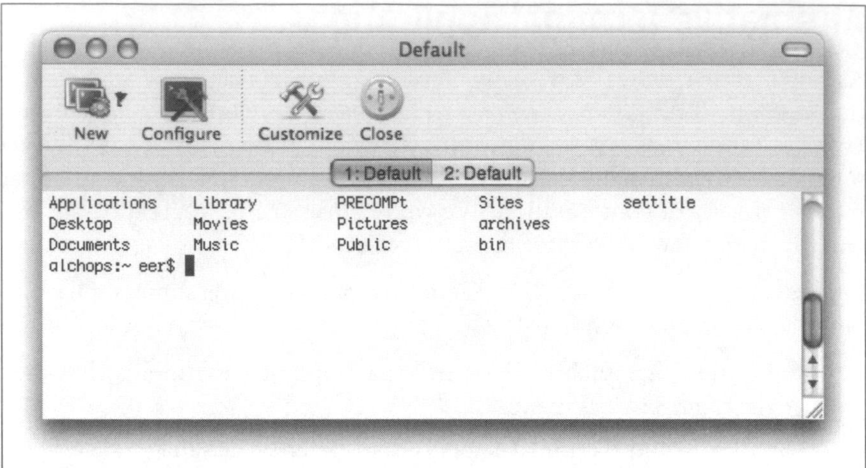

Figure 1-4. Using tabs with iTerm

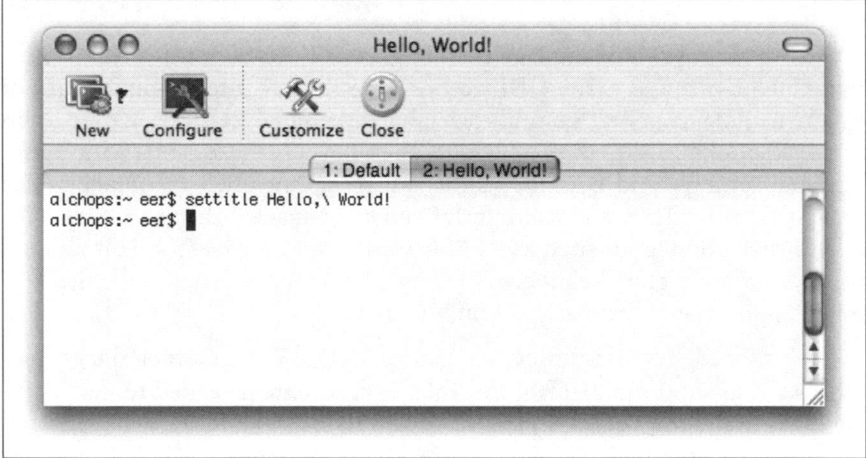

Figure 1-5. Customized tab labels in iTerm

click the plus sign to add a bookmark and specify its name, which is used when you open a session from the New icon in iTerm's toolbar. Figure 1-6 shows the Bookmark preferences window in which we have defined several bookmarks after the Default Session, but before the automatically and dynamically generated Bonjour bookmarks.

The bookmark *OpenSafari* opens Safari, while the *OpenSitesFolder* bookmark opens the *~/Sites* folder in the Finder. To add a bookmark that opens another login session with various characteristics that differ from the Default, you must first create a new Profile. For example, suppose your Default login session has black text and you want to create a bookmark

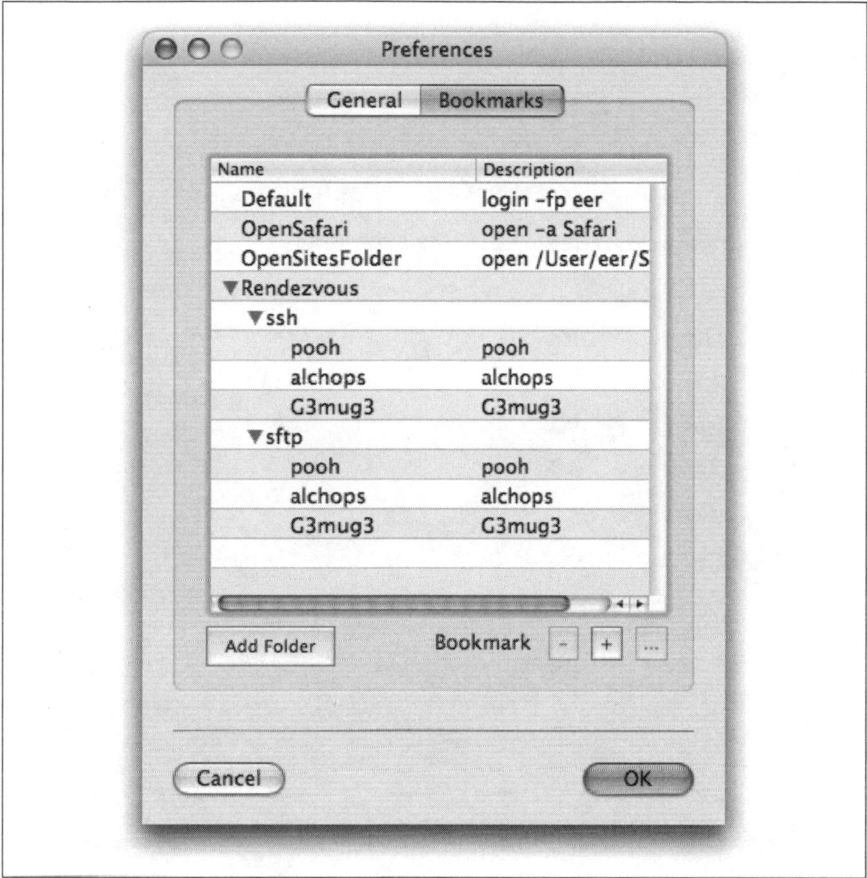

Figure 1-6. Bookmarks in iTerm

named *bluetext* for a login session with blue text. First, select iTerm → Preferences. Then, click the General tab, followed by the Profiles button. To add a profile with the display characteristic of blue text, click the Display tab, set the colors you want, and click the plus sign to name the new profile as shown in Figure 1-7.

To add the new profile as a bookmark, select iTerm → Preferences and click the Bookmarks tab in Preferences window. In the Bookmarks Preferences window, click the plus sign to add the new bookmark as shown in Figure 1-8.

iTerm's contextual menu consists of the following items: New Tab (which allows you to choose a session from the bookmarks), Browser (which opens the selected URL in your default web browser), Mail (which opens a compose mail window with the selected email address as the recipient), Copy, Paste, Save, Select All, Clear Buffer, Close, and Configure.

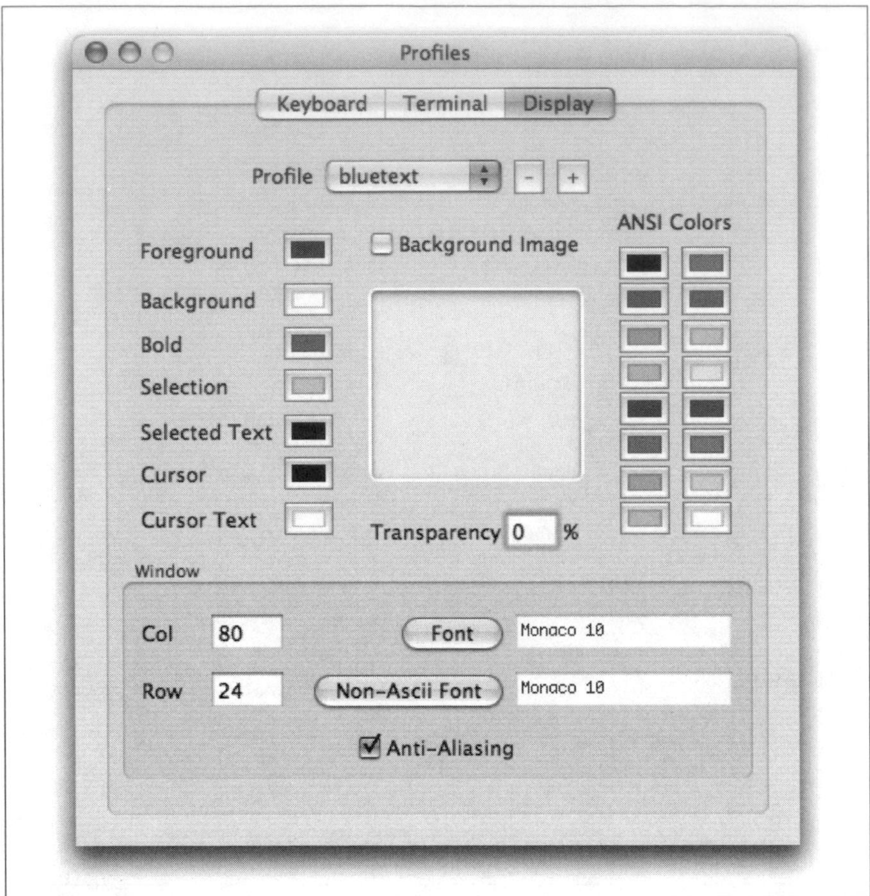

Figure 1-7. Defining profiles in iTerm

The open Command

The *open* shell command lets you open Finder windows and launch Aqua applications. To open a directory in the Finder, use *open*, followed by the name of the directory. For example, to open a Finder window containing the current directory, enter the following command:

```
open .
```

To open your Public folder (*~/Public*) in a Finder window, use the following:

```
open ~/Public
```

To open the */Applications* folder in a Finder window, use the following:

```
open /Applications
```

Figure 1-8. Defining a bookmark to a new profile in iTerm

To open an application, you need only its name. To open Xcode (*/Developer/Applications*), you would use the following:

```
open -a Xcode
```

You are not required to enter the path for the application, only its name, even if it is a Classic application. The only time you are required to enter the path is if you have two different versions of an application with similar names on your system.

You can use the *-a* option to open a file with something other than the application with which it's associated. For example, to open an XML file in Xcode instead of the default XML editor, the Property List Editor, enter this command:

```
open -a Xcode data.xml
```

To open multiple files, you can use wildcards:

```
open *.c
```

To force a file to be opened with TextEdit, use *-e*:

```
open -e *.c
```

The *-e* option directs the file to be opened in TextEdit; it cannot be used to open a file in another text editor, such as BBEdit (though BBEdit includes its own command-line application for this purpose). However, if you want to open a file using BBEdit, use the following:

```
open -a BBEdit filename
```

If you want to use TextEdit on a file that is owned by an administrator (or *root*), *sudo open -e* won't work. You'll need to specify the full path to the TextEdit executable, as in:

```
$ sudo /Applications/TextEdit.app/Contents/MacOS/TextEdit filename
```

If you find yourself doing this often, you might want to create an alias for the path to TextEdit's executable file. For example, you could enter the following into your *.bash_profile* file:

```
alias sudotext="sudo /Applications/TextEdit.app/Contents/MacOS/TextEdit "
```

Then the next time you want to open a text file that would otherwise require use of the *sudo* command, you could just use the following:

```
$ sudotext filename
```

When you enter that command, you'll be prompted for the admin password; once authenticated, the file you've specified is opened in TextEdit, just as you hoped it would.

Similar to the *open* command, the *open-x11* command is used to open applications. However, it is for opening X11-based apps in Apple's X11 environment. You can learn more about X11 and the *open-x11* command in Chapter 7.

CHAPTER 2

Searching and Metadata

If a Unix Geek needs to find something, she'll probably use *locate* or *find*, depending on what she's looking for. Because *locate* is based on a static database that's only regenerated periodically (see "Scheduling Tasks in Chapter 4), it would be the choice for things that don't change a lot (virtually anything in */usr*). It's also much faster because it has that database to consult. And trusty old *find*, slow as molasses, it what you need when you need more control over the search or when you're looking for something that *locate* doesn't know about, such as files that have been created recently.

But Tiger introduces a new search capability, Spotlight, which stores and sifts through file metadata faster than a herd of sheep can clear a field. Spotlight comes in two forms: a GUI interface accessible from the menubar, and a suite of command-line utilities. This chapter introduces you to Spotlight and shows you how to take advantage of all it has to offer.

Spotlight

Remember the relentless disk grinding you heard after you first installed the operating system? That was Spotlight creating its initial database. Spotlight is a repository of metadata for certain types of files—Spotlight gathers information about any file (or data record, such as an iCal event) for which it has an *importer* (an operating system plug-in that extracts metadata from a document). To see all the importers on your system, look in */System/Library/Spotlight* and */Library/Spotlight*.

By default, Spotlight has importers for the following files and data:

- Address Book records
- AppleWorks files
- Applications

- Audio files
- Safari bookmarks
- iChat transcripts
- Fonts
- iCal events
- Images
- Keynote presentations
- Mail messages
- Microsoft Office documents
- Pages documents
- PDF and PostScript files
- QuickTime movies
- RTF documents
- Source code
- System preferences

To perform a spotlight query, simply click the magnifying glass icon in the upper right of the menu bar or press ⌘-Space. A Spotlight search field drops down, in which you enter a search term, as shown in Figure 2-1.

You can get a more detailed Spotlight search window by pressing Option-⌘-Space. This window, shown in Figure 2-2, lets you configure a number of aspects of your search, such as location, date, and result grouping.

Performing Spotlight Searches

Unix geeks might never use Spotlight if Mac OS X didn't include some command-line goodies for performing searches. You can perform a simple Spotlight search from the shell with the following syntax:

```
mdfind term
```

For example:

```
$ mdfind burroughs
/Developer/Documentation/DeveloperTools/Tcl/Trf/bz2.html
/Volumes/Macintosh HD/Users/bjepson/Music/iTunes/iTunes Music/William
     S. Burroughs
/Volumes/Macintosh HD/Users/bjepson/Music/iTunes/iTunes Music/William
     S. Burroughs/Dead City Radio/02 A Thanksgiving Prayer.m4p
/Volumes/Macintosh HD/Users/bjepson/Music/iTunes/iTunes Music Library.xml
/Volumes/Macintosh HD/Users/bjepson/Sites/radio/2003/04/11.html
```

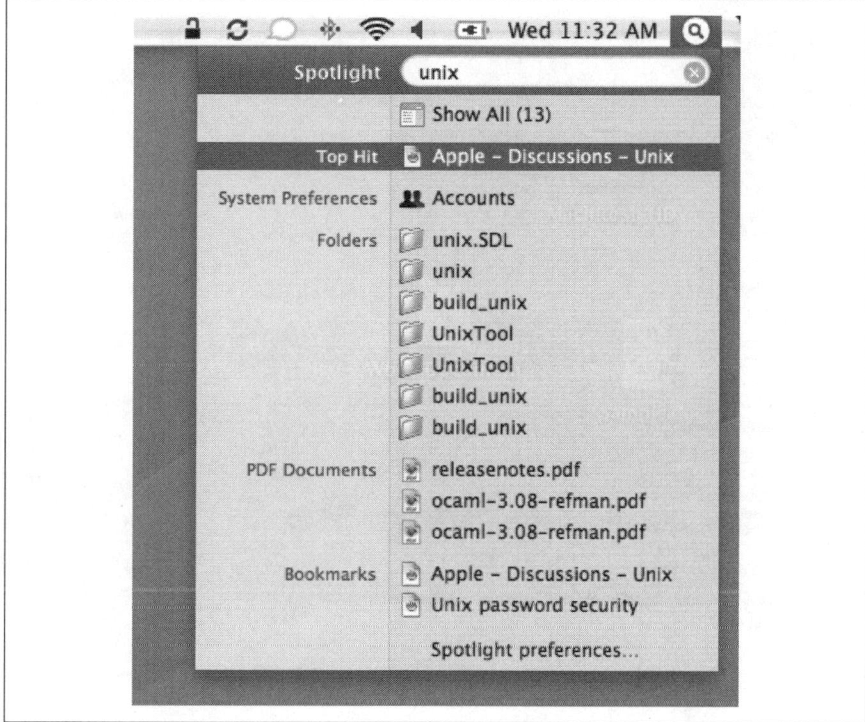

Figure 2-1. Using the Spotlight menu

If you have a good idea of where you want to search, you can use the *-onlyin* option as shown here:

```
$ mdfind -onlyin /Developer burroughs
/Developer/Documentation/DeveloperTools/Tcl/Trf/bz2.html
```

You can use the *-live* option to update the results in real time as they change, and as quickly as Spotlight can index them.

Although you can find interesting results with simple keyword searches, you can refine your search by specifying any of the metadata attribute keys. For example, to find all the songs written by Robert Hunter, you could use this search:

```
$ mdfind "kMDItemComposer == '*Robert Hunter*'"
/Users/bjepson/Music/iTunes/iTunes Music/Grateful Dead/Hundred Year
  Hall (Disc 1) [Live]/1-01 Bertha.m4a
/Users/bjepson/Music/iTunes/iTunes Music/Grateful Dead/Hundred Year
  Hall (Disc 1) [Live]/1-04 China Cat Sunflower.m4a
/Users/bjepson/Music/iTunes/iTunes Music/Grateful Dead/Hundred Year
  Hall (Disc 1) [Live]/1-06 Jack Straw.m4a
/Users/bjepson/Music/iTunes/iTunes Music/Grateful Dead/Hundred Year
  Hall (Disc 1) [Live]/1-08 Playing In The Band.m4a
```

Figure 2-2. Searching with the Spotlight window

```
/Users/bjepson/Music/iTunes/iTunes Music/Grateful Dead/Dick's Picks
  Volume 12 (Disc 1)/1-02 China Cat Sunflower _.m4a
/Users/bjepson/Music/iTunes/iTunes Music/Grateful Dead/Dick's Picks
  Volume 12 (Disc 1)/1-06 Truckin' _.m4a
[... and so forth ...]
```

Without the wildcard characters (*), you wouldn't match a thing, since Robert Hunter coauthored all those songs with Jerry Garcia. You can perform more complex queries with *mdfind*, as well. For example, the following query uses the and (&&) operator to combine two search criteria: the composer name contains "Jerry" and the performer (author) name does not contain "Grateful Dead":

```
$ mdfind "kMDItemComposer == '*Jerry*' && \
    kMDItemAuthors != '*Grateful Dead*'"
/Users/bjepson/Music/iTunes/iTunes Music/Compilations/Box of Pearls - The
  Janis Joplin Collection/3-11 Piece of My Heart (Live at Woodstock).m4p
/Users/bjepson/Music/iTunes/iTunes Music/The Who/Live At Leeds/11
  Summertime Blues.m4a
```

Inspecting a File's Attributes

Now that we've found a couple songs written by someone named Jerry who's not in the Grateful Dead, how do we figure out what his deal is? The *mdls* utility lets you see all of the metadata for a given file:

```
$ cd ~/Music/iTunes/iTunes\ Music/Compilations/
$ cd Box\ of\ Pearls\ -\ The\ Janis\ Joplin\ Collection/
$ mdls 3-11\ Piece\ of\ My\ Heart\ \(Live\ at\ Woodstock\).m4p
3-11 Piece of My Heart (Live at Woodstock).m4p -------------
kMDItemAlbum                   = "Box of Pearls - The Janis Joplin
Collection"
kMDItemAttributeChangeDate     = 2005-02-19 17:43:08 -0500
kMDItemAudioBitRate            = 125240
kMDItemAudioChannelCount       = 2
kMDItemAudioTrackNumber        = 11
kMDItemAuthors                 = ("Janis Joplin")
kMDItemCodecs                  = ("")
kMDItemComposer                = "Bert Berns & Jerry Ragovoy"
kMDItemContentCreationDate     = 2004-04-02 11:46:40 -0500
kMDItemContentModificationDate = 2004-04-02 11:46:40 -0500
kMDItemContentType             = "com.apple.protected-mpeg-4-audio"
kMDItemContentTypeTree         = (
    "com.apple.protected-mpeg-4-audio",
    "public.audio",
    "public.audiovisual-content",
    "public.data",
    "public.item",
    "public.content"
)
kMDItemDisplayName             = "3-11 Piece of My Heart (Live at
Woodstock).m4p"
kMDItemDurationSeconds         = 391.3483333333334
kMDItemFSContentChangeDate     = 2004-04-02 11:46:40 -0500
kMDItemFSCreationDate          = 2004-04-02 11:46:40 -0500
kMDItemFSCreatorCode           = 1752133483
kMDItemFSFinderFlags           = 0
kMDItemFSInvisible             = 0
kMDItemFSLabel                 = 0
kMDItemFSName                  = "3-11 Piece of My Heart (Live at
Woodstock).m4p"
kMDItemFSNodeCount             = 0
kMDItemFSOwnerGroupID          = 501
kMDItemFSOwnerUserID           = 501
kMDItemFSSize                  = 6522800
kMDItemFSTypeCode              = 1295274016
kMDItemID                      = 128067
kMDItemKind                    = "MPEG-4 Audio File (Protected)"
kMDItemLastUsedDate            = 2004-04-02 11:46:40 -0500
kMDItemMediaTypes              = (Sound)
kMDItemMusicalGenre            = "Rock"
```

```
kMDItemStreamable              = 0
kMDItemTitle                   = "Piece of My Heart (Live at Woodstock)"
kMDItemTotalBitRate            = 125240
kMDItemUsedDates               = (2004-04-02 11:46:40 -0500)
```

That's a lot of information, but this sampling gives you an idea of what sort of search terms you can use with your *mdfind* queries. Table 2-1 lists some of the most common metadata attributes, but as you can see from the music file example, importers (in this case, the iTunes importer) are free to define their own attributes.

Keep in mind an important distinction when speaking of metadata: the owner (in terms of file system permissions) of the file is not necessarily its author. For example, if you rip an MP3 file from a CD-ROM, you're the owner. However, iTunes consults CDDB (the Gracenote CD Database, located at *http://www.gracenote.com/gn_products/cddb*) and uses the information it finds there to determine the authors of the file. On the other hand, if you create a Word document on your Mac, you'll not only be the owner of the file, but you're also the author. Another way to think about this is that Spotlight metadata is not so much about *files*, but the *contents* of files.

Table 2-1. Common Spotlight metadata attributes

Attribute	Description
kMDItemAttributeChangeDate	The date and time that a metadata attribute was last changed.
kMDItemAudiences	The intended audience of the file.
kMDItemAuthors	The authors of the document.
kMDItemCity	The document's city of origin.
kMDItemComment	Comments regarding the document.
kMDItemContactKeywords	A list of contacts associated with the document.
kMDItemContentCreationDate	The document's creation date.
kMDItemContentModificationDate	Last modification date of the document.
kMDItemContentType	The qualified content type of the document, such as *com.adobe.pdf* for PDF files and *com.apple.protected-mpeg-4-audio* for an Apple Advanced Audio Coding (AAC) file.
kMDItemContributors	Contributors to this document.
kMDItemCopyright	The copyright owner.
kMDItemCountry	The document's country of origin.
kMDItemCoverage	The scope of the document, such as a geographical location or a period of time.
kMDItemCreator	The application that created the document.
kMDItemDescription	A description of the document.
kMDItemDueDate	Due date for the item represented by the document.

Table 2-1. Common Spotlight metadata attributes (continued)

Attribute	Description
kMDItemDurationSeconds	Duration (in seconds) of the document.
kMDItemEmailAddresses	Email addresses associated with this document.
kMDItemEncodingApplications	The name of the application (such as "Acrobat Distiller") that was responsible for converting the document in its current form.
kMDItemFinderComment	This contains any Finder comments for the document.
kMDItemFonts	Fonts used in the document.
kMDItemHeadline	A headline-style synopsis of the document.
kMDItemInstantMessageAddresses	IM addresses/screen names associated with the document.
kMDItemInstructions	Special instructions or warnings associated with this document.
kMDItemKeywords	Keywords associated with the document.
kMDItemKind	Describes the kind of document, such as "iCal Event."
kMDItemLanguages	Language of the document.
kMDItemLastUsedDate	The date and time the document was last opened.
kMDItemNumberOfPages	Page count of this document.
kMDItemOrganizations	The organization that created the document.
kMDItemPageHeight	Height of the document's page layout in points.
kMDItemPageWidth	Width of the document's page layout in points.
kMDItemPhoneNumbers	Phone numbers associated with the document.
kMDItemProjects	Names of projects (other documents such as an iMovie project) that this document is associated with.
kMDItemPublishers	The publisher of the document.
kMDItemRecipients	The recipient of the document.
kMDItemRights	A link to the statement of rights (such as a Creative Commons or old-school copyright license) that govern the use of the document.
kMDItemSecurityMethod	Encryption method used on the document.
kMDItemStarRating	Rating of the document (as in the iTunes "star" rating).
kMDItemStateOrProvince	The document's state or province of origin.
kMDItemTitle	The title.
kMDItemVersion	The version number.
kMDItemWhereFroms	Where the document came from, such as a URI or email address.

Managing Spotlight

Spotlight is modestly configurable; you can use System Preferences → Spotlight to control the order in which results are presented, exclude certain file types, and specify directories that must never be indexed. You can do quite a bit from the shell prompt as well.

The *mdutil* command controls Spotlight settings on a volume-by-volume basis, and *mdimport* lets you work with the various importers installed on your system. For example, *mdutil* can turn indexing on or off for an entire volume with the *-i* option (it takes an argument of *on* or *off*):

```
# mdutil -i off /Volumes/Macintosh\ HD
/Volumes/Macintosh HD:
        Indexing disabled for volume.
```

This setting is persistent across reboots. You can inspect a volume's setting with the *-s* option:

```
# mdutil -s /Volumes/Macintosh\ HD/
/Volumes/Macintosh HD/:
        Status: Indexing Disabled
```

You can use *mdimport* to list all the importers installed on your system:

```
$ mdimport -L
2005-02-26 22:10:53.296 mdimport[268] Paths: id(501) (
    "/System/Library/Spotlight/Image.mdimporter",
    "/System/Library/Spotlight/Audio.mdimporter",
    "/System/Library/Spotlight/Font.mdimporter",
    "/System/Library/Spotlight/PS.mdimporter",
    "/Library/Spotlight/Microsoft Office.mdimporter",
[... and so forth ...]
```

And if the list of attributes in Table 2-1 isn't enough to keep you busy, you can also use *mdimport* to list all the attributes supported by the importers on your system:

```
$ mdimport -A
'kMDItemAcquisitionMake'                'Device make'
     'Make of the device used to acquire this document'
'kMDItemAcquisitionModel'               'Device model'
     'Model of the device was used to acquire this document'
'kMDItemAlbum'          'Album'
     'Title for a collection of media, such as a record album'
'kMDItemAperture'               'Aperture'
     'Aperture setting of the camera when the picture was taken'
[... and so forth ...]
```

mdimport also has a number of features of interest to people developing their own metadata importers. For example:

- *-X* prints out an XML schema for the metadata on your system
- *-f* forces *mdimport* to import a directory or file (overriding any exceptions you've made in System Preferences)
- *-p* displays performance statistics for a run of *mdimport*

Resource Forks and HFS+ Metadata

Apple's HFS+ filesystem has been stashing metadata away since its introduction in Mac OS X 8.1. *Resource forks* are generally invisible portions of files used for stashing additional information (the primary portion of the file—indeed the only part of a file most Unix Geeks are used to thinking about—is called the *data fork*). Before Mac OS X, resource forks contained application resources. These are now contained in the application bundle itself, although resource forks are still used in classic applications and a few odd places (such as text clippings, which you can create by dragging and dropping text selections to the Finder).

You can inspect a resource fork by appending */rsrc* to a file name, as in:

```
$ ls -l Sample.textClipping
-rw-r--r--   1 bjepson  bjepson  0 Feb 27 11:05 Sample.textClipping
$ ls -l Sample.textClipping/rsrc
-rw-r--r--   1 bjepson  bjepson  1770 Feb 27 11:05 Sample.textClipping/rsrc
```

The contents of a resource fork, even for something simple like a text clipping, are not necessarily human-readable, but there's usually something you can dig out:

```
$ file Sample.textClipping/rsrc
Sample.textClipping/rsrc: ms-windows icon resource
$ strings Sample.textClipping/rsrc
KApple's HFS+ filesystem has been stashing metadata away since its
introduction in Mac OS X 8.1. Resource forks are generally invisible
portionsof files used for stashing additional information (the primary
portion of the...
```

Mac OS X Tiger also makes use of HFS+ metadata, which consists of extended attributes that are associated with files. For example, if you look at the root of your Mac's hard drive in the Finder, you'll only see a small subset of the files (at the very least, Library, System, Applications, Users). But if you drop down into the Terminal, there are plenty more. The files that don't appear have an attribute (`I`) that makes them invisible to the Finder.

You can inspect this metadata with *GetFileInfo* and set it with *SetFile*, both of which are located in */Developer/Tools*:

```
$ GetFileInfo Sample.doc
file: "/Users/bjepson/Desktop/Sample.doc"
type: "W8BN"
creator: "MSWD"
attributes: avbstclinmedz
created: 02/27/2005 11:20:47
modified: 02/27/2005 11:21:01
```

An uppercase attribute indicates that the attribute is toggled on, and lowercase means it is off. The *SetFile* manpage describes all these attributes. For example, to hide the file extension in the Finder, set the `E` (extension is hidden) attribute:

```
$ SetFile -a E Sample.doc
```

You can also change the creator code and file type with *-c* and *-t*, respectively. For example, to change *Sample.doc* so it's owned by NeoOffice/J (*http://www.neooffice.org*), set the creator code to the empty string and the file type to `NO%F`, as shown in the following listing and in Figure 2-3.

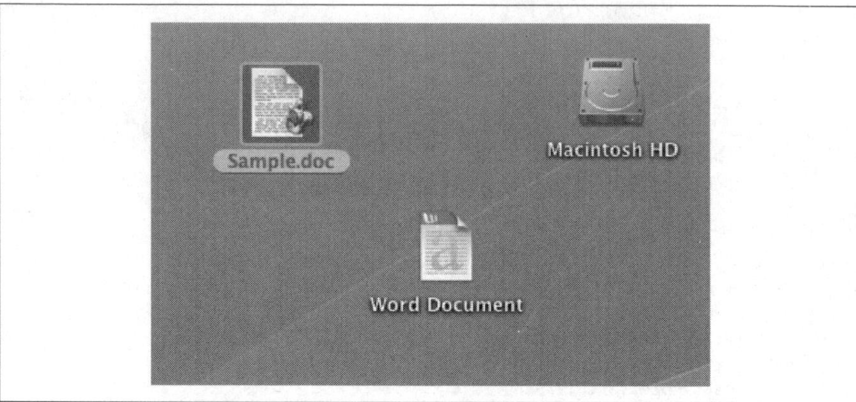

Figure 2-3. NeoOffice owns Sample.doc now

```
$ SetFile -c "" -t "NO%F" Sample.doc
$ GetFileInfo Sample.doc
file: "/Users/bjepson/Desktop/Sample.doc"
type: "NO%F"
creator: ""
attributes: avbstclinmEdz
created: 02/27/2005 11:20:47
modified: 02/27/2005 11:21:01
```

UFS

Although UFS doesn't natively support resource forks or HFS+ attributes, Mac OS X finds a place to stash that info. If the file has either a resource fork or any attributes that depend on HFS+ semantics, this information goes into a file named *._`filename`*, where *`filename`* is the name of the original file (this is known as the Apple Double format):

```
$ touch Foo
$ ls -al
total 4
drwxr-xr-x   2 bjepson  bjepson  1024 Feb 21 20:54 .
```

```
drwxr-xr-x   6 bjepson  bjepson  1024 Feb 21 20:53 ..
-rw-r--r--   1 bjepson  bjepson     0 Feb 21 20:54 Foo
$ SetFile -a S Foo
$ ls -al
total 6
drwxr-xr-x   2 bjepson  bjepson  1024 Feb 21 20:54 .
drwxr-xr-x   6 bjepson  bjepson  1024 Feb 21 20:53 ..
-rw-r--r--   1 bjepson  bjepson    82 Feb 21 20:54 ._Foo
-rw-r--r--   1 bjepson  bjepson     0 Feb 21 20:54 Foo
```

Preserving Metadata

Before Mac OS X Tiger, you had to be very careful with what you did at the command line. If you used *cp*, *mv*, *rsync*, or any of the other command line utilities that move stuff around, you could have lost part of your file. It was easy to miss this sort of mayhem, since this metadata isn't apparent until you go looking for it, and it wasn't always a disaster. For example, you could have copied a graphics file that kept its preview in its resource fork, and you probably wouldn't have missed it—after all, the next time you opened the image, the application most likely regenerated the preview. But with other files, such as text clippings and Internet locations (drag a URL from Safari to the Finder to create one of these), you lost everything, since all of these files' contents are contained in the resource fork. Here's how it would go on Mac OS X 10.3 and earlier:

```
$ ls -l Resource\ Fork\ Example.webloc
-rw-r--r--   1 bjepson  bjepson  0 Feb 21 15:54 Resource Fork Example.webloc
$ ls -l Resource\ Fork\ Example.webloc/rsrc
-rw-r--r--   1 bjepson  bjepson  624 Feb 21 15:54 Resource Fork Example.
webloc/rsrc
$ cp Resource\ Fork\ Example.webloc foo.webloc
$ ls -l foo.webloc
-rw-r--r--   1 bjepson  bjepson  0 Feb 26 23:18 foo.webloc
$ ls -l foo.webloc/rsrc
-rw-r--r--   1 bjepson  bjepson  0 Feb 26 23:18 foo.webloc/rsrc
```

It's not just the resource fork that got clobbered, you also lost the HFS+ metadata:

```
[Before...]
$ GetFileInfo Resource\ Fork\ Example.webloc
file: "/Users/bjepson/Desktop/Resource Fork Example.webloc"
type: "ilht"
creator: "MACS"
attributes: avbstclinmEdz
created: 02/26/2005 23:18:33
modified: 02/26/2005 23:18:33

[After...]
$ GetFileInfo foo.webloc
```

```
file: "/Users/bjepson/Desktop/foo.webloc"
type: ""
creator: ""
attributes: avbstclinmedz
created: 02/26/2005 23:18:52
modified: 02/26/2005 23:18:52
```

Fortunately, Mac OS X Tiger finally makes this problem (mostly) go away by making all the *cp*, *mv*, and *rsync* command-line utilities aware of the resource forks and HFS+:

```
$ cp Resource\ Fork\ Example.webloc foo.webloc
$ ls -l foo.webloc/rsrc
-rw-r--r--   1 bjepson  bjepson  717 Feb 26 23:25 foo.webloc/rsrc
$ GetFileInfo foo.webloc
file: "/Users/bjepson/Desktop/foo.webloc"
type: "ilht"
creator: "MACS"
attributes: avbstclinmEdz
created: 02/26/2005 23:25:21
modified: 02/26/2005 23:27:15
```

If you copy or move the file to a non-Mac system such as a FAT-formatted memory card, Apple Double comes in to save the day:

```
$ cp Resource\ Fork\ Example.webloc /Volumes/NO\ NAME/
$ ls -al /Volumes/NO\ NAME/ | grep Res
-rwxrwxrwx   1 bjepson  bjepson   4434 Feb 27 09:45 ._Resource Fork Example.
webloc
-rwxrwxrwx   1 bjepson  bjepson      0 Feb 27 09:45 Resource Fork Example.
webloc
```

And if you *rm* a file on a volume that's using Apple Double (including UFS as well), it cleans up the ._ file:

```
$ rm /Volumes/NO\ NAME/Resource\ Fork\ Example.webloc
remove /Volumes/NO NAME/Resource Fork Example.webloc? y
$ ls -al /Volumes/NO\ NAME/ | grep Res
[... no results ...]
```

For the most part, Mac OS X has you covered when it comes to preserving resource forks. There are a few gotchas that you need to watch out for: *sftp*, *ftp*, and *scp* won't create the resource fork for you.

Also, some tools, such as the Unison File Synchronizer (*http://www.cis.upenn.edu/~bcpierce/unison/*), will try to create the resource forks on the Unix, Linux, or Windows end of the transaction. While this sort of thing works smoothly for the most part, it can occasionally trip you up. We'll talk about those issues and many others in the next chapter.

CHAPTER 3

The Mac OS X Filesystem

HFS+ has a lot going for it. Although its case-insensitivity caused problems back in the very early days of Mac OS X, is hasn't proved to be a problem in the long run. Its transparent support of the metadata that is so crucial to Mac OS X, coupled with its excellent support for journaling, make it the filesystem of choice for Mac OS X. But even if your hard disk, iPods, and external drives are all happily formatted with HFS+, you'll have to exchange files with something other than a Mac one of these days.

Mac OS X files are complicated constructs. Chapter 2 introduced you to the metadata that can lurk on the HFS+ filesystem and also discussed how it's stored on other types of filesystems using the Apple Double format. With much more than the usual contents of files to worry about, it's very easy to drop bits of your files all over the place, especially on foreign filesystems. This chapter talks a bit more about these details, explains what you need to consider when you move files from HFS+ to other filesystems, and ends with a description of how files are laid out on a Mac.

Working with Foreign Filesystems

If you're going to move files between your Mac and another operating system, there are some things you need to watch out for. As we discussed in Chapter 2, the Apple Double format will sprinkle some files with odd names across the filesystem, such as *._filename*. You'll also find a few files created in the root, such as *Temporary Items* and *.Trashes* (see Table 3-1).

The most significant problem you'll run into is moving large files around: if you're not using a third-party utility, the only common filesystem that Mac OS X, Windows, and Linux can read and write is the ancient FAT32, which has a limit of 2 GB per file.

If at all possible, we suggest that you use the network to transfer large files. If you're using an AirPort (or even a 100BaseT) network, it's worth running a cable between your Mac and the other system and setting up a TCP/IP connection for large file transfers. If you can get Gigabit Ethernet or even IP over FireWire, you'll be pleased with the zippy file transfer speeds. Even if you're not moving large files, the network is often the best way to exchange information. The are several solutions you can use for exchanging files across the network:

Netatalk
: Netatalk (*http://netatalk.sourceforge.net*) is best known as a suite for introducing Unix servers to AppleTalk networks. However, it has a daemon, *afpd*, which can share files over TCP/IP using the native Apple sharing protocol, AFP (Apple Filing Protocol). Early versions (and often the versions that are bundled with many Linux distributions) only supported an earlier version of AFP, and were limited in the length of file names. The most recent version of Netatalk works great with Mac OS X, with the exception of its non-standard Apple Double implementation, described later in this section.

Unison
: Unison (*http://www.cis.upenn.edu/~bcpierce/unison*) is a powerful file synchronizer that lets you keep Windows, Mac OS X, Linux, and Unix files in sync. It does so by maintaining a replica on each side of the synchronization, comparing the state of the filesystem against the last-known replica, and making intelligent decisions about which files are the most recent. In cases where it can't figure something out (perhaps you changed the file in both places), it prompts you to tell it what to do.

Samba
: Samba (*http://www.samba.org*) is a file and printer sharing solution that's compatible with the SMB/CIFS (Server Message Block/Common Internet Filesystem) protocol used by Windows. Although it has no native support for HFS+ metadata or resource forks, Mac OS X creates Apple Double files (described in Chapter 2) on Samba shares as needed.

Howl
: Howl (*http://www.porchdogsoft.com/products/howl*) is not a file sharing utility, but rather a great Bonjour implementation for Linux, Unix, and Windows that makes your life easier. Howl is packaged with many Linux distributions, but you can always build it from source.

  If you only use one feature of Howl, it will be its Multicast DNS feature. mDNS frees you from either having to maintain an */etc/hosts* file or remember IP addresses. As with the Mac OS X implementation of Bonjour, you can reach a host on the local network with *hostname.local*, which you'll see in action in some of the following examples. (You can also obtain a Rendezvous/Bonjour implementation direct from Apple at *http://developer.apple.com/networking/bonjour*.)

If you use multiple solutions in combination, you may run into trouble if they disagree with what's going on under the hood of their Apple Double implementation. For example, suppose you have a single Internet location (*.webloc*) file in the *~/Test* directory on your Mac:

```
$ cd Test/
$ ls -l
total 8
-rw-r--r--    1 bjepson  bjepson  0 Mar  5 13:38 Safari.webloc
```

Next, suppose you sync your Mac to a Linux server using Unison:

```
$ unison /Users/bjepson/Test ssh://bjepson@homer.local//home/bjepson/Test
Contacting server...
Password: ********
Looking for changes
  Waiting for changes from server
Reconciling changes

local          homer
new file ---->            Safari.webloc  [f]

Proceed with propagating updates? [] y
Propagating updates


UNISON started propagating changes at 14:21:13 on 05 Mar 2005
[BGN] Copying Safari.webloc
  from /Users/bjepson/Test
  to //homer//home/bjepson/Test
[END] Copying Safari.webloc
UNISON finished propagating changes at 14:21:13 on 05 Mar 2005


Saving synchronizer state
Synchronization complete  (1 item transferred, 0 skipped, 0 failures)
```

If you log into the Linux server and inspect the filesystem, you'll see the same kind of Apple Double file format that's used by Mac OS X. All is well with the world:

```
$ ls -al
total 12
drwxr-xr-x    2 bjepson  bjepson      4096 2005-03-05 14:21 .
drwxr-xr-x   39 bjepson  bjepson      4096 2005-03-05 14:18 ..
-rw-------    1 bjepson  bjepson       741 2005-03-05 14:21 ._Safari.webloc
-rw-r--r--    1 bjepson  bjepson         0 2005-03-05 14:21 Safari.webloc
```

Now, suppose this directory on the Linux server is also shared using Netatalk's *afpd*. Things would get weird if you created another Internet location file on the Mac, and then used the Finder to drag and drop that file across to the AFP share on the Linux box.

Netatalk is going to do a couple of surprising things. First, when it creates a dot file such as *.DS_Store*, it does a hexadecimal conversion and creates *:2eDS_Store*. Second, instead of creating a file that adheres to the Apple Double format used by Apple and Unison, it's going to create a *.AppleDouble* directory that contains the metadata that HFS+ would normally store transparently. Here's what you've got on the Linux side now:

```
$ ls -al
total 36
drwxr-xr-x    3 bjepson  bjepson      4096 2005-03-05 14:34 .
drwxr-xr-x   40 bjepson  bjepson      4096 2005-03-05 14:34 ..
-rw-r--r--    1 bjepson  bjepson      6148 2005-03-05 14:34 :2eDS_Store
drwxr-xr-x    2 bjepson  bjepson      4096 2005-03-05 14:34 .AppleDouble
-rw-r--r--    1 bjepson  bjepson      6148 2005-03-05 14:26 .DS_Store
-rw-r--r--    1 bjepson  bjepson       254 2005-03-05 14:23 Google.webloc
-rw-------    1 bjepson  bjepson       741 2005-03-05 14:21 ._Safari.webloc
-rw-r--r--    1 bjepson  bjepson         0 2005-03-05 14:21 Safari.webloc
$ ls -l .AppleDouble/
total 8
-rw-rw-rw-    1 bjepson  bjepson       741 2005-03-05 14:34 :2eDS_Store
-rw-rw-rw-    1 bjepson  bjepson      1191 2005-03-05 14:34 Google.webloc
```

As you might imagine, the next time you run Unison from the Mac side, all hell breaks loose. Unison is forced to skip two files:

```
$ unison /Users/bjepson/Test ssh://bjepson@homer.local//home/bjepson/Test
Contacting server...
Password:
Looking for changes
  Safari.webloc
  Waiting for changes from server
Reconciling changes

local          homer
         error            .AppleDouble
[root 2]: The name of this Unix file is not allowed in Windows/OSX (.
AppleDouble/:2eDS_Store)
         error            :2eDS_Store
The name of this Unix file is not allowed in Windows/OSX (:2eDS_Store)
new file ====> new file   Google.webloc  [] >
changed  ---->            .DS_Store  [f]

Proceed with propagating updates? [] y
Propagating updates


UNISON started propagating changes at 14:36:39 on 05 Mar 2005
```

```
[ERROR] Skipping .AppleDouble
  [root 2]: The name of this Unix file is not allowed in Windows/OSX (.
AppleDouble/:2eDS_Store)
[ERROR] Skipping :2eDS_Store
  The name of this Unix file is not allowed in Windows/OSX (:2eDS_Store)
[BGN] Updating file Google.webloc
  from /Users/bjepson/Test
  to //homer//home/bjepson/Test
[BGN] Updating file .DS_Store
  from /Users/bjepson/Test
  to //homer//home/bjepson/Test
[END] Updating file .DS_Store
[END] Updating file Google.webloc
UNISON finished propagating changes at 14:36:39 on 05 Mar 2005


Saving synchronizer state
Synchronization complete  (2 items transferred, 2 skipped, 0 failures)
  skipped: .AppleDouble
  skipped: :2eDS_Store
```

We'd suggest that you only use one point of entry (either Unison *or* Netatalk) for a given directory, but if you need to have it both ways, there are solutions.

One workaround is to add `options:ro,noadouble` to the filesystem's entry in *AppleVolumes.default* on the Linux server. This makes the AFP share read-only and also disables the creation of *.AppleDouble* (except when a resource fork is created, which won't happen because you're accessing it read-only). This gives you quick and dirty access to the files on the Linux server via AFP when you need it, but forces you to update them through only Unison.

Another solution is to keep everything read/write, mount the remote server's filesystem before you run Unison, and simply have Unison treat the remote server as a local filesystem instead of going through SSH:

```
$ unison /Users/bjepson/Test /Volumes/Home\ Directory/Test
```

You'll still have crufty files (such as *:2eDS_Store*) appear on the Linux side, but they won't get in the way when you synchronize files and folders. However, this is a suboptimal configuration for Unison, which benefits greatly from having local filesystem access to the files on both ends of the synchronization.

Files and Directories

If you do an *ls -a /* on your Tiger system, you'll see some familiar things, such as */etc* and */var*, but you'll also notice some unfamiliar things, such as

/TheVolumeSettingsFolder, */Library*, and */Documents*. Mac OS X's filesystem contains traces of Unix, NeXTSTEP, and Mac OS 9. The tables in the rest of this chapter list directory entries and provide a description of each file or directory.

Table 3-1 describes the files and directories (indicated with a trailing slash) you may find in your / (the root) directory. The remaining tables in this chapter describe significant subdirectories.

Table 3-1. Mac OS X's root directory

File or directory	Description
.DS_Store	Contains Finder settings, such as icon location and window size. The file will appear in any directory that you've viewed with the Finder.
.Spotlight-V100/	Contains metadata used by Spotlight. For more information, see Chapter 2.
.Trashes/	Contains files that have been dragged to the Trash. On a boot volume, such files are stored in *~/.Trash*. On a non-boot volume, these files are in */.Trashes/uid/*.
.vol/	Maps HFS+ file IDs to files. If you know a file's ID, you can open it using */.vol/id*.
Applications/	Holds all your Mac OS X applications. Its *Utilities* subdirectory includes lots of useful things, such as the Terminal, Console, and the Activity Monitor.
Applications (Mac OS 9)/	Contains all your OS 9 applications if you've got Mac OS X and Mac OS 9 installed.
automount/	Handles static NFS mounts for the *automount* daemon.
bin/	Contains essential system binaries.
botlib.log	Quake III players have this.
cores/	A symbolic link (or *symlink*) to */private/cores*. If core dumps are enabled (with *tcsh*'s *limit* and *bash*/*sh*'s *ulimit* commands—see the *tcsh* and *bash* manpages for more details)—they are created in this directory as *core.pid*.
Desktop DB	Along with *Desktop DF*, contains the desktop database that is rebuilt when you click Rebuild Desktop in System Preferences → Classic.
Desktop DF	See Desktop DB.
Desktop Folder/	The Mac OS 9 desktop folder.
dev/	Contains files that represent various devices. See Table 3-6.
Developer/	Contains Apple's Xcode Tools and documentation. Available only if you have installed the Xcode Tools.
Documents/	The Mac OS 9 documents folder.
etc/	Contains system configuration files. See Table 3-2. The directory is a symbolic link to */private/etc*.
Installer Log File	May be left by some third-party application installers.
Library/	Contains support files for locally installed applications, among other things. See Table 3-4.
lost+found	Stores orphaned files discovered by *fsck*. You'll only find this on UFS volumes.
mach	A symbolic link to the */mach.sym* file.

Table 3-1. Mac OS X's root directory (continued)

File or directory	Description
mach.sym	Contains kernel symbols. It is generated during each boot by */etc/rc*.
mach_kernel	The Darwin kernel.
Network/	Contains network-mounted *Application*, *Library*, and *Users* directories, as well as a *Servers* directory, which contains directories mounted by the *automount* daemon.
private/	Contains the *tmp*, *var*, *etc*, and *cores* directories.
sbin/	Contains executables for system administration and configuration.
sw/	Contains the Fink installation (see Chapter 13).
Shared Items/	Gives OS 9 multiuser systems a place where users can store files for other users to access.
System/	Contains a subdirectory, *Library*, which holds support files for the system and system applications, among other things. See Table 3-3.
System Folder/	The Mac OS 9 System Folder.
Temporary Items/	Contains temporary files used by Mac OS 9.
TheFindByContentFolder/	Created by Sherlock 2 (the Classic version).
TheVolumeSettingsFolder/	Keeps track of shared volume details, such as open windows and desktop printers.
tmp/	Holds temporary files. It is a symbolic link to */private/tmp*.
Trash/	Where Mac OS 9 stores deleted files until the Trash is emptied.
User Guides And Information/	An alias to */Library/Documentation/User Guides and Information*, and contains hardware-specific documentation and information about Mac OS X.
Users/	Contains home directories for the users on the system. The *root* user's home directory is */var/root*.
usr/	Contains BSD Unix applications and support files.
var/	Contains frequently modified files, such as log files. It is a symbolic link to */private/var*.
VM Storage	Mac OS 9 virtual memory file.
Volumes/	Contains all mounted filesystems, including removable media and mounted disk images.

The /etc Directory

The */etc* directory contains configuration files for Unix applications and services, as well as scripts that control system startup. Table 3-2 lists the contents of the */etc* directory.

Table 3-2. The /etc directory

File or directory	Description
6to4.conf	Configuration file for encapsulating IPv6 within IPv4. See *ip6config(8)*.
afpovertcp.cfg	Causes Mac OS X to use TCP/IP as the default transport for Apple File Protocol (AFP). Use this file to configure the defaults for AFP over TCP/IP.

Table 3-2. The /etc directory (continued)

File or directory	Description
aliases	Mail aliases file. Symbolic link to */etc/postfix/aliases*.
aliases.db	Mail aliases db file created when you run *newaliases*.
appletalk.cfg	AppleTalk configuration file for routing or multihoming. See the *appletalk.cfg(5)* manpage.
authorization	Controls how applications, such as installers, can temporarily obtain *root* privileges.
authorization.cac	Undocumented.
bashrc	Global configuration file for *bash*, the Bourne-again shell.
crontab	*root*'s *crontab*.
csh.cshrc	Global *csh* configuration file, processed when the shell starts up. If you have a *.cshrc* or *.tcshrc* file in your home directory, *tcsh* executes its contents as well.
csh.login	Global *csh* login file, processed when a login shell starts up. If you have a *.login* file in your home directory, *tcsh* will execute its contents as well.
csh.logout	Global *csh* logout file, processed when a user logs out of a login shell.
cups/	Contains configuration files for Common Unix Printing System (CUPS).
daily	*cron* job that is run once a day (see *crontab*). This is a symlink to */etc/periodic/daily/500.daily*.
defaults/	Contains default configuration files for applications and utilities.
dumpdates	Dump date records created by *dump(5)*, which is run by */etc/daily*.
efax.rc	Configuration file for *fax(1)*.
find.codes	Undocumented.
fonts/	Configures fonts for X11.
fstab.hd	Undocumented.
ftpusers	List of users who are prohibited from using FTP.
gdb.conf	Global *gdb* configuration file.
gettytab	Terminal configuration database.
group	Group permissions file. See Chapter 5.
hostconfig	System configuration file that controls many of the startup items described in Chapter 3.
hosts	Host database; a mapping of IP addresses to hostnames. You can use this as a supplement to other Directory Services, such as DNS. Mac OS X 10.1 and earlier consulted this file only in single-user mode, but as of Mac OS X 10.2 (Jaguar), this file is used at other times. For more information, see Chapter 5.
hosts.equiv	List of trusted remote hosts and host-user pairs. This is used by *rsh* and is inherently insecure. You should use *ssh* instead, which is a secure alternative. See *ssh-keygen(1)* to generate key pairs that can be used to set up a trust relationship with remote users.
hosts.lpd	List of hosts that are allowed to connect to the Unix *lpd* service.
httpd/	Contains Apache's configuration files.

Table 3-2. The /etc directory (continued)

File or directory	Description
inetd.conf	Internet super-server (*inetd*) configuration file.
kcpassword	Stores an encrypted version of a user's password for auto-login.
kern_loader.conf	Mach's kernel server loader configuration file. Empty in the current version of Mac OS X.
localtime	Symbolic link to your system's time zone, such as: */usr/share/zoneinfo/US/Eastern*.
mach_init.d/	Mach bootstrap daemons. See Chapter 4.
mach_init_per_user.d/	Per-user Mach bootstrap daemons. See Chapter 4.
mail.rc	Global configuration file for */usr/bin/mail*.
master.passwd	Shadow *passwd* file, consulted only in single-user mode. During normal system operation, Open Directory manages user information (see Chapter 5).
memberd.conf	Configuration file for the group membership resolution daemon, *memberd(8)*.
moduli	System-wide prime numbers used for cryptographic applications such as *ssh*.
monthly	Monthly *cron* job (see *crontab*); a symlink to */etc/periodic/monthly/500. monthly*.
motd	Message of the day; displayed each time you launch a new Terminal or log in remotely.
named.conf	Configuration file for *named*, the DNS daemon. For more details, see *named(8)*.
nanorc	Configuration file for the *nano* text editor.
networks	Network name database.
notify.conf	Configuration for the Notification Center.
openldap/	Contains configuration files for OpenLDAP, an implementation of the Lightweight Directory Access Protocol.
pam.d/	Contains configuration files for PAM.
passwd	Password file. For more information, see Chapter 5.
pear.conf	Configuration file for *pear*, the PHP Extension and Application Repository.
periodic/	Contains configuration files for the *periodic* utility, which runs *cron* jobs on a regular basis.
php.ini.default	Default PHP initialization file.
postfix/	Contains *postfix* configuration files.
ppp/	Contains configuration files for Point-To-Point Protocol (PPP).
printcap	Printer configuration file for *lpd*. CUPS automatically generates this file. For more information, see *cupsd(8)*.
profile	Global profile for the Bourne-again shell.
protocols	Network protocol database.
racoon/	Contains configuration files for *racoon*, the IKE key management daemon.
rc	Startup script for multiuser mode.
rc.common	Common settings for startup scripts.
rc.netboot	Startup script for booting from the network using NetBoot.

Table 3-2. The /etc directory (continued)

File or directory	Description
rc.shutdown	System shutdown script.
resolv.conf	DNS resolver configuration. Symlink to */var/run/resolv.conf*.
rmtab	Remote NFS mount table.
rpc	RPC number-to-name mappings. Mac OS X 10.1 and earlier consulted this file only in single-user mode, but newer versions of Mac OS X use this file at other times.
rtadvd.conf	Configuration file for the router advertisement daemon. For more details, see *rtadvd(8)*.
services	Internet service name database. Mac OS X 10.1 and earlier consulted this file only in single-user mode, but Mac OS X 10.2 (Jaguar) uses this file at other times. For more information, see Chapter 5.
shells	List of shells.
slpsa.conf	Configuration file for the service locator daemon (*slpd*).
smb.conf	Samba configuration file.
smb.conf.template	Template configuration file for Samba.
snmpd.conf	Configuration file for the ucd-snmp *snmpd* agent.
ssh_config	Global configuration file for OpenSSH client programs.
ssh_host_dsa_key	Private DSA host key for OpenSSH. This file, and the other *ssh_host_** files, are created the first time you start Remote Login in the Sharing System Preferences.
ssh_host_dsa_key.pub	Public DSA host key for OpenSSH.
ssh_host_key	Private host key for OpenSSH when using SSH 1 compatibility.
ssh_host_key.pub	Public host key for OpenSSH when using SSH 1 compatibility.
ssh_host_rsa_key	Private RSA host key for OpenSSH.
ssh_host_rsa_key.pub	Public RSA host key for OpenSSH.
sshd_config	Configuration file for the OpenSSH *sshd* daemon.
sudoers	Configuration file for the *sudo* command. Make sure you use the *visudo* command only to edit this file.
syslog.conf	*syslogd* configuration file.
ttys	Terminal initialization file.
weekly	Weekly *cron* job (see *crontab*). This is a symlink to */etc/periodic/weekly/500.weekly*.
X11/	X11 configuration directory. This file is present only if you have installed X11.
xgrid/	Configuration files for Xgrid.
xinetd.conf	Configuration file for *xinetd*, the extended Internet superserver daemon.
xinetd.d/	Contains service-specific configuration files for *xinetd*.
xtab	Lists current NFS exports.

The /System/Library Directory

Table 3-3 lists the directories stored under the */System/Library* directory. You should not modify the contents of these directories or add new files to them. Instead, use their counterparts in the */Library* folder. For example, to install a new font, drag it into */Library/Fonts*, not */System/Library/Fonts*.

Table 3-3. The /System/Library directory

File or directory	Description
Automator/	Contains Automator actions and supporting files.
Caches/	Contains caches used by various parts of the operating system.
CFMSupport/	Holds shared libraries used by Carbon applications.
ColorPickers/	Includes localized resources for Mac OS X color pickers.
Colors/	Contains the names and values of colors used in the color picker control.
ColorSync/	Contains ColorSync profiles.
Components/	Contains application building blocks (components), such as AppleScript and color pickers. Components are not applications themselves and are generally shared between applications.
Contextual Menu Items/	Contains plug-ins for the Finder's contextual menu (Control-click or Right-click).
CoreServices/	Contains system applications, such as *SystemStarter*, *BootX*, the Finder, and the login window.
Dictionaries/	Contains dictionaries used by the Dictionary application.
Displays/	Contains ColorSync information for external monitors.
DTDs/	Contains document type definitions for XML documents used by the system, such as property lists.
Extensions/	Holds Darwin kernel extensions.
Extensions.kextcache	Contains information about extensions in the cache; a compressed XML document.
Extensions.mkext	Contains the kernel extension cache. It is created at boot by */etc/rc*.
Filesystems/	Contains drivers and utilities for various filesystems (MS-DOS, AppleShare, UFS, etc.).
Filters/	Contains Quartz Filters that are used in the Print dialog's ColorSync section.
Find/	Includes support files for Sherlock's content indexing.
Fonts/	Contains core Mac OS X fonts.
Frameworks/	Holds a collection of reusable application frameworks, including shared libraries, headers, and documentation.
Image Capture/	Contains device support files for the Image Capture application.
Java/	Contains Java *class* and *jar* files.
Keyboard Layouts/	Contains bundles that support internationalized keyboard layouts.
Keychains/	Contains system-wide keychain files.
LaunchAgents/	Undocumented.
LaunchDaemons/	Contains startup configuration files for *launchd* as described in Chapter 4.

Table 3-3. The /System/Library directory (continued)

File or directory	Description
LocalePlugins/	Plug-ins for locale-specific text handling.
LoginPlugins/	Contains helper applications that are launched as you log in.
Modem Scripts/	Contains modem configuration scripts.
MonitorPanels/	Includes panels used by System Preferences → Displays.
OpenSSL/	Holds OpenSSL configuration and support files.
Perl/	Holds Perl Libraries.
PreferencePanes/	Contains all the preference panes for the Preferences application.
Printers/	Contains printer support files.
PrivateFrameworks/	Holds private frameworks meant to support Mac OS X. These frameworks are not meant for programmers' use.
QuickTime/	Holds QuickTime support files.
QuickTimeJava/	Includes support files for the QuickTime/Java bridge.
Rulebooks/	Contains information used for text handling, such as word-breaking rules for hyphenation.
Screen Savers/	Contains screensavers that you can select from System Preferences → Desktop & Screen Saver.
ScriptingAdditions/	Includes AppleScript plug-ins and libraries.
Security/	Undocumented.
ServerSetup/	Contains a script to toggle whether *postfix* is loaded on demand.
Services/	Contains services that are made available through the Services menu.
Sounds/	Contains sounds that are available in System Preferences → Sound.
Speech/	Includes speech recognition and generation support files.
Spotlight/	Contains metadata importers for Spotlight (see Chapter 2).
StartupItems/	Contains startup scripts as described in Chapter 4.
SyncServices/	Contains iSync conduits.
SystemConfiguration/	Contains plug-ins used to monitor various system activities (for Apple use only).
SystemProfiler/	Contains support files for System Profiler.
Tcl/	Holds Tcl Libraries.
TextEncodings/	Contains localized text encodings.
User Template/	Holds localized skeleton files for user directories. See "Creating a User's Home Directory" in Chapter 5.
WidgetResources/	Contains support files for Dashboard.

The /Library Directory

Table 3-4 lists the contents of the */Library* directory. The */Library* directory contains counterparts to many directories found in */System/Library*. You can use the */Library* counterparts for system-wide customization. If you find a directory of the same name in your home *Library* directory (*~/Library*), you can use that for user-level customization. For example, you can install fonts for one particular user by moving them into *~/ Library/Fonts*. Table 3-4 lists only the directories found in */Library* that are not also found in */System/Library* (with the exception of *Java* and *Perl*, which bear additional discussion included in the table).

Table 3-4. The /Library directory

File or directory	Description
Address Book Plug-Ins/	Contains plug-ins for the Address Book application.
Application Support/	Contains support files for locally installed applications.
Audio/	Contains audio plug-ins and sounds.
ColorSync/	Contains user-installed ColorSync profiles and scripts.
Desktop Pictures/	Contains desktop pictures used by System Preferences → Desktop & Screen Saver.
Documentation/	Provides documentation for locally installed applications.
Graphics/	Undocumented.
Internet Plug-Ins/	Contains locally installed browser plug-ins.
Java/	Contains locally installed Java classes (you can drop jar files into */Library/Java/Extensions*), as well as a suitable directory to use as your `$JAVA_HOME` (*/Library/Java/Home*).
Logs/	Holds logs for services such as Apple File Services, the Crash Reporter, and the Directory Service.
Mail/	Includes support files for *Mail.app*.
Perl/	Contains locally installed Perl modules (MakeMaker's `INSTALLSITELIB`).
Preferences/	Holds global preferences.
Python/	Contains locally installed Python modules.
Receipts/	Leaves a receipt in the form of a *.pkg* directory after you install an application with the Mac OS X installer. The *.pkg* directory contains a bill of materials file (*.bom*), which you can read with the *lsbom* command.
Scripts/	Contains a variety of AppleScripts installed with Mac OS X.
User Pictures/	Contains user pictures that are used in the login panel.
WebServer/	Contains the Apache CGI and document *root* directories.

The /var Directory

The */var* directory contains transient and volatile files, such as PID files (which tell you the process ID of a currently running daemon), log files, and many others. Table 3-5 lists the contents of the */var* directory.

Table 3-5. The /var directory

File or directory	Description
at/	Contains information about jobs scheduled with the *at* command.
audit/	Undocumented.
backups/	Contains backups of the NetInfo database.
cron/	Contains user *crontab* files.
db/	Includes a grab bag of configuration and data files, including the *locate* database, the NetInfo database, and network interface information.
empty/	Used as an unwritable *chroot(8)* environment.
launchd/	Contains *launchd*'s working files.
log/	Contains a variety of log files, including *syslog*, mail, and web server logs.
mail/	Contains inboxes for local users' email.
msgs/	Holds system-wide messages that were delivered using *msgs -s*.
named/	Includes various files used for local DNS services.
netboot/	Contains various files used for NetBoot.
root/	Serves as the *root* user's home directory.
run/	Holds PID files for running processes. Also contains working files used by programs such as *sudo*.
rwho/	Contains information used by the *rwho* command.
slp.regfile	List of servers found with Service Location Protocol (SLP).
spool/	Serves as a spool directory for mail, printer queues, and other queued resources.
tmp/	Serves as a temporary file directory.
vm/	Contains your swap files.
xgrid/	Holds working files used by Xgrid.
yp/	Contains files used by NIS.

The /dev Directory

The */dev* directory contains files that represent devices attached to the system, including physical devices, such as serial ports, and pseudo-devices, such as a random number generator. Table 3-6 lists the contents of the */dev* directory.

Table 3-6. The /dev directory

File or directory	Description
bpf[0-3]	Berkeley Packet Filter devices. See *bpf(4)*.
console	The system console. This is owned by whoever is currently logged in. If you write to it, the output ends up in */var/tmp/console.log*, which you can view with the Console application (*/Applications/Utilities*).

Table 3-6. The /dev directory (continued)

File or directory	Description
*cu.**	Modem devices for compatibility with the Unix *cu* (call up) utility.
disk[0-n]	Disk device.
disk[0-n]s[0-n]	Disk partition. For example, */dev/disk0s1* is the first partition of */dev/disk0*.
fd/	Devices that correspond to file descriptors. See the *fd* manpage for more details.
fsevents	Undocumented.
klog	Device used by *syslogd* to read kernel messages.
kmem	Image of kernel memory.
mem	Image of the system memory.
nsmb0	Device file used for *smbfs*.
null	Bit bucket. You can redirect anything here, and it disappears.
ptyp[0-f]	Master ends of the first sixteen pseudo-*ttys*.
pty[q-w][0-f]	Master ends of the remaining pseudo-*ttys*.
random	Source of pseudorandom data. See *random(4)*.
rdisk[0-n]	Raw disk device.
rdisk[0-n]s[0-n]	Raw disk partition.
stderr	Symbolic link to */dev/fd/2*.
stdin	Symbolic link to */dev/fd/0*.
stdout	Symbolic link to */dev/fd/1*.
tty	Standard output stream of the current Terminal or remote login.
*tty.**	Various modem and serial devices.
ttyp[0-f]	Slave ends of the first sixteen pseudo-*ttys*.
tty[q-w][0-f]	Slave ends of the remaining pseudo-*ttys*.
urandom	Source of pseudorandom data, not guaranteed to be strong. See *random(4)*.
vn[0-3]	Pseudo disk devices.
zero	Infinite supply of null characters. Often used with *dd* to create a file made up of null characters.

CHAPTER 4

Startup

The most striking difference between Mac OS X and other flavors of Unix is in how Mac OS X handles the boot process. Gone are */etc/inittab*, */etc/init.d*, and */etc/rc.local* from traditional Unix systems. In their place is a BSD-like startup sequence sandwiched between a Mach* foundation and the Aqua user interface.

This chapter describes Mac OS X Tiger's startup sequence, beginning with the *BootX* loader and progressing to full multiuser mode, at which time the system is ready to accept logins from normal users. The chapter also covers custom startup items, network interface configuration, and Mac OS X's default *periodic* jobs.

Booting Mac OS X

When the computer is powered up, the firmware is in complete control. After the firmware initializes the hardware, it hands off control to the *BootX* loader, which bootstraps the kernel. After a trip into Mach, the control bubbles up into the BSD subsystem, and eventually into the Aqua user interface.

By default, Mac OS X boots graphically. If you'd like to see console messages as you boot, hold down ⌘-V (the "V" stands for "verbose") as you start the computer. If you'd like to always boot in verbose mode, you can specify a flag in the boot arguments that are stored in your system's firmware. First, use the command *nvram boot-args* to make sure there aren't any flags already set (if there are, and you didn't set them, you probably should not change this setting). Set your boot arguments to *-v* with this command:

```
sudo /usr/sbin/nvram boot-args="-v"
```

* Mach is a microkernel operating system developed at Carnegie Mellon University. The Mac OS X kernel, *xnu*, is a hybrid of Mach and BSD.

The next time you boot your Mac, it boots in verbose mode. To turn this setting off, use the command:

```
sudo /usr/sbin/nvram boot-args=
```

To boot in single-user mode, hold down ⌘-S as you start the computer. In single-user mode, your filesystem is mounted as read-only, which limits what you can do. Single-user mode should generally be used only to repair a system that has been damaged (for example, see "Restoring the Directory Services Database" in Chapter 5). Unlike with other Unix systems, we do not suggest that you use single-user mode to perform *fsck* repairs manually. Instead, restart your Mac and boot from Tiger's install DVD (hold down the C key as your Mac starts up), and then run the Disk Utility (Installer → Open Disk Utility) to repair a problem disk volume.

The BootX Loader

BootX is located in */System/Library/CoreServices*. It draws the Apple logo on the screen and proceeds to set up the kernel environment. *BootX* first looks for kernel extensions (drivers, also known as *kexts*) that are cached in the *mkext cache*. If this cache does not exist, *BootX* loads only those extensions in */System/Library/Extensions* that have the *OSBundleRequired* key in their `ExtensionName.kext/` *Info.plist* file. Example 4-1 is an excerpt from the */System/Library/Extensions/System.kext/Info.plist* file.

Example 4-1. A portion of a kernel extension's Info.plist file

```
<?xml version="1.0" encoding="UTF-8"?>
<!DOCTYPE plist PUBLIC "-//Apple Computer//DTD PLIST 1.0//EN"
        "http://www.apple.com/DTDs/PropertyList-1.0.dtd">
<plist version-"1.0">
  <dict>
    <key>CFBundleDevelopmentRegion</key>
    <string>English</string>
    <!-- multiple keys and strings omitted -->
  </dict>
</plist>
```

After the required drivers are loaded, *BootX* hands off control to the kernel (*/mach_kernel*).

Initialization

The kernel first initializes all the data structures needed to support Mach and BSD. Next, it initializes the I/O Kit, which connects the kernel with the set of extensions that correspond to the machine's hardware configuration. Then, the kernel finds and mounts the root filesystem. The kernel then launches the first process on the system, *launchd*, which is responsible for bootstrapping the system as well as launching daemons on behalf of the system or users.

Mac OS X Panther (10.3) and earlier did things differently. The first process the kernel loaded was *mach_init*, which started Mach message handling. *mach_init* then launched the BSD *init* process. In keeping with Unix conventions, *init* was process ID (PID) 1, even though it was started second. *mach_init* was given PID 2, and its parent PID was set to 1 (*init*'s PID). As of Mac OS X Tiger (10.4), *launchd* replaces both of these processes.

The /etc/rc Script

If you're booting normally, *launchd* loads the */etc/rc* shell script to start the system (if you're booting in single user mode, */etc/rc* is not run at all). This *rc* script sources the */etc/rc.common* script, which sets the initial environment, defines some common functions, and loads the */etc/hostconfig* file, which controls the system services that get started at boot. Example 4-2 is an excerpt from the *hostconfig* file.

Example 4-2. A portion of /etc/hostconfig

```
# Services
AFPSERVER=-NO-
CUPS=-AUTOMATIC-
```

This excerpt shows the settings that determine whether Apple File Sharing and CUPS (Common Unix Printing System) are launched at startup. See "The startup script" later in this chapter, for an explanation of how */etc/hostconfig* can be used to control services that you install yourself. Table 4-1 describes the default entries from */etc/hostconfig*.

Table 4-1. Default entries from the hostconfig file

Entry	Default value	Description
HOSTNAME	-AUTOMATIC-	Specifies a hostname. A setting of -AUTOMATIC- causes *configd* to use the value from the system configuration database.
ROUTER	-AUTOMATIC-	This specifies the default router. -AUTOMATIC- causes Mac OS X to use the router supplied by DHCP or BOOTP. The settings in System Preferences → Network override this.
AFPSERVER	-NO-	Controls whether Apple File Sharing (Personal File Sharing in System Preferences → Sharing) is enabled. This corresponds to the AppleShare startup item. (For information on startup items, see "SystemStarter," later in this chapter.)

Table 4-1. Default entries from the hostconfig file (continued)

Entry	Default value	Description
AUTHSERVER	-NO-	Specifies whether the NetInfo authentication server for legacy clients (*/usr/sbin/tim*) should be started. This corresponds to the AuthServer startup item.
AUTOMOUNT	-YES-	Determines whether the NFS *automount* daemon should be started. The NFS startup item consults this setting.
CUPS	-AUTOMATIC-	Controls whether Printing Services are started up. This corresponds to the *PrintingServices* startup item. However, this is not controlled by the Printer Sharing option in System Preferences → Sharing (that setting instead inserts the appropriate settings into the */etc/cups/cupsd.conf* file).
IPFORWARDING	-NO-	Determines whether the Network startup item enables IP forwarding.
IPV6	-YES-	Specifies whether the Network startup item should turn on IPv6 support.
NFSLOCKS	-AUTOMATIC-	If your Mac is running as an NFS server, a setting of -AUTOMATIC- enables locking for NFS files. As an NFS client, a value of -YES- enables locking, but -AUTOMATIC- loads the appropriate daemons (*rpc.statd* and *rpc.lockd*) so they are only used when needed. The NFS startup item consults this setting.
NISDOMAIN	-NO-	Specifies the NIS Domain that your Mac should participate in. Leave it set to -NO- to disable NIS, otherwise set it to the appropriate domain. The NIS startup item uses this setting.
TIMESYNC	-YES-	Controls whether the network time daemon (*ntpd*) is started. You can configure these settings with System Preferences → Date & Time. This setting affects the NetworkTime startup item.
QTSSERVER	-NO-	Specifies whether the QuickTime Streaming Server is started at boot time. Although it's not included with the desktop version of Mac OS X, you can download it from *http://developer.apple.com/darwin/projects/streaming/*.
WEBSERVER	-NO-	Controls whether the Apache web server (Personal Web Sharing in System Preferences → Sharing) is started. This corresponds to the Apache startup item.
SMBSERVER	-NO-	This setting has no effect. Older versions of Mac OS X used it to control Samba, the Windows file sharing server. This setting can be toggled using Windows Sharing in System Preferences → Sharing, which toggles the `disable` setting in */etc/xinetd.d/smbd*.
SNMPSERVER	-NO-	Specifies whether the SNMP agent is to be started. This corresponds to the SNMP startup item.
CRASHREPORTER	-YES-	Controls whether the crash reporter is started. You can refine the crash reporter settings with */Developer/Utilities/CrashReporterPrefs*.
ARDAGENT	-NO-	Specifies whether Apple Remote Desktop (also specified in System Preferences → Sharing) is started.

After *rc* has loaded in values from */etc/rc.common* and */etc/hostconfig*, it performs a check of the filesystem (*fsck*) if needed. If the *fsck* fails, *rc* tries an *fsck -fy*, which forces a check and assumes a "Yes" answer to all the questions that *fsck* asks. If that fails, the system halts.

If you find yourself with *fsck* problems, you should boot from the Mac OS X installation DVD. You can boot from a DVD by holding down the C key at startup. When the Installer appears, choose Installer → Disk Utility from the menu bar and use it to inspect and repair the damaged disk.

Next, */etc/rc* performs the following steps (among others, that is; this list describes the most significant):

Mounts local filesystems
: By this point, the root filesystem is already mounted, but the *rc* script now mounts any additional HFS+ and UFS volumes listed in */etc/fstab*, as well as the */dev* filesystem. This step does not, however, perform the automatic mounting of local volumes under the */Volumes* directory. This is handled by the disk arbitration daemon, which is started as a Mach bootstrap daemon (see "Mach Bootstrap Services," later in this chapter).

Launches BootCacheControl
: The *rc* script initializes the boot-time performance cache (*BootCacheControl*), which implements intelligent read-ahead strategies for the boot volume.

Tunes the system
: Next, a series of *sysctl* calls tune kernel variables such as the maximum number of *vnodes* (data structures the kernel uses to represent files) and various shared memory settings.

Enables virtual memory
: At this point, the *dynamic_pager* daemon starts running. This daemon manages swap files in the */var/vm/* subdirectory. The kernel uses these files to allocate virtual memory as it is needed.

Starts kextd, the kernel extension daemon
: The kernel initially boots with the minimum set of extensions needed to mount the root filesystem on all supported hardware. Some of these extensions are not needed, so */etc/rc* starts the *kextd* daemon (*/usr/libexec/kextd*) to unload unnecessary extensions. For example, the *iPodDriver* includes the *OSBundleRequired* key to support booting from your iPod. If you don't have your iPod plugged in, *kextd* can safely unload that driver. The *kextd* daemon is also responsible for loading

and unloading extensions on demand for the duration of the system's uptime. Extensions live in the */System/Library/Extensions* directory.

Creates the NetInfo Database
: NetInfo is a Directory Services database for standalone machines. See Chapter 3 for a complete discussion. In this step, the *rc* script creates a default NetInfo database (only if none exists).

Launches Mach bootstrap services
: Next, the *rc* script runs *register_mach_bootstrap_servers* on all the services listed in */etc/mach_init.d*. That directory contains a collection of XML *.plist* files containing a description of services, the path to the corresponding executable, and whether the service should be loaded on demand. See "Mach Bootstrap Services," later in this chapter.

Starts up Launch Daemons
: As of Mac OS X 10.4 Tiger, the *SystemStarter* (see "SystemStarter," later in this chapter) method for starting up daemons is reserved for core system components such as Apache, Spotlight, and Apple Remote Desktop. In its place, *launchd*, which is also the first process on the system, takes care of bootstrapping most of the services on the system. See "launchd," later in this chapter.

Sets the system language
: If this system is not fully configured (if the file */var/db/.AppleSetupDone* does not exist), the language chooser appears at this point and prompts the user to choose a default language for the system. Whether that chooser appears, the *rc* script reads in */var/log/CDIS.custom* and exports the variable it contains into subsequent environments.

After these steps are completed, */etc/rc* hands off control to */sbin/SystemStarter*, which is described in the "SystemStarter" section later in this chapter.

It's true—there are three ways to start a daemon on Mac OS X: using *SystemStarter*, Mach Bootstrap Services, and *launchd*. Of the three of these, *launchd* is the latest, but for some purposes, you'll find the *SystemStarter* scheme to be best. For more information, see "SystemStarter" and "Adding Startup Items," later in this chapter.

Mach Bootstrap Services

Mac OS X Panther introduced Mach bootstrap services, a new approach for starting daemons. Daemons can be loaded at two points: system startup and user login, which includes local and remote (such as SSH) logins. System startup scripts go into */etc/mach_init.d*, and user login scripts go into */etc/mach_init_per_user.d*. Bootstrap daemons are identified to the system using the `ServiceName` in their *.plist* files, and the operating system can load that service on demand if the `OnDemand` option is set to `true` (this is the default). Mac OS X will launch these services on demand or wake sleeping bootstrap services (when a bootstrap service goes unused for a period of time, it can sleep). Table 4-2 describes the services started in this stage.

Table 4-2. Mach bootstrap services

Item	Description
ATSServer.plist	Launches the Apple Type Solution server.
configd.plist	Starts the Configuration server daemon. See "scutil" in Chapter 17 for information on working with the Configuration server's database.
coreaudiod.plist	Starts the Core Audio daemon.
coreservicesd.plist	Launches the Core Services daemon.
DirectoryService.plist	Starts The DirectoryService daemon. For more information, see Chapter 5 and the *DirectoryService* manpage.
diskarbitrationd.plist	Launches the disk arbitration daemon, which coordinates the mounting of filesystems. For more information, see the *diskarbitrationd* manpage.
distnoted.plist	Starts the distributed notifications daemon.
hdiejectd.plist	Unknown or undocumented.
IIDCAssistant.plist	Starts a daemon required to support iSight audio.
KerberosAutoConfig.plist	Configures the single sign-on service. See the *kerberosautoconfig* manpage .
kuncd.plist	Starts the Kernel-User Notification daemon, which kernel-level code can use to pop up dialogs when user action is needed. See the "Kernel-User Notification" topic in *Writing an I/O Kit Device Driver*, which you can find at *http://developer.apple.com/documentation/DeviceDrivers/*.
lookupd.plist	Starts *lookupd*, a thin layer that acts as a frontend to Directory Services. For more information, see the *lookupd* manpage and Chapter 5.
mds.plist	Starts the *mds* daemon used by Spotlight.
memberd.plist	Starts the group membership daemon.
notifyd.plist	Launches the server for the Mac OS X notification system. For more information, see the *notify(3)* manpage.
ocspd.plist	Starts the Online Certificate Status Protocol daemon, used to check the status of a certificate.
scsid.plist	Launches a daemon used by the SCSI subsystem.
securityd.plist	Starts the security server, which manages keychain items and other cryptographic operations.
WindowServer.plist	Starts the Mac OS X WindowServer, the service that manages the screen and the windows drawn upon it.

launchd

Mac OS X Tiger introduces the latest and greatest startup scheme, *launchd*. It has launch-on-demand capabilities and also supports on-demand launching via Mach ports (as does the *mach_init.d* scheme). *launchd* also offers the ability to launch on demand based on file system and Unix domain socket events. The property list (*.plist*) files for system-installed daemons are in */System/Library/LaunchDaemons*. Locally-installed daemons can be installed into */Library/LaunchDaemons*. Table 4-3 lists and describes the system-installed daemons, most of which have counterparts in Linux and Unix systems.

For an example of a launch daemon property list, see "Periodic Jobs," later in this chapter.

You can control launch daemons with the *launchctl* utility. For example, to enable and load a daemon that's disabled (there will be a `Disabled` key in its property list file), use `launchctl load -w` followed by the path to the property list. For example, the following command would enable and start the telnet server:

```
# launchctl load -w /System/Library/LaunchDaemons/telnet.plist
```

You can stop and disable this daemon with `unload -w`:

```
# launchctl unload -w /System/Library/LaunchDaemons/telnet.plist
```

For more information, see the *launchctl* manpage.

Table 4-3. Default Mac OS X launch daemons

Property List File	Description	Enabled by default?
bootps.plist	Starts the DHCP/BOOTP daemon.	No
com.apple.atrun.plist	Launches the *atrun* daemon.	Yes
com.apple.KernelEventAgent.plist	Runs the kernel event agent, which responds to low-level kernel events (such as disk and network events).	Yes
com.apple.mDNSResponder.plist	Starts the Multicast DNS responder, needed by Bonjour.	Yes
com.apple.nibindd.plist	Launches the NetInfo binder daemon.	Yes
com.apple.periodic-daily.plist	Runs the daily *periodic* job.	Yes
com.apple.periodic-monthly.plist	Runs the monthly *periodic* job.	Yes
com.apple.periodic-weekly.plist	Runs the weekly *periodic* job.	Yes
com.apple.portmap.plist	Starts the portmapper.	Yes
com.apple.syslogd.plist	Launches the system log daemon.	Yes
com.apple.xgridagentd.plist	Runs the Xgrid agent.	No

Table 4-3. Default Mac OS X launch daemons (continued)

Property List File	Description	Enabled by default?
com.apple.xgridcontrollerd.plist	Runs the Xgrid controller.	No
com.vix.cron.plist	Starts the *cron* daemon.	Yes
eppc.plist	Runs the Apple Events server.	No
exec.plist	Starts *rexecd*, the remote execution server.	No
finger.plist	Launches the finger daemon.	No
ftp.plist	Starts the FTP server.	No
login.plist	Starts the remote login (*rlogin*) daemon.	No
nmbd.plist	Launches Samba's *nmbd* daemon.	No
ntalk.plist	Starts the *ntalk* daemon.	No
org.isc.named.plist	Runs *named*.	No
org.postfix.master.plist	Launches the postfix master process.	Yes
org.xinetd.xinetd.plist	Starts the Internet superserver (*xinetd*).	Yes
printer.plist	Starts the CUPS *lpd* server.	No
shell.plist	Starts the remote shell daemon (*rshd*).	No
smbd.plist	Launches Samba's *smbd* daemon.	No
ssh.plist	Starts the SSH server.	No
swat.plist	Runs the Samba Web Administration Tool.	No
telnet.plist	Launches the telnet server.	No
tftp.plist	Starts the Trivial FTP server daemon.	No

SystemStarter

SystemStarter examines */System/Library/StartupItems* and */Library/StartupItems* for applications that should be started at boot time. */Library/StartupItems* contains items for locally installed applications. */System/Library/StartupItems* contains items for the system. You should not modify these or add your own items here. Table 4-4 lists Mac OS X's available startup items.

Because much of *SystemStarter*'s responsibilities have been handled by *launchd*, the number of startup items has dramatically decreased since Mac OS X 10.3.

Table 4-4. Mac OS X default startup items

Item	Description
Apache	Starts the Apache web server. Enable this with the `WEBSERVER` entry in */etc/hostconfig* or by turning on Web Sharing (System Preferences → Sharing).
AppServices	Starts the desktop database, input managers, and printing services.

Table 4-4. Mac OS X default startup items (continued)

Item	Description
AppleShare	Starts Apple file sharing. Enable this with the `AFPSERVER` entry in */etc/hostconfig* or by turning on File Sharing (System Preferences → Sharing).
AuthServer	Starts the authentication server. Enable this with the `AUTHSERVER` entry in */etc/hostconfig*.
CrashReporter	Enables automatic crash report generation when an application crashes. Enable this with the `CRASHREPORTER` entry in */etc/hostconfig*.
Disks	Mounts local filesystems.
FibreChannel	Starts support for Fibre Channel controllers.
IFCStart	Launches *ifcstart*, which is used for international components of Mac OS X.
IPServices	Starts *xinetd* and, optionally, Internet address sharing.
Metadata	Launches the daemons required for Spotlight.
NFS	Starts the NFS client. The NFS server is started if NetInfo or */etc/exports* has been configured to export one or more filesystems.
NIS	Starts the Network Information Service unless `NISDOMAIN` is set to `-NO` in */etc/hostconfig*.
NetworkTime	Starts the NTP client. Enable this with the `TIMESYNC` entry in */etc/hostconfig* or with System Preferences → Date & Time.
PrintingServices	Starts the Common Unix Printing System (CUPS).
RemoteDesktopAgent	Starts the remote desktop server. Enable it with the `ARDAGENT` entry in */etc/hostconfig* or by enabling Apple Remote Desktop in System Preferences → Sharing.
SNMP	Starts *snmpd*, the SNMP daemon. Enable it with the `SNMPSERVER` entry in */etc/hostconfig*.

The Login Window

Once *SystemStarter* is finished, *getty* is launched. In */etc/ttys*, the console entry launches the Login Window (*/System/Library/CoreServices/loginwindow.app*). At this point, the system is fully functional and ready to accept logins.

Adding Startup Items

To automatically start applications, you have two choices: start them when a user logs in, or start them when the system boots up. On most Unix systems, startup applications either reside in the */etc/rc.local* script or the */etc/init.d* directory. Under Mac OS 9, you could add a startup item by putting its alias in *System Folder/Startup Items*. Mac OS X has a different approach, described in the following sections.

Login Preferences

To start an application each time you log in, use the Accounts panel of System Preferences and select the Login Items tab. This is good for user applications, such as Stickies or an instant messenger program. For system daemons, you should set up a directory in */Library/StartupItems*, as described in the next section.

Startup Items

If you compile and install a daemon, you'll probably want it to start at boot time. For example, MySQL will build out of the box on Mac OS X (you can download it from *http://www.mysql.com*).

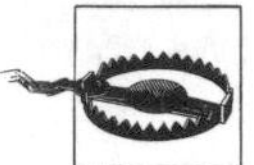

In some cases, you can start a daemon by creating a launch daemon property list in */Library/LaunchDaemons*. However, there are many restrictions on launch daemons—for example, they are not allowed to change the user or group id. Also, launch daemons do not have a facility for shutting down. For complete details on these restrictions, see the *launchd.plist* manpage. If you are setting up a daemon that either cannot abide by the *launchd* restrictions, or one that needs to be shutdown gracefully, you should create a Startup Item as described in this section.

A startup item is controlled by three things: a folder (such as */Library/StartupItems/MyItem*), a shell script with the same name as the directory (such as *MyItem*), and a property list named *StartupParameters.plist*. The shell script and the property list must appear at the top level of the startup item's folder. You can also create a *Resources* directory to hold localized resources, but this is not mandatory.

To set up the MySQL startup item, create the directory */Library/StartupItems/MySQL* as root. Then, create two files in that directory, the startup script *MySQL* and the property list *StartupParameters.plist*. The *MySQL* file must be an executable since it is a shell script. After you set up these two files as directed in the following sections, *MySQL* is launched at each boot.

The startup script

The startup script should be a shell script with `StartService()`, `StopService( )`, and `RestartService( )` functions. The contents of */Library/StartupItems/MySQL/MySQL* are shown in Example 4-3. The function call at the bottom of the script invokes the `RunService()` function from *rc.common*, which in turn invokes `StartService( )`, `StopService( )`, or `RestartService( )`, depending on whether the script was invoked with an argument of `start`, `stop`, or `restart`.

Although previous versions of Mac OS X did not invoke the `StopService( )` code when the system was shut down, Mac OS X Tiger does. Database developers everywhere can breathe a sigh of relief.

Example 4-3. A MySQL startup script

```
#!/bin/sh

# Source common setup, including hostconfig.
#
. /etc/rc.common

StartService( )
{
    # Don't start unless MySQL is enabled in /etc/hostconfig
    if [ "${MYSQL:=-NO-}" = "-YES-" ]; then
        ConsoleMessage "Starting MySQL"
        /usr/local/mysql/bin/mysqld_safe --user=mysql &
    fi
}

StopService( )
{
    ConsoleMessage "Stopping MySQL"
    # If you've set a root password within mysql, you may
    # need to add --password=password on the next line.
    /usr/local/mysql/bin/mysqladmin shutdown
}

RestartService( )
{
    # Don't restart unless MySQL is enabled in /etc/hostconfig
    if [ "${MYSQL:=-NO-}" = "-YES-" ]; then
        ConsoleMessage "Restarting MySQL"
        StopService
        StartService
    else
        StopService
    fi
}

RunService "$1"
```

Because it consults the settings of the $MYSQL environment variable, the startup script won't do anything unless you've enabled MySQL in the */etc/hostconfig* file. To do this, add the following line to */etc/hostconfig*:

```
MYSQL=-YES-
```

Mac OS X does not recognize any special connections between *hostconfig* entries and startup scripts. Instead, the startup script sources the */etc/rc.common* file, which in turn sources *hostconfig*. The directives in *hostconfig* are merely environment variables, and the startup script checks the value of the variables that control its behavior (in this case, $MYSQL).

The property list

The property list (*StartupParameters.plist*) can be in XML or NeXT format, and the list contains attributes that describe the item and determine its place in the startup sequence. The NeXT format uses NeXTSTEP-style property lists, as shown in Example 4-4.

Example 4-4. The MySQL startup parameters as a NeXT property list

```
{
  Description     = "MySQL";
  Provides        = ("MySQL");
  Requires        = ("Network");
  OrderPreference = "Late";
}
```

The XML format adheres to the *PropertyList.dtd* Document Type Definition (DTD). You can use your favorite text editor or the *Property List Editor* (*/Developer/Applications/Utilities*) to create your own property list. Example 4-5 shows the property list in XML.

Example 4-5. The MySQL startup parameters as an XML property list

```
<?xml version="1.0" encoding="UTF-8"?>
<!DOCTYPE plist
  SYSTEM "file://localhost/System/Library/DTDs/PropertyList.dtd">
<plist version="0.9">
<dict>
    <key>Description</key>
    <string>MySQL</string>
    <key>Provides</key>
    <array>
        <string>MySQL</string>
    </array>
    <key>Requires</key>
    <array>
        <string>Network</string>
    </array>
```

Example 4-5. The MySQL startup parameters as an XML property list (continued)

```
    <key>OrderPreference</key>
    <string>Late</string>
</dict>
</plist>
```

The following list describes the various keys you can use in a startup parameters property list:

`Description`
: This is a phrase that describes the item.

`Provides`
: This is an array of services that the item provides (for example, Apache provides *Web Server*). These services should be globally unique. In the event that *SystemStarter* finds two items that provide the same service, it starts the first one it finds.

`Requires`
: This is an array of services that the item depends on. It should correspond to another item's `Provides` attribute. If a required service cannot be started, the system won't start the item.

`Uses`
: This is similar to `Requires`, but it is a weaker association. If *SystemStarter* can find a matching service, it will start it. If it can't, the dependent item still starts.

`OrderPreference`
: The `Requires` and `Uses` attributes imply a particular order, in that dependent items will be started after the services they depend on. You can specify `First`, `Early`, `None` (the default), `Late`, or `Last` here. *SystemStarter* does its best to satisfy this preference, but dependency orders prevail.

You can now manually start, restart, and stop MySQL by invoking *SystemStarter* from the command line:

```
$ sudo SystemStarter start MySQL
$ sudo SystemStarter restart MySQL
$ sudo SystemStarter stop MySQL
```

Scheduling Tasks

Like other flavors of Unix, Mac OS X uses *cron* to schedule tasks for periodic execution. Each user's *cron* jobs are controlled by configuration files that you can edit with *crontab -e*. (To list the contents of the file, use *crontab -l*.)

Periodic Jobs

In Mac OS X Tiger, the global *crontab* (*/etc/crontab*) has been replaced with three launch daemons. The original *crontab* looked like this:

```
15 3 * * *        root    periodic daily
30 4 * * 6        root    periodic weekly
30 5 1 * *        root    periodic monthly
```

But now, each line is replaced by a file in */System/Library/LaunchDaemons* (*com.apple.periodic-daily.plist*, *com.apple.periodic-weekly.plist*, and *com.apple.periodic-monthly.plist*) that uses the StartCalendar tag to specify when it is to be run. For example, here is the *com.apple.periodic-daily.plist* file:

```
<?xml version="1.0" encoding="UTF-8"?>
<!DOCTYPE plist PUBLIC "-//Apple Computer//DTD PLIST 1.0//EN" "http://www.
apple.
com/DTDs/PropertyList-1.0.dtd">
<plist version="1.0">
<dict>
        <key>Label</key>
        <string>com.apple.periodic-daily</string>
        <key>ProgramArguments</key>
        <array>
                <string>/usr/sbin/periodic</string>
                <string>daily</string>
        </array>
        <key>LowPriorityIO</key>
        <true/>
        <key>Nice</key>
        <integer>1</integer>
        <key>StartCalendarInterval</key>
        <dict>
                <key>Hour</key>
                <integer>3</integer>
                <key>Minute</key>
                <integer>15</integer>
        </dict>
</dict>
</plist>
```

These three launch daemons run the scripts contained in subdirectories of the */etc/periodic* directory: */etc/periodic/daily*, */etc/periodic/weekly*, and */etc/periodic/monthly*. Each of these directories contains one or more scripts:

```
/etc/periodic/daily/100.clean-logs
/etc/periodic/daily/500.daily
/etc/periodic/monthly/500.monthly
/etc/periodic/weekly/500.weekly
```

By default, the launch daemons runs them in the wee hours of the night. If your Mac is not usually turned on at those times, you could either edit the *com.apple.periodic-*.plist* files or remember to run them periodically using the following syntax:

```
sudo periodic daily weekly monthly
```

As you'll see in Chapter 5, it is vitally important that you run these jobs to ensure that your local NetInfo database is backed up.

You should not modify these files, because they may be replaced by future system updates. Instead, create a */etc/daily.local*, */etc/weekly.local*, or */etc/monthly.local* file to hold your site-specific *cron* jobs. The *cron* jobs are simply shell scripts that contain commands to be run as *root*. The local *cron* jobs are invoked at the end of the *500.daily*, *500.weekly*, and *500.monthly* scripts found in the */etc/periodic* subdirectory.

CHAPTER 5

Directory Services

A *directory service* manages information about users and resources such as printers and servers. It can manage this information for anything from a single machine to an entire corporate network. The Directory Service architecture in Mac OS X is called *Open Directory*. Open Directory encompasses flat files (such as */etc/hosts*), NetInfo (the legacy directory service brought over from earlier versions of Mac OS X and NeXTSTEP), LDAPv3, and other services through third-party plug-ins.

This chapter describes how to perform common configuration tasks, such as adding a user or host on Mac OS X with the default configuration. If your system administrator has configured your Macintosh to consult an external directory server, some of these instructions may not work. If that's the case, you should ask your system administrator to make these kinds of changes anyhow.

Understanding Directory Services

In Mac OS X 10.1.*x* and earlier, the system was configured to consult the NetInfo database for all directory information. If you needed to do something simple, such as adding a host, you couldn't just add it to */etc/hosts* and be done with it. Instead, you had to use the NetInfo Manager (or NetInfo's command-line utilities) to add the host to the system.

However, as of Mac OS X 10.2 (Jaguar), NetInfo functions started to become more of a legacy protocol and were reduced to handling the local directory database for machines that did not participate in a network-wide directory, such as Active Directory or OpenLDAP. NetInfo is still present in Mac OS X 10.3 and 10.4, but you can perform many configuration tasks by editing the standard Unix flat files. By default, Mac OS X is now configured to consult the local directory (also known as the NetInfo database) for authentication, which corresponds to */etc/passwd* and */etc/group* on other Unix systems. You can override this setting with the Directory Access application. For more information, see "Configuring Directory Services," later in this chapter.

For users whose network configuration consists of an IP address, a default gateway, and some DNS addresses, this default configuration should be fine. You'll need to tap into Open Directory's features for more advanced configurations, such as determining how a user can log into a workstation and find his home directory, even when that directory is hosted on a shared server.

In order to work with Mac OS X's Directory Services, you must first understand the overall architecture, which is known as Open Directory. Directory Services is the part of Mac OS X (and the open source Darwin operating system) that implements this architecture. Figure 5-1 shows the relationship of Directory Services to the rest of the operating system. On the top, server processes, as well as the user's desktop and applications, act as clients to Directory Services, which delegates requests to a directory service plug-in (see "Configuring Directory Services," later in this chapter, for a description of each plug-in).

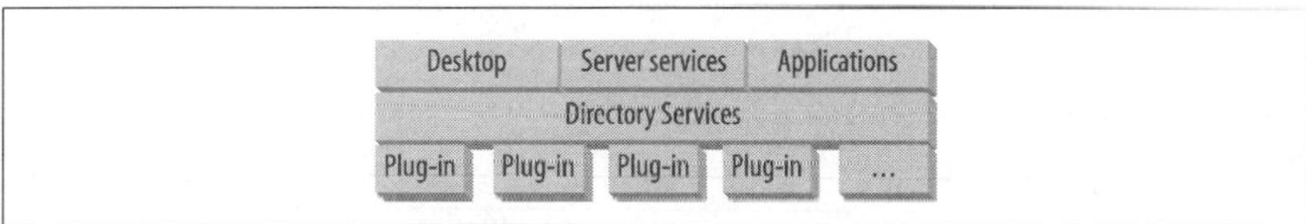

Figure 5-1. The Directory Services architecture

Programming with Directory Services

As a programmer, you frequently need to deal with directory information, whether you realize it or not. Your application uses Directory Services each time it looks up a host entry or authenticates a password. The Open Directory architecture unifies what used to be a random collection of flat files in */etc*. The good news is that the flat files still work. The other good news is that there is a brave new world just beyond those flat files. So, while all your old Unix code should work with the Open Directory architecture, you should look for new ways to accomplish old tasks, especially if you can continue writing portable code.

To get at directory information, Unix applications typically go through the C library using such functions as `gethostent()`. The C library connects to *lookupd*, a thin shim that is the doorway to the *DirectoryService* daemon. The *DirectoryService* daemon consults the available plug-ins until it finds the one that can answer the directory query.

Working with Passwords

One traditional route to user and password information was through the getpw* family of functions. However, those functions are not ideal for working with systems that support multiple directories (flat files, NetInfo, LDAP, etc.). Also, in the interest of thwarting dictionary attacks against password files, many operating systems have stopped returning encrypted passwords through those APIs. Many Unix and Linux systems simply return an "x" when you invoke a function like getpwnam( ). However, those systems can return an encrypted password through functions like getspnam( ), which consult shadow password entries and can generally be invoked by the root user only. Example 5-1 shows the typical usage of such an API, where the user enters her plaintext password, and the program encrypts it and then compares it against the encrypted password stored in the system.

Example 5-1. Using getpwnam( ) to retrieve an encrypted password

```
/*
 * getpw* no longer returns a crypted password.
 *
 * Compile with gcc checkpass.c -o checkpass
 * Run with: ./checkpass
 */

#include <pwd.h>
#include <stdio.h>
#include <stdlib.h>

int main(int argc, char *argv[])
{
  const char *user = NULL;
  struct passwd *pwd;

  /* Set the user name if it was supplied on the command
   * line.  Bail out if we don't end up with a user name.
   */
  if (argc == 2)
    user = argv[1];
  if(!user)
  {
    fprintf(stderr, "Usage: checkpass <username>\n");
    exit(1);
  }

  /* Fetch the password entry. */
  if (pwd = getpwnam(user))
  {
    char *password = (char *) getpass("Enter your password: ");

    /* Encrypt the password using the encrypted password as salt.
```

Example 5-1. Using getpwnam( ) to retrieve an encrypted password (continued)

```
     * See crypt(3) for complete details.
     */
    char *crypted  = (char *) crypt(password, pwd->pw_passwd);

    /* Are the two encrypted passwords identical? */
    if (strcmp(pwd->pw_passwd, crypted) == 0)
      printf("Success.\n");
    else
    {
      printf("Bad password: %s != %s\n", pwd->pw_passwd, crypted);
      return 1;
    }
  }
  else
  {
    fprintf(stderr, "Could not find password for %s.\n", user);
    return 1;
  }
  return 0;

}
```

As of Mac OS X Panther (v 10.3), your code no longer has a chance to look at an encrypted password. There are no functions such as `getspnam( )`, and if you invoke a function like `getpwnam( )`, you'll get one or more asterisks as the result. For example:

```
$ gcc checkpass.c -o checkpass
$ ./checkpass bjepson
Enter your password:
Bad password: ******** != **yRnqib5QSRI
```

There are some circumstances where you can obtain an encrypted password, but this is not the default behavior of Mac OS X. See the *getpwent(3)* manpage for complete details.

Instead of retrieving and comparing encrypted passwords, you should go through the Linux-PAM APIs. Since Linux-PAM is included with (or available for) many flavors of Unix, you can use it to write portable code. Example 5-2 shows a simple program that uses Linux-PAM to prompt a user for his password.

Example 5-2. Using Linux-PAM to authenticate a user

```
/*
 * Use Linux-PAM to check passwords.
 *
```

Example 5-2. Using Linux-PAM to authenticate a user (continued)

```
 * Compile with gcc pam_example.c -o pam_example -lpam
 * Run with: ./pam_example <username>
 */
#include <stdio.h>
#include <pam/pam_appl.h>
#include <pam/pam_misc.h>

int main(int argc, char *argv[])
{

  int retval;
  static struct pam_conv pam_conv;
  pam_conv.conv = misc_conv;
  pam_handle_t *pamh = NULL;
  const char *user = NULL;

  /* Set the username if it was supplied on the command
   * line. Bail out if we don't end up with a username.
   */
  if (argc == 2)
    user = argv[1];
  if(!user)
  {
    fprintf(stderr, "Usage: pam_example <username>\n");
    exit(1);
  }

  /* Initialize Linux-PAM. */
  retval = pam_start("pam_example", user, &pam_conv, &pamh);
  if (retval != PAM_SUCCESS)
  {
    fprintf(stderr, "Could not start pam: %s\n",
        pam_strerror(pamh, retval));
    exit(1);
  }

  /* Try to authenticate the user. This could cause Linux-PAM
   * to prompt the user for a password.
   */
  retval = pam_authenticate(pamh, 0);
  if (retval == PAM_SUCCESS)
    printf("Success.\n");
  else
    fprintf(stderr, "Failure: %s\n", pam_strerror(pamh, retval));

  /* Shutdown Linux-PAM. Return with an error if
   * something goes wrong.
   */
  return pam_end(pamh, retval) == PAM_SUCCESS ? 0 : 1;
}
```

In order for this to work, you must create a file called *pam_example* in */etc/pam.d* with the following contents (the filename must match the first argument to pam_start( ), which is shown in bold in Example 5-2):

```
auth        required  pam_securityserver.so
account     required  pam_permit.so
password    required  pam_deny.so
```

Be careful when making any changes in the */etc/pam.d* directory. If you change one of the files that is consulted for system login, you may lock yourself out of the system. For more information on Linux-PAM, see the *pam(8)* manpage.

Once you've compiled this program and created the *pam_example* file in */etc/pam.d*, you can test it out:

```
$ gcc pam_example.c -o pam_example -lpam
$ ./pam_example bjepson
Password: ********
Success.
```

Configuring Directory Services

In order to configure Directory Services, use the Directory Access application (*/Applications/Utilities*), shown in Figure 5-2. You can enable or disable various directory service plug-ins, or change their configuration.

Directory Access supports the following plug-ins:

Active Directory
: This plug-in lets Mac OS X consult an Active Directory domain on a server running Windows 2000 or Windows 2003.

AppleTalk
: This is the ultimate Mac OS legacy protocol. AppleTalk was the original networking protocol supported by Mac OS versions prior to Mac OS X. Linux and the server editions of Windows also support AppleTalk.

Bonjour
: Formerly known as Rendezvous, Bonjour is Apple's zero-configuration protocol for discovering file sharing, printers, and other network services. It uses a peer-to-peer approach to announce and discover services automatically as devices join a network.

BSD Flat File and NIS
: This includes the Network Information Service (NIS) and the flat files located in the */etc* directory, such as *hosts*, *exports*, and *services*. By default, this option is switched off. After you enable it, click Apply, switch to the Authentication tab, choose Custom Path from the search menu, click the Add button, choose */BSD/Local*, and click Apply again.

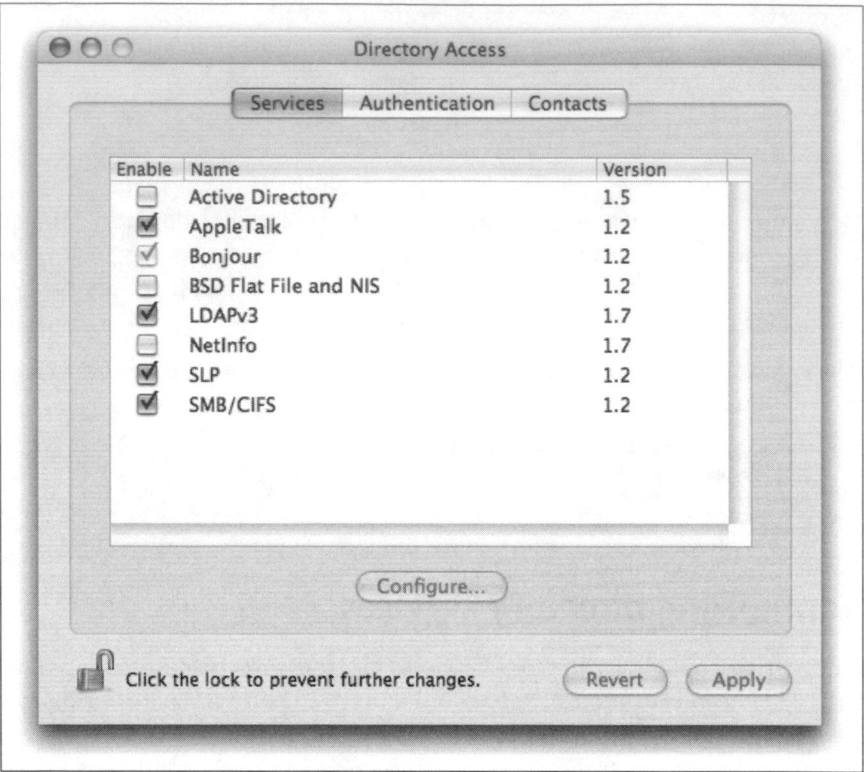

Figure 5-2. The Directory Access application shows the available plug-ins

LDAPv3
This is the same version of LDAP used by Microsoft's Active Directory and Novell's NDS. In addition to the client components, Mac OS X includes *slapd*, a standalone LDAP daemon. Mac OS X's LDAP support comes through OpenLDAP (*http://www.openldap.org*), an open source LDAPv3 implementation.

NetInfo
This is a legacy Directory Services protocol introduced in NeXTSTEP. If the checkbox is off (the default), NetInfo uses the local domain but does not consult network-based NetInfo domains. If the checkbox is on, NetInfo also looks for and potentially uses any network-based domains that it finds.

NetInfo and LDAP both use the same data store, which is contained in */var/db/netinfo/*. The data store is a collection of embedded database files.

SLP
: This is the Service Location Protocol, which supports file and print services over IP.

SMB/CIFS
: This is the Server Message Block protocol (a.k.a., Common Internet File System), which is Microsoft's protocol for file and print services.

Under the Services tab, everything except NetInfo and BSD Configuration Files is enabled by default. However, if you go to the Authentication tab (Figure 5-3), you'll see that NetInfo is the sole service in charge of authentication (which is handled by */etc/passwd* and */etc/group* on other Unix systems).

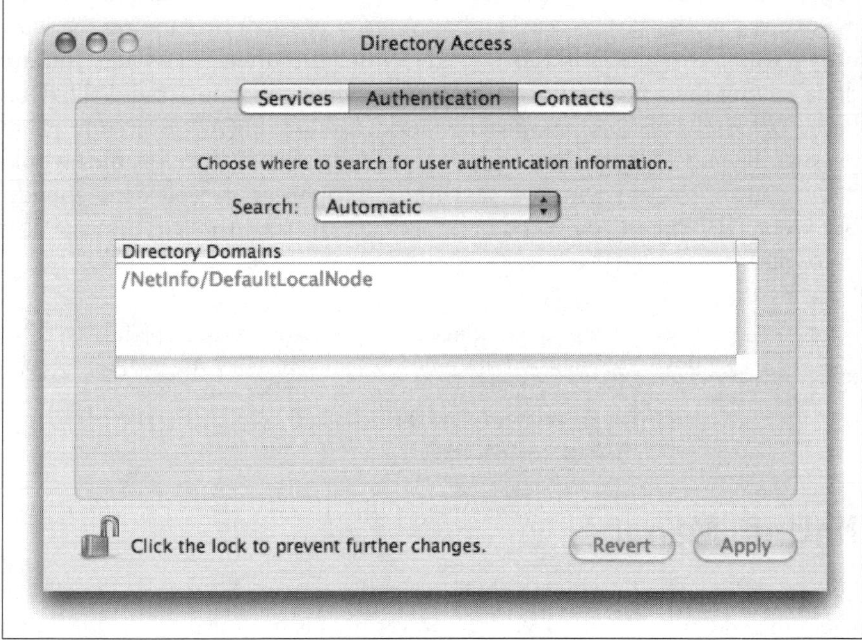

Figure 5-3. The Directory Access Authentication tab

By default, the Authentication tab is set to Automatic. You can set the Search popup to any of the following:

Automatic
: This is the default, which searches (in order) the local NetInfo directory, a shared NetInfo domain, and a shared LDAPv3 domain.

Local directory
: This searches only the local NetInfo directory.

Custom path

This allows you to use BSD flat files (*/etc/passwd* and */etc/group*). After you select Custom path from the pop up, click Add and select */BSD/local*.

After you have changed the Search setting, click Apply. The Contact tab is set up identically to the Authentication tab and is used by programs that search Directory Services for contact information (office locations, phone numbers, full names, etc.).

Enabling BSD flat files does not copy or change the information in the local directory (the NetInfo database). If you want to rely only on flat files, you would need to find all the user entries from the local directory (you could use the command *nidump passwd .* to list them all) and add them to the password flat files (*/etc/passwd* and */etc/master.passwd*) by running the *vipw* utility with no arguments (do not edit either file directly). When you are done editing the password file, *vipw* invokes *pwd_mkdb* to rebuild the databases (*/etc/spwd.db* and */etc/pwd.db*) used for looking up usernames and passwords, and also updates */etc/passwd*. Switching over to flat files would allow you to access encrypted passwords through `getpwnam()` and friends, but would also mean you could no longer use the GUI tools to manage user accounts.

If you change any settings in the Directory Access applications, you may find that some invalid credentials are temporarily cached by Directory Services. To clear out the cache immediately, run the following command as *root*:

```
$ lookupd -flushcache
```

NetInfo Manager

The local directory is organized hierarchically, starting from the *root*, which, like a filesystem's *root*, is called */*. However, this is not meant to suggest that there is a corresponding directory or file for each entry. Instead, the data is stored in a collection of files under */var/db/netinfo*.

You can browse or modify the local directory using NetInfo Manager, which is located in */Applications/Utilities*. Figure 5-4 shows NetInfo Manager displaying the properties of the *mysql* user.

Directory Services Utilities

This chapter demonstrates four Directory Services utilities: *dscl*, *nireport*, *nidump*, and *niload*. Table 5-1 describes these and other NetInfo utilities.

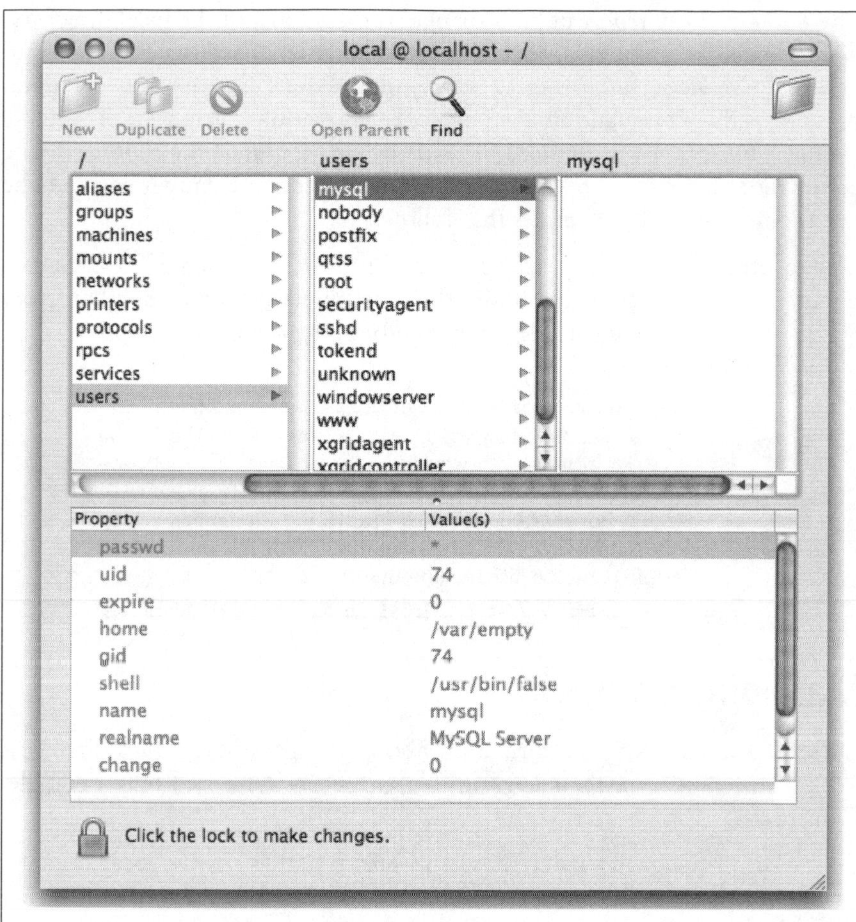

Figure 5-4. Browsing the local directory

Table 5-1. NetInfo tools

Tool	Description
dscl	Provides a command-line interface to Directory Services.
nicl	Provides a command-line interface to NetInfo.
nidump	Extracts flat file format data (such as */etc/passwd*) from NetInfo.
nifind	Finds a NetInfo directory.
nigrep	Performs a regular expression search on NetInfo.
niload	Loads flat file format data (such as */etc/passwd*) into NetInfo.
nireport	Prints tables from NetInfo.
niutil	NetInfo utility for manipulating the database.

The *nidump* and *nireport* utilities display the contents of the local directory. *niload* loads the contents of flat files (such as */etc/passwd* or */etc/hosts*) into Directory Services. *niutil* directly manipulates the Directory Services database; it's the command-line equivalent of NetInfo Manager. To make changes, use *sudo* with these commands or first log in as the *root* user. The commands that can be performed as a normal user are shown without the *sudo* command in the examples that follow.

Unlike other *ni** utilities, *nicl* acts directly on the database files. Consequently, you can use *nicl* to modify the local directory even when Directory Services is not running (such as when you boot into single-user mode).

When you use any of these utilities you are making potentially dangerous changes to your system. But even if you trash the local directory with reckless usage of these commands, you can restore the NetInfo database from your last backup. For more details, see "Restoring the Directory Services Database," later in this chapter. To back up the local NetInfo database, use the command:

```
$ nidump -r / -t localhost/local > backup.nidump
```

Managing Groups

Directory Services stores information about groups in its */groups* directory. This is different from the */etc/group* file, which is consulted only in single-user mode.

To list all of the group IDs (GIDs) and group names for the local domain, invoke *nireport* with the NetInfo domain (., the local domain), the directory (*/groups*), and the properties you want to inspect—in this case, *gid* and *name*:

```
$ nireport . /groups gid name
-2      nobody
-1      nogroup
0       wheel
1       daemon
2       kmem
3       sys
4       tty
5       operator
6       mail
7       bin
20      staff
26      lp
27      postfix
28      postdrop
29      certusers
```

```
45      utmp
66      uucp
68      dialer
69      network
70      www
74      mysql
[... and so on ...]
```

Although the flat file format is called *group* (after the */etc/group* file), the group directory is */groups*. If you forget that last *s*, *nireport* looks for the wrong directory. However, if you want to dump the groups directory in the */etc/group* file format, use the command *nidump group* . without that last *s*.

Creating a Group with niload

The *niload* utility can be used to read the flat file format used by */etc/group* (`name:password:gid:members`). To add a new group, you can create a file that adheres to that format, and load it with *niload*. For ad hoc work, you can use a here document (an expression that functions as a quoted string, but spans multiple lines) rather than a separate file:

```
$ sudo niload group . <<EOF
> writers:*:1001:
> EOF
```

Creating a Group with dscl

To create a group with *dscl*, you'll need to create a directory under */groups* and set the *gid* and *passwd* properties. An asterisk (*) specifies no password; be sure to quote it so that the shell does not attempt to expand it. The following creates a group named *writers* as GID 5005 with no password and no members:

```
$ sudo dscl . create /groups/writers gid 5005
$ sudo dscl . create /groups/writers passwd '*'
```

Adding Users to a Group

You can add users to the group by appending values to the *users* property with *dscl*'s *merge* command at the command line (or by using the *merge* command interactively; start *dscl* in interactive mode with *sudo dscl* .). If the *users* property does not exist, *dscl* creates it. If the users are already part of the group, they are not added to the list (contrast this with the *-append* command, which can result in the same user being added more than once if the command is invoked multiple times):

```
$ sudo dscl . merge /groups/writers users bjepson rothman
```

Listing Groups with nidump

Use *nidump* to confirm that the new group was created correctly. To list groups with *nidump*, pass in the format (in this case, the *group* file) and the domain (., the local domain):

```
$ nidump group . | grep writers
writers:*:5005:bjepson,rothman
```

Because you can use *nireport* to dump any directory, you could also use it to see this information:

```
$ nireport . /groups name passwd gid users | grep writers
writers *       5005    bjepson,rothman
```

Deleting a Group

To delete a group, use *dscl*'s *delete* command. Be careful with this command, since it deletes everything in and below the specified NetInfo directory:

```
$ sudo dscl . delete /groups/writers
```

Managing Users and Passwords

The Directory Services equivalent of the *passwd* file resides under the */users* portion of the directory. Although Mac OS X includes */etc/passwd* and */etc/master.passwd* files, they are consulted only while the system is in single-user mode, or if the system has been reconfigured to use BSD Flat Files (see "Configuring Directory Services," earlier in this chapter).

To add a normal user to your system, you should use System Preferences → Accounts. However, if you want to bulk-load NetInfo with many users or create a user while logged in over *ssh*, you can use *dscl* or *niload*.

You can list all users with the *nireport* utility. Supply the NetInfo domain (., the local domain), the directory (*/users*), and the properties you want to inspect (*uid*, *name*, *home*, *realname*, and *shell*):

```
$ nireport . /users uid name home realname shell
-2      nobody  /var/empty      Unprivileged User       /usr/bin/false
0       root    /var/root       System Administrator    /bin/sh
1       daemon  /var/root       System Services /usr/bin/false
99      unknown /var/empty      Unknown User    /usr/bin/false
26      lp      /var/spool/cups Printing Services       /usr/bin/false
27      postfix /var/spool/postfix      Postfix User    /usr/bin/false
70      www     /Library/WebServer      World Wide Web Server   /usr/bin/
false
71      eppc    /var/empty      Apple Events User       /usr/bin/false
74      mysql   /var/empty      MySQL Server    /usr/bin/false
```

```
75      sshd    /var/empty      sshd Privilege separation       /usr/bin/
false
76      qtss    /var/empty      QuickTime Streaming Server      /usr/bin/
false
77      cyrusimap       /var/imap       Cyrus IMAP User /usr/bin/false
78      mailman /var/empty      Mailman user    /usr/bin/false
79      appserver       /var/empty      Application Server      /usr/bin/
false
[... and so on ...]
```

Creating a User with niload

The *niload* utility understands the flat file format used by */etc/passwd* (which is `name:password:uid:gid:class:change:expire:gecos:home_dir:shell`). See the *passwd(5)* manpage for a description of each field. To add a new user, create a file that adheres to that format and load it with *niload*. You can use a here document rather than a separate file. This example creates a user for Ernest Rothman with a UID of 701 and membership in the group numbered 701, which you'll create next:

```
$ sudo niload passwd . <<EOF
> rothman:*:701:701::0:0:Ernest Rothman:/Users/rothman:/bin/bash
> EOF
```

Next, create a group with the same name as the new user and a GID that matches his UID (as of Mac OS X 10.3, users are given their own groups):

```
$ sudo niload group . <<EOF
> rothman:*:701:
> EOF
```

As you can see from the example, we set the user's password field to *, which disables logins for that account. To set the password, we'll use the *passwd* command:

```
$ sudo passwd rothman
Changing password for rothman.
New password: ********
Retype new password: ********
```

If you *niload* a user that already exists, that user's entry will be updated with the new information. Before the user can log in, you must create his home directory (see "Creating a User's Home Directory," later in this chapter).

Creating a User with dscl

To create a user with *dscl*, you'll need to create a directory under */users*, and set the *uid*, *gid*, *shell*, *realname*, and *home* properties.

The following commands will create the same user shown in the previous section:

```
$ sudo dscl . create /users/rothman uid 701
$ sudo dscl . create /users/rothman gid 701
$ sudo dscl . create /users/rothman shell /bin/bash
$ sudo dscl . create /users/rothman home /Users/rothman
$ sudo dscl . create /users/rothman realname "Ernest Rothman"
$ sudo dscl . create /users/rothman passwd \*
$ sudo dscl . create /groups/rothman gid 701
$ sudo dscl . create /groups/rothman passwd \*
```

Be sure to quote or escape the asterisk (*) in the `passwd` entries. After you create the user, you should set the password as shown in the previous section.

Creating a User's Home Directory

One thing that NetInfo can't do for you is create the user's home directory. Mac OS X keeps a skeleton directory under the */System/Library/User Template* directory. If you look in this directory, you'll see localized versions of a user's home directory. To copy the localized English version of the home directory, use the *ditto* command with the *--rsrc* flag to preserve any resource forks that may exist:

```
$ sudo ditto --rsrc \
  /System/Library/User\ Template/English.lproj /Users/rothman
```

Then, use *chown* to recursively set the ownership of the home directory and all its contents (make sure you set the group to a group of which the user is a member):

```
$ sudo chown -R rothman:rothman /Users/rothman
```

This change makes the new user the owner of his home directory and all its contents.

Granting Administrative Privileges

To give someone administrative privileges, add that user to the *admin* group (*/groups/admin*). This gives him or her the ability to use *sudo* and run applications (such as software installers) that require such privileges:

```
$ sudo dscl . merge /groups/admin users rothman
```

If you want this setting to take place immediately, you can run the command *sudo lookupd -flushcache* to flush any cached credentials.

Modifying a User

You can change a user's properties by using the *create* command, even if that property already exists. For example, to change *rothman*'s shell to *zsh*, use:

```
$ sudo dscl . -create /users/rothman shell /bin/zsh
```

You can also modify most user settings with System Preferences → Accounts. If you want to do things the traditional Unix way, Mac OS X includes *chsh*, *chfn*, and *chpass* in Version 10.3 and beyond.

Listing Users with nidump

Use *nidump* to confirm that *rothman* was added successfully. To list users with *nidump*, pass in the format (in this case, the *passwd* file) and the domain (use . for the local domain):

```
$ nidump passwd . | grep rothman
rothman:********:701:701::0:0:Ernest Rothman:/Users/rothman:/bin/zsh
```

Deleting a User

To delete a user, use *dscl*'s *delete* command. Since *delete* recursively deletes everything under the specified directory, use this command with caution:

```
$ sudo dscl . delete /users/rothman
```

If you want to also delete that user's home directory, you'll have to do it manually.

Be sure to delete the group you created for this user as well ("rothman" in this example), as shown in "Deleting a Group," earlier in this chapter.

Managing Hostnames and IP Addresses

Mac OS X consults both the */etc/hosts* file and the */machines* portion of the local directory. For example, the following entry in */etc/hosts* would map the hostname *xyzzy* to 192.168.0.1:

```
192.168.0.1    xyzzy
```

Creating a Host with niload

The *niload* utility understands the flat file format used by */etc/hosts* (`ip_address name`). See the *hosts(5)* manpage for a description of each field. To add a new host, create a file using that format and load it with *niload*. This example ads the host *xyzzy*:

```
$ sudo niload hosts . <<EOF
> 192.168.0.1 xyzzy
> EOF
```

If you add an entry that already exists, it will be overwritten.

The */etc/hosts* file takes precedence over the local directory, so if you enter the same hostname with different IP addresses in both places, Mac OS X uses the one in */etc/hosts*.

Exporting Directories with NFS

You can use the */etc/exports* file to store folders that you want to export over NFS. For example, the following line exports the */Users* directory to two hosts (192.168.0.134 and 192.168.0.106):

```
/Users  -ro 192.168.0.134 192.168.0.106
```

The NFS server will start automatically at boot time if there are any exports in that file. After you've set up your exports, you can reboot, and NFS should start automatically. NFS options supported by Mac OS X include the following (see the *exports(5)* manpage for complete details):

`-maproot=user`
: Specifies that the remote *root* user should be mapped to the specified user. You may specify either a username or numeric user ID.

`-maproot=user:[group[:group...]]`
: Specifies that the remote *root* user should be mapped to the specified user with the specified group credentials. If you include the colon with no groups, as in `-maproot=`*`username`*:, it means the remote user should have no group credentials. You may specify a username or numeric user ID for *`user`* and a group name or numeric group ID for *`group`*.

`-mapall=user`
: Specifies that all remote users should be mapped to the specified user.

`-mapall=user:[group[:group...]]`
: Specifies that all remote users should be mapped to the specified user with the specified group credentials. If you include the colon with no groups, as in `mapall=`*`username`*:, it specifies that the remote user should be given no group credentials.

`-kerb`
: Uses a Kerberos authentication server to authenticate and map client credentials.

`-ro`
: Exports the filesystem as read-only. The synonym `-o` is also supported.

Flat Files and Their Directory Services Counterparts

As mentioned earlier, Directory Services manages information for several flat files in earlier releases of Mac OS X, including */etc/printcap*, */etc/mail/aliases*, */etc/protocols*, and */etc/services*. For a complete list of known flat file formats, see the *nidump* and *niload* manpages.

Although you can edit these flat files directly as you would on any other Unix system, you can also use Directory Services to manage this information. You can use *niload* with a supported flat file format to add entries, or you can use *dscl* or NetInfo Manager to directly manipulate the entries. Table 5-2 lists each flat file, the corresponding portion of the directory, and important properties associated with each entry. See the *netinfo(5)* manpage for complete details. Properties marked with (list) can take multiple values using the *dscl merge* command (for an example, see "Adding Users to a Group," earlier in this chapter.)

The "Flat files or local database?" column in Table 5-2 indicates whether Directory Services consults the flat file, the local database, or both. You can use Directory Access to modify the way information is looked up on your Macintosh.

Table 5-2. Flat files and their NetInfo counterparts

Flat file	NetInfo directory	Important properties	Flat files or local database?
/etc/exports	*/exports*	name, clients (list), opts (list)	Flat files
/etc/fstab	*/mounts*	name, dir, type, opts (list), passno, freq	Local database
/etc/group	*/groups*	name, passwd, gid, users (list)	Local database
/etc/hosts	*/machines*	ip_address, name (list)	Both; entries in */etc/hosts* take precedence
/etc/mail/aliases	*/aliases*	name, members (list)	Flat files
/etc/networks	*/networks*	name (list), address	Flat files
/etc/passwd, /etc/master.passwd	*/users*	name, passwd, uid, gid, realname, home, shell	Local database

Table 5-2. Flat files and their NetInfo counterparts (continued)

Flat file	NetInfo directory	Important properties	Flat files or local database?
/etc/printcap	*/printers*	*name*, and various *printcap* properties (see the *printcap(5)* manpage)	Flat files
/etc/protocols	*/protocols*	name (list), number	Flat files
/etc/rpc	*/rpcs*	name (list), number	Flat files
/etc/services	*/services*	*name* (list), *port*, *protocol* (list)	Flat files

Restoring the Directory Services Database

If the local directory database is damaged, boot into single-user mode by holding down ⌘-S as the system starts up. Next, check to see if you have a backup of the NetInfo database. The *daily periodic* job backs up the database each time it is run. You can find the backup in */var/backups/local.nidump*. If you don't have a backup, you won't be able to restore. The *local.nidump* file is overwritten each time the *cron* job runs, so make sure you back it up regularly (preferably to some form of removable media).

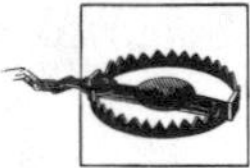

If your computer is generally not turned on at 3:15 a.m. (the default time for the *daily periodic* job), you'll never get a backup of your local directory. You can solve this problem by editing *com.apple.periodic-daily.plist* to run this job at a different time, or to run the job periodically with the command *sudo periodic daily*. See "Periodic Jobs" in Chapter 4 for more details.

If you totally mess up and find that you forgot to backup your NetInfo database, you can stop at step 5 and issue the command *rm /var/db/.AppleSetupDone*. This makes Mac OS X think that it's being booted for the first time when you restart, forcing it to run the Setup Assistant so you can create the initial user for the system, thus bringing your system to a usable state for further repairs.

After the system boots in single-user mode, you should:

1. Wait for the root# prompt to come up.
2. Fix any filesystem errors:

   ```
   # /sbin/fsck -fy
   ```

3. Mount the *root* filesystem as read/write:

   ```
   # /sbin/mount -uw /
   ```

4. Change directories and go to the NetInfo database directory:

   ```
   # cd /var/db/netinfo/
   ```

5. Move the database out of the way and give it a different name:

   ```
   # mv local.nidb/ local.nidb.broken
   ```

6. Start enough of the system to use NetInfo. The */etc/rc* script also creates a blank NetInfo database when it sees that it no longer exists:

   ```
   # sh /etc/rc
   ```

7. Wait for a while for the system to become ready—just before it's ready, you should see the screen go blue as though it's going to show you the login window, However, it will return to the verbose boot screen with the black background, and you can press Control-L or Return to get your shell prompt back. Next, load the backup into NetInfo:

   ```
   # /usr/bin/niload  -d -r / . < /var/backups/local.nidump
   ```

8. When it saw that the NetInfo database needed to be recreated, */etc/rc* deleted the *.AppleSetupDone* file, so you need to recreate it:

   ```
   # touch /var/db/.AppleSetupDone
   ```

After you have completed these steps, reboot the system with the *reboot* command.

CHAPTER 6

Printing

Mac OS X offers a rich and flexible set of tools for administering and using a wide variety of printers. Common Unix tools—such as *lpr*, *lpq*, and *lprm*—are here as well, along with a few new ones just for Mac OS X.

This chapter starts out with a basic discussion of how to use the Printer Setup Utility (*/Applications/Utilities*), a GUI tool for configuring local and network printers. Then we'll move on to discuss the Mac OS X implementations of the Unix printing tools. In particular, we will discuss the Common Unix Printing System (CUPS), Gimp-Print, and HP InkJet Server (HPIJS).

Printer Setup Utility

If you're using a popular USB printer under Mac OS X, it is likely that all you'll need to do is connect it to the USB port and choose the printer in the Print dialog when you want to print a document. However, there are some circumstances where it's not so simple:

- Perhaps your USB printer does not automatically show up as an available printer in the Print dialog
- Maybe you want to share your printer with other computers on your LAN
- Perhaps you want to use a network printer such as one listed in Open Directory, an AppleTalk printer, or one for which all you have is an IP address

If you haven't already set up a printer using the Printer Setup Utility, there are three ways to add a new printer in Mac OS X:

Add a printer automatically
: Attempting to print a document from virtually any application automatically launches the Printer Setup Utility. Mac OS X first informs you that you have no printers available, and then asks if you'd like to add a printer. Click on the Add button to start the setup procedure.

Launch Print Center
: You can also add a new printer in the Printer Setup Utility by clicking the Add button. The */Applications/Utilities* folder also contains an icon for Print Center. In Tiger, the Print Center is provided as an alias to Printer Setup Utility, to maintain backward compatibility with earlier versions of Mac OS X.

Use System Preferences
: Open System Preferences, choose Print & Fax → Printing, click the + sign, and click Add when the Printer Setup Utility appears. To share your printers with other computers, open System Preferences, choose Print & Fax → Sharing, select the printers you want to share, and click "Share these printers with other computers."

Whichever way you end up clicking the Add button, Printer Setup Utility automatically searches for Rendezvous-enabled printers on your network. If a Rendezvous-enabled printer is found, you can easily add this printer and you'll be ready to use it immediately. If a Rendezvous-enabled printer is not found, a dialog box appears, informing you that "You have no printers available"; you're then asked if you want to add a printer to your list. If you click Add you can kick off the setup procedure in the Printer Browser window as shown in Figure 6-1.

Adding an IP Printer

If you have a printer on your network that is not Rendezvous-enabled, you'll need to have some information about it on hand:

- The printer's IP address or hostname.
- The manufacturer and model of the printer.

If you don't know the exact model of the printer, you may be able to set up the printer, albeit with reduced functionality. For example, if all you know is that you've got some kind of HP DeskJet, you could configure the printer as a generic DeskJet by selecting ESP → HP New DeskJet Series CUPS from the Printer Model options when you are adding the printer. However, knowing the exact model will probably let you take advantage of special printing features such as duplex printing.

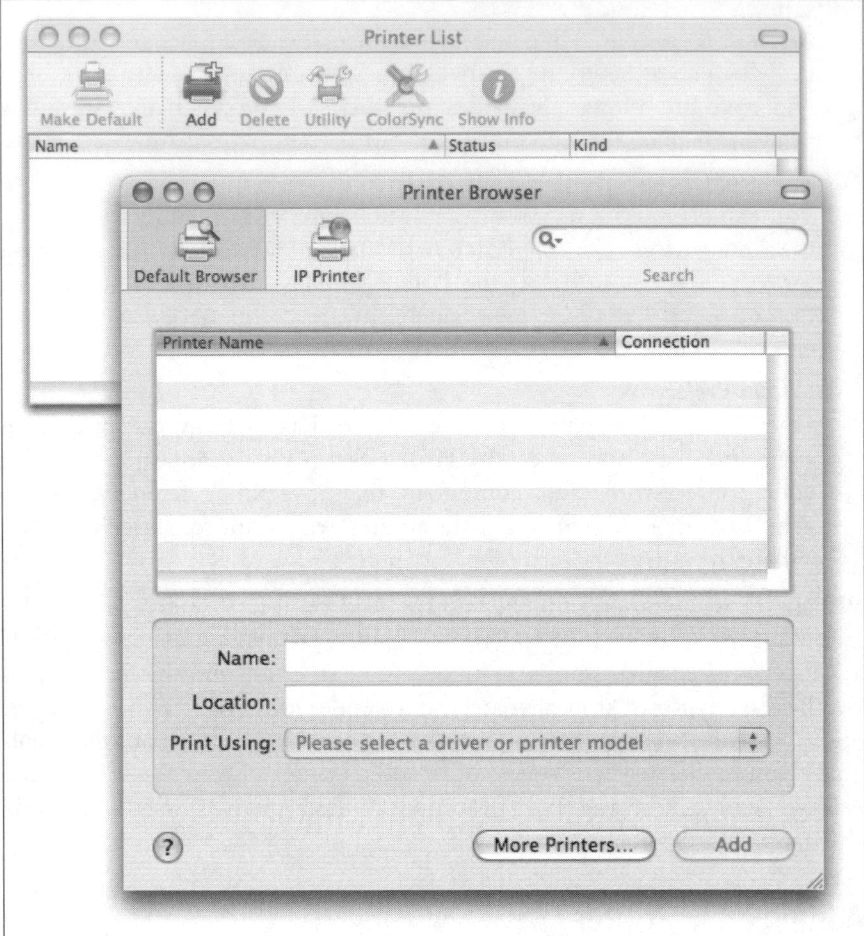

Figure 6-1. Specifying the printer type in the Printer Setup Utility

To set up an IP printer, click the IP Printer icon in the printer Browser window, and select the protocol as shown in Figure 6-2.

You need to select a Protocol from the following choices:

- Internet Printing Protocol - IPP
- Line Printer Daemon - LPD
- HP Jet Direct - Socket

For example, suppose you have a Tektronix Phaser 750P with Plus Features on your LAN and that its IP address is 192.168.0.77. In this case, you would select Line Printer Daemon - LPD as the Printer Type, enter 192.168.0.77 as the Address, specify a Queue Name if required (otherwise it is called

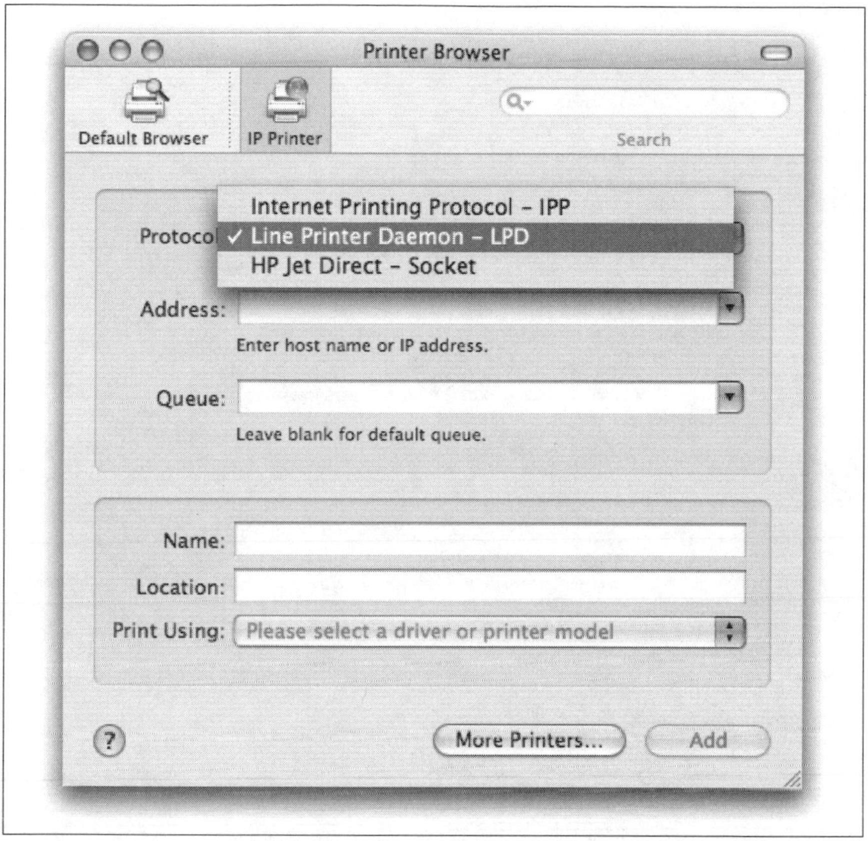

Figure 6-2. Selecting the IP printing protocol in the Printer Setup Utility's Printer Browser

"default"), and select Tektronix in the Print Using box and Tektronix Phaser 750P with Plus Features under Model as shown in Figure 6-3.

After clicking the Add button, you are be prompted to enter printer-specific information such as printer installable options, as shown in Figure 6-4.

Once you've added a printer, the printer shows up in the Print & Fax preference pane, as shown in Figure 6-5.

If you can't find your printer model, try selecting the Generic option; in most instances, that should work.

Setting up an LPD printer in this manner allows you to print documents not only by selecting Print from GUI-based applications, but to also manipulate

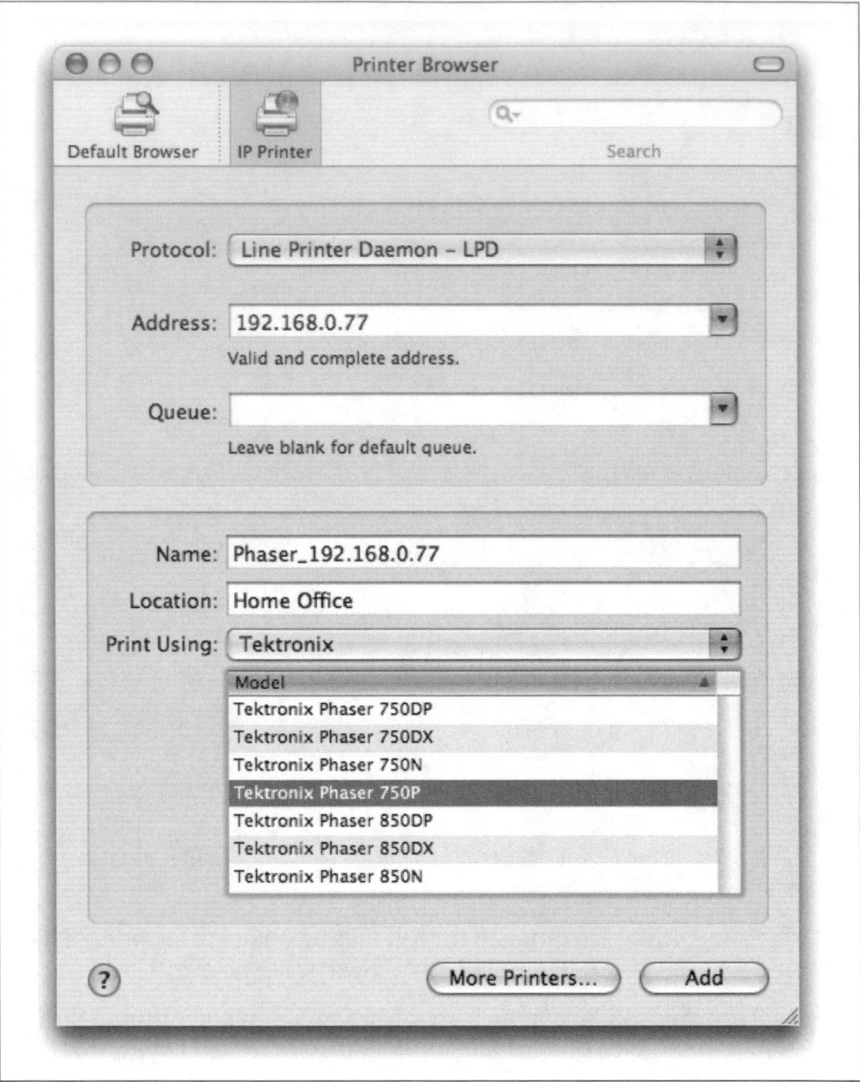

Figure 6-3. Adding an IP printer in the Printer Setup Utility's Printer Browser

the print queue from the Terminal using the CUPS *lp*, *lpstat*, and *cancel* shell commands. By selecting "More Printers..." in the Printer Browser window, you'll see options for selecting your IP printer, as well as any of the following printer types:

- AppleTalk
- Bluetooth
- Windows Printing

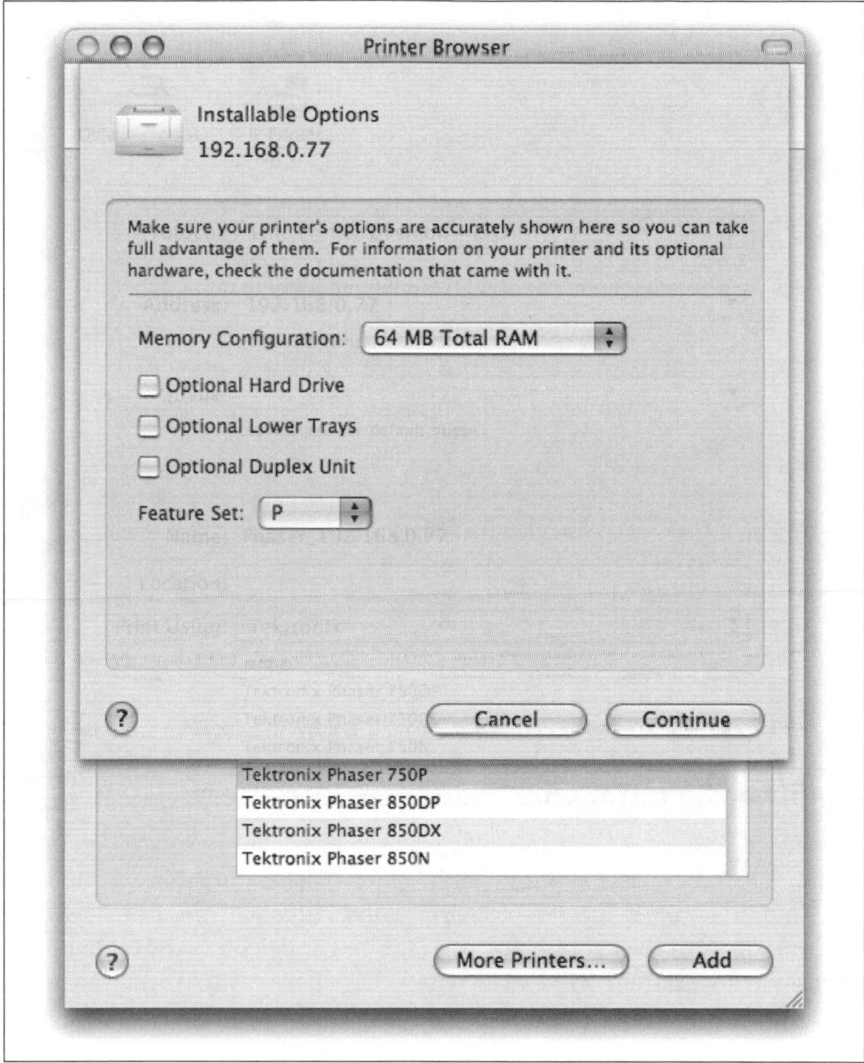

Figure 6-4. Specifying printer model-specific installable options

- Canon BJ Network
- EPSON AppleTalk
- EPSON FireWire
- EPSON TP/IP
- EPSON USB
- HP IP Printing
- Lexmark Inkjet Networking

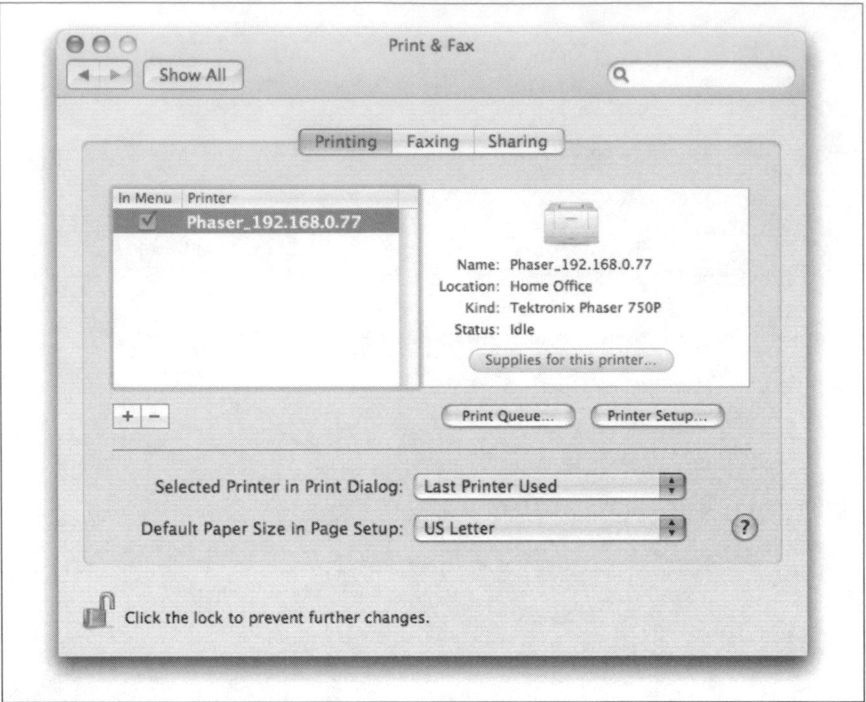

Figure 6-5. Print & Fax System Preference

Modifying a Printer's Settings

Once your printer has been added, you can change some of its settings (location, printer model, and any installable options) using the Printer Setup Utility. To do this, open the Printer Setup Utility, highlight the printer whose settings you want to change, and click the Show Info icon in the toolbar; this opens the Printer Info window, which you can use to make the changes. Click Apply Changes to make your changes take effect.

Creating a Desktop Icon for a Printer

You can use the Printer Setup Utility to create and place an icon for your printer on the Desktop. To do this, open the Printer Setup Utility, highlight the printer in the list, and choose Printers → Create Desktop Printer from the menu bar. You can save the printer's Desktop icon to the desktop or to any folder in which you have write permission. After you create the icon, you can place it in the left section of the Dock with icons of applications, in the lower section of the Finder's Places sidebar, or just leave it on your Desktop. In each case, you'll be able to print a document by dragging its icon to the printer's icon.

Double-clicking a Desktop printer icon opens a window that shows you the status of the printer and any items in the print queue. This comes in handy for times when you need to quickly cancel a print job or start/stop the print queue to service a printer.

Printer Sharing

Printers with a network adapter are not necessarily the only printers available on your LAN. You can share a printer that's connected to your computer with other computers. For example, you can share your USB printer with all the computers on your LAN by opening Preferences → Sharing, clicking the Services tab, and enabling Printer Sharing.

When you change a system preference you may need to click the lock in the lower left corner to authenticate yourself as an administrative user before you make any changes.

If you've activated the firewall, enabling Printer Sharing opens up ports 631 (Internet Printing Protocol) and 515 (*lpd*) for printing. As noted earlier, you can share selected printers using the Print & Fax preference panel's Sharing pane, as shown in Figure 6-6.

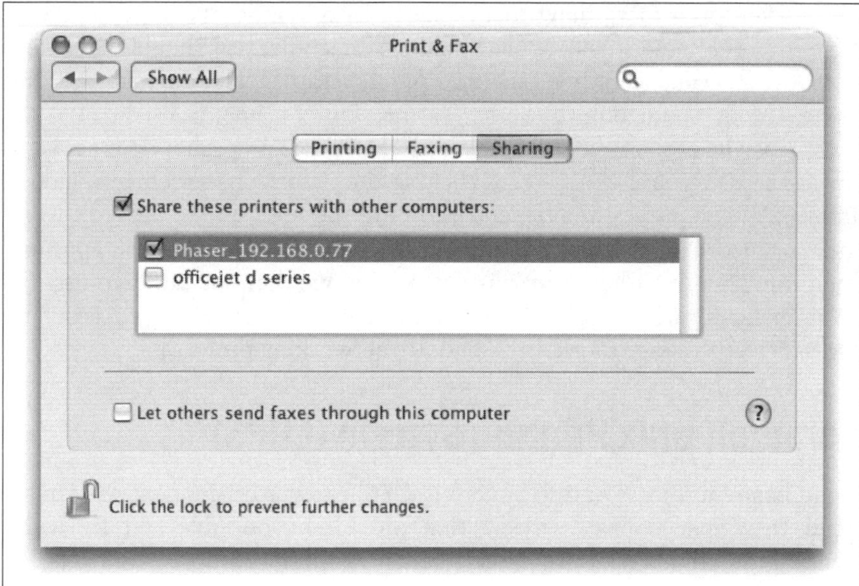

Figure 6-6. Print & Fax Sharing interface

Once you've shared your printer, other Macs on your subnet should automatically see your printer in their Print dialog boxes. If a user is on your local network, but not on your subnet, she can connect to the printer using the IP address or hostname of your Macintosh.

In addition to sharing your printer with Mac users, you can also share it with Linux, Unix, and Windows users. If a Unix or Linux computer is on the same subnet as the computer sharing its printers and has CUPS installed, it sees the shared printer (assuming it's capable of browsing for printers). If not, you will need to provide the IP address of the computer sharing the printer (see "Printing from Remote Systems," later in this chapter).

To let Windows users connect to your printer, activate both Printer Sharing and Windows Sharing in the Sharing pane of System Preferences. Windows users on your network can now add the printer.

After you've activated printer sharing, you may want to add some information about the physical location of the printer. You can do this by opening the Printer Setup Utility, highlighting the shared printer, clicking the Show Info icon, and entering that information in the Location field. For example, if the marketing group is sharing a printer, type Marketing in the Location field.

It is easy to print to a printer that is shared by a Windows computer. If your Mac is on the same subnet as the Windows machine, you should see it listed with other available printers in the Printer Setup Utility. In this case, just check the In Menu box to the left of the printer name. Subsequently, this printer will be available in Print dialogs. If the Windows printer does not show up in the list, you can add it by clicking the Add icon, selecting Windows Printing in the pop-up dialog, and choosing the appropriate network workgroup. Once you've done this, any available Windows printers will appear in the Printer Setup Utility printer list; select the one that you'd like to use. For additional information, select Help → Printer Setup Utility Help and search for SMB (Server Message Block, the Windows networking protocol).

Common Unix Printing System (CUPS)

The Common Unix Printing System (CUPS), a core component of Mac OS X, is free, open source software that provides a portable and extensible printing system for the Unix-based Internet Printing Protocol (IPP/1.1).

Extensive documentation and source code is available for CUPS online (*http://www.cups.org*). As noted in online documentation, the goal of CUPS is "to provide a complete, modern printing system for Unix that can be used to support new printers, devices, and protocols while providing compatibility with existing Unix applications."

CUPS provides System V- and Berkeley-compatible command-line interfaces and a web-based interface to extensive documentation, status monitoring, and printer administration. You access the web-based administration interface by pointing your web browser to port 631 on the localhost (*http://127.0.0.1:631*). (To access CUPS from a remote machine, enable Printer Sharing (System Preferences → Sharing), and use your machine's IP address instead of 127.0.0.1.) The main page of the web-based administrative interface is shown in Figure 6-7.

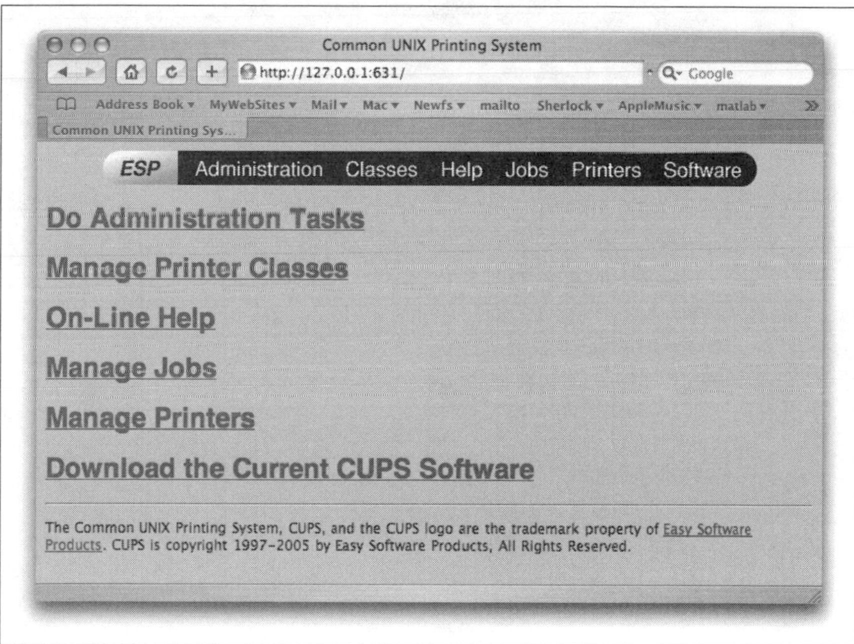

Figure 6-7. CUPS' web-based interface

Printing from Remote Systems

CUPS is available on a wide variety of Unix-based systems and makes both the administration and use of shared printers easy. For example, a shared USB printer connected to your Mac is immediately visible to a Solaris-based

SUN workstation running CUPS, provided the Solaris machine is on the same subnet (if not, remote users can connect to the printer by supplying your Mac's IP address or hostname).

GNOME and KDE, the most popular desktop environments for Linux, have utilities that make it easy to connect to a printer you've shared from your Mac. Before you proceed, you should find out the queue name of your printer, as described in the following steps:

1. Open the Printer Setup Utility (*/Applications/Utilities*).
2. Select your printer and click the Show Info icon.
3. The Printer Info dialog appears; make sure Name & Location is selected at the top of the dialog. Figure 6-8 shows the settings for an HP OfficeJet D135 connected to the USB port. The queue name for this printer is "officejet d series."

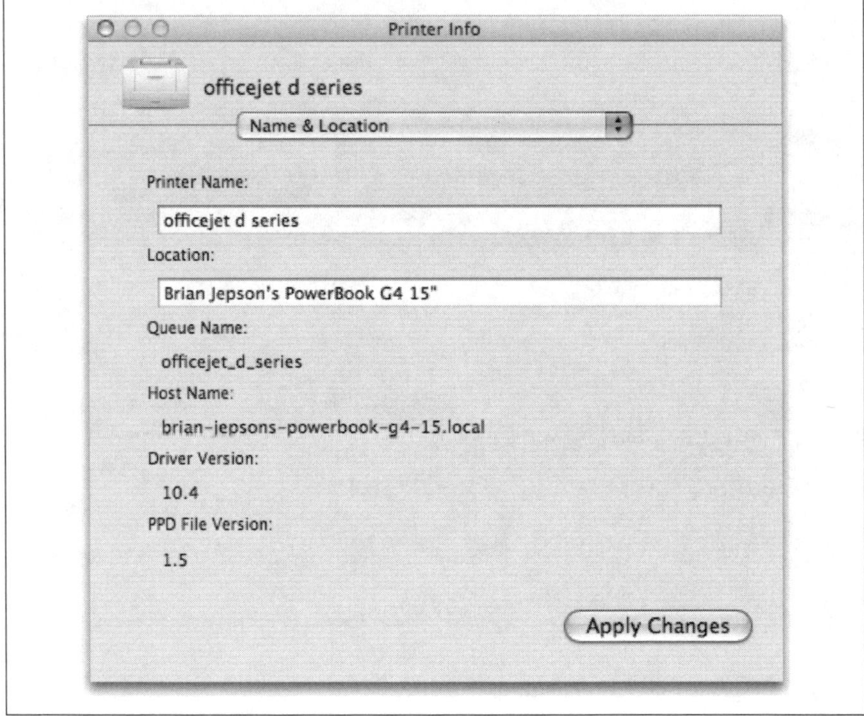

Figure 6-8. Inspecting the properties for an HP OfficeJet

GNOME

To connect to your Mac's printer from GNOME:

1. Launch the GNOME CUPS Manager. This may appear in a menu (on Ubuntu Linux, select Computer → System Configuration → Printing), or you can run the command *gnome-cups-manager*. The CUPS Manager appears as shown in Figure 6-9.
2. Double-click New Printer; the Add a Printer wizard appears.
3. In Step 1, select Network Printer (CUPS Printer) and specify the URL of your printer. The URL is of the form *http://HOST:631/printers/queuename*, as shown in Figure 6-10. Click Next.
4. In Step 2 (Figure 6-11), select the manufacturer and printer model. Click Apply. The Add a Printer dialog box disappears, and you'll be back in the GNOME CUPS Manager (an icon should now be visible for your newly-added printer).
5. Print a test page. Right-click on the printer you just added, select Properties, and click Print Test Page from the dialog that appears (Figure 6-12).

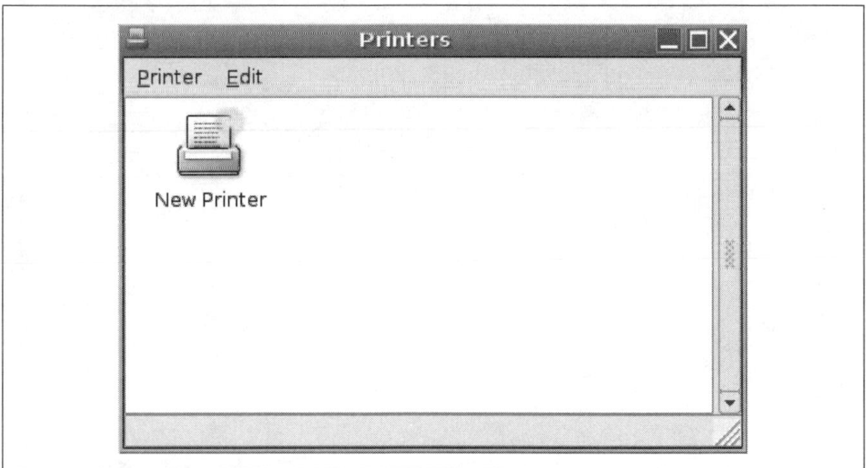

Figure 6-9. The GNOME CUPS Manager

KDE

To connect to your Mac's printer using KDE, launch the KDE Control Panel and choose Peripherals → Printers. You may find that your printer is already detected, as shown in Figure 6-13. Depending on whether your Linux system can resolve your Mac's hostname properly, this printer may work as-is.

Add a Printer

Step 1 of 2: Printer Connection

This assistant helps you set up a printer.

Printer Type: Local Printer

Network Printer CUPS Printer (IPP)

URI: http://192.168.254.150:631/printers/officejet_d_series

Cancel Back Forward

Figure 6-10. Adding a new printer under GNOME

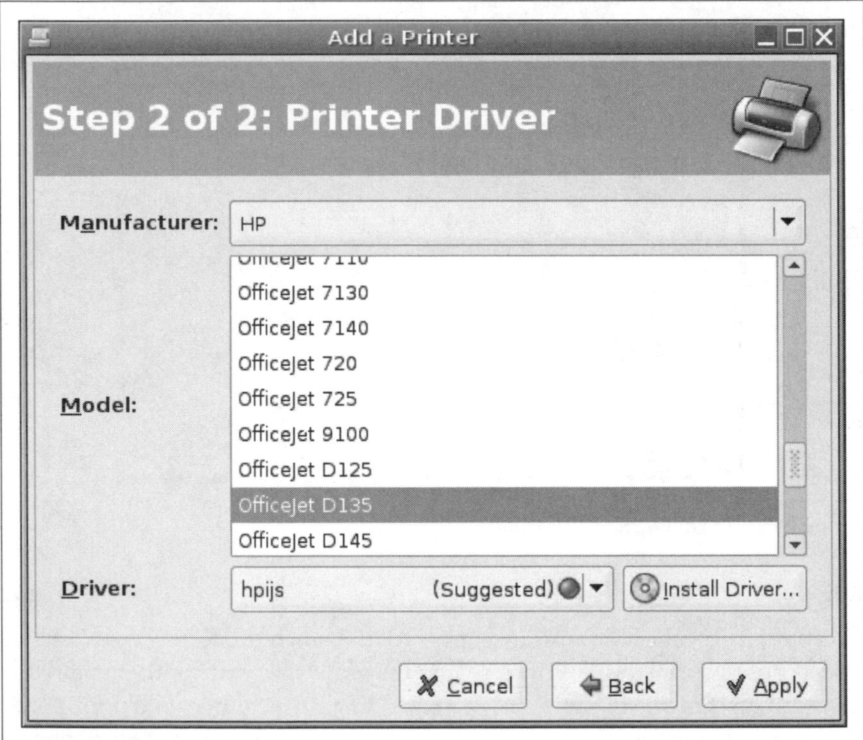

Figure 6-11. Specifying the printer's make and model

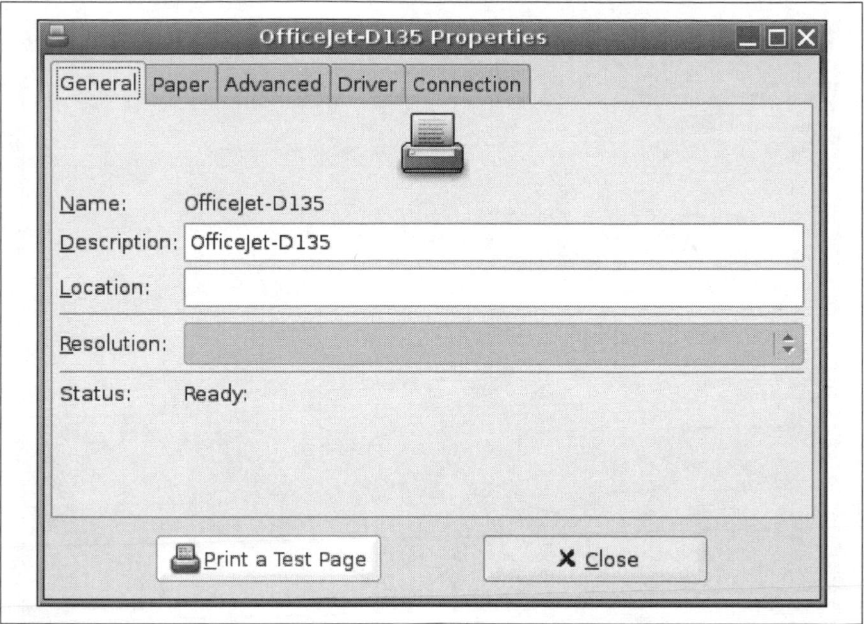

Figure 6-12. Printing a test page

Right-click on the printer, select Printer IPP Report, and browse the results. If you see "Unknown host" and/or "Unable to lookup host" in the printer-state-message, it probably won't work out of the box.

In our case, it didn't work out of the box. You can follow these steps to add the printer manually:

1. Click Add → Add Printer/Class.
2. The Add Printer Wizard appears. Click Next to start the wizard.
3. The Backend Selection appears (Figure 6-14). Choose Remote CUPS Server (IPP/HTTP) and click Next.
4. The next screen asks for use identification. Leave this set to the default (Anonymous) and click Next.
5. Specify your Mac's IP address and CUPS port (normally 631) as shown in Figure 6-15. Click Next.
6. You'll see a list of shared printers on your Mac, as shown in Figure 6-16. Choose one and click Next.
7. The next screen asks you to select the printer manufacturer and model. Click Next when you're done.

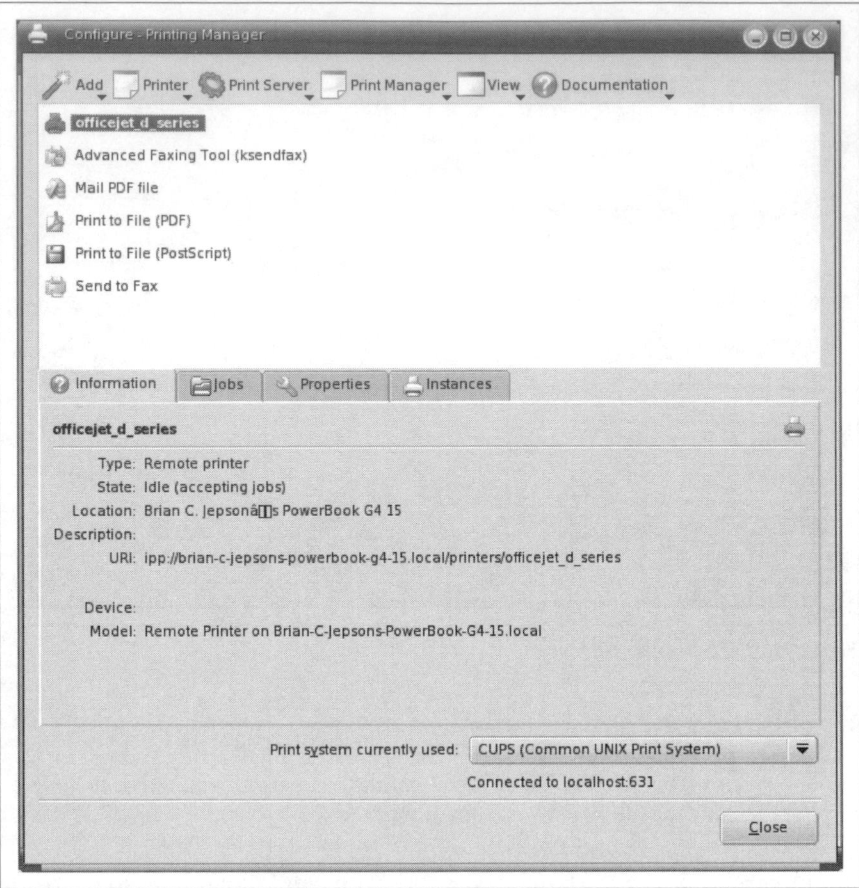

Figure 6-13. KDE will usually detect your shared printer

8. The Driver Selection screen appears. This displays all the detected drivers for your printer, as shown in Figure 6-17. Choose the correct one, and click Next.
9. At this point, you're prompted to test the printer. When we tried it, it didn't work, but it wasn't a showstopper. If it doesn't work for you, click Next anyway and keep on moving through the Wizard.
10. There are a few more screens: Banner Selection, Printer Quota Settings, and Users Access Settings. Leave the defaults and click Next for each one.

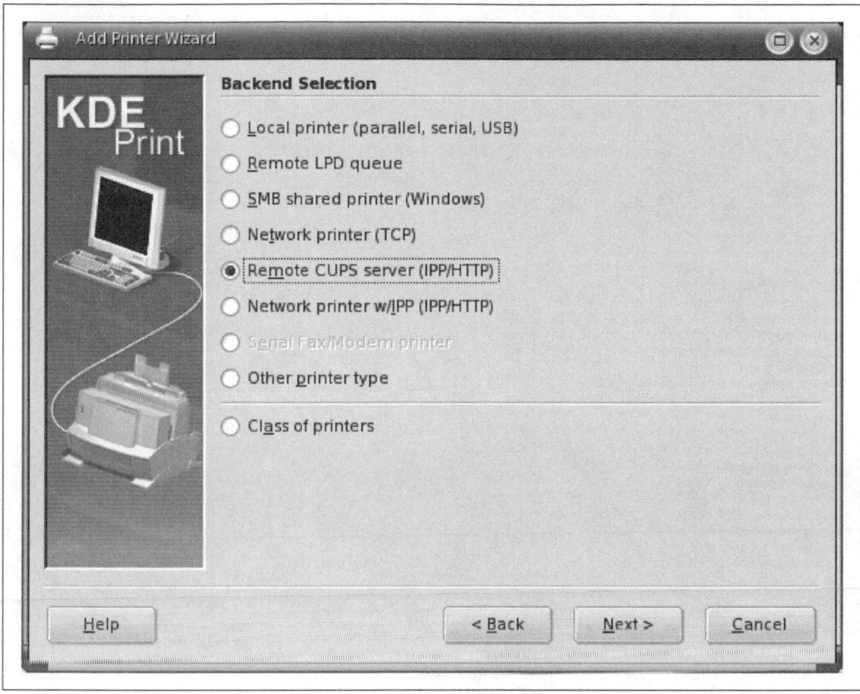

Figure 6-14. Specifying the CUPS backend for your printer

11. The next screen asks for the printer name, location, and description. Specify something that you think is useful, and then click Next.
12. The final screen shows you a summary of the selected settings. Review them, clicking Back if necessary to change anything, and click Finish when you are ready.
13. After the printer is installed, you can right-click on it in the Printing Manager and select Test Printer to send it a test page.

Manual printer configuration (Linux and Unix)

You can also configure a CUPS client manually. To add your Mac OS X printer as the default printer, edit */etc/cups/printers.conf* on the Linux (or other Unix) machine, and add the following entry, replacing `OfficeJet-D135`, `192.168.254.150`, and `officejet_d_series` with the appropriate values:

```
<DefaultPrinter OfficeJet-D135>
Info OfficeJet-D135
DeviceURI http://192.168.254.150:631/printers/officejet_d_series
State Idle
Accepting Yes
```

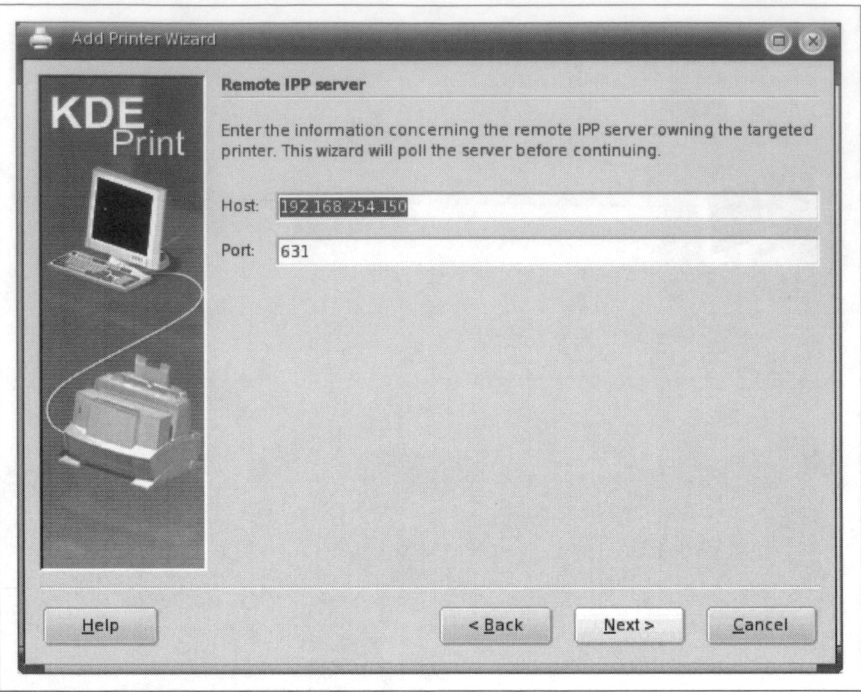

Figure 6-15. Setting the host and port

```
JobSheets none none
QuotaPeriod 0
PageLimit 0
KLimit 0
</Printer>
```

If you don't want the printer as the default printer, change `DefaultPrinter` to `Printer`. After you've added the entry, stop and restart CUPS on the Linux (or other Unix) machine to load the new printer configuration.

Printing from Linux

After you get your Mac and its printer to appear in the list, you don't need to do any further configuration. To print from an application such as Firefox, select the Print option from the application's main menu. Your Mac's printer will either appear by name, or show up as something simple like "PostScript/default," as shown in Figure 6-18.

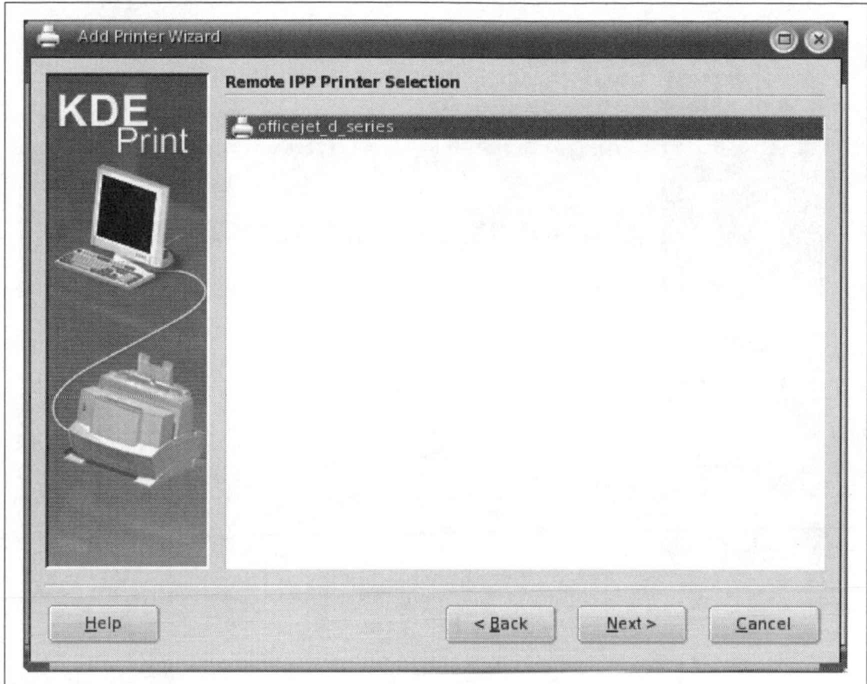

Figure 6-16. Choosing the shared printer on your Mac

Gimp-Print

Gimp-Print (*http://gimp-print.sourceforge.net*) is a package of printer drivers that is bundled with Mac OS X Tiger. The Gimp-Print drivers support printers from Epson, Canon, Lexmark, HP, and others. In many cases, drivers for these printers are not available from the printer manufacturer themselves. Even if drivers are available, the Gimp-Print drivers are often of better quality than those offered by the manufacturer.

If you are using a version of Mac OS X prior to Panther, you'll need to download the drivers from the Mac OS X Gimp-Print web site (*http://gimp-print.sourceforge.net/MacOSX.php3*).

Figure 6-17. Choosing from the available drivers

HP InkJet Server (HPIJS) Project

The Hewlett-Packard InkJet Server (HPIJS) Project is a collection of drivers from Hewlett-Packard that has been released as open source software. Although HPIJS was originally released for Linux, it has been ported to Mac OS X (*http://www.linuxprinting.org/macosx/hpijs/*). HPIJS supports over 200 Hewlett-Packard printer models.

Although Gimp-Print is included with Mac OS X Tiger, if you find both a Gimp-Print driver and the HPIJS driver we suggest that you try both and compare the quality. For example, the only Gimp-Print driver we found for the Hewlett-Packard OfficeJet d135 was the HP New DeskJet Series CUPS v1.1 that came with Mac OS X Tiger. It supports neither duplex printing nor the higher resolutions that this printer model is capable of. However, the HPIJS OfficeJet D135 driver supports these higher resolutions and duplex printing.

Figure 6-18. Printing to your Macintosh's shared printer from Ubuntu Linux

CHAPTER 7
The X Window System

Although the X in “Mac OS X” is not the same X as in “The X Window System,” you can get them to play nice together.

Most Unix systems use the X Window System as their default GUI. (We'll refer to the X Window System as X11 instead of X, to avoid confusion with Mac OS X.) X11 includes development tools and libraries for creating graphical applications for Unix-based systems. Mac OS X does not use X11 as its GUI, relying instead on Quartz (and, on compatible hardware, Quartz Extreme), a completely different graphics system. However, Apple's own implementation of X11 for Mac OS X, based on the open source XFree86 Project's X11 (*http://www.xfree86.org*), was initially released as a beta for Jaguar and is bundled with Mac OS X Tiger as an optional installation. Apple also provides an X11 software development kit (the X11 SDK) as an optional installation with Xcode, which is located in the Xcode Tools folder on the Mac OS X Tiger Installation DVD.

This chapter highlights some of the key features of Apple's X11 distribution and explains how to install Apple's X11 and the X11 SDK. It also explains how to use X11 in both rootless and full-screen modes (using the GNOME and KDE desktops). You'll also learn how to connect to other X Window systems using Virtual Network Computing (VNC), as well as how to remotely control the Mac OS X Aqua desktop from other X11 systems.

From Aqua to X11, there's no shortage of graphical environments for Mac OS X. The operating system's solid Unix underpinnings and powerful graphics subsystem make it possible for developers to support alternative graphical environments. For this reason, a humble iBook can make a fine cockpit for a network of heterogeneous machines!

About Apple's X11

As noted earlier, Apple's X11 distribution is based on the open source XFree86 Project's XFree86, Version 4.4. The X11 package has been optimized for Mac OS X and has the following features:

- X11R6.6 window server.
- Support for the RandR (Resize and Rotate) extension.
- Strong integration with Mac OS X environment.
- A Quartz window manager that provides Aqua window decorations, ability to minimize windows to the Dock, and pasteboard integration.
- Can use other window managers.
- Compatible with Exposé.
- Supports rootless and full-screen modes.
- A customizable Application menu, which allows you to add applications for easy launching and to map keyboard shortcuts.
- A customizable Dock menu, which allows you to add applications for easy launching, to map keyboard shortcuts, and to list all open windows.
- Finder integration, which supports auto-detection of X11 binaries and double-clicking to launch X11 binaries, starting the X server if it is not already running.
- Preference settings for system color map, key equivalents, system alerts, keyboard mapping, and multi-button mouse emulation.
- Hardware acceleration support for OpenGL (GLX) and Direct CG (AIPI).

Installing X11

Apple's X11 for Mac OS X is available as an optional installation bundled with Mac OS X. To install it when you first install Mac OS X Tiger (or upgrade an existing installation), you must customize the installation (in the Selection Type phase) and select the X11 checkbox. If you don't install X11 during the Mac OS X installation, you can install it later by inserting the Install Mac OS X DVD, then double-clicking the *System* folder, followed by the *Installation* folder, and then the *Packages* folder. Here you'll find the *X11User.pkg* package, which you must also double-click to start the installation process.

The installation places the double-clickable X11 application in the */Applications/Utilities* folder. If you're going to build X11-based applications, you'll need to install the Xcode Tools, which installs X11SDK by default. To install Xcode Tools along with X11SDK, insert the Mac OS X Install DVD, and double-click the Xcode Tools folder to find XcodeTools.mpkg, which you must double-click to begin the installation process.

If you don't install X11SDK when you install Xcode Tools, you can install it later by once again inserting the Mac OS X Install DVD, double-clicking the Xcode Tools folder, followed by the Packages folder, where you will find the X11SDK.pkg installer. Double-click the *X11SDK.pkg* installer to begin the installation of X11SDK. Instructions for building X11 applications are included in Chapter 11; this chapter simply focuses on using X11.

The *X11User.pkg* can be downloaded from *http://www.apple.com/macosx/features/x11/download*, while Xcode Tools can be downloaded from the Apple Developer Connection located at *http://developer.apple.com*.

Running X11

X11 can be run in two modes, *full screen* or *rootless* (the default). Both of these modes run side-by-side with Aqua, although full-screen mode hides the Finder and Mac OS X's desktop. (To hide X11 and return to the Finder, press Option-⌘-A.)

To launch the X server, double-click the X11 application (in */Applications/Utilities*). An *xterm* window (which looks similar to a Mac OS X Terminal window) opens, sporting Aqua-like buttons for closing, minimizing, and maximizing the window. Also, X11 windows minimize to the Dock, just like other Aqua windows. Figure 7-1 shows a Terminal window and an *xterm* window side-by-side.

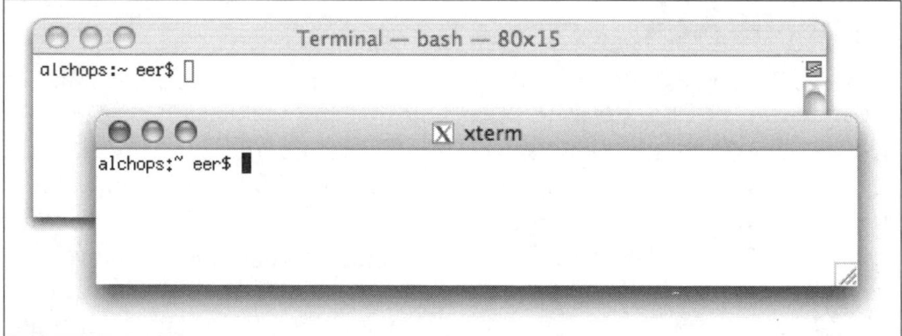

Figure 7-1. A Terminal and an xterm sporting the Aqua look

If you're using the default configuration, you'll also notice three obvious differences from a Terminal window. In particular:

- The *xterm* window has a titlebar that reads "xterm"
- The *xterm* window does not have vertical and/or horizontal scrollbars
- The *xterm* window does not have a split window option

A less obvious difference between a Terminal window and an X11 *xterm* window is that Control-clicking (or right-clicking) in an *xterm* window does not invoke the same contextual menu that it does in a Terminal window. Control-clicking, Control-Option-clicking, and Control-⌘-clicking in an *xterm* invokes *xterm*-specific contextual menus, as shown in Figures 7-2, 7-3, and 7-4. If you have a three-button mouse, Control-clicking with the right mouse button does the same thing as Control-⌘-clicking; Control-clicking with the middle button does the same thing as Control-Option-clicking.

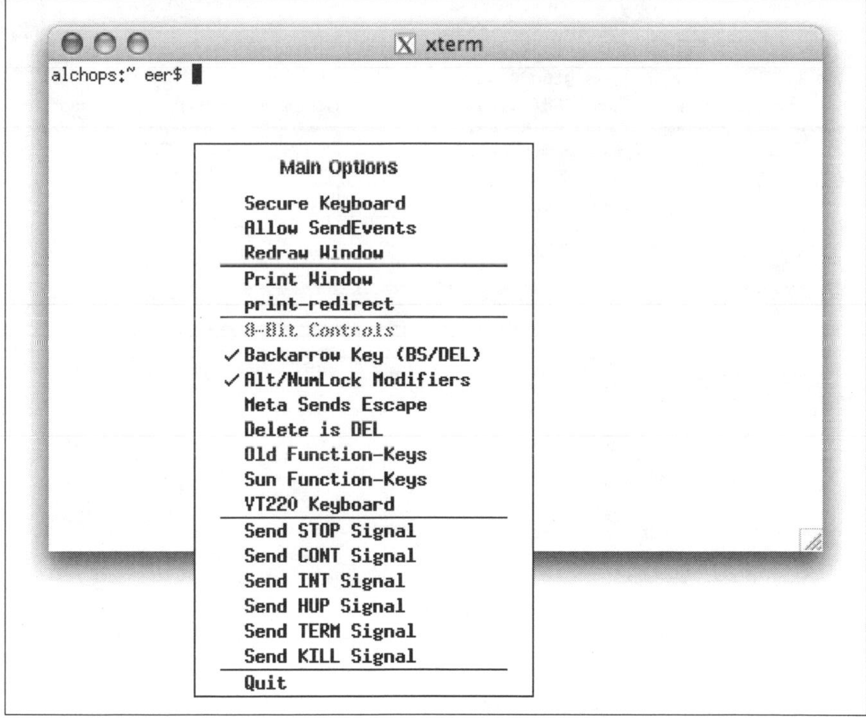

Figure 7-2. Control-click (or Control-left-click) in an xterm window

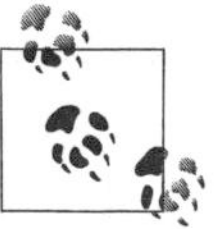

You can use Fink to install an *xterm* replacement such as *rxvt* or *eterm*. See Chapter 13 for more information on Fink.

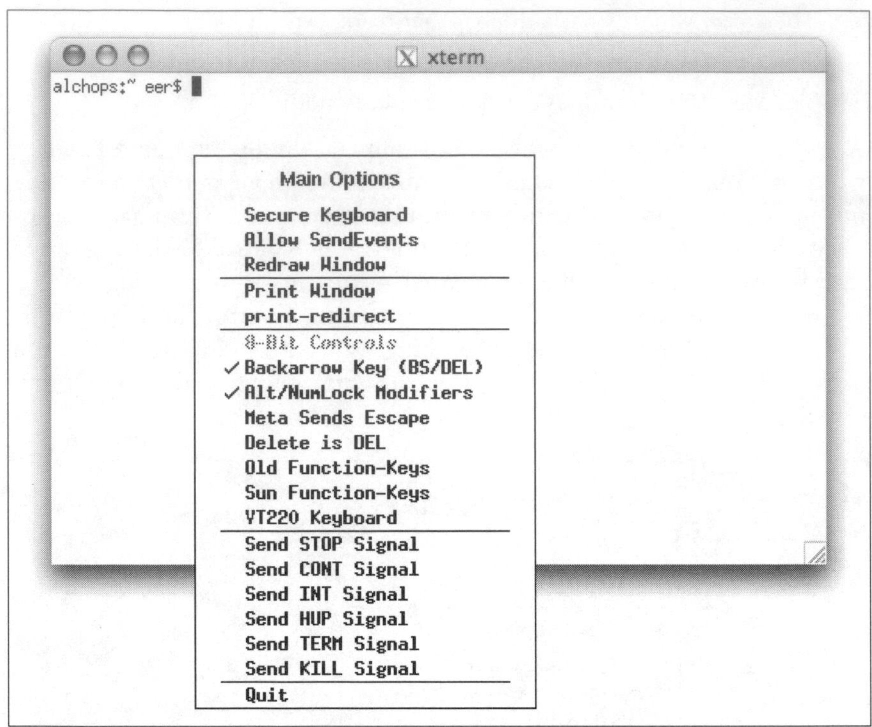

Figure 7-3. Control-click (or Control-left-click) in an xterm window

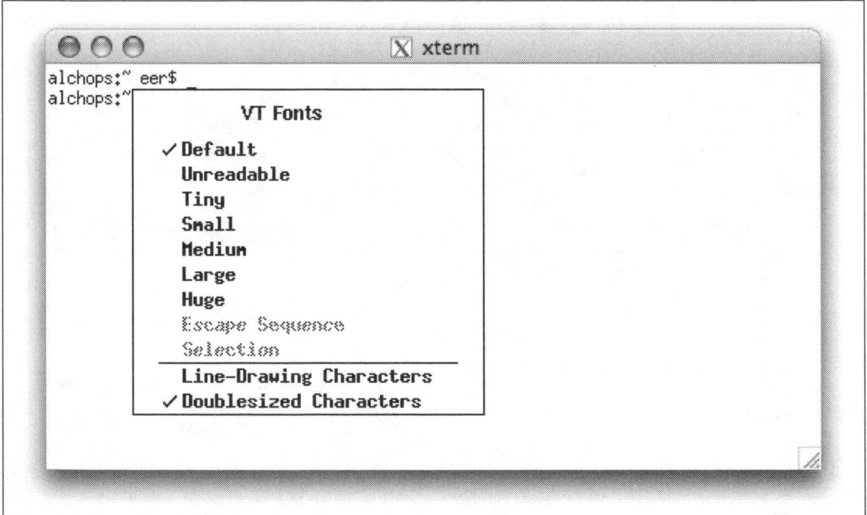

Figure 7-4. Control-⌘-click (or Control-right-click) in an xterm window

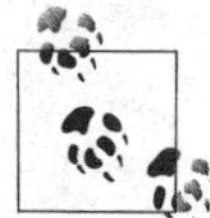

Mac OS X emulates right-mouse clicks with Control-click. In X11, you can configure key combinations that simulate two- and three-button mice.

By default, Option-click simulates the middle mouse button, and ⌘-click simulates the right mouse button. You can use X11 → Preferences to enable or disable this, but you cannot change which key combinations are used (although you can use *xmodmap* as you would under any other X11 system to remap pointer buttons).

In rootless mode, X11 applications take up their own window on your Mac OS X desktop. In full-screen mode, X11 takes over the entire screen and is suitable for running an X11 desktop environment (DTE) like GNOME, KDE, or Xfce. If you want to run X11 in full-screen mode, you'll have to enable this mode in the X11's preferences by clicking the Output tab and selecting the full-screen mode checkbox.

You can still access your Mac OS X desktop while in full-screen mode by pressing Option-⌘-A. To go back to the X11 desktop, click on the X11 icon in the Dock or use ⌘-Tab and then press Option-⌘-A.

Customizing X11

There are a number of things you can customize in X11. For example, you can customize your *xterm* window, set X11 application preferences, customize the X11 application and Dock menus, and specify which window manager to use.

Dot-files, Desktops, and Window Managers

To customize X11, you can create an *.xinitrc* script in your Home directory. A sample *.xinitrc* script is provided in */etc/X11/xinit/xinitrc*.

Using the script as a starting point, you can specify which X11-based applications to start when X11 is launched, including which window manager you'd like to use as your default. The default window manager for X11 is the Quartz window manager (or *quartz-wm*). The tab window manager (or *twm*) is also bundled with X11, but many other window managers are available. You can visit the following web sites to get instructions and binaries for a wide variety of window managers and DTEs:

Fink
: *http://fink.sourceforge.net*

DarwinPorts
: *http://darwinports.opendarwin.org*

GNU-Darwin
: *http://gnu-darwin.sourceforge.net*

OroborOSX
: *http://oroborosx.sourceforge.net*

If you're going to use your own *.xinitrc* file and want to use the Quartz window manager, make sure you start the Quartz window manager with the command:

```
exec /usr/X11R6/bin/quartz-wm
```

Once you've installed X11, you'll probably want to install additional X11 applications, window managers, and perhaps other DTEs. (Even if you are using Apple's window manager, you can still run most binaries from other DTEs, such as GNOME and KDE, without using that DTE as your desktop.) One of the easiest ways to install additional window managers is to use Fink. Table 7-1 lists some of the window managers and desktops offered by Fink. (See Chapter 13 for information on installing and updating Fink.)

Table 7-1. Window managers available for Fink

Window manager/desktop	Fink package name
Blackbox	Blackbox
Enlightenment	enlightenment
FVWM	fvwm, fvwm2
GNOME	bundle-gnome
IceWM	Icewm
KDE	bundle-kde
mwm	Lesstif
Oroborus	Oroborus, oroborus2
PWM	Pwm
Sawfish	Sawfish
Window Maker	windowmaker
XFce	Xfce

Fink has entire sections (*http://fink.sourceforge.net/pdb/sections.php*) devoted to GNOME and KDE, where you will find an extensive set of libraries, utilities, and plug-ins. Also included in the GNOME section are GTK+, *glib*, and Glade. Installing GNOME and KDE may be especially useful if you want to develop software for these desktops.

Fink installs everything in its */sw* directory. So, for example, if you've installed *lesstif* and want to use the *mwm* window manager, you must include */sw/bin* in your path, or include `/sw/bin/mwm &` in your *.xinitrc* file to start the Motif window manager. However, if you've installed Fink according to its instructions, */sw/bin* is automatically added to your command path (see Chapter 16).

You can customize the *xterm* window in Apple's X11 in the same way you would customize *xterm* on any other system running X11. You can, for example, set resources in an *.Xdefaults* file in your home directory or use escape sequences to set the title bar (see "Customizing the Terminal on the Fly" in Chapter 1).

X11 Preferences, Application Menu, and Dock Menu

You can also customize your X11 environment by setting X11's preferences via the X11 → Preferences window (⌘-,) and adding programs to its Application menu. X11's preferences are organized into two categories: Input and Output. The X11 preferences have the following options:

Input

The following options are used for controlling how X11 interacts with input devices:

Emulate three-button mouse
: Determines whether Option-click and ⌘-click mimic the middle and right buttons.

Use the system keyboard layout
: Allows input menu changes to overwrite the current X11 keymap.

Enable keyboard shortcuts under X11
: Enabled menu bar key equivalents, which may interfere with X11 applications that use the Meta modifier.

By default, all three of these options are enabled.

Output

The following options are used for configuring X11's look and feel:

Colors
: This pop-up menu offers the following options:

  - From Display
  - 256 Colors

- Thousands
- Millions

By default, the Color pop-up is set to "From Display"; if you change this setting to something else, you will need to relaunch X11 for the change to take effect.

Enable the Enter Full Screen Menu
: This option is unchecked by default. When unchecked, X11 runs in rootless mode, which means that X11 windows can reside side-by-side with Aqua windows. In full-screen mode, use Option-⌘-A to toggle full-screen X11 and Aqua.

Use system alert sounds
: Determines whether X11's beeps use the system alert sound, as specified in the Sound Effects preference pane (System Preferences → Sound → Sound Effects). If left unchecked, X11 windows use the standard Unix system beep to sound an alert.

Customizing X11's Applications menu

X11's Applications menu can be used to quickly launch X11 applications, so you don't have to enter their command path. You can add other X11 applications to this menu and assign keyboard shortcuts by selecting Applications → Customize to bring up the X11 Application Menu dialog window, shown in Figure 7-5.

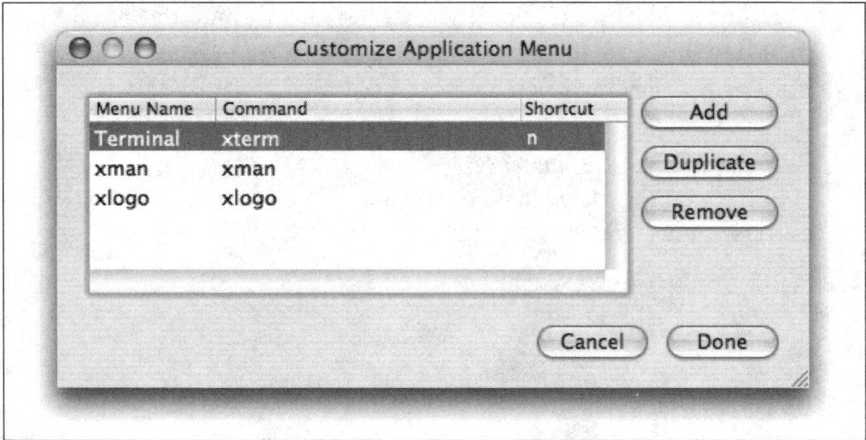

Figure 7-5. X11 Application Menu customization window

The same X11 Application Menu customization window can be opened by Control-clicking on X11's Dock icon and selecting Applications → Customize from the contextual menu. When you Control-click on X11's Dock icon, you'll see that the applications shown in Figure 7-5 are listed there as well. X11's contextual menu allows you to quickly launch other X11 applications and to switch between windows of currently running X11 applications.

X11-based Applications and Libraries

You can use Fink or DarwinPorts to install many X11-based applications, such as the GNU Image Manipulation Program (GIMP), *xfig/transfig*, ImageMagick, *nedit*, and many others. Since Fink understands dependencies, installing some of these applications will cause Fink to first install several other packages. For example, since the text editor *nedit* depends on Motif libraries, Fink will first install *lesstif*. (This also gives you the Motif window manager, *mwm*.) Similarly, when you install the GIMP via Fink, you will also install the packages for GNOME, GTK+, and *glib* since Fink handles any package dependencies you might encounter. DarwinPorts can be used in a similar manner.

You can also use Fink (see Chapter 13) or DarwinPorts (see Chapter 14) to install libraries directly. For example, the following command can be used to install the X11-based Qt libraries with Fink:

```
$ sudo fink install qt
```

There is an Aqua version of Qt for Mac OS X (available from Trolltech, *http://www.trolltech.com*); however, Qt applications won't automatically use the library. Instead, you'll need to recompile and link the application against the Aqua version of Qt, which may not always be a trivial task. If you want the Aqua version of qt, you can alternatively use DarwinPorts to install it with the following command:

```
$ sudo port install qt3-mac
```

Another interesting development is the port of KDE to Mac OS X. As of this writing, Konqueror had been ported and a port of Koffice was underway. To keep abreast of developments pertaining to KDE on Mac OS X, see *http://ranger.befunk.com/blog/*.

Aqua-X11 Interactions

Since X11-based applications rely on different graphics systems, even when running XDarwin in rootless mode, you would not necessarily expect to see GUI interactions run smoothly between these two graphics systems. But actually, there are several such interactions that run very well.

First, it is possible to open X11-based applications from the Terminal application. To launch an X11-based application from the Terminal, use the *open-x11* command as follows:

```
$ open-x11 /sw/bin/gimp
```

You can also copy and paste between X11 and Mac OS X applications. For example, to copy from an *xterm* window, select some text with your mouse and use the standard Macintosh keyboard shortcut to copy, ⌘-C. This places the selected text into the clipboard. To paste the contents of the clipboard into a Mac OS X application (such as the Terminal), simply press ⌘-V to paste the text.

To copy from a Mac OS X application, highlight some text and press ⌘-C. The copied text can be pasted into an *xterm* window by pressing the middle button of a three-button mouse or by Option-clicking in the X11 application.

TKAqua

Although TKAqua has been available for pre-Tiger releases of Mac OS X (from *http://tcltkaqua.sourceforge.net/*), Tiger is the first release of Mac OS X that ships with this Aqua-fied version of the Tcl scripting language and its Tk toolkit. The double-clickable Wish Shell is installed in */Developer/Applications/Utilities* when you install Xcode. An X11-based version of Tcl/Tk can be installed with Fink (see Chapter 13) or DarwinPorts (see Chapter 14).

Connecting to Other X Window Systems

You can connect from Mac OS X to other X Window systems using *ssh* with X11 forwarding. If you use OpenSSH (which is included with Mac OS X), you must use the *-X* option to request X11 forwarding. When used with the *ssh* command, the *-2* option specifies the SSH Version 2 protocol, as opposed to the older Version 1 protocol. For example:

```
$ ssh -2 -X remotemachine -l username
```

As long as X11 is running, this can be entered in either an *xterm* window or in the Terminal. To have the X11 forwarding enabled in Terminal, you must have the `DISPLAY` variable set prior to making the connection. Under the *bash* shell (and other Bourne-compatible shells) use:

```
DISPLAY=:0.0; export DISPLAY
```

Under *csh* and *tcsh*, use:

```
setenv DISPLAY :0.0
```

It is also possible to create a double-clickable application that connects to a remote machine via SSH 2, with X11 forwarding enabled. For example, you can use the following script for this purpose:

```
#!/bin/sh
DISPLAY=:0.0; export DISPLAY
/usr/X11R6/bin/xterm -e ssh -2 -X remotemachine -l username
```

If you've installed the commercial version of SSH from *http://www.ssh.com*, the equivalent of the preceding script is as follows:

```
#!/bin/sh
DISPLAY=:0.0; export DISPLAY
/usr/X11R6/bin/xterm -e ssh2 remotemachine -l username
```

The X11 forwarding flag is *+x* with the commercial SSH, but it is enabled by default, so you need not include it in the command.

Using Apple's X11, you can add an Application menu item to accomplish the same task. To do this, start by saving the above script to whatever you'd like to call this application. For example, suppose we want to connect to a remote machine named *mrchops* with a username of *eer*. We'll name the application *sshmrchops* and save it as *~/bin/sshmrchops.sh*. In X11, select Applications → Customize, and then click the Add button, as shown in Figure 7-6.

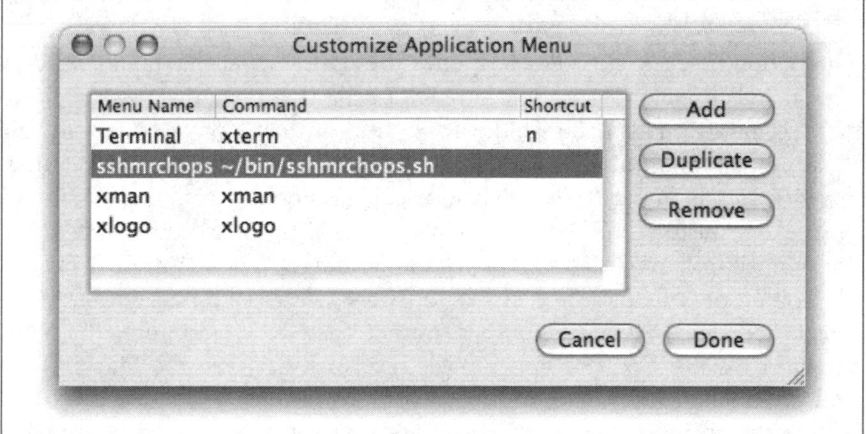

Figure 7-6. Adding an item to the X11 application menu

That's it! Now you'll be ready to launch the connection to the remote machine via the menu bar and the Dock. Once you've connected to a machine running X11, you can start X11-based applications on the remote machine and display them on your Mac OS X machine.

You can also do the reverse (SSH to your Mac and run X11 applications on the Mac, but display them on the local machine), but be sure to edit */etc/sshd_config* and change this line:

```
#X11Forwarding no
```

to this:

```
X11Forwarding yes
```

You also need to stop and restart Remote Login using System Preferences → Sharing for this change to take effect.

OSX2X

These days, it's fairly common to find a Mac sitting next to a Linux or Unix system running an X11-based desktop. You may also have more than one Mac on your desk. In such situations, it would be convenient to use only one keyboard and mouse to control all of your Mac OS X and X11-based desktops, saving valuable desktop space. Enter Michael Dales' free BSD-licensed application *osx2x* (*http://opendarwin.org/projects/osx2x/*).

To use this handy little application, log into your Linux/Unix box running an X11 server, and enter the command:

```
xhost + mymachost
```

Then, double-click the *osx2x* application, and once the main window appears, click New Connection to open a drop-down window. In the drop-down window's Hostname field, supply the hostname or IP address of the Unix box running the X11 desktop, followed by either `:0` or `:0.0` (without any spaces), as in *`myhost`*`:0.0`. Next, select the Edge detection (East, West, North, or South), and the connection type X11. If, on the other hand, you are connecting your Mac to a machine running a VNC (Virtual Network Computer, described in the next section) server (for example, another Mac), select VNC as the Connection type rather than X11, and enter the VNC server password. You can switch back and forth between the Mac and the remote machine with Control-T, or you can enable edge detection and choose the position of your X11 system relative to your Mac. For example, if your Mac is to the right of your destination X11 machine, select West as illustrated in Figure 7-7.

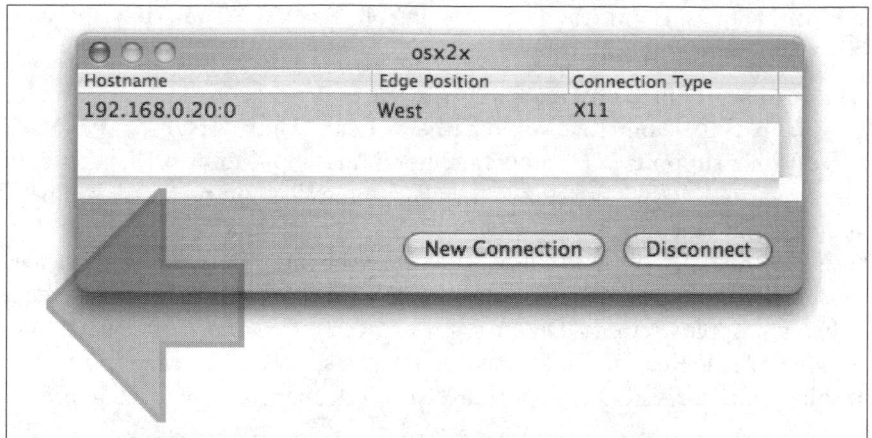

Figure 7-7. Controlling a neighboring X11 desktop with osx2x

In addition to using one keyboard and mouse to control up to four systems, you can use *osx2x* to copy text from an X11 clipboard using ⌘-C and paste on the Mac OS X side using ⌘-V.

Virtual Network Computing

One of the attractive features of Mac OS X is the ease with which you can integrate a Mac OS X system into a Unix environment consisting of multiple Unix workstations that typically rely on X11 for their GUI. In the previous section, for example, we explained how to log in to a remote Unix machine, launch an X11 application, and display the application on your Mac. The reverse process is also possible. You can log into a remote Mac OS X machine from another computer, launch an application on the remote Mac OS X machine, and have the application display on your local machine. The local machine, meanwhile, can be running the X Window System, Microsoft Windows, or any another platform supported by Virtual Network Computing (VNC).

VNC consists of two components:

- A VNC server, which must be installed on the remote machine
- A VNC viewer, which is used on the local machine to view and control applications running on the remote machine

The VNC connection is made through a TCP/IP connection.

The VNC server and viewer may not only be on different machines, but they can also be installed on different operating systems. This allows you to, for example, connect from Solaris to Mac OS X. Using VNC, you can launch and run both X11 and Aqua applications on Mac OS X, but view and control them from your Solaris box.

VNC can be installed on Mac OS X with the Fink package manager (look for the *vnc* package), but that version (the standard Unix version of the VNC server) only supports X11 programs, not Aqua applications. This standard Unix version of VNC translates X11 calls into the VNC protocol. All you need on the client machine is a VNC viewer. Two attractive Mac-friendly alternatives to the strictly X11-based VNC server are *OSXvnc* (*http://www.redstonesoftware.com/vnc.html*), and Apple's powerful desktop management software, Apple Remote Desktop 2.x. (ARD2) *OSXvnc* is freeware, and although Apple Remote Desktop is commercial software, the client portion of it ships with Tiger and includes a full VNC server, named *AppleVNCServer*.

The standard Unix version of the VNC server is quite robust. Rather than interacting with your display, it intercepts and translates the X11 network protocol. (In fact, the Unix version of the server is based on the XFree86 source code.) Applications that run under the Unix server are not displayed on the server's screen (unless you set the `DISPLAY` environment variable to `:0.0`, in which case it would be displayed only on the remote server, but not on your VNC client). Instead, they are displayed on an invisible X server that relays its virtual display to the VNC viewer on the client machine. *OSXvnc* and *AppleVNCServer* work in a similar manner except they support the Mac OS X Aqua desktop instead of X11. With either *OSXvnc* or *AppleVNCServer* running on your Mac OS X system, you can use a VNC client on another system—for example, a Unix system—to display and control your Mac OS X Aqua desktop. You can even tunnel these VNC connections (both X11 and Aqua) through SSH.

Launching VNC

If you installed VNC on your Mac OS X system via Fink (or on any Unix system for that matter), you can start the VNC server by issuing the following command:

```
vncserver
```

If you don't have physical access to the system on which you want to run the VNC server, you can login into it remotely and enter the command before logging out:

```
nohup vncserver
```

This starts the VNC server, and `nohup` makes sure that it continues to run after you log out. In either case, the first time you start `vncserver`, you need to supply a password, which you need anyway when connecting from a remote machine. (This password can be changed using the command *vncpasswd*.) You can run several servers; each server is identified by its hostname with a *:number* appended. For example, suppose you start the VNC server twice on a machine named *abbott*; the first server is identified as *abbott:1* and the second as *abbott:2*. You need to supply this identifier when you connect from a client machine.

By default, the VNC server runs *twm*. So, when you connect, you will see an X11 desktop instead of Mac OS X's desktop. You can specify a different window manager in *~/.vnc/xstartup*. To terminate the VNC server, use the following command syntax:

```
vncserver -kill :display
```

For example, to terminate *abbott:1*, you would issue the following command while logged into *abbott* as the user who started the VNC server:

```
vncserver -kill :1
```

VNC and SSH

VNC passwords and network traffic are sent over the wire as plaintext. However, you can use SSH with VNC to encrypt this traffic.

There is a derivative of VNC, called TightVNC (*http://www.tightvnc.com*), which is optimized for bandwidth conservations. (If you are using Fink, you can install it with the command *fink install tightvnc*). TightVNC also offers automatic SSH tunneling on Unix and backward compatibility with the standard VNC.

If you want to tunnel your VNC connection through SSH, you can do it even without TightVNC. To illustrate this process, let's consider an example using a SUN workstation running Solaris named *mrchops* and a PowerBook G4 named *mug* running Mac OS X Tiger. In the following example, the VNC server is running on the Solaris machine and a VNC client on the Mac OS X machine. To display and control the remote Solaris GNOME desktop on your local Mac OS X system, do the following:

1. Log into the Solaris machine, *mrchops*, via SSH if you need to login remotely.
2. On *mrchops*, enter the following command to start the VNC server on *display :1*:

   ```
   nohup vncserver :1
   ```

3. In your *~/.vnc* directory, edit the *xstartup* file so *gnome* starts when you connect to the VNC server with a VNC client. In particular, your *xstartup* file should look like this:

   ```
   #!/bin/sh
   xrdb $HOME/.Xresources
   ```

```
xterm -geometry 80x24+10+10 -ls -title "$VNCDESKTOP Desktop" &

exec /usr/bin/gnome-session
```

4. Logout from the Solaris box, *mrchops*.
5. From a Terminal window (or *xterm*) on your Mac OS X machine, log into *mrchops* via *ssh:*

   ```
   ssh -L 5902:127.0.0.1:5901 mrchops
   ```

   Any references to *display :2* on your Mac will connect to the Solaris machine's *display :1* through an SSH tunnel (*display :1* uses port 5901, *display :2* uses 5902). You may need to add the *–l* option to this command if your username on the Solaris machine is different from the one you're using on your Mac OS X machine. For example, say your username on *mrchops* is *brian,* but on *mug* it's *ernie*. The following command would be issued instead of the one above:

   ```
   ssh -L 5902:127.0.0.1:5901 mrchops -l brian
   ```

   Additionally, you may need to open ports through any firewalls you may have running. Open ports 5900-5902 for VNC, and 22 for *ssh*.
6. On your Mac, you can either start X11 or run *vncviewer* from the command line:

   ```
   vncviewer localhost:2
   ```

   You can also run an Aqua VNC client like *VNCDimension* (*http://www.mdimension.com/*) or *Chicken of the VNC* (*http://sourceforge.net/projects/cotvnc/*). Figure 7-8 shows a Chicken of the VNC connection to a Solaris GNOME desktop.

Connecting to the Mac OS X VNC Server

To connect to a Mac OS X machine that is running a VNC server, you need to install a VNC viewer. We mentioned two Mac OS X viewers (*VNCDimension* and *Chicken of the VNC*) earlier, and additional Mac OS X viewers can be found on Version Tracker or MacUpdate (*http://www.versiontracker.com/macosx/* or *http://www.macupdate.com*) by searching for "VNC". VNC or TightVNC provide viewers for Unix systems. These viewers can be used to display and control the Mac OS X client machines.

To connect, start your viewer and specify the hostname and display number, such as *chops:1* or *chops:2*. If all goes well, you'll be asked for your password and then be connected to the remote Mac OS X desktop. VNC connections to Mac OS X Aqua desktops can be established through SSH tunnels.

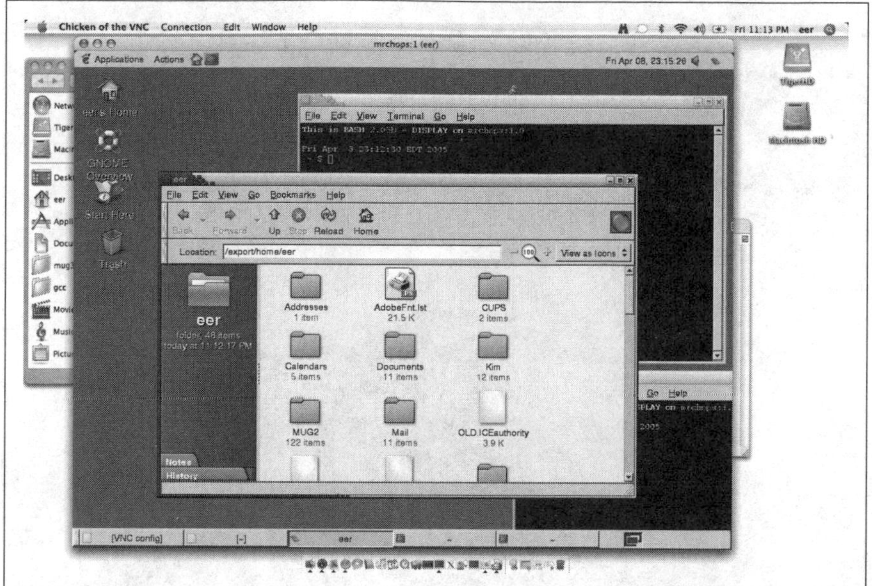

Figure 7-8. Chicken of the VNC displaying a remote GNOME desktop

To illustrate this process, let's do the reverse of what we did in our last example; let's make an SSH-secured connection from a Solaris machine to the Mac OS X machine running the VNC server. Again, let's assume that the name of the Solaris machine is *mrchops* and the Mac OS X machine has a hostname of *alchops*.

1. On *alchops*, double-click the *OSXvnc* application. Select a display number (we've selected 1 in this example). The port number will be filled in automatically once you've selected the display number. Next, enter a password that will be used to connect to the VNC server and click the Start Server button. This step is illustrated in Figure 7-9.

   You can also *ssh* to *alchops* and start *OSXvnc* from the command line. For a list of command-line options enter:

   ```
   /Applications/OSXvnc.app/OSXvnc-server -help
   ```

2. On the Solaris machine, *mrchops*, enter:

   ```
   ssh -L 5902:localhost:5901 alchops
   ```

3. In another *xterm* window on *mrchops*, enter:

   ```
   vncviewer -depth 24 -truecolor localhost:2
   ```

4. The resulting VNC connection is shown in shown in Figure 7-10.

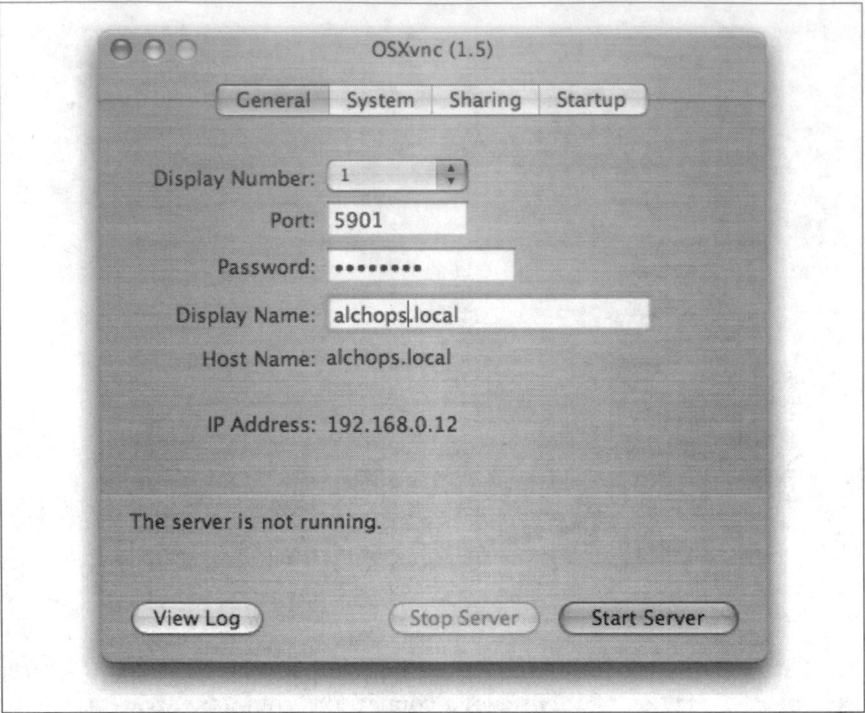

Figure 7-9. Starting the OSXvnc server

If you're running *OSXvnc* on your Mac, you can control the Mac OS X desktop from the SUN Solaris machine, but the image quality of the Mac OS X desktop will be poor unless you invoke the *vncviewer* with the options *-depth 24 -truecolor*. In our testing, these options are needed to connect the Solaris *vncviewer* to the *AppleVNCServer*.

OSXvnc has several configuration options. If you click the System button when you open *OSXvnc*, you can select Swap Mouse Buttons 2 and 3, and two energy savings: Allow Display Dimming and Allow machine to Sleep. You can choose from several sharing options under *OSXvnc*'s Sharing button, as shown in Figure 7-11.

If you want *OSXvnc-server* to run whenever the Mac OS X system is running, *OSXvnc* provides a way to install and configure a system-wide VNC server that starts when you boot your Mac. To take advantage of this feature, click the Startup button in *OSXvnc*, click the Configure Startup Item, and authenticate as an administrative user, as shown in Figure 7-12.

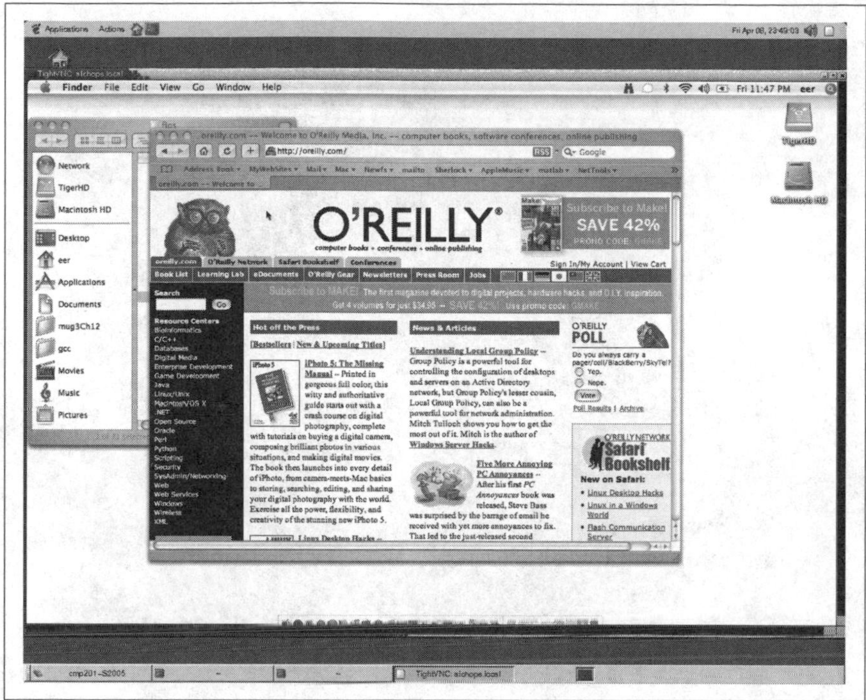

Figure 7-10. Mac OS X desktop displayed and controlled on a Solaris GNOME desktop

Configuring *OSXvnc* as a startup item places *OSXvnc* in */Library/StartupItems*. Subsequently, the `OSXvnc-server` application starts automatically when you boot up your Mac. In this case, the *OSXvnc* GUI doesn't run, and you won't have access to the pasteboard between machines.

To enable *AppleVNCServer* check Apple Remote Desktop in the Sharing System Preference, click the Access Privileges button, check "VNC viewers may control screen with password," select a password, and click OK, as shown in Figure 7-13.

At the time of this writing *OSXvnc* does not support multiple monitors, while *AppleVNCServer* does. Though, according to the *OSXvnc* web site, support for multiple monitors is planned for a future release. You can run both *OSXvnc* and *AppleVNCServer* on the same system, but since *AppleVNCServer* listens for clients on port 5900, you'll need to avoid using this port for *OSXvnc*.

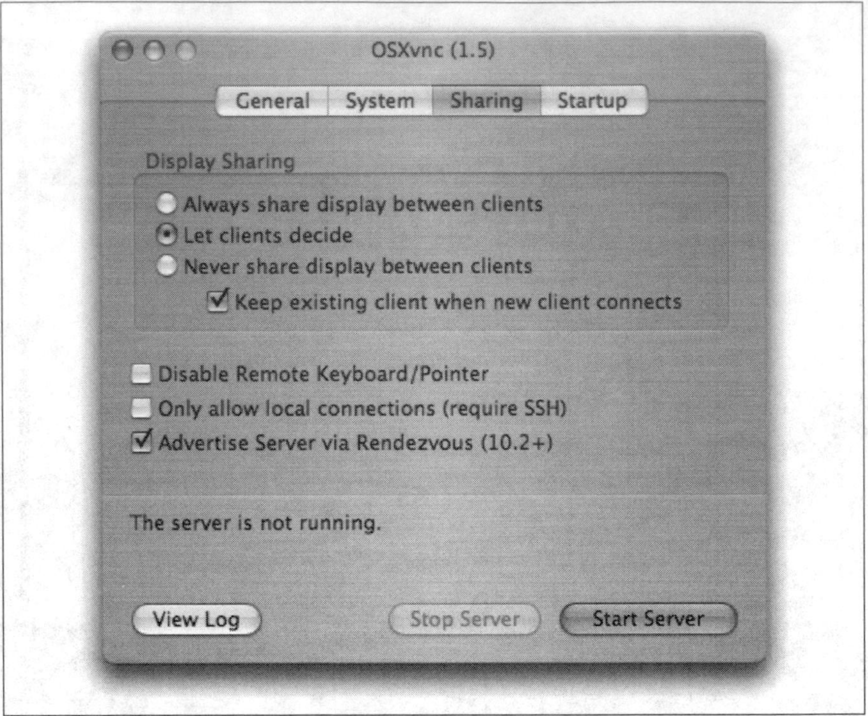

Figure 7-11. Sharing configuration in OSXvnc

VNC clients and servers are available for Windows machines, so Windows clients can connect to Mac OS X and other UNIX VNC servers. Mac OS X clients can also connect to and control Windows VNC servers. (See *http://www.realvnc.com/*.) As an alternative to VNC, you can use Microsoft's free Remote Desktop Client (RDC, available at *http://www.microsoft.com/mac/otherproducts/otherproducts.aspx?pid=remotedesktopclient*) to remotely control a Windows desktop from a Mac OS X machine. An open source X11-based remote desktop client for Windows, named rdesktop (*http://www.rdesktop.org*), is also available and can be installed with DarwinPorts or Fink. (See Chapters 13 and 14 for information on DarwinPorts and Fink, respectively.)

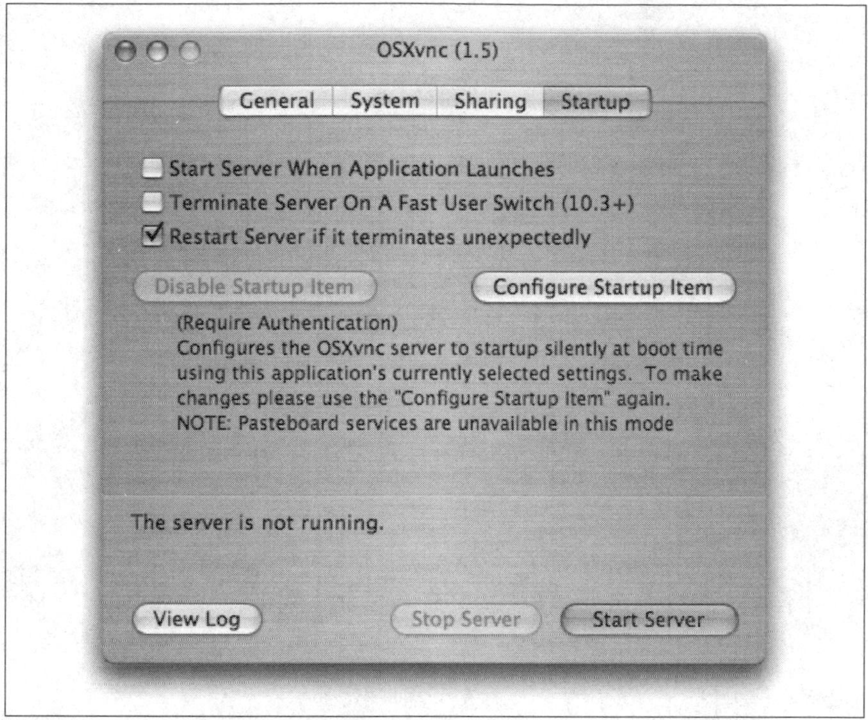

Figure 7-12. Installing OSXvnc as a Startup Item

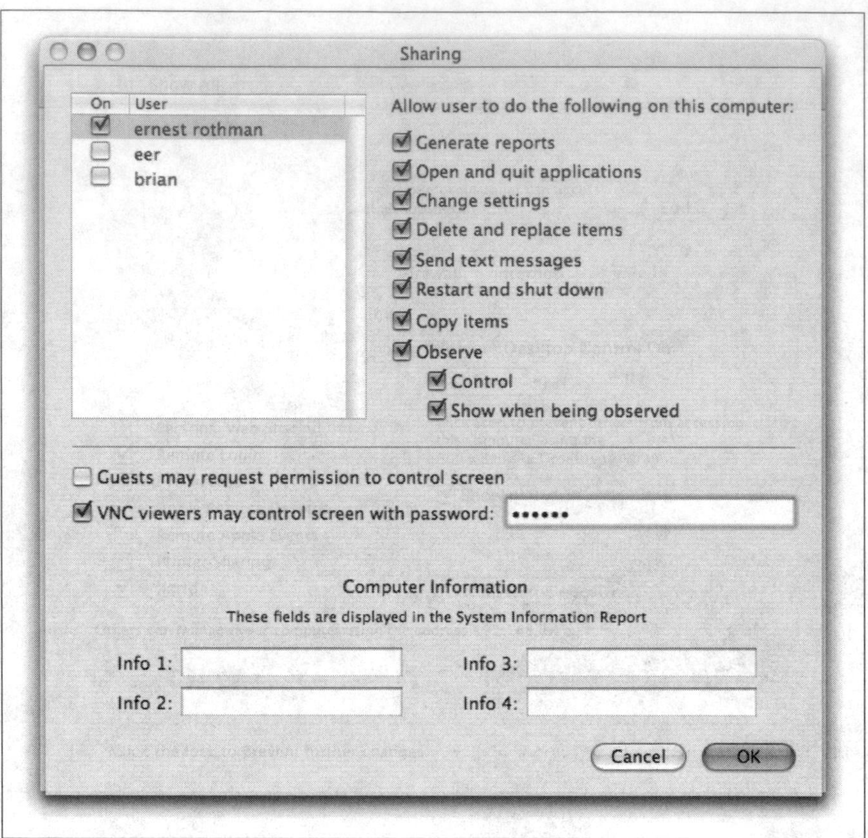

Figure 7-13. Enabling AppleVNCServer

CHAPTER 8
Multimedia

Since its introduction, the Macintosh has earned a reputation as a strong computing platform for multimedia applications. With the maturation of Mac OS X and its support for open source applications, coupled with Apple's Digital Hub strategy, the Macintosh has become an even better choice for multimedia applications.

This chapter highlights a few multimedia applications that may be especially interesting to those Mac OS X users who have used similar (and in some cases, the same) applications in Linux and/or various flavors of Unix. We begin with a brief discussion on how to burn CDs in Mac OS X using both GUI and command-line tools. The chapter then moves on to discuss some familiar (to Linux/Unix users) open source and bundled applications for playing videos, image editing, and 3D modeling.

Burning CDs

There are several ways to burn CDs in Mac OS X. Which method of CD-burning you should use depends largely on what kind of data you are burning to the CD. Let's consider an example in which we'll use a CD-R to backup *~/Documents/tex-docs*. The same procedure can be applied to other data. We'll discuss how to accomplish this task with the GUI-based Disk Utility application located in */Applications/Utilities,* with a burnable folder, and by using the command line in Terminal. In either case, you should make a disk image before burning your data to a CD-R.

To make a disk image of *~/Documents/tex-docs* using Disk Utility, select File → New → Disk Image From Folder and choose *~/Documents/tex-docs* from the Open dialog that appears. A New Image From Folder pop-up window will prompt you to enter the name of the image you want to save, where you want to save the disk image and in what format, and whether you want to encrypt the disk image. This is illustrated in Figure 8-1, where we've chosen to save the disk image as *tex-docsBAK* to the Desktop in read-only format and without encryption (although you can't see the file extension in that dialog, it's automatically appended, giving you *tex-docsBAK.dmg*).

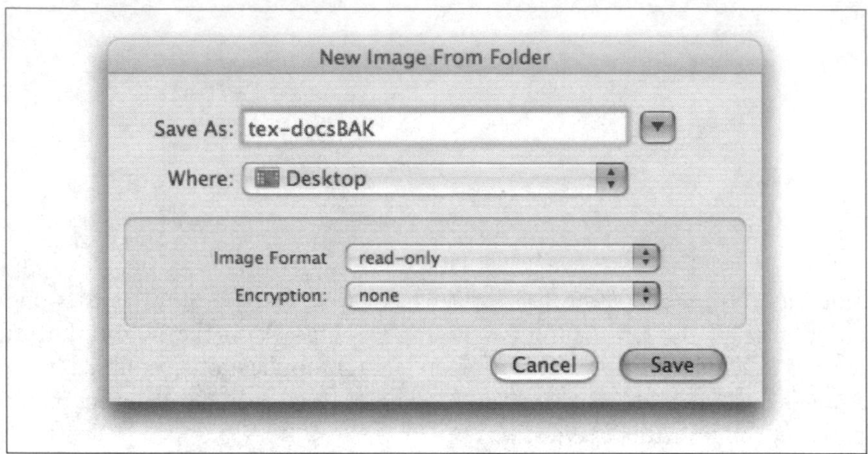

Figure 8-1. Creating a disk image with the Disk Utility

When the disk image has been created, it will appear in the list on the left side of the Disk Utility window. To burn this image to a CD-R, select the disk image in Disk Utility's window and click the Burn icon in the toolbar. Disk Utility then prompts you to insert a blank disc and to select some options for burning the CD, as shown in Figure 8-2.

You can also do this using *burnable folders*, a feature introduced in Mac OS X Tiger to make it easier to copy files to a CD. To create a burnable folder, Control-click (or right-click) in the Finder and select New Burn Folder from the contextual menu. This creates a folder with a radioactive burn icon and named with a *.fpbf* extension. When you drag and drop a file into the Burn Folder, an alias for the file is placed inside the folder (see Appendix A for details on aliases). For example, if you drag and drop a folder named *tex-docs* into the burnable folder, an alias named *tex-docs* is created in the Burn Folder. This, along with a yellow bar containing a Burn button just under the titlebar, can be seen when you open the burnable folder, as shown in Figure 8-3.

When you click the burn button (or select File → Burn Disk from the menu bar), you are prompted to insert a blank disc (e.g., a CD-R or DVD-R). When you insert a disc, the actual file (in this example, the *tex-docs* folder) is written to disc. You can leave the Burn Folder and its alias on your system so you can reuse it for subsequent backups. When you initiate a burn in the burnable folder, the current contents of *tex-docs* are written to the disc.

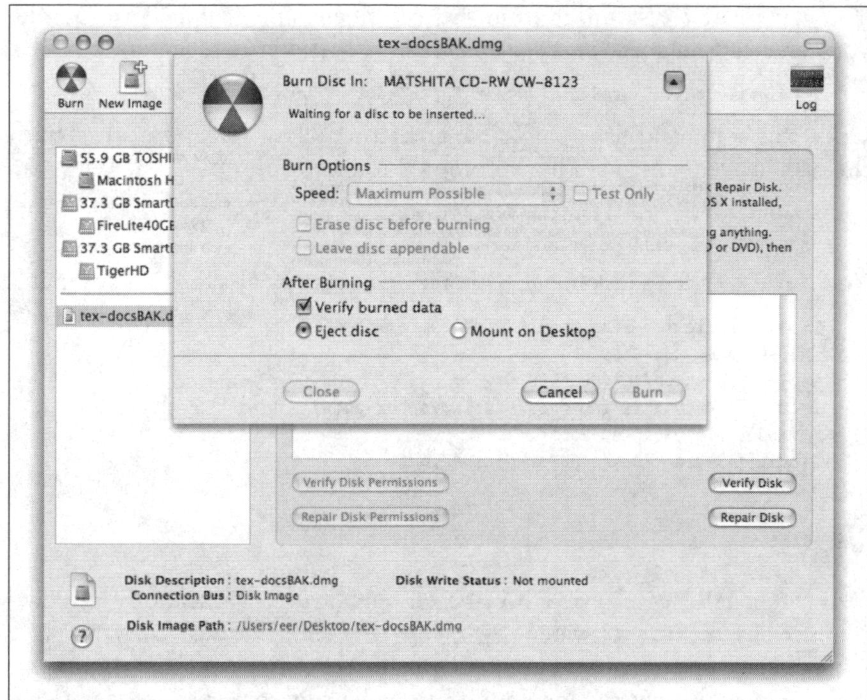

Figure 8-2. Burning a disk image with the Disk Utility

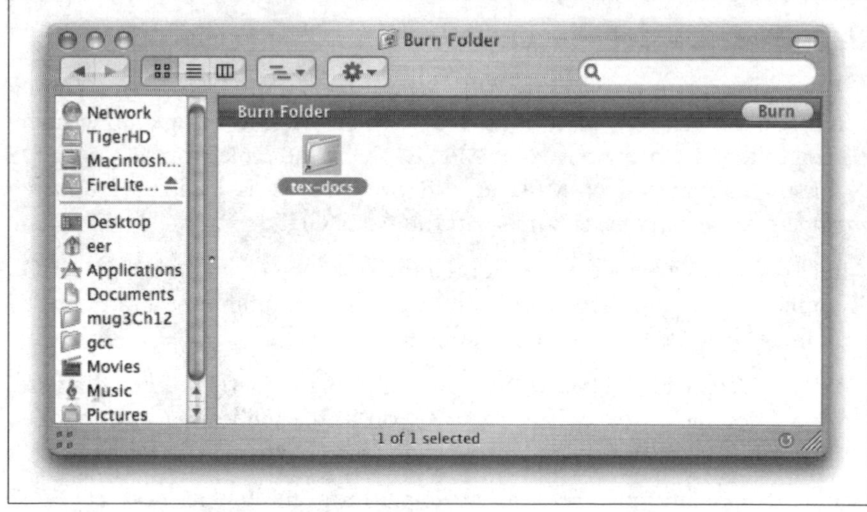

Figure 8-3. A burnable folder containing an alias of a folder to be burned to a CD

You can create a disk image from the Terminal using *hdiutil*. For example, you can create an image of *~/Documents/tex-docs* with this command:

```
$ hdiutil create -srcdir ~/Documents/tex-docs ~/Desktop/tex-docsBAK.dmg
```

Once this command has completed, enter the following command to burn the disk image to disc (you'll be prompted to insert a disc):

```
$ hdiutil burn ~/Desktop/tex-docsBAK.dmg
Please insert a disc:
```

You can also create a disk image with a fixed size, copy files to it, and burn it:

```
$ hdiutil create -size 200m ~/Desktop/tex-docsBAK.dmg -fs HFS+ \
    -volname tex-docs
$ open ~/Desktop/tex-docsBAK.dmg
$ cp -R ~/Documents/tex-docs/ /Volumes/tex-docs/
$ umount /Volumes/tex-docs/
$ hdiutil burn ~/Desktop/tex-docsBAK.dmg
```

Video

You can install any of several X11-based open source applications for viewing various formats of video by using the Fink package manager (see Chapter 13). These applications will run under Apple's X11 environment. Also, some open source video applications have been ported to Mac OS X using Aqua, rather than relying on X11.

Open Source Video Players

MPlayer (*http://www.mplayerhq.hu*), a popular audio/video player among Linux/Unix users, runs under Mac OS X. In addition to being among many packages that are being ported to Mac OS X by the Fink Project, a Mac OS X binary distribution of MPlayer, MPlayer OS X, is available at *http://mplayerosx.sourceforge.net/* and sports an Aqua GUI.

After you've downloaded and mounted the disk image, drag the MPlayer OS X application to your Applications folder, and then unmount and trash the disk image if you don't plan to install it anywhere else.

To play videos with MPlayer OS X (shown in Figure 8-4), you can drag and drop a video file on the MPlayer OS X icon in the Finder, or select a video from the MPlayer OS X menu bar by using File → Open.

Another popular open source, cross-platform multimedia player, VLC (shown in Figure 8-5), has been ported to Mac OS X and sports an Aqua-native GUI. VLC, distributed by the VideoLAN project (*http://www.videolan.org*), supports a wide variety of video and audio formats. To play a

Figure 8-4. MPlayer OS X

video using VLC, choose either File → Open from the menu bar or drag and drop the video file onto the VLC icon in the Finder.

VideoLAN supports some formats that Apple's QuickTime Player does not. If you find that QuickTime does not support a particular file, you may want to try it with VLC or MPlayer OS X.

Image Editing

The GIMP (*http://www.gimp.org*) is one of the best-known open source image manipulation programs. You can get GIMP for Mac OS X from Fink (see Chapter 13). With the GIMP, you can create drawings, touch up photographs, convert images, and do much more.

You can even use the GIMP as iPhoto's default image editor. To do this, use the Script Editor (found in */Applications/AppleScript*) to create the following AppleScript, and save it as an Application named */Applications/LaunchGIMP* (select File → Save As, and specify Application under File Format):

```
on open all_images
  tell application "X11" to activate
```

Figure 8-5. VLC

```
    repeat with image in all_images

      (* replace colons with slashes, prefix path with /Volumes *)
      do shell script "perl -e '$f=shift; $f =~ s/:/\\//g;  " & ¬
        "print \"/Volumes/$f\";' \"" & image & "\""
      set image to the result

      (* set the X11 DISPLAY variable, and launch gimp-remote *)
      do shell script "DISPLAY=:0.0; export DISPLAY; " & ¬
       "PATH=$PATH:/sw/bin; export PATH; " & ¬
       "gimp-remote -n \"" & image & "\""

    end repeat
  end open
```

Next, go to iPhoto's Preferences window (iPhoto → Preferences, or ⌘-,) and follow these steps:

1. In the Double-Click section under General, click on the radio button next to "Opens photo in". You'll be prompted to select an application (if not, click the Select button).
2. Choose *LaunchGIMP* as the application.
3. Close the Preferences window (⌘-W).
4. Quit iPhoto (⌘-Q).

When you relaunch iPhoto, you are able to use the GIMP as your image editing tool the next time you select an image file for editing.

> Another solution would be to use Gimp.app, a self-contained installation of GIMP for Mac OS X that does not rely on Fink. You can find it at *http://gimp-app.sourceforge.net*. With Gimp.app, you can simply specify Gimp as the helper application for iPhoto.

There is a modified version of the GIMP, CinePaint (*http://cinepaint.sourceforge.net/*) that is designed to meet the needs of film professionals. It has been used in the *Harry Potter* movies, *Scooby Doo*, and other movies. CinePaint was originally known as Film GIMP, and an earlier version was available through Fink at the time of this writing. Check out the CinePaint web site for the latest version.

3D Modeling

Blender (*http://www.blender3d.org*) is a popular cross-platform, open source, integrated 3D graphics package for modeling, animation, rendering, post-production, real-time interactive 3D, and game creation and playback. A complete list of features can be found on Blender's web site. In addition to source code, binaries are available for a variety of platforms, including Mac OS X.

To install Blender on Mac OS X, download the appropriate disk image from Blender's site and, after it has mounted, copy Blender to your *Applications* folder. To run Blender, double-click its icon.

As you can see in Figure 8-6, the look and feel of Blender on Mac OS X is different from most standard Aqua applications. The reason is that OpenGL is used to draw Blender's interface.

Since Blender makes extensive use of OpenGL, you'll find that drawing images in large windows can be slow if your Mac's graphics card does not have sufficient memory. In this case, you can switch to fewer screen colors in System Preferences → Displays, and then click on the Display button and choose the Thousands option as the number of colors to display onscreen.

Although Blender is designed for use with a three-button mouse, the standard single-button Apple mouse can also be used in combination with various keystrokes.

- The left button of a three-button mouse is used to activate screen menus and buttons in the GUI, to resize subwindows, and to set the 3D cursor. The same effect can be achieved with the single button of a standard one-button Apple mouse.

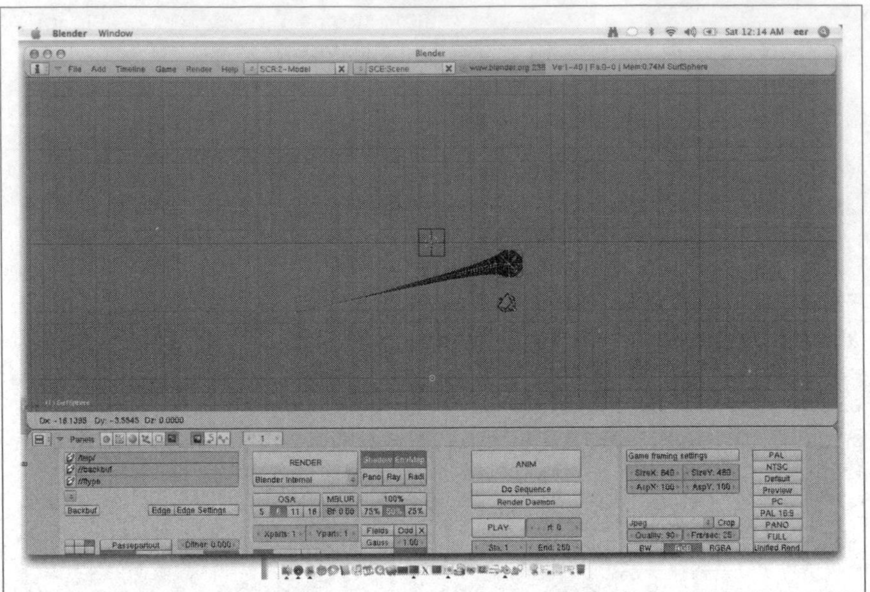

Figure 8-6. Blender, running on Mac OS X

- The middle button of a three-button mouse is used to move, rotate, and zoom the 3D views. To access this functionality with a one-button mouse, simultaneously press the Shift-Control-Option keys with the mouse button.
- The right button is used to select 3D objects. The right mouse button effect can be achieved by Command-clicking.

There are more Mac OS X-specific details to be aware of when using Blender. For example, on other platforms, the F12 key is used to render an image in Blender; however, on Mac OS X, you must press either Control-F12 or Option-F12 to render an image. This is because the F12 key is used on a Mac to activate Dashboard.

CHAPTER 9

Third-Party Tools and Applications

Although Mac OS X ships with an impressive number of applications, including Mail, Safari, Address Book, iCal, iSync, Automator, and the Xcode Tools (just to name a few), there are many third-party freeware and shareware applications available for Mac OS X that further enrich the Mac OS X experience. This chapter provides an overview of a few applications that we feel will appeal to Unix aficionados.

Virtual Desktops and Screens

One desktop feature that has long been a staple of the Unix world is the virtual desktop. For example, if you've used GNOME or KDE, you are probably accustomed to having multiple workspaces in which to run various applications or open different sets of windows. Nearly all Unix/Linux desktop environments have this feature, and yet Mac OS X does not.

Although Mac OS X's desktop does not include virtual desktops or workspaces, it does include several desktop real estate-saving features. Moreover, virtual desktops (or screens) are available as third-party applications.

The primary desktop real estate-saving features of Aqua are provided by options on the application menu (the leftmost menu that has the same name as the front most application), Exposé, and third-party applications, described in the following sections.

The Application Menu

The ability to *hide* an application is particularly useful for applications that you don't frequently need to interact with, such as the OSXvnc server. The Hide option, found in the application menu of most Mac OS X applications (for example, OSXvnc → Hide OSXvnc), can usually be invoked with the ⌘-H keyboard shortcut to hide the currently running application.

To un-hide the application, simply click on the application's Dock icon or use the application switcher (⌘-Tab) to locate the application. The Hide Others menu selection (sometimes available with the keyboard shortcut Option-⌘-H) hides all other open applications.

Finally, the Show All menu option, which is located in the application menu, brings all running applications out of hiding.

Exposé

Exposé found its way into Mac OS X Panther as a nifty hack by one of the Apple engineers. Exposé was previewed and quickly added to Mac OS X's codebase as a must-have for the Panther release and has been retained in Tiger. Exposé uses Quartz rendering to quickly give you access to all of the open windows for running applications, or to scoot them out of the way so you can quickly see what's on your Desktop.

Exposé can be activated in three ways:

- Function keys
- Hot corners (as defined in System Preferences → Dashboard & Exposé)
- By programming the buttons of a multi-button mouse, which can be defined in System Preferences → Keyboard & Mouse

By default, F9 tiles all open windows (as shown in Figure 9-1), F10 tiles all open windows of the current application, and F11 forces all open windows out of the way so you can see what's on the Desktop. In each case, pressing the given function key a second time reverses the effect of pressing it the first time. For example, if you press F11 to hide all open windows, pressing F11 again will undo this action and return all open windows to the Desktop.

Other tricks you can try with Exposé include:

- If you hold down the Shift key and press either of the F9, F10, or F11 keys, Exposé works in slow motion.
- If you've pressed F9 to separate the windows (as shown in Figure 9-1), you can use the arrow keys on your keyboard to highlight a particular window. The window is shaded light blue, and its filename is superimposed on the window.
- If you've pressed F10 to separate the windows for the current application, hit the Tab key to switch to another application and bring its windows—again, separated by Exposé—to the front. Also, Shift-Tab cycles backward through the window stack, so if you've gone too far with the Tab key, try hitting Shift-Tab to return to the application you need.

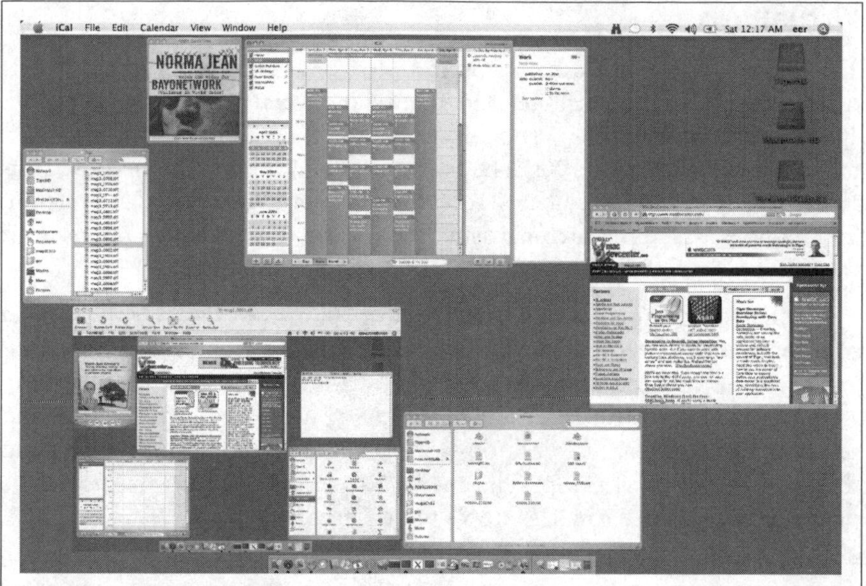

Figure 9-1. An Exposé-tiled desktop

- If you've done the last trick, combine that with the previous and use the arrow keys to highlight a window; pressing Return brings that window to the front of the stack.
- If you've used F11 to push the windows out of the way so you can see the Desktop, the window that previously had the focus is still active, even though it isn't really visible. For example, if you have a Terminal window open and you hit F11, try issuing a simple command like *ls*, then hit F11 to bring the windows back; you should see the output of *ls* in the Terminal window. (F9 and F10 take the focus away.)

Virtual Desktops

Although Exposé adds some useful and interesting features, it doesn't provide you with the virtual desktops that many X11 users are used to. Mac OS X users can, however, add this feature with one of at least two third-party applications. These third-party applications include:

- CodeTek's shareware VirtualDesktop (*http://www.codetek.com/php/virtual.php*)
- Marco Coïsson's freeware Virtual Screens (*http://homepage.mac.com/marco_coisson/VirtualScreens/VirtualScreensEn.html*)

In both cases, the Exposé feature is still available—these third-party applications add features to the Mac OS X desktop rather than replace them.

VirtualDesktop

The shareware VirtualDesktop application from CodeTek Studios, Inc. is rich in features, customizable, and comes with extensive documentation. The two licensed versions, Pro and Lite, both allow up to 100 virtual desktops and support Apple's X11, Exposé, and AppleScript, among other features. The Pro version includes several features not found in the Lite version, for example, desktop switching using the mouse. A detailed comparison of the Lite and Pro versions is available on CodeTek's web site.

The default configuration of VirtualDesktop, shown in Figure 9-2, places a pager in the lower-left corner of the screen. This pager is used to switch to any available virtual desktop or to drag a window from one virtual desktop to another. A menu bar tool is also added—you can use it to click on and select any available virtual desktop, a foreground application, or window in the selected virtual desktop. The menu bar tool also hides or shows the pager and can open VirtualDesktop's preferences.

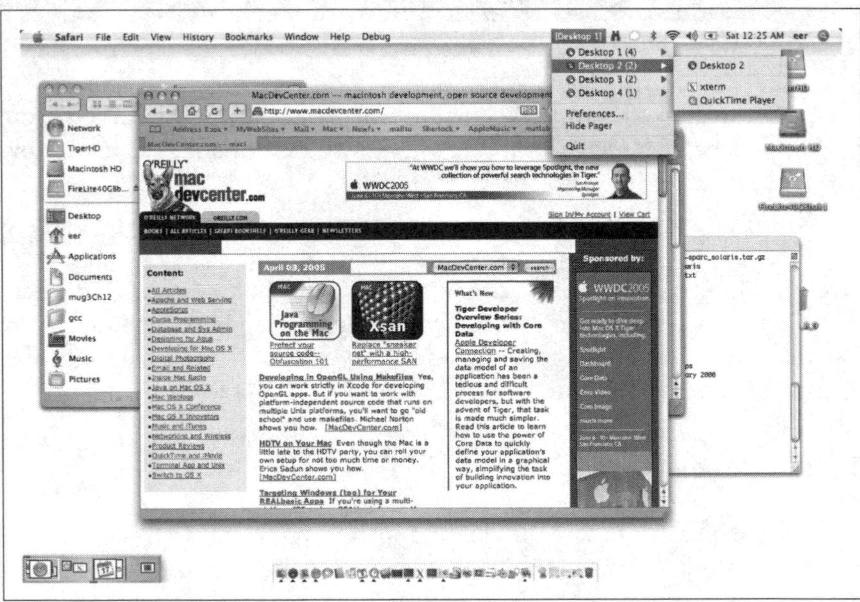

Figure 9-2. CodeTek VirtualDesktop

VirtualDesktop also allows you to open multiple windows of an application in more than one virtual desktop. This is useful in many situations, and is especially convenient for X11 users accustomed to having at least one *xterm* window open in each virtual desktop. You can also assign particular applications to specific desktops and customize keyboard shortcuts in the application's preferences. There are many additional features of VirtualDesktop that we have not covered here; see the program's web site for more information. You can obtain a fully functional 15-day demo registration key, if you'd like to evaluate Virtual Desktop before purchasing it.

Virtual Screens

Virtual Screens is similar to VirtualDesktop, but is not as rich in features and capabilities. Nevertheless, Virtual Screens is a useful product that places no limit on the number of virtual screens in which to run different applications.

When you start Virtual Screens, you can add screens by selecting Screens → New Screen from the menu bar, and assigning a screen name and "hot key" or keyboard shortcut, which is typically of the form Option-Control-*number*. At least one of the Option and the Control keys is required, while the ⌘ key is not allowed. Once you have at least two screens, you can switch to any screen either by pressing its keyboard shortcut or by selecting its name from a menu bar tool to the right of the system status menu bar.

By default, when you switch screens, the applications that are not hidden in the current screen will be hidden in the new screen, while the applications that were not hidden last time in the selected screen will be shown. This behavior can be modified by locking applications that you want to be shown when switching screens. Effectively, Virtual Screens hides applications. If you lock an application, Virtual Screens won't hide that particular application. You can lock an application in a couple of ways. One way is by making it the foremost application in the Finder, and then locking it from the menu bar tool. The other way to lock an application is by selecting Screens → Configure Screens from the menu bar to launch the Screens and Apps Configuration window. If an application is set to lock in the Screens and Apps Configuration window, all of its windows appear in each virtual screen.

In addition to locking applications, you can associate a running application with a particular screen so that whenever the screen is active, the application is shown. You can define a default application for a screen in one of two ways. The first way is to place a dot in the appropriate row and column in the Screens and Apps Configuration window. The second way is by making the desired application the front application and selecting Set *screen name* as default for app *application name*.

A limitation of Virtual Screens is that you cannot have different windows open for a single application in different virtual screens, as you can with VirtualDesktop. For example, if you want a Terminal window open in each virtual screen, you must lock the Terminal application; then you'll have

Terminal windows open in every virtual screen. Clicking on a running application's icon in the Dock moves that particular application to the current virtual screen.

SSH GUIs

OpenSSH is a free version of the SSH suite of network connectivity tools that provides encrypted replacements for *telnet*, *ftp*, *rlogin*, *rcp*, and more. As noted earlier in the book, OpenSSH is bundled with Mac OS X. Although the SSH tools are fully functional from the command line, several GUIs are available for SSH. One such front-end, familiar to Unix/Linux users, is Brian Masney's GTK+/glib-based *gftp* (*http://www.gftp.org*). *gftp* can be installed on Mac OS X using Fink.

Another option is Fugu (*http://rsug.itd.umich.edu/software/fugu/*), which is a graphical interface to OpenSSH, bundled with Mac OS X. Fugu is developed and provided as freeware by the University of Michigan's Research Systems Unix Group. As noted on its web site (which should always be consulted for the most up-to-date version and information), Fugu has many useful features including, but not limited to, the following:

- Support for SFTP, SCP
- Support for SSH command-line options
- Ability to create SSH Tunnels
- Drag and drop files on its interface to upload/download files
- External editor support
- Image previews
- Show/hide hidden files (i.e., beginning with a period)
- Directory upload
- Permissions, owner and group modification
- Directory histories
- Unicode character support
- Support for connections to alternate ports
- Compression support
- Keychain support
- Favorites list for frequently visited hosts
- Support for Bonjour

When Fugu is launched, you will be greeted with a dialog window that includes a file browser showing your local Home directory, and blank fields that you must fill in to make an *sftp* connection to a remote site, as illustrated in Figure 9-3.

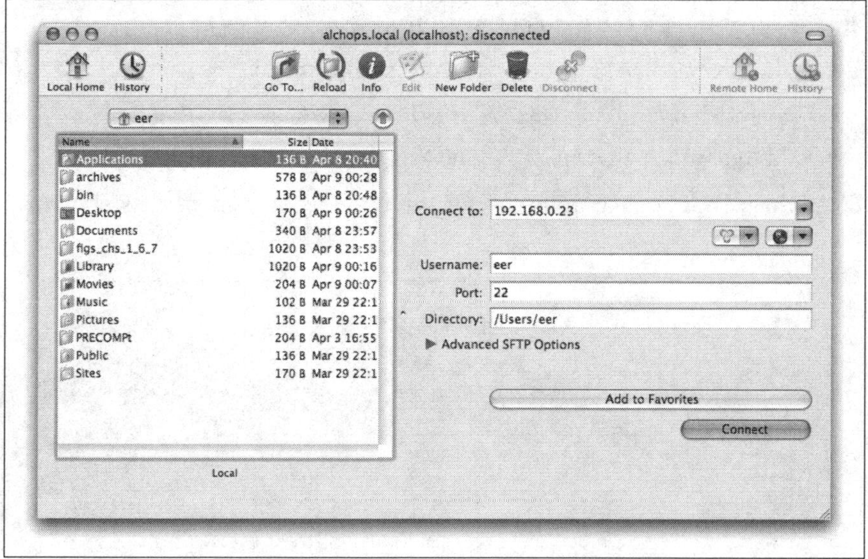

Figure 9-3. Fugu's sftp connection

To use Fugu, enter the IP address or domain name, remote username, port, and directory that you want to access. Under Advanced SFTP Options, you can enable features such as compression or enter additional SSH options. Once you've added this information, add the host to a list of Favorites so you can quickly connect to that site in the future, instead of entering all of its information each time.

Once you've entered this information as shown in Figure 9-3, click the Connect button. If you're connecting to this host for the first time, you'll be prompted to enter a password and add it to your Keychain. Click the Authenticate button and, if all goes well, the right column of Fugu's window displays the remote directory in its file browser.

You can now drag and drop to upload or download files. However, at the time of this writing, you could not use Fugu to drag and download directories with *sftp*. To download folders in Fugu, you must use *scp*.

As noted earlier, Fugu can be used to remotely delete files simply by selecting the filename and then clicking on the Delete icon. At the time of this writing, Fugu could not delete recursively. In other words, if you want to delete a directory and all of the files contained within it, you'll have to delete the files manually. Only then can you delete the empty directory.

You can also change certain attributes of a file, regardless of whether a file is local or remote, by selecting the file in Fugu's file browser and clicking the Get Info icon. In the resulting pop-up window, you'll be able to change, among other things, the file's permissions.

Two other freeware SSH frontends worth mentioning are:

- Cyberduck (*http://www.cyberduck.ch/*)
- SSH Agent (*http://www.phil.uu.nl/~xges/ssh/*)

Cyberduck is another graphical user interface to *ftp* and *sftp*, as shown in Figure 9-4.

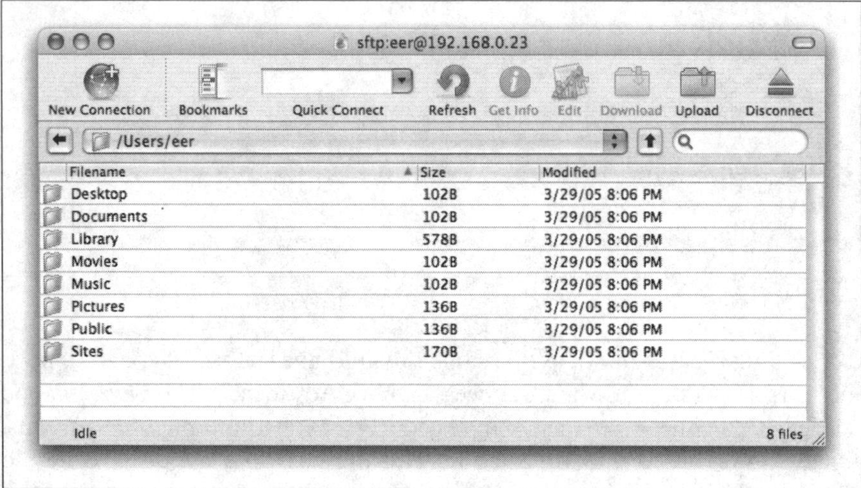

Figure 9-4. An sftp connection via Cyberduck

Cyberduck's set of features is similar to has many useful features including, but not limited to, the following:

- Support for FTP and SFTP
- Drag and drop files on its interface to upload/download files
- Multiple simultaneous connections
- External editor support
- Show/hide hidden files (i.e., beginning with .)
- Directory upload
- Permissions, owner and group modification
- Directory histories
- Live filtering of directory listings

- Move, create, and delete remote files
- Unicode character support
- Support for connections to alternate ports
- Keychain support
- Bookmarks list for frequently visited hosts
- Support for Bonjour

SSH Agent can be used to (among other things) start an SSH-agent, generate identities, add identities to agents, and establish a secure tunnel. Figure 9-5 illustrates how to use the SSH Agent to set up an SSH tunnel in order to make a secure connection to a VNC server.

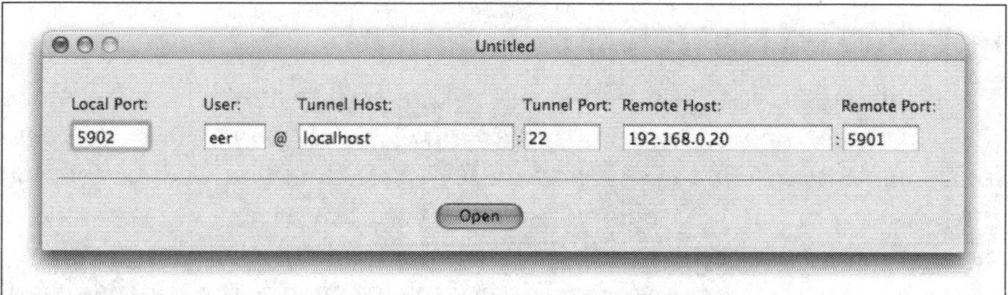

Figure 9-5. Setting up an SSH tunnel to a VNC server with SSH Agent

LaTeX

TeX was developed by computer scientist Donald Knuth as a special programming language used to typeset mathematical and scientific publications. LaTeX, developed by Leslie Lamport and subsequently further developed by Frank Mittelbach among others, is essentially a rather large set of macros built on top of TeX.

The TeX Users Group (TUG) web site (*http://www.tug.org*) contains an enormous amount of information on TeX-related projects and resources. One distribution of TeX for Unix systems, teTeX (*http://www.tug.org/teTeX*), is provided by Thomas Esser. teTeX is commonly found on Unix- and Linux-based systems, especially those used by mathematicians, scientists, and engineers.

The Mac-TeX web site (*http://www.esm.psu.edu/mac-tex*), maintained by Gary L. Gray and Joseph C. Slater, is devoted to tracking TeX developments for the Mac platform. This site is a must-visit if you're interested in using TeX on Mac OS X.

teTeX can be installed on a Mac OS X system with Fink. You could also use the installation provided by Gerben Wierda's i-Installer to install TeX Live-teTeX, a superset of teTeX.

In this section, we'll discuss how to install TeX Live-teTeX with i-Installer and then briefly describe two graphical frontends to LaTeX: TeXShop and iTeXMac. TeXShop and iTeXMac are actually more than frontends; they provide unified LaTeX environments, complete with editors and other tools. We'll round out this section with two more applications, Equation Service and LaTeX Equation Editor, which allow you to easily use your LaTeX installation to add mathematical typesetting capabilities to applications such as Mail, iChat, and Keynote.

Installing TeX Live-teTeX

To install TeX Live-teTeX (*http://www.rna.nl/tex-org.html*), first download the i-Installer application from *ftp://ftp.nluug.nl/pub/comp/macosx/volumes/ii2/II2.dmg* and install it in */Applications/Utilities*. Once you've done this you can use it to install TeX. Before installing TeX, however, you may want to use i-Installer to install five optional packages, Freetype 2, libwmf, Ghostscript 8, ImageMagick, and FontForge, which enhance the capabilities of TeX. Specifically, Ghostscript 8 is recommended if you want *dvips* support, while the other four packages are needed if you want full support for TeX4ht TeX to HTML conversion as well as graphics file format conversion using ImageMagick's convert tool. According to the advice given on the TeXShop web site (*http://www.uoregon.edu/~koch/texshop/texshop.html*), you should install the five optional packages in the order as listed above.

No matter what package you're installing with i-Installer, double-click the i-Installer in the Finder, and then select i-Package → Known Packages i-Directory. A window listing many packages opens, as shown in Figure 9-6.

In the Known Packages i-Directory listing, find and double-click the desired package to open a pop-up window, which can be used either to view the package's Readme and Pkg Properties or to Install or Uninstall the package. Pkg Properties lists, among other things, the URL for the binary, the size of the download, whether or not the package is already installed on your system, and the installation location. Simply click Install in the pop-up window, and authenticate as an administrative user to download and install the package. When you install TeX, you should click Install & Configure. There are several options for installation, depending on your level of expertise with LaTeX as well as your requirements for optional LaTeX components. These options are described in great detail in the Readme, which can be viewed in the pop-up window, as shown in Figure 9-7.

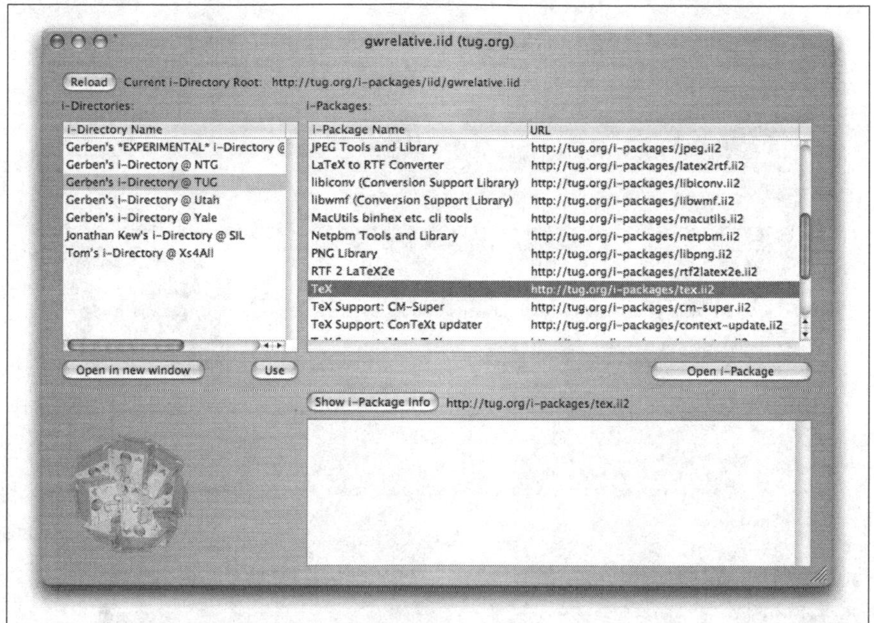

Figure 9-6. Known packages listed in the i-Directory window

Clicking Install & Configure downloads, and installs the teTeX Foundation package in */usr/local/teTeX* with a symbolic link */Library/teTeX* pointing to */usr/local/teTeX*. If you select the Expert installation mode, when installation of TeX nears completion, you'll be prompted to configure items such as language selection, paper size, and formats. Otherwise these configuration options will be set automatically.

Local system modifications, for example, addition of new LaTeX packages (i.e., **.sty* files) can be made to */usr/local/teTeX/share/texmf.local*. Modifications can also be made on a per-user basis by modifying *~/Library/texmf*. If you subsequently upgrade your LaTeX installation with i-Installer, these local modifications are not affected. The teTeX search order for files is:

1. *~/Library/texmf*
2. */usr/local/teTeX/share/texmf.local*
3. */usr/local/teTeX/share/texmf.gwtex*
4. */usr/local/teTeX/share/texmf.tetex*
5. */usr/local/teTeX/share/texmf*

Once the installation and configuration of TeX Live-teTeX is complete, you can run *latex* from the command line. However, even the most hardcore command-line fanatics may find the available Aqua-based interfaces enticing.

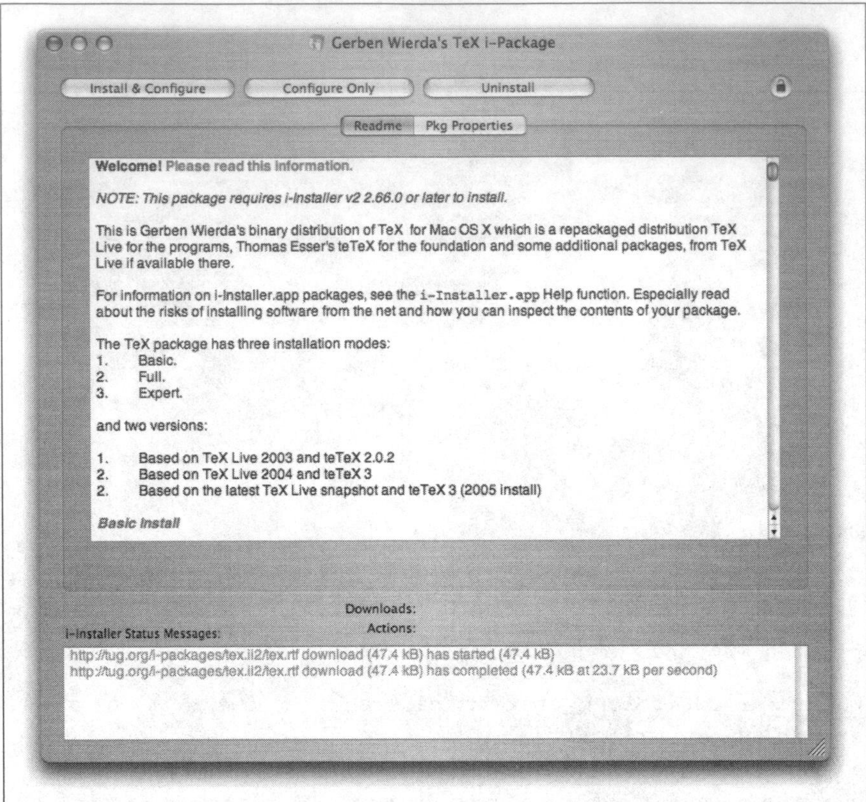

Figure 9-7. TeX Package's Readme

Finally, Gerben Wierda's TeX Live-teTeX can coexist with a teTeX that you've installed using Fink. Fink, which installs software in */sw*, actually provides an option (*install system-tetex*) to place symbolic links in */sw* instead of installing a second version of teTeX. This method allows you to maintain only one version of teTeX and ensures that Fink is aware of it when checking dependencies.

TeXShop

To install TeXShop, download the *TeXShop.dmg* file from the TeXShop web site (*http://darkwing.uoregon.edu/~koch/texshop/texshop.html*), mount the disk image by double-clicking on it, and then drag the TeXShop application to your Applications folder. Individual users should also drag the *texmf* folder, located in the "To Your Library" folder on TeXShop's disk image, to their *~/Library* folders.

TeXShop includes a specialized editor with syntax highlighting, LaTeX macros accessible from a toolbar menu, and a previewer. The LaTeX macros can be used to insert LaTeX code into your document.

By default, TeXShop uses *pdftex* and *pdflatex* (part of standard teTeX distribution) to produce output in PDF instead of the more traditionally used DVI format. Figure 9-8 shows TeXShop's built-in editor, while Figure 9-9 shows TeXShop's previewer.

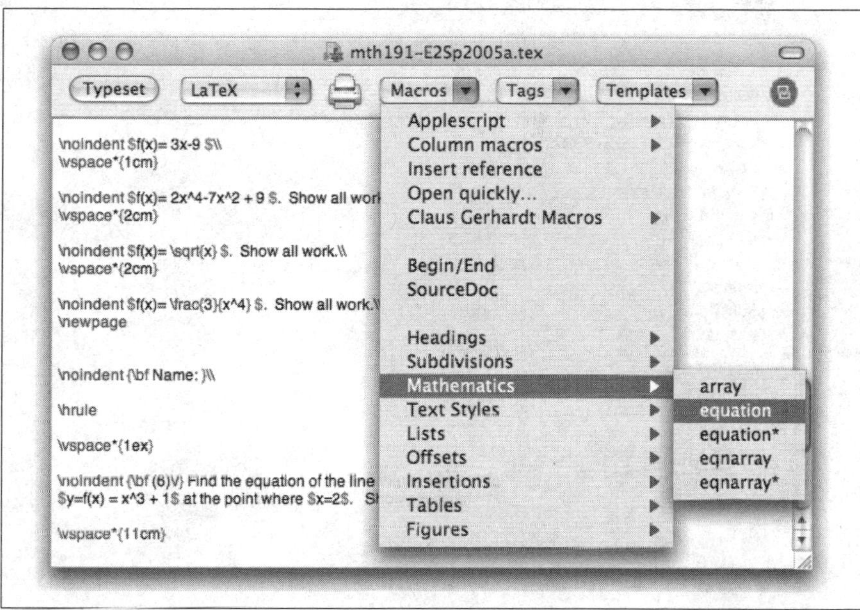

Figure 9-8. TeXShop editor with its LaTeX Macros menu

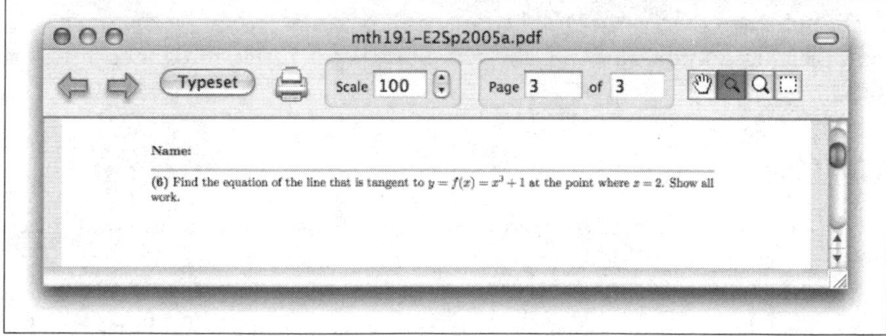

Figure 9-9. TeXShop's built-in previewer

Among its many useful features, TeXShop supports AppleScript and is highly configurable. In particular, you can configure the Latex Panel, Auto

Completion, the Keyboard Menu Shortcuts, and the Macro menu. These user-level configurations are written to four *plist* files, stored in *~/Library/TeXShop*: *completion.plist*, *autocompletion.plist*, *KeyEquivalents.plist*, and *Macros.plist*. Figure 9-10 shows TeXShop's Macro Editor, which can be opened from the Macros toolbar. Select Window → LaTeX Panel to open the LaTeX Panel.

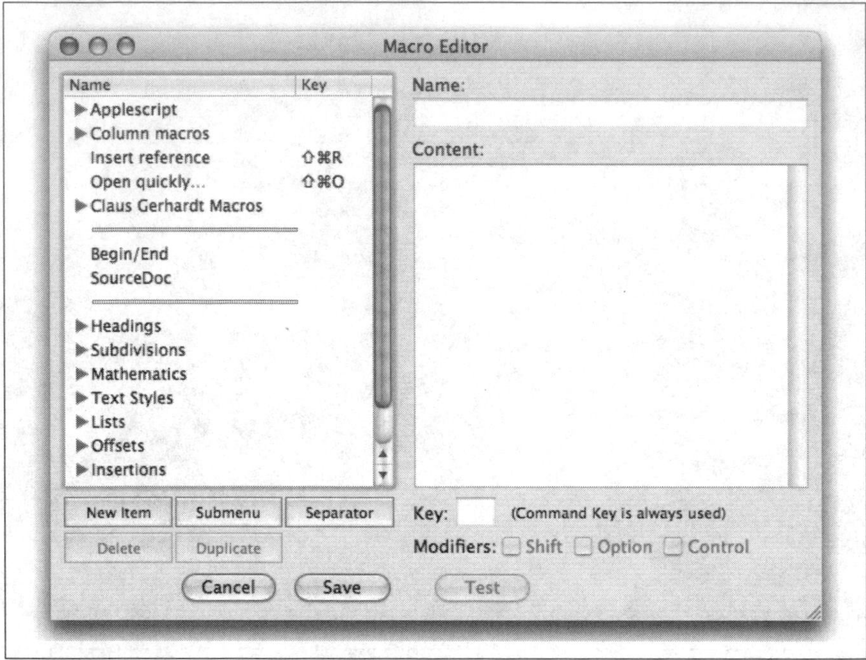

Figure 9-10. TeXShop's Macro Editor

TeXShop (together with TeX Live-teTeX) provides a highly customizable, complete, and unified LaTeX environment that is nicely integrated for Mac OS X.

iTeXMac

iTeXMac (*http://itexmac.sourceforge.net/Download.html*), is a feature-rich alternative to TeXShop. Installation involves dragging and dropping the iTeXMac application file to your Applications folder. You may also want to download *LaTeX.help* and *TeX Catalogue Online.help*, since both provide extensive help on LaTeX from within Mac OS X's Help Viewer (*/Library/System/CoreServices*). If you opt to download the two *.help* files, you must drop them in */Library/Documentation/Help* before you can view them in Help Viewer.

iTeXMac provides a customizable, integrated LaTeX environment, including a specialized editor with syntax highlighting and extensive LaTeX macros accessible from the toolbar menu. These macros can be used to insert LaTeX code into your document from a menu selection. While TeXShop also has this ability, iTeXMac comes with a larger selection of macros. Figure 9-11 shows iTeXMac's built-in editor and LaTeX macro menu.

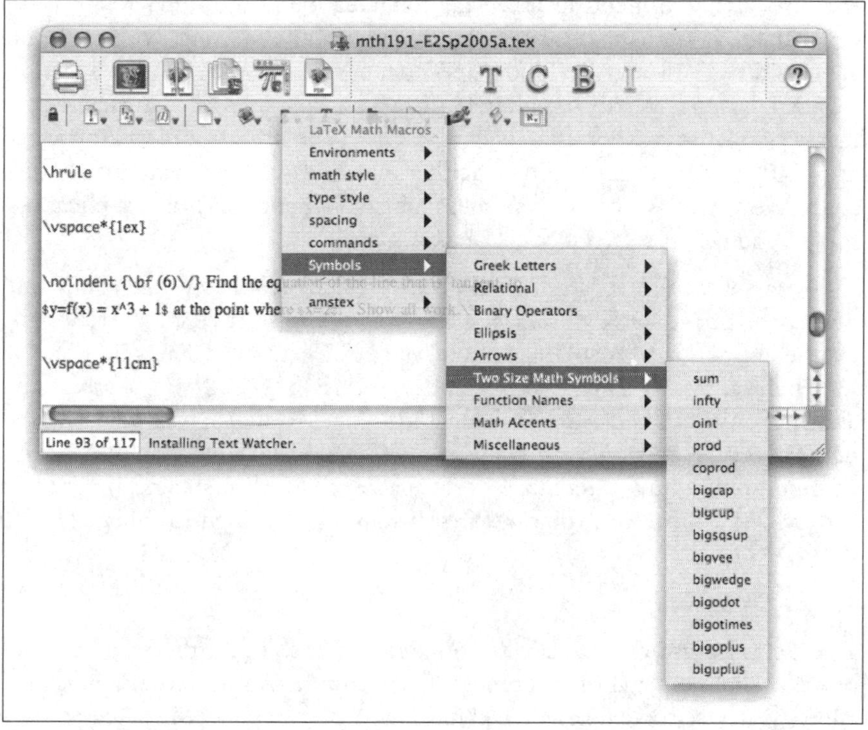

Figure 9-11. iTeXMac's editor and LaTeX Macro menu

Additional features of iTeXMac include:

- Customizable macros
- Customizable key bindings
- Extensive support for project design
- iTeXMac Help, LaTeX Help, and TeX Catalogue Online Help, each accessible from the Help Viewer
- AppleScript support
- Aside from PDF, iTeXMac's viewer can view PS, EPS, and DVI files, which are processed by iTeXMac to produce PDF output
- Extensive set of Dock menu items

Although iTeXMac is designed to use Gerben Wierda's TeX Live-teTeX distribution, you can use it with teTeX installed by Fink, provided that you enable Fink teTeX in iTeXMac's Preferences → teTeX Assistant menu.

iTeXMac and TeXShop share many of the same features. The differences between these two applications are essentially that iTeXMac has a few more features and those features are more extensively implemented. For example, the LaTeX macro menu in iTeXMac includes many more macros. On the other hand, it seems that (at least at the time of this writing, with iTeXMac at Version 1.3.15 and TeXShop at Version 1.35), TeXShop has a performance advantage when compiling large LaTeX files, as well as in viewing the resulting PDF files. Fortunately, these two very useful and well-designed applications can coexist. Since neither occupies a large amount of disk space, you may want to keep them both on hand in your Applications folder, and perhaps even in your Dock.

An open source X11-based WYSIWYM (What You See Is What You Mean) document processor, LyX (*http://www.lyx.org*), uses teTeX as a rendering engine and runs on most Unix/Linux systems, Windows OS/2, and Mac OS X. There are essentially two versions of LyX: one built on *xforms*, and another on *Qt*. Thanks to Qt/Mac (*http://www.trolltech.com/download/qt/mac.html*), an Aqua-native port of LyX, named LyX/Mac (*http://www.18james.com/lyx_on_aqua.html*), is available as a self-installing binary. To run LyX/Mac, however, you must first install teTeX using i-Installer or Fink.

LaTeX Services

One great feature of Mac OS X is its Services menu and the many options offered there by some programmers. For example, Apple's Mail application allows you to select text in an email message and then select Mail → Services → Speech → Start Speaking Text. When you select "Start Speaking Text," Mac OS X's speech synthesis component jumps into action and speaks the selected text back to you. There are at least two LaTeX-related applications that use *pdflatex* (included with teTeX) to produce small PDF images of LaTeX-processed code. One of these two applications creates a Services menu item that can be used with other applications.

Equation Service (*http://www.esm.psu.edu/mac-tex/EquationService*) provides inline typesetting of LaTeX code. To install this Service, download and install the Equation Service application in your Applications folder. When you run it the first time, configuration files are placed in *~/Library/Application Support*.

There two ways to use Equation Service: by highlighting LaTeX code in an application and selecting one of several choices from the Services menu or by creating and previewing equations in the Equation Service application's main window. To use Equation Services to typeset LaTeX within an application (for example, iChat), highlight LaTeX string in an iChat chat window, and select iChat → Services → Equation Service → Typeset Equation. Normally Equation Service replaces the LaTeX code with an image file when it typesets the LaTeX code. At the time of this writing, however, Equation Service adds an image file just after the LaTeX code in iChat. When this happens, you should delete the LaTeX code after the image has been added. Figure 9-12 illustrates the result of this process.

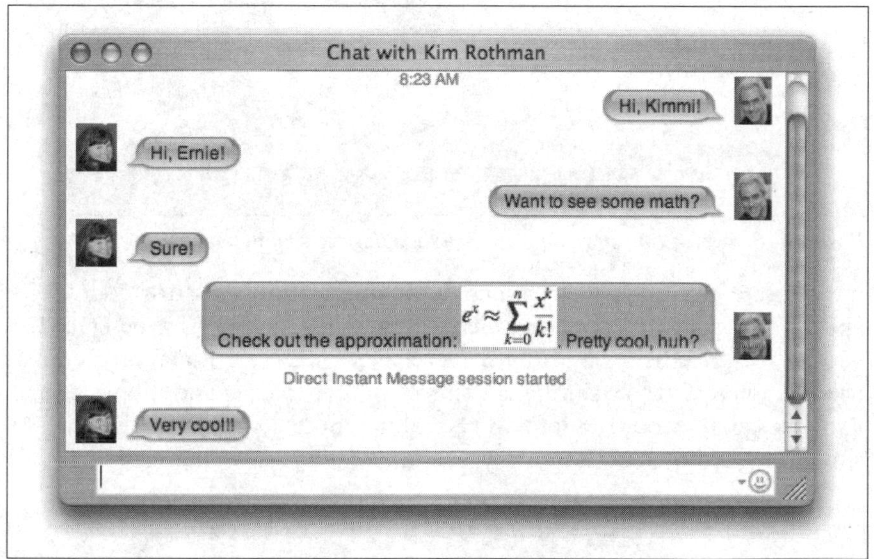

Figure 9-12. An iChat message with an equation rendered by Equation Service

Equation Service is known to work with TextEdit, and OmniGraffle. In both of these applications, Equation Service replaces the LaTeX code with an appropriate image file containing the mathematical typesetting. Although Equation Service works in many cases from the Services item in the Mac OS X menu bar, LaTeX strings can also be typeset in the main window of Equation Service, as Figure 9-13 illustrates.

Once you've typeset an equation in the main window of Equation Service, you can drag and drop the resulting PDF image into a number of applications, such as Microsoft Office or Apple's Keynote. There are several preferences you can set in Equation Service's preferences including font size, text color, and background color of the typeset equations.

LaTeX Equation Editor (*http://evolve.lse.ac.uk/software/EquationEditor/*) is similar to LaTeX Equation Service, but it operates in one mode only: you

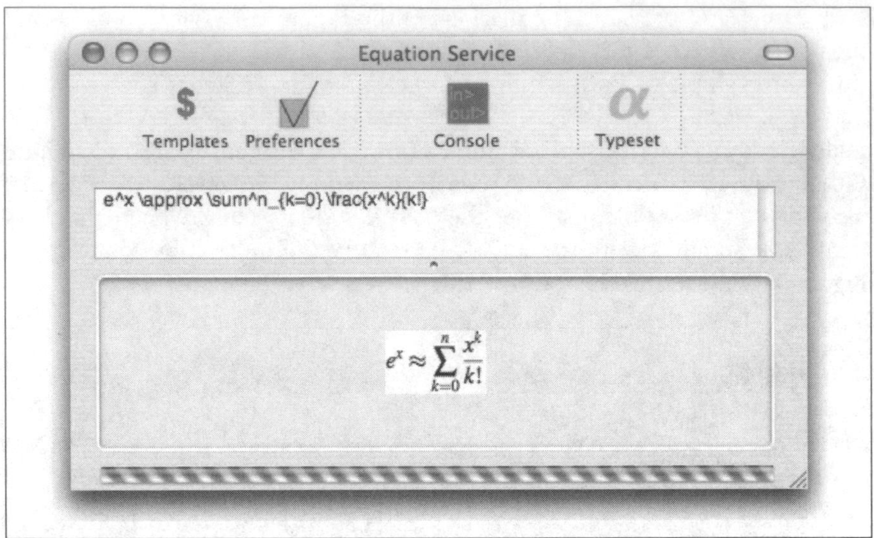

Figure 9-13. Typesetting an equation in Equation Service's main window

must create and preview equations in the application's main window. This application does not provide a Services menu selection to typeset LaTeX strings within other applications. Nevertheless, LaTeX Equation Editor is useful and easy to use, since it is a simple matter to drag and drop the small PDF image it produces into Mail and Keynote documents. Figure 9-14 shows LaTeX Equation Editor's typesetting of a LaTeX string.

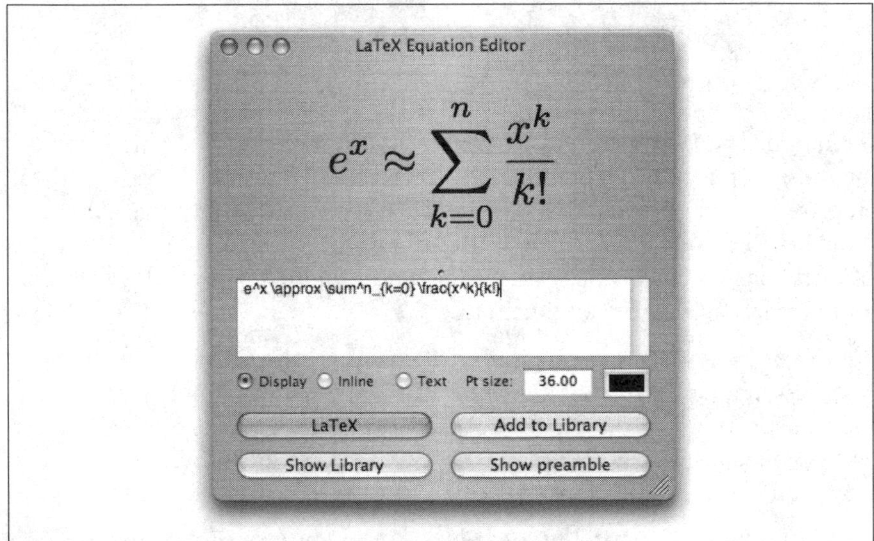

Figure 9-14. Typesetting an equation with LaTeX Equation Editor

R with an Aqua GUI

The open source statistical computing package R is a GNU project to develop a package similar to Bell Laboratories' S statistical package. R runs on a variety of platforms, including most X11-based systems and Windows. Although an X11-based version of R can be installed with Fink, another port of R that supports both X11 and Mac OS X, R.app, has been developed by Stefano M. Iacus and others associated with the R-Core/R-Foundation. A binary distribution of R for Mac OS X, among other systems, is distributed through the Comprehensive R Network (CRAN; *http://cran.r-project.org/*).

The installer places an application named R in your Applications folder. Double-clicking the R icon opens an Aqua-based console window, in which you enter R commands as shown in Figure 9-15.

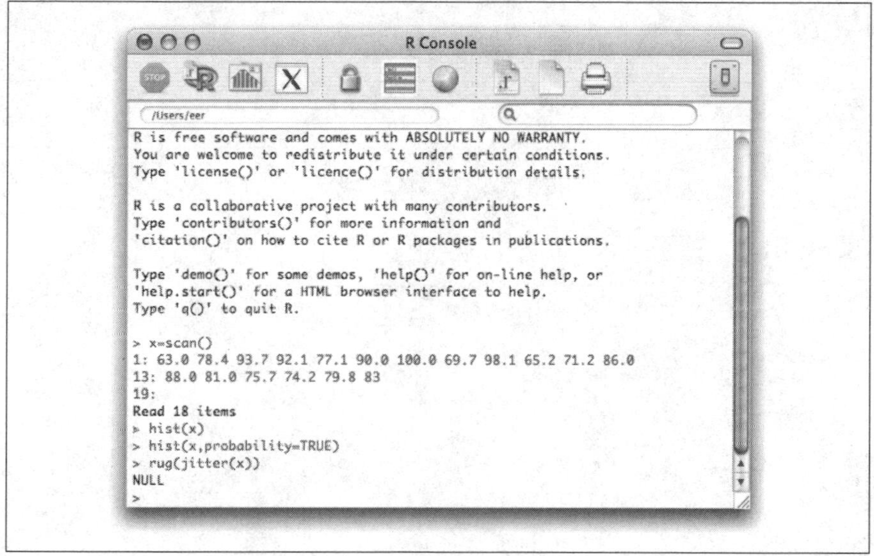

Figure 9-15. The R Console

Figure 9-16 shows an R graphics window containing a histogram.

R is also AppleScriptable. Example 9-1 shows an AppleScript that instructs R to store some values in a variable x, and display a histogram corresponding to these values. You can use X11 graphics with R from the R console or from a Terminal (or xterm) window. To use X11 graphics from the R console, you must first click the X icon in the R Console's toolbar to start the X11 Window server. If, on the other hand, you start R from the Terminal, you'll need to start X11 before displaying graphics in an X11 window. Figure 9-17 shows the same histogram shown in Figure 9-16, but this time it's displayed in an X11 window.

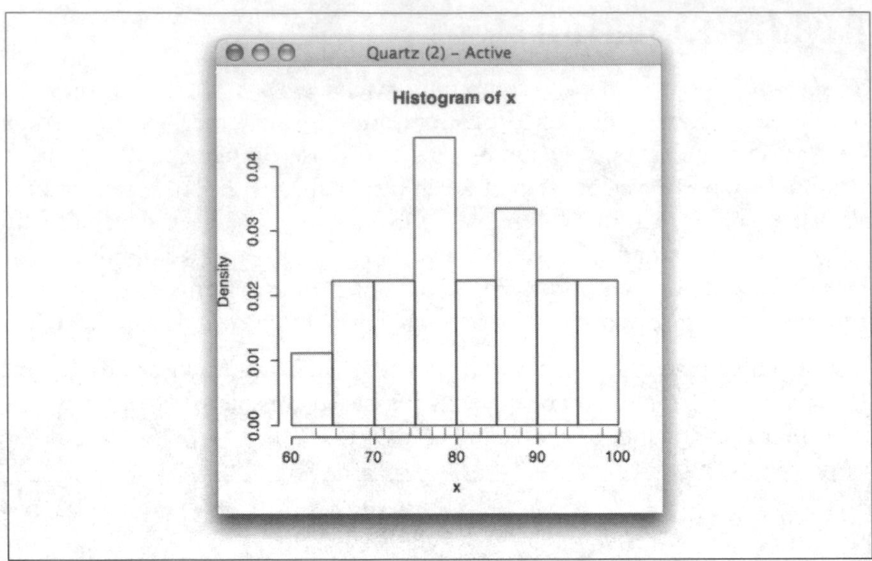

Figure 9-16. R's graphics window

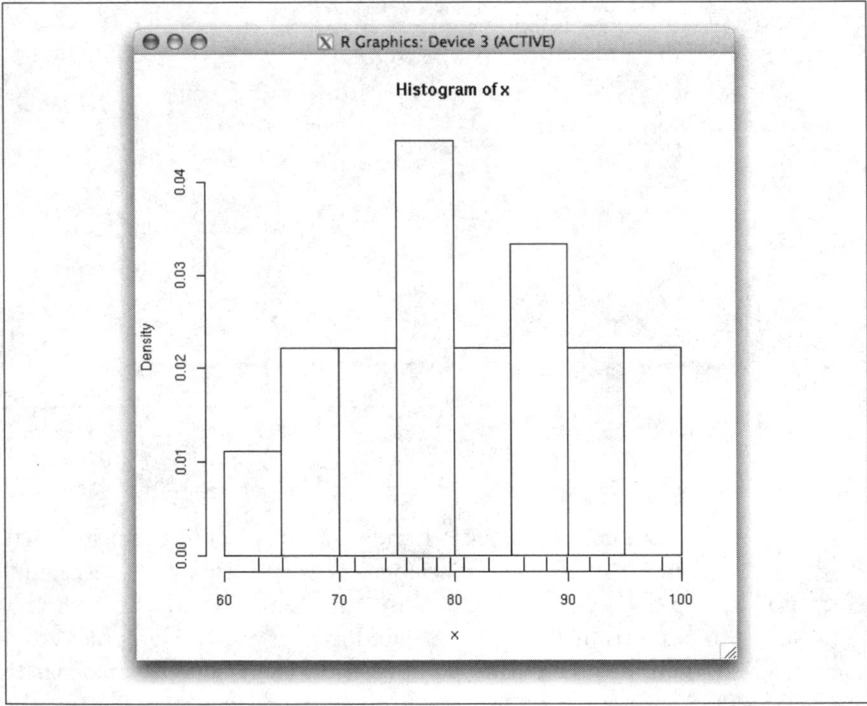

Figure 9-17. R graphics, X11 style

Example 9-1. AppleScript to interact with R

```
try
    tell application "RAqua"
    activate
        with timeout of 1000 seconds
            cmd "x = c(77, 79, 90, 69, 75, 73, 71, 69, 84)"
            cmd "hist(x)"
            cmd "hist(x,probability=TRUE)"
            cmd "rug(jitter(x))"
        end timeout
    end tell
end try
```

We have presented a situation that corresponds to Release R-2.01, which was available at the time of this writing. Be sure to consult the CRAN web site for up-to-date information.

NeoOffice/J and OpenOffice

OpenOffice (*http://www.openoffice.org*) is well-known in the Unix/Linux community as a powerful and free X11-based alternative to the Microsoft Office productivity suite. Open Office includes the word processor Writer, the spreadsheet Calc, the presentation tool Impress, and the drawing tool Draw. OpenOffice also includes a set of database tools and a mathematical equation editor. Aside from providing a powerful set of productivity tools, OpenOffice can import and export to Microsoft Office documents.

At the time of this writing, of port of OpenOffice 1.1.2 is available for a number of platforms, including an X11-based port for Mac OS X. Also at the time of this writing, OpenOffice 2.0 beta ports are available for Linux, Solaris, and Windows, while an X11-based port is planned.

In addition to the OpenOffice.org-supported X11-based Mac OS X port, the NeoOffice group (*http://www.neooffice.org*) provides Carbon- and Java-based Mac OS X versions of OpenOffice, NeoOffice/J. Binaries for both X11 and non-X11-based Mac OS X ports are available from the OpenOffice web site (*http://porting.openoffice.org/mac/ooo-osx_downloads.html*). The X11-based port is a little more mature and functional and looks the same on Mac OS X as it does on other X11-based platforms.

NeoOffice/J, however, has better integration with Mac OS X and runs natively on the Mac as a Java application. Among other things, NeoOffice/J uses Mac OS X fonts, uses native printer drivers, and uses Mac OS X's menu bar, unlike the X11 version. If you have the space on your hard drive, you can install both the X11-basedOpenOffice and NeoOffice/J on the same system, but our experience leans toward using NeoOffice/J. Figure 9-18 shows a Word document that has been imported into NeoOffice/J.

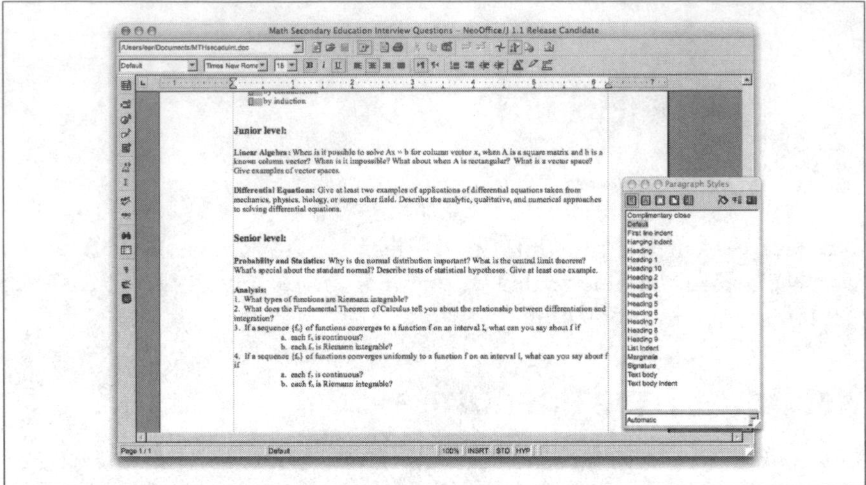

Figure 9-18. An MS Word document opened in NeoOffice/J

CHAPTER 10

Dual-Boot and Beyond

Mac OS X isn't the only operating system you can run on your Mac. Right about now, some of you are probably saying to yourself, "Huh?", but stay with me here. There are many PowerPC-based operating systems that run great on Apple hardware, including Linux, NetBSD, BeOS, and many others. But who says you have to run one operating system at a time? And who says it has to be a PowerPC-based operating system?

There is an array of bewildering choices when it comes to mixing and matching operating systems. Do you need run Linux on your PowerBook so you can write code for a client? Sure, no problem. How about running Linux under Mac OS X? Also, no problem. Do you want to run Mac OS X on an x86 Linux machine? You can even do that, if you are patient. Here are some of the combinations we'll look at in this chapter:

Running on the Bare Metal
: If you want to run an alternative operating system on your Mac, there are many choices available. Linux and NetBSD will run on just about any kind of Mac, all the way back to the 68k-based Macintoshes. BeOS can run on many of the pre-G3 Power Macs, but most of the current BeOS development is on the x86 version, so this might be of curiosity value only. To boot into another operating system on your Mac, you'll need to erase or repartition your drive. We'll talk about this in the "Linux on Mac Hardware" section of this chapter; much of what you read in that section will apply to other operating systems as well.

Running on Mac OS X
: There is a good selection of emulators that run on Mac OS X. With Microsoft's Virtual PC ($99 and up; *http://www.microsoft.com/mac/products/virtualpc/virtualpc.aspx*), you can run x86-based operating systems. Amit Singh's legendary "Many Systems on a PowerBook" article (*http://kernelthread.com/mac/vpc*) documents dozens of operating

systems that run under Virtual PC. In addition to Virtual PC, there are two open source x86 emulators of note: Bochs, a portable (but very slow) x86 emulator and QEMU, a highly tuned x86 emulator that comes close to Virtual PC in speed. We'll discuss Virtual PC and QEMU in the "Emulators on Mac OS X" section.

Running Mac OS X under Another OS
: This is probably the oddest one of the bunch. Although it may sound like some sort of sick fantasy, you can run Mac OS X on PC hardware using PearPC (*http://pearpc.sourceforge.net*). You'll need a fairly fast computer to even approximate the speed of entry-level Macs. Running Mac OS X Tiger on my PC (a 2.4GHz Prescott-core Pentium IV with 512MB of PC3200 RAM and a Radeon 9600 graphics adapter) felt a lot like my first Mac OS X machine (a PowerMac 7500 with a Sonnet G3 add-in card, 128 MB of RAM, Radeon MAC Edition, and XPostFacto, which allowed me to even install Mac OS X on the unsupported hardware). In other words, the system was just barely usable, and constantly pushed the limits of my patience. But with a fast enough PC and some more time for PearPC to mature, it could become a very interesting way to run Mac OS X. Read all about it in the "Emulating the Mac" section of this chapter.

All of these operating systems wouldn't be very useful if they didn't talk to the outside world. Whether you're running an alternative operating system on the bare hardware or under an emulator, getting the network up and running can be tricky in some cases. When it gets tricky, we'll cover this essential configuration step in detail in this chapter.

Why Bother?

All this discussion of how to do it raises the question of why you'd even do it in the first place. After all, if you need to run Linux, you could always buy an inexpensive x86-based system. As it turns out, there are a number of really good reasons to run Linux on your Mac:

Portability
: First and foremost, emulation gives you portability. Wherever you travel with your Mac, why not bring a dozen Linux distributions and flavors of Windows around with you?

Software Testing
: If you're developing an application that has to run on Linux, there are a lot of flavors of Linux. You *could* set up a multiboot x86 box with all the flavors of Linux, but working with virtual machines is much easier and

requires less time spent juggling partition configurations. With emulation, you can run all these systems at once, albeit at something of a performance hit (although Virtual PC and QEMU let you pause background operating systems if you desire).

Further, with Virtual PC and QEMU, you can suspend an operating system and restore it later. This is much like the ACPI (Advanced Configuration and Power Interface) suspend-to-disk feature, but without all the incompatibilities and unpredictable bugs. So, if you have some testing to do, you can get in and out quickly.

Browser Testing

Nothing beats virtual machines for browser testing. You can develop your web application (or site) on your Mac, and in very little time, fire up several emulated operating systems and test your application in a wide array of browsers ranging from Safari and Camino on Mac OS X, to Internet Explorer and Firefox on Windows or Firefox, Epiphany, and KDE's Konqueror on Linux.

Konqueror's rendering engine, KHTML, is an open source code-base that Apple leveraged when building Safari. When Apple announced Safari at Macworld San Francisco in 2004, they stunned a lot of people by coming out with their own web browser. But even more so, Apple shocked the Open Source community by promptly submitting their changes back to the KDE team. To learn more about Konqueror, visit its development web site at *http://www.konqueror.org*.

Freeze and Thaw

When you set up an operating system with an emulator, the system's hard disk is just a file on your Mac's filesystem. If you keep this under 4 GB or so, you can burn a snapshot of the operating system to a DVD for a very quick restore. This is ideal in testing scenarios where you frequently need to test your software on a clean install or standardized software configuration.

Fun

Got an old MS-DOS game you want to play on your Mac? Nothing beats an emulator for running these old games (see Figure 10-1), except maybe an old Tandy home computer. Furthermore, there's plenty to be said for running an old operating system just for the fun of it.

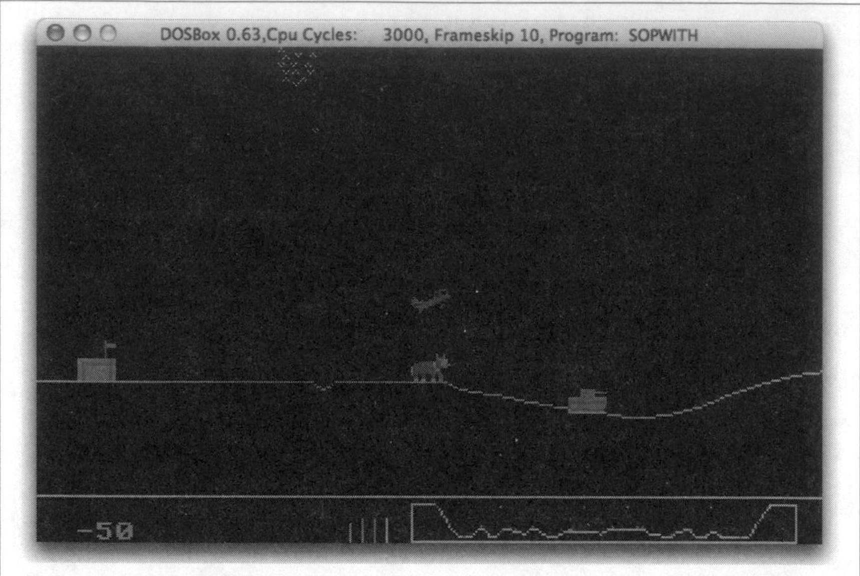

Figure 10-1. A little Sopwith, anyone?

Your best bet for MS-DOS emulation is DOSBox (*http://dosbox.sourceforge.net/*), which has one feature that sets it apart from other emulators: it lets you mount parts of the host file system as DOS drives. So, you can download that old MS-DOS game, unzip it into *~/Games*, and mount *~/Games* as your *D:* drive in DOS box. Figure 10-1 shows a real classic running under DOSBox.

Linux on Mac Hardware

Linux will run on Apple hardware based on the Motorola 68020 (and higher) as well as PowerPC-based Macs. However, this section talks only about what you need to do to get it running on a Mac OS X-capable Mac.

You can learn how to get Linux running on that old Centris you're using as a doorstop at the Linux/mac68k Project (*http://www.linux-m68k.org*), or the Debian on Motorola 680x0 pages (*http://www.debian.org/ports/m68k*).

There are several distributions of Linux you can choose for your PowerPC Macintosh. Speaking of an old Centris, if you want to see something really wild, how about a 25 MHz Centris running Linux running PearPC running Mac OS X Panther? See all the gory details at *http://www.appletalk.com.au/articles/68kpanther*.

Picking a Linux Distribution

Of course, if you're going to run Linux on your Mac, you'll need to know which brand will work with your hardware, and there are a few to choose from. This list should give you an idea of what's available for your Linux hacking needs:

Yellow Dog Linux
: Based on Red Hat's Fedora Core, Yellow Dog Linux (*http://www.yellowdoglinux.com*) is one of the most popular Mac-based Linux distributions, and it runs on Macintoshes based on the G3 (with built-in USB), G4, and G5. If your Mac can run Mac OS X, then it will probably run YDL.

Gentoo Linux
: Gentoo Linux (*http://www.gentoo.org*) is a hacker's dream. Although you can install it using pre-built binaries, the preferred method is to bootstrap a minimal system and compile the bulk of it by source. Gentoo is one of the few Linux distributions where you need to run *chroot* as a standard part of the installation process. Install it sometime, and you may learn a lot about Linux. Gentoo will run on the PowerPC chipset, as well as pre-G3, G3, G4, and G5 Macs.

Debian GNU/Linux
: Debian (*http://www.debian.org/ports/powerpc*) runs on a lot of different hardware, including PowerPC (including pre-G3 all the way up to G5s) Macs. Debian is known for its wide selection of packages, hacker-friendly configuration, and bleeding-edge releases that are hard to resist even when you know better.

Ubuntu
: If you like Debian, there's a very good chance you'll adore Ubuntu (*http://www.ubuntulinux.org*), a Debian-based Linux distro that is an excellent desktop Linux—but it's not dumbed-down. Ubuntu detects and configures your oddball hardware and launches X11 with a very pretty face, but still lets you take control. You can find Ubuntu Linux for Power PC Macs (pre-G3 through G4s).

Compatibility Details

Although Linux for PowerPC is generally compatible with Macintosh hardware, there are a few areas that you need to watch out for: hardware on newer Macs, AirPort Extreme, Bluetooth, and power management.

The newest-generation Macs are likely to be untested with the most current release of Linux for the PowerPC, and also may have glitches that won't be fixed until a new version of the Linux kernel is released. For example, at the time of this writing, the Yellow Dog Linux hardware compatibility pages (*http://www.yellowdoglinux.com/support/hardware/breakdown/index.php*) indicates that the 17-inch PowerBook does not support sleep, external video, and the built-in modem, audio is iffy, and Bluetooth is untested (and therefore not supported). However, the older Titanium PowerBooks get better scores with iffy audio and no external video.

It's quite likely that AirPort Extreme won't work either, since the chipset maker (Broadcom) has not released the information necessary for Linux developers to support their product. So, if you want to run PowerPC Linux on a Macintosh with AirPort Extreme, you'll need to use either a supported PC card or a USB Wi-Fi adapter.

Partitioning for Linux

If you have the benefit of planning ahead, partitioning for Linux is a piece of cake. That is, if you are installing Mac OS X from scratch, you may as well partition your drive and leave some space for Linux. If you aren't installing Mac OS X from scratch, you *really* should consider reinstalling. If you don't want to reinstall, use Carbon Copy Cloner (*www.bombich.com/software/ccc.html*) to clone your Mac OS X install to an external drive, then reformat your internal drive to accommodate Linux, and finally clone Mac OS X back to your internal drive.

When you (re-) partition your hard drive, take the following steps:

1. Create one extra partition of at least 4 GB (enough room to run Linux comfortably).
2. Set its format to Free Space as shown in Figure 10-2.
3. Use the rest of the space for any Macintosh partitions you need.

When you install Linux, tell it to use that free space. The distribution you're installing creates the Linux and swap partitions in that space. Some Linux distributions may offer to use the entire disk by default, so you'll need to override this. For example, in Ubuntu 4.10 (Warty), select "Manually Edit Partition Table," scroll down to the partition marked FREE SPACE, press Enter, and then select "Automatically partition the free space" from the menu that appears.

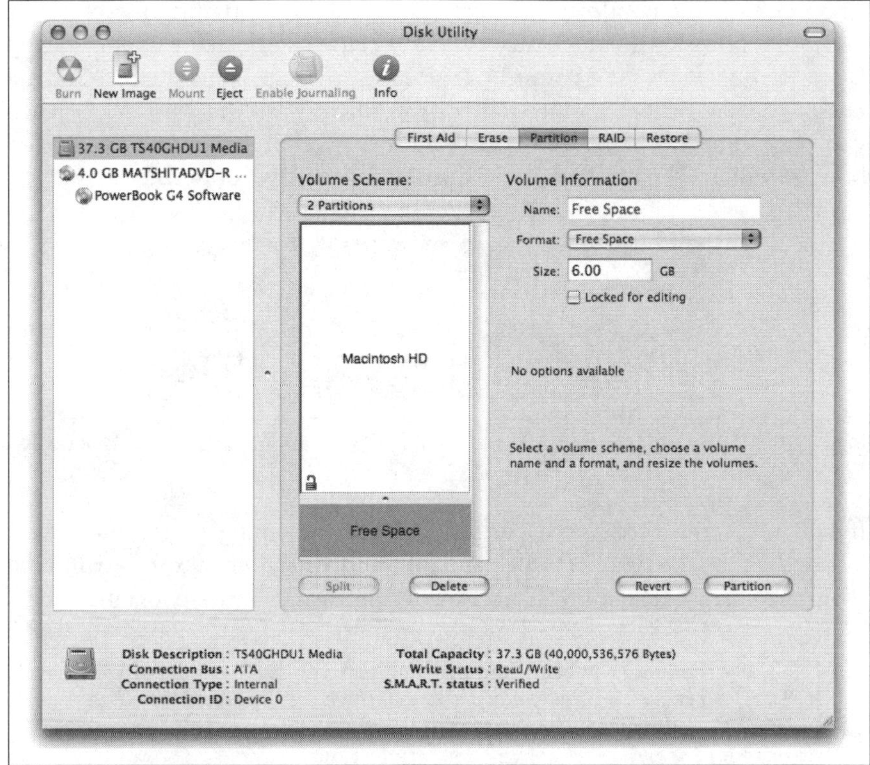

Figure 10-2. Partitioning your hard drive for Linux

If you don't want to repartition, you could install Linux on a separate drive. Given that storage is cheap (as little as 50 cents a GB if you find the right deal), it shouldn't be hard for you to put a second drive in your Mac. If you're running Linux on a PowerBook, some intrepid souls have managed to boot Linux on an external drive, but it is notoriously difficult. For some details, see the discussion thread at *http://www.ubuntuforums.org/showthread.php?t=3952*. As of this writing, Terra Soft Solutions, the developers of Yellow Dog Linux, have just announced support for external FireWire drives, and have begun selling FireWire drives preloaded with Yellow Dog Linux. For more information, see *http://www.terrasoftsolutions.com*.

Booting into Linux

Linux installs a *bootloader*, such as Yaboot (*http://penguinppc.org/bootloaders/yaboot/*), which the distribution uses to boot the Linux distribution, much in the same way Mac OS X boots with help from BootX (see

Chapter 3). If the bootloader is installed on the Linux partition, you'll only see the bootloader if your Linux partition remains selected as your Startup Disk. If you switch the Startup Disk settings (System Preferences → Startup Disk), you can easily boot into Linux by holding down the Option key when you boot your Mac. Choose the disk with the Linux penguin (Tux) logo to boot into Linux. Figure 10-3 shows three bootable disk options.

Figure 10-3. From left to right: partitions for Mac OS X Panther, Linux, and Mac OS X Tiger

If you place the Free Space partition at the beginning of the hard disk, Yaboot will be the first bootable partition, and your Mac hardware will boot that partition by default if you reset Open Firmware to factory defaults.

For more information, see the Yaboot HOWTO at *http://penguinppc.org/bootloaders/yaboot/doc/yaboot-howto.shtml/*.

Mac-on-Linux

Mac-on-Linux (*http://www.maconlinux.org*) is a hardware "virtualizer" that provides a virtual machine environment that is Mac-compatible enough for you to run Linux, Mac OS (7.5.2 through 9.2.2), and Mac OS X (10.1 through 10.3.3 as of this writing). Mac-on-Linux emulates the bits that it needs to, but when the operating system running in the virtual machine accesses the hardware of the virtual environment, Mac-on-Linux virtualizes the call and passes it right on down to the real hardware.

Emulators on Mac OS X

Emulation has been a hot area of the past few years. It's emerged as a way to defeat obsolescence by letting you run software for obsolete computers. Have a favorite Atari 800 game but your old Atari won't boot? You can download the emulator, point it at the disk image containing that old game, and start playing. Repeat as necessary for Apple II, Commodore 64, Atari VCS, and more.

Copyrights and Vintage Games

If your favorite old game isn't shareware or in the public domain, there are some legal issues involved with obtaining copies of your old game, but at the time of this writing, there weren't any effective barriers that would keep you from finding and running them.

There are a several sites with information about vintage game and computer emulators for the Mac, including:

- *http://www.zophar.net/mac/mac.phtml*
- *http://www.macemu.com*
- *http://www.emaculation.com*
- *http://www.emulation.net*
- *http://www.bannister.org/software/emu.htm*

Given the speeds of today's Macs, it's not surprising that you can easily emulate a 1 MHz computer from the old days. But what's fantastic is how you can emulate near-current PC hardware on your Mac. Microsoft's Virtual PC is capable of running even the resource-hungry Windows XP quite comfortably on current Macintoshes, and the open source QEMU comes close, although it's not quite as fast as Virtual PC. Both are capable of running Linux comfortably.

Virtual PC

Microsoft's Virtual PC, formerly Connectix Virtual PC, has been letting Mac users run Windows and DOS on their Macs for years. You can also run dozens of other operating systems—some are easier to install than others—including Linux, Darwin, and Net/Free/OpenBSD.

Virtual PC 7 is available without an operating system (it's basically a bare-metal virtual machine) for approximately $129. If you're planning to run Windows on it, you could splurge on one of the editions of Virtual PC that is bundled with a Windows operating system (Windows 2000, Windows XP Home, or Windows XP Professional).

Once you've got Virtual PC up and running, you can install an operating system. You can install from an ISO image, CD-ROM, or DVD. For example, here's how to install Ubuntu Linux from an ISO image:

1. Select File → New. You'll be prompted to select a setup method.
2. Select Install Your Own Operating System, and then click Begin.

3. You're prompted to choose an operating system and hard disk format (see Figure 10-4). One of the choices you'll notice that is missing is the size of the drive. Virtual PC defaults to a 15 GB drive, but it doesn't use up all the space at once. Instead, it grows as you add files to the drive. Select Linux for the operating system and Unformatted for the hard disk format and click Continue.
4. Now you need to choose a filename for the virtual machine, as well as a location, as shown in Figure 10-5.

The file that gets created is actually a bundle, so if you locate it in the Finder, right-click on it and select Show Package Contents from the contextual menu and you'll see all sorts of files, including configuration data, the hard disk image, and any saved states.

5. Next, Virtual PC prompts you to start the PC. Click Start PC to begin. When the Virtual PC starts up, the first thing you'll see is an annoying help document and an error message in the virtual machine (see Figure 10-6).
6. You now need to "capture" the CD-ROM and reboot the virtual machine. Select Drives → Capture CD Image and choose the CD-ROM ISO image. If you want to capture a CD-ROM that's sitting in your optical drive, you can select Drives → Capture Disc.

After you've captured the drive, select PC → Reset to reboot the PC. You'll be launched into the installer. In theory, everything should go smoothly, and probably will for most operating systems. However, here are some troubleshooting hints:

Linux doesn't find the network adapter

If Linux doesn't detect your network hardware, you can try to force its hand. Virtual PC emulates a DECChip Ethernet adapter that Linux is happy to support with the de2104x driver. For example, here's how you can get Ubuntu to recognize the network hardware and proceed as though nothing's gone wrong. First, wait for the Ubuntu installer to complain about its failure to detect the network interface, then:

1. Switch to virtual console (Option-F2).
2. Press Enter to activate the console and get a root prompt.
3. Run the command `modprobe de2104x`.

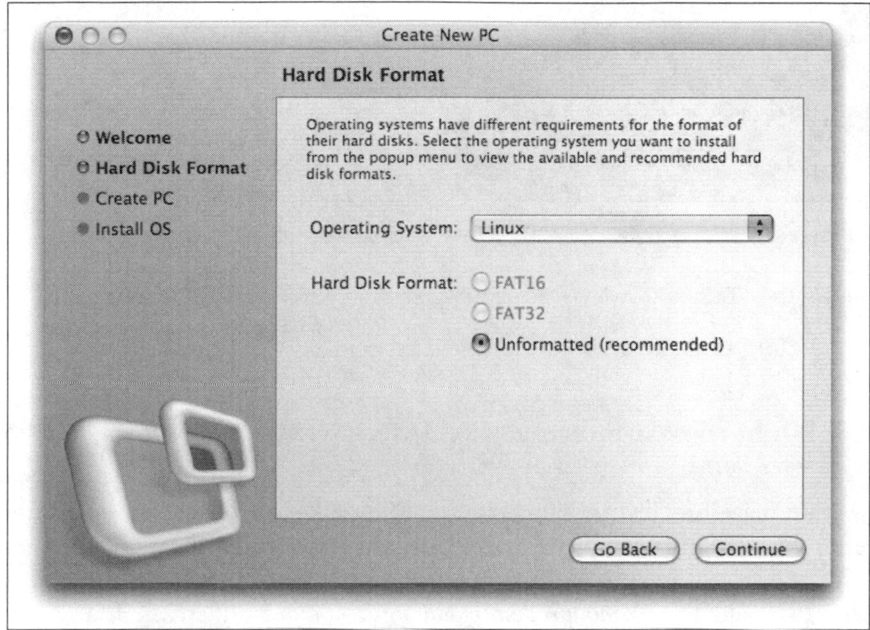

Figure 10-4. Create your virtual hard drive

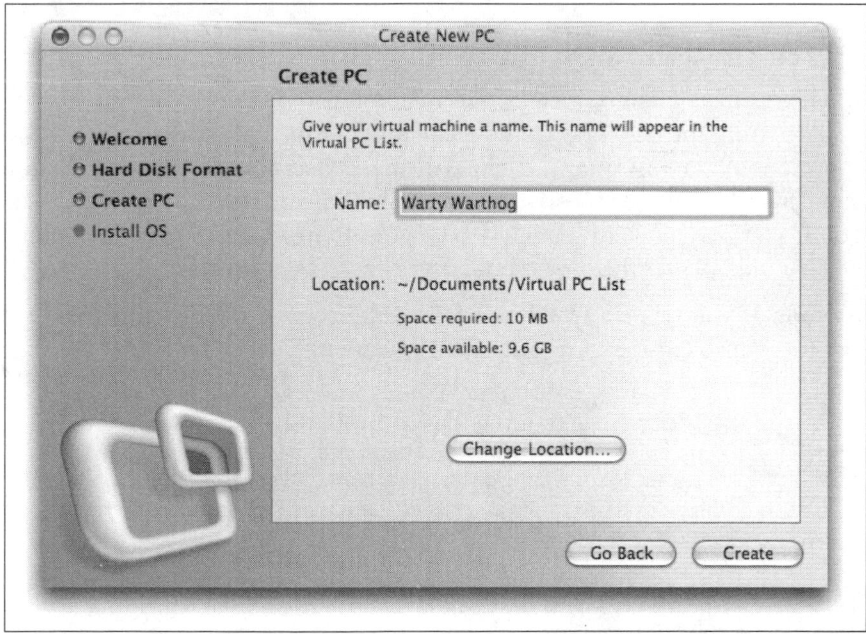

Figure 10-5. Choose a location and name for your virtual machine

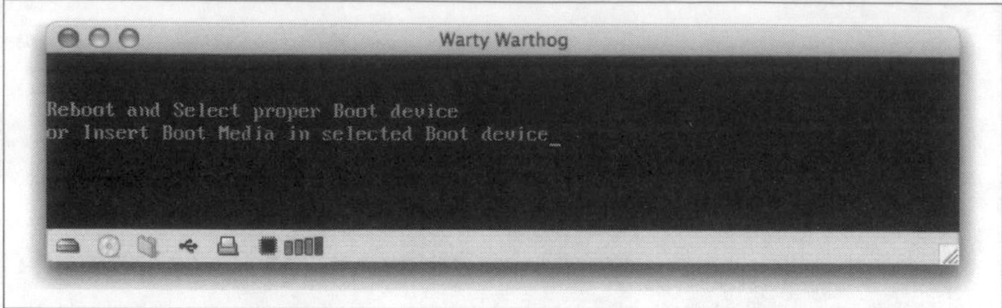

Figure 10-6. This DOS-style error message reminds you to insert a CD-ROM

4. Return to the first virtual console (Option-F1).
5. Select Go Back.
6. When you get to the menu, select Detect Network Hardware, and setup will resume.

With other Linux distributions, such as Mandrake, you can safely wait until after installation is complete to configure the network hardware. For example, under Mandrake 10.0 Community Edition, you can add `de2104x` (on a line by itself) to */etc/modprobe.preload* (*/etc/modules* under 2.4 and earlier kernels) and reboot the virtual machine. You may also find that the *tulip* driver works just fine.

Linux can't configure TCP/IP

After you install Linux, one of the first things you'll need to do is fetch updates from the network. Under Debian, Ubuntu, and other *apt*-based distributions, your operating system will make decisions during installation about which package repositories to use. If the network isn't working at this point, you may have to manually configure things later. So, the first thing you should do after that first reboot is to check the network.

As soon as you reboot, switch to an alternate console (Option-F2 if you are at a text console, Control-Option-F2 if you are in X11) and log in.

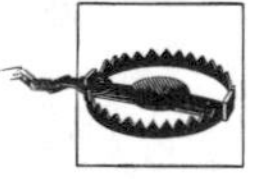

> Wait a minute—if your Linux distribution hasn't let you set up a new user or set the *root* password, you won't be able to log in. If so, wait until the installer lets you create the *root* user or a user who can use *sudo*, and then switch to the alternate console and log in.

Try to FTP or SSH to a known good host (don't use *ping*, since ICMP may be discarded by some NAT routers, and Virtual PC's default configuration puts an additional NAT layer between the virtual machine and the network). If you can't reach any hosts, you can manually configure networking in the virtual machine. You'll need to set the network as shown in Table 10-1.

Table 10-1. Network Settings for Virtual PC

Setting	Value
IP Address	192.168.131.175
Gateway/Router	192.168.131.254
DNS Servers	192.168.254.254, 192.168.254.252

For example, under Debian, you can edit */etc/network/interfaces* and change:

```
iface eth0 inet dhcp
```

to:

```
iface eth0 inet static
        address 192.168.131.175
        netmask 255.255.255.0
        gateway 192.168.131.254
```

and then set */etc/resolv.conf* to read:

```
nameserver 192.168.131.254
nameserver 192.168.131.252
```

Now restart networking with */etc/init.d/networking restart*. Make sure you can reach something with FTP or SSH, and return to the post-install setup with Option-F1 (for the main text console) or Option-F7 (for X11-based setups).

With many other Linux distributions, you can wait until installation is complete to configure the network. For example, under Mandrake 10.0 Community Edition, replace the contents of */etc/sysconfig/network-scripts/ifcfg-eth0* with:

```
DEVICE=eth0
IPADDR=192.168.131.175
NETMASK=255.255.255.0
GATEWAY=192.168.131.254
ONBOOT=yes
```

And configure */etc/resolv.conf* as shown for Debian earlier in this section. Then restart networking with */etc/init.d/network restart*.

Even after these changes, you may still see a [FAILED] status next to "Bringing up interface eth0." However, the network may still be working, so test it before you give up.

For more information, see Microsoft's knowledge base entry on troubleshooting Virtual PC's network at *http://support.microsoft.com/kb/825372*.

Launching X11 displays garbage on the screen

Virtual PC's emulated S3 Trio64 graphics adapter doesn't play well with X11 in 24/32-bit color. Reconfigure X11 to use 16-bit or lower color. In a Debian-based system, you can use the command *dpkg-reconfigure xserver-xfree86*. You can also edit */etc/X11/XF86Config-4* on most Linux distributions and set the color depth to 16 (look for `Depth` and `DefaultDepth` settings in that file). Figure 10-7 shows how to configure this during the installation of Mandrake 10.

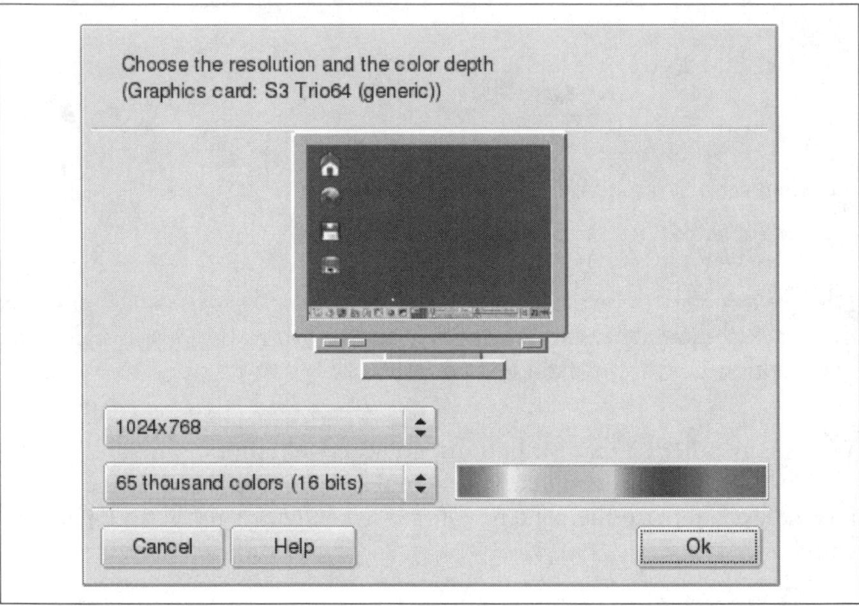

Figure 10-7. Setting color depth in Mandrake 10

QEMU

QEMU (*http://fabrice.bellard.free.fr/qemu*) is a state-of-the-art open source emulator. Like Bochs (*http://bochs.sourceforge.net*), QEMU can emulate an x86 CPU. However, QEMU is significantly faster than Bochs, and can also emulate a number of other CPUs, including SPARC and PowerPC. Most important, QEMU is fast enough for day-to-day use, although for top performance, you'll find that Virtual PC wins (see the sidebar "Virtual PC Versus QEMU," later in this chapter).

To get started with QEMU, you can either grab a binary package from *http://www.freeoszoo.org/download.php*, or download the source from QEMU's web page (noted earlier) and compile it yourself. If you're chasing the latest release, you may need to compile it yourself. You'll also need to compile a Mac OS X native build of SDL; see *http://www.libsdl.org/index.php*.

Once you've got QEMU installed, you should have at least *qemu-img* and *qemu* in someplace such as */usr/local/bin* or */opt/local/bin*. You may also have *qemu-system-ppc* and *qemu-system-sparc* (the Power PC and SPARC system emulators). Now you're ready to either run one of the pre-packaged virtual machines from *http://www.freeoszoo.org/download.php*, or install one by hand.

Installing an operating system

To create a virtual machine with QEMU:

1. Create a new blank disk image with *qemu-img*. For example, to create a 4 GB image named *ubuntu.img*:

   ```
   $ qemu-img create ubuntu.img 4G
   ```

2. It's best if you have your installation media available as ISO images. Don't even bother to burn them to CD. Instead, keep them handy on some kind of secondary storage, such as a FireWire drive or heck, even burn a few of them to a DVD-R.
3. Make sure you have time. If you are installing the operating system from scratch, it could take hours, unless you have the fastest, latest, and greatest. So, open up System Preferences → Energy Saver and tell your Mac not to sleep. This might be a good time to consider going to FreeOSZoo for a pre-built image.

If you have a fast x86 Linux machine, you should perform the initial setup there, since x86 emulation on an x86 machine is faster than on PowerPC. You can move QEMU disk images between the Linux, Windows, and Mac OS X versions of QEMU without hassle. The disk images get big, so we suggest you use Fast Ethernet, Gigabit Ethernet, or FireWire to transfer the images between machines. As fast as AirPort Extreme is, it still takes a painfully long time to transfer a 4 GB or larger disk image.

4. Once you've got everything set up, you'll have an ISO image and a blank QEMU disk image sitting around:

   ```
   $ ls -1
   total 9459264
   -rw-r--r--  1 bjepson  unknown  4294967296  2 Feb 22:05 ubuntu.img
   ```

```
-rwxr-xr-x  1 bjepson  unknown   548175872  2 Feb 22:01 warty-install-
i386.iso
```

5. Launch *qemu* with the ISO image as your CD-ROM drive (*boot -d* tells QEMU to boot from the second IDE device, which happens to be the CD-ROM). Use the disk image as the first hard drive. Use the *-monitor* option to give you a console from which you can control QEMU, and use *-localtime* to use the local system time:

   ```
   $ qemu -m128 -cdrom warty-install-i386.iso -hda ubuntu.img -boot d \
       -monitor stdio -localtime
   ```

In a matter of seconds, you'll see the installation splash screen as shown in Figure 10-8.

Once you're done installing the virtual machine, you'll need to make a change to the command line when you want to reboot it; change the *-boot d* option to *-boot c* to boot from the first virtual hard drive instead of the CD-ROM image.

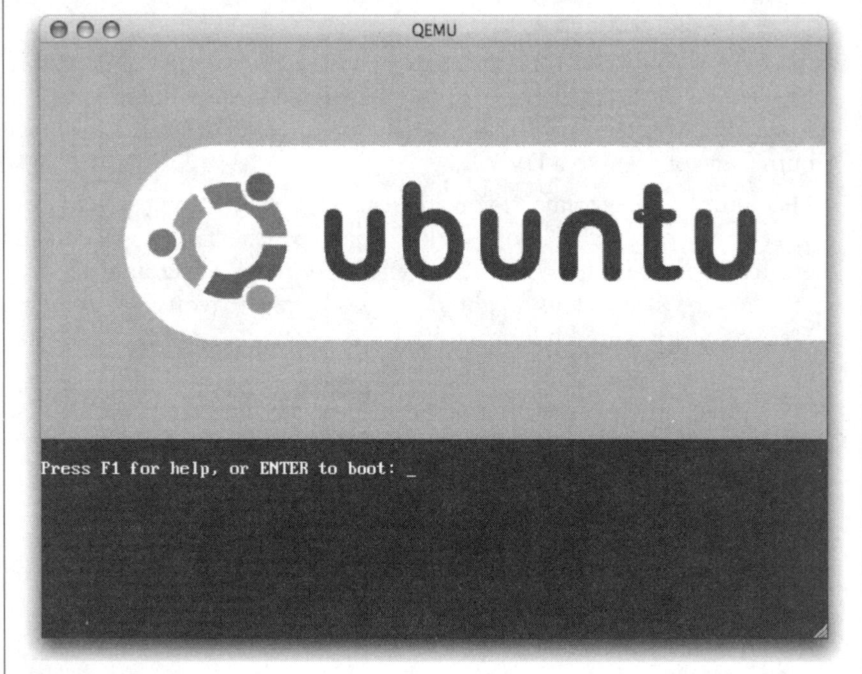

Figure 10-8. Ubuntu is ready to install

If you switch back to the Terminal window from which you launched QEMU, you'll see the console up and running. Type *help* and press Return to see a list of the commands that are available:

```
QEMU 0.6.1 monitor - type 'help' for more information
(qemu) help
help|? [cmd] -- show the help
commit  -- commit changes to the disk images (if -snapshot is used)
info subcommand -- show various information about the system state
q|quit  -- quit the emulator
eject [-f] device -- eject a removable media (use -f to force it)
change device filename -- change a removable media
screendump filename -- save screen into PPM image 'filename'
log item1[,...] -- activate logging of the specified items to '/tmp/qemu.
log'
savevm filename -- save the whole virtual machine state to 'filename'
loadvm filename -- restore the whole virtual machine state from 'filename'
stop  -- stop emulation
c|cont  -- resume emulation
gdbserver [port] -- start gdbserver session (default port=1234)
x /fmt addr -- virtual memory dump starting at 'addr'
xp /fmt addr -- physical memory dump starting at 'addr'
p|print /fmt expr -- print expression value (use $reg for CPU register
access)
i /fmt addr -- I/O port read
sendkey keys -- send keys to the VM (e.g. 'sendkey ctrl-alt-f1')
system_reset  -- reset the system
(qemu)
```

You'll need to use this console to switch CD-ROMs during installation. Use *eject* to eject the ISO, and *change* to insert a new one:

```
(qemu) eject cdrom
(qemu) change cdrom warty-install-i386.iso
```

You can now install your operating system as you would on an actual PC (follow the prompts, partition your virtual disk, select packages, and then go drink a long slow cup of coffee).

Suspending and resuming

The user interface may not be as fancy as Virtual PC's, but you can suspend (pause and save state to disk) and resume your virtual machines under QEMU. However, if you mix any of this up, such as forgetting to stop before you issue the *savevm* command, you could get the contents of the saved memory and your hard disk image out of sync.

To save state, stop the virtual machine, save the memory, and quit:

```
(qemu) stop
(qemu) savevm savedstate.sav
(qemu) quit
```

To resume where you left off, start QEMU as you normally would, but use the *-loadvm* option to specify the saved state:

```
$ qemu -m128 -cdrom warty-install-i386.iso -hda ubuntu.img -boot c \
    -monitor stdio -localtime -loadvm savedstate.sav
```

Networking

QEMU sets up a NAT network for your virtual machine, so if the operating system cooperates, you won't need to do anything special to get networking working correctly. QEMU emulates a PCI NE2000 adapter, so you should be able to use a generic NE2000 driver for that card.

If you try to use *ping* to test the network, it probably won't work due to the NAT implementation. Use *ftp*, *ssh*, or a web browser to test the network.

Virtual PC Versus QEMU

At the time of this writing, Virtual PC 7 is significantly faster than QEMU. But Virtual PC 7 is pretty fast to begin with—QEMU is fast enough for light usage, but we wouldn't recommend it for day-to-day tasks such as running office applications, surfing the web, email, or instant messenger. Use your Mac for that.

We tested Virtual PC and QEMU with Ubuntu Warty. We used the *w3c-libwww-5.4.0* source code from *http://www.w3.org/Library* for testing. We ran *make* three times on each emulator, and took the average. We ran this under the lightweight `icewm` Window manager rather than the text console, so as to stress the GUI a bit while we ran the tests.

The Mac OS X tests were performed on a 1.25 GHz G4 PowerBook with 1 GB of RAM and 128 MB allocated to the virtual machine. The virtual disk image was located on an external FireWire drive.

The Linux tests were performed on a 2.4 GHz Pentium IV system with 512 MB of RAM running Xandros 2.5 and 128 MB allocated to the virtual machine. The virtual disk image was located on an internal SATA drive.

Emulator	Host operating system	Time
QEMU	Mac OS X	1 hour, 41 minutes
QEMU	Linux	38 minutes
Virtual PC	Mac OS X	1 hour, 11 minutes

Emulating the Mac

So far, this chapter has covered getting other operating systems to run on your Mac, but you can also go in the other direction, running Mac OS X on other operating systems.

PearPC

PearPC (*http://pearpc.sourceforge.net*) emulates a Macintosh surprisingly well, and runs on Linux and Windows. At the time of this writing, PearPC isn't quite ready for daily use, but it certainly makes a great conversation piece at parties, assuming that you throw or attend the kind of parties where geeks gather around computers.

PearPC is quite complicated to set up. You'll need to tweak a configuration file a few times during installation, use Darwin for PowerPC to partition the virtual hard drive, and perform some manual steps to get networking going.

First, download PearPC from *http://pearpc.sourceforge.net*, install it, then follow the instructions in the rest of this section.

To create and partition your virtual drive image:

1. Use the *dd* command to create a blank image. The seek option lets you specify a size without actually writing the data. Be sure to use a block size of 516,096, as this is what PearPC expects. You can specify a size in gigabytes as a multiple of 2080:

```
$ dd if=/dev/zero of=macosxpanther.img bs=516096 \
seek=`expr 2080 \* 4` count=0
```

2. Make sure you have a Darwin ISO handy (we used *darwin-701.iso*, which you can get from *http://devworld.apple.com/darwin*).
3. Create a configuration file for booting Darwin, with the filename *ppccfg.darwin_bootstrap* and these contents:

```
prom_env_machargs="-v"

# Hard disk
pci_ide0_master_installed=1
pci_ide0_master_image="macosxpanther.img"
pci_ide0_master_type="hd"

# boot cd
pci_ide0_slave_installed=1
pci_ide0_slave_image="darwin-701.iso"
pci_ide0_slave_type="cdrom"
```

4. Boot PearPC with the following command, and then select the CD as the boot device when prompted:

   ```
   ppc ppccfg.darwin_bootstrap
   ```

5. When Darwin's installer boots, *don't* choose to install Darwin. Instead, type *shell* and press Return to drop into a shell.
6. Run *pdisk* and select */dev/disk0* as the disk to operate on.
7. Create a new Apple_HFS partition with a starting block of 64 and a length in blocks equal to the size of the Apple_Free partition as shown in Figure 10-9. (Use `w` to write your changes and `q` to exit pdisk.)
8. Type *halt* to shut down Darwin.

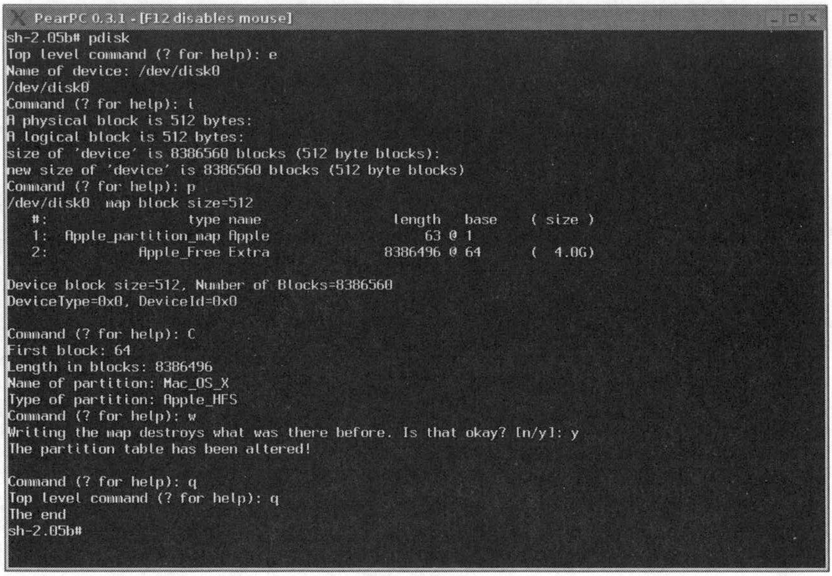

```
PearPC 0.3.1 - [F12 disables mouse]
sh-2.05b# pdisk
Top level command (? for help): e
Name of device: /dev/disk0
/dev/disk0
Command (? for help): i
A physical block is 512 bytes:
A logical block is 512 bytes:
size of 'device' is 8386560 blocks (512 byte blocks):
new size of 'device' is 8386560 blocks (512 byte blocks)
Command (? for help): p
/dev/disk0  map block size=512
   #:                type name                length   base    ( size )
   1: Apple_partition_map Apple                  63 @ 1
   2:          Apple_Free Extra             8386496 @ 64      (  4.0G)

Device block size=512, Number of Blocks=8386560
DeviceType=0x0, DeviceId=0x0

Command (? for help): C
First block: 64
Length in blocks: 8386496
Name of partition: Mac_OS_X
Type of partition: Apple_HFS
Command (? for help): w
Writing the map destroys what was there before. Is that okay? [n/y]: y
The partition table has been altered!

Command (? for help): q
Top level command (? for help): q
The end
sh-2.05b#
```

Figure 10-9. Partitioning your virtual disk

To install Mac OS X:

1. Copy the *video.x* graphics driver into the directory that holds your virtual drive:

   ```
   $ cp ../src/pearpc-0.3.1/video.x .
   ```

2. Create a configuration file, *ppccfg*, with the following contents:

   ```
   prom_env_machargs="-v"
   prom_driver_graphic="video.x"

   # Hard disk
   pci_ide0_master_installed=1
   ```

```
pci_ide0_master_image="macosxpanther.img"
pci_ide0_master_type="hd"

# boot cd
pci_ide0_slave_installed=1
pci_ide0_slave_image="/dev/cdrom"
pci_ide0_slave_type="cdrom"
```

3. Insert your Mac OS X installation CD in your CDROM drive, and run the command *ppc ppccfg*.
4. You'll be prompted to select a partition to boot. At this point, there's only one choice, as shown in Figure 10-10. Select it and the Mac OS X installer will launch.
5. Continue through the dialogs as you would on a real Mac. When you reach the Select a Destination screen, you probably won't see any available volumes. Select Open Disk Utility from the Installer menu, and erase the virtual drive as shown in Figure 10-11.
6. Choose the hard disk you just formatted as your destination, and click Continue to proceed to the Easy Install.
7. To avoid disk swapping, click Customize and trim the installation choices down to the bare minimum as shown in Figure 10-12. Click Install to begin.
8. After it's done, Mac OS X will try to reboot, but may instead just shutdown (or perhaps panic, repeating the error message "Event processing timed out. Event dropped."). You can kill PearPC if necessary.
9. Put your second CD-ROM in the drive, and restart PearPC (with the command *ppc ppccfg* again). Select your hard drive when prompted to select a partition to boot (option 2 in Figure 10-13)
10. After Mac OS X boots up, the Installer may install some more software at this point before launching the Setup Assistant.
11. Answer the questions the Setup Assistant asks you. You should skip the Internet connection setup for now. We'll explain how to get that up and running in the next section.

Mac OS X should now be running, as shown in Figure 10-14.

To configure your PearPC virtual machine to support networking:

1. Shut down the virtual machine.
2. Make sure your Linux kernel has support for the *tun* and *bridge* modules. If you get an error running the following two commands, you may need to rebuild your kernel:

```
# modprobe tun
# modprobe bridge
```

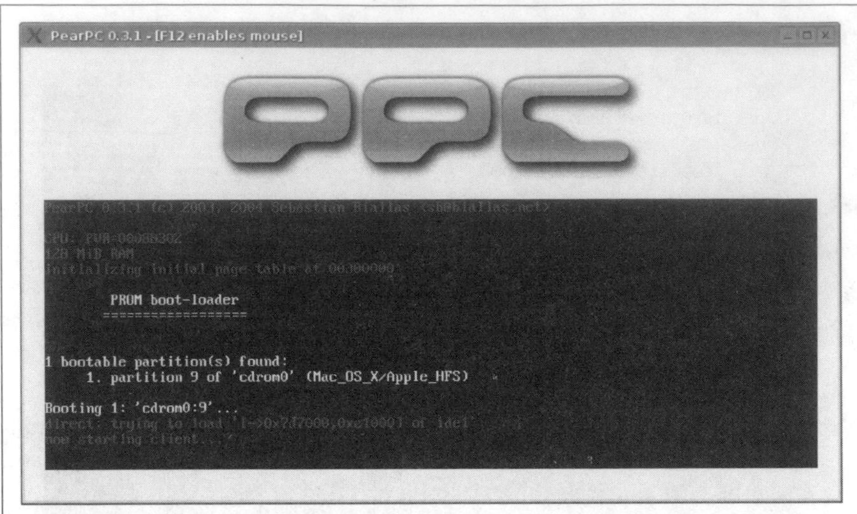

Figure 10-10. Select the installation CD to get things started

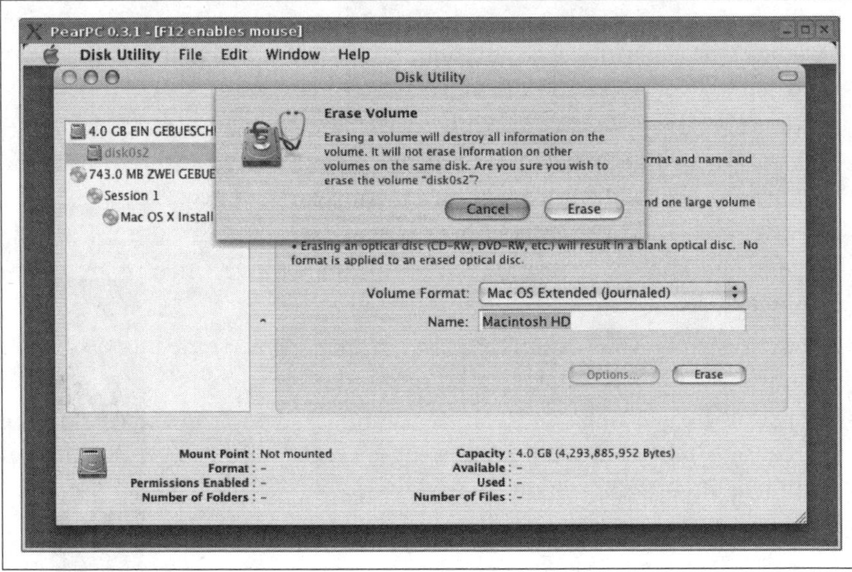

Figure 10-11. Erasing the virtual hard drive

3. Make sure that the user under which you plan to run PearPC has access to the *tun* device:

```
# chown :bjepson /dev/net/tun
# chmod g+rw /dev/net/tun
```

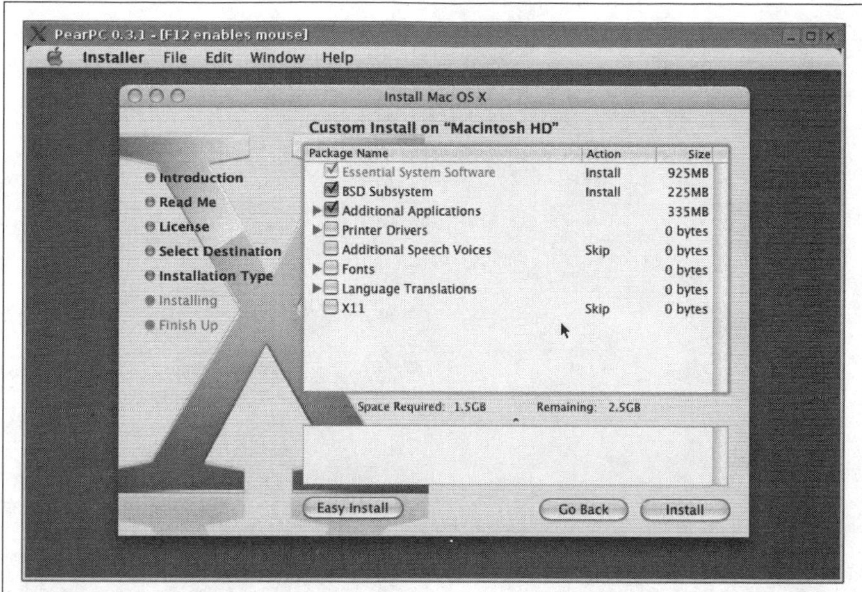

Figure 10-12. Install a minimal system

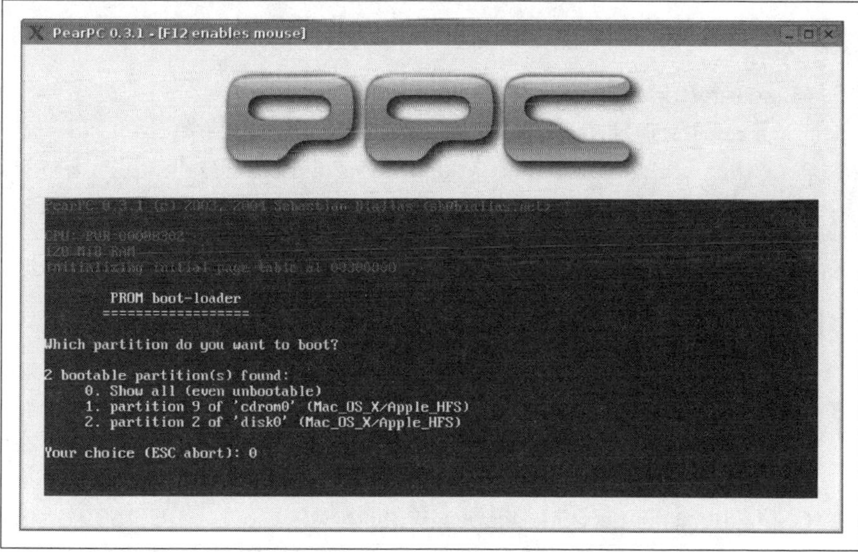

Figure 10-13. Select disk0 to boot your new Mac OS X installation

4. Copy the PearPC networking scripts to the same directory as the virtual machine and give yourself access to them (but make *root* the owner):

```
# cp -R ~/src/pearpc-0.3.1/scripts .
# chown root:bjepson scripts/ifppc*
```

Figure 10-14. Mac OS X up and running under PearPC

5. Make some of the *ifppc** scripts *suid root*:

```
# chmod 4755 scripts/ifppc_*setuid
```

6. Add the following lines to your config file (*ppccfg* in the previous example):

```
#network
pci_rtl8139_installed = 1
pci_rtl8139_mac = "de:ad:ca:fe:12:35"
```

7. Start PearPC:

```
$ ppc ppccfg
```

8. Open System Preferences → Network. The first time you do this, Mac OS X announces that it's detected a new PCI Ethernet Slot. This is the virtual Ethernet card. Select it from the Show menu, and select TCP/IP.
9. Configure your network adapter with the IP address 192.168.1.1 and the router 192.168.1.80 as shown in Figure 10-15. Use the same DNS server as you do for the rest of your network (shown as 192.168.254.1 in this example).

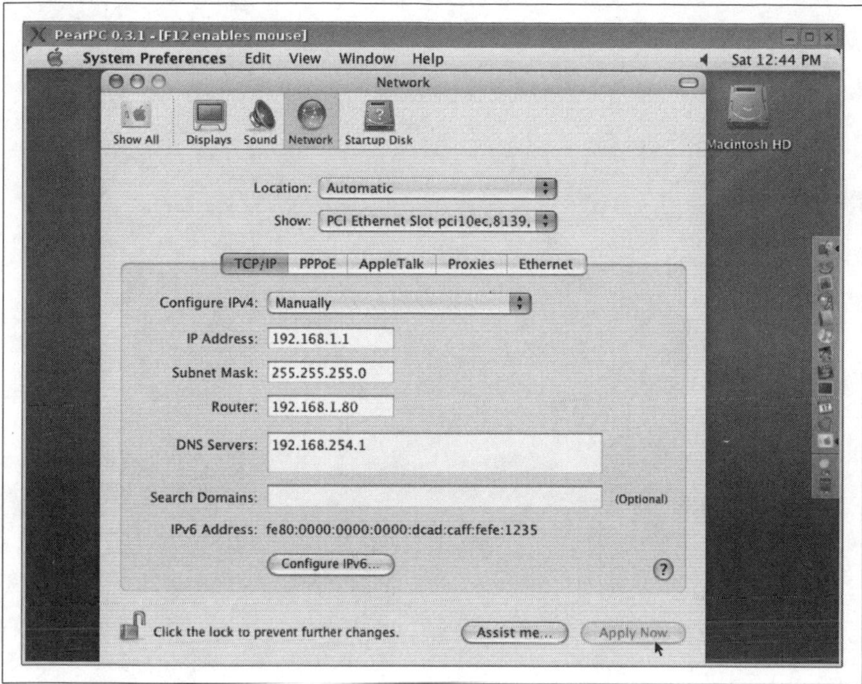

Figure 10-15. Configuring the network under PearPC

PART II
Building Applications

Although Apple's C compiler is based on the GNU Compiler Collection (GCC), there are important differences between compiling and linking on Mac OS X and on other platforms. This part of the book describes these differences.

CHAPTER 11

Compiling Source Code

The Xcode Tools that ship with Tiger provide a development environment for building applications with Cocoa, Carbon, Java, and even AppleScript. Xcode Tools include utilities that should be familiar to any Unix developer who works with command-line compilers. For details about obtaining these tools, see the "Xcode Tools" section in the Preface. Xcode Tools include all sorts of other goodies, including an advanced Integrated Development Environment (IDE), but coverage of those tools is beyond the scope and intent of this book. To learn more about the Xcode Tools, go to */Developer/ADC Reference Library/documentation/DeveloperTools/index.html*.

The C compiler that comes with Xcode is based on the Free Software Foundation's GNU Compiler Collection, or GCC. Apple's modifications to GCC include an Objective-C compiler, as well as various modifications to deal with the Darwin operating system. The development environment in Mac OS X includes:

AppleScript
: This is an English-like language used to script applications and the operating system. AppleScript is installed as part of the Mac OS X operating system and does not require Xcode. Instead, to write AppleScripts, use the Script Editor (*/Applications/AppleScript*).

AppleScript Studio
: This is a high-level development environment based on AppleScript that allows you to build GUI applications by hooking AppleScript into the Cocoa framework. If you plan to build AppleScript Studio applications, you will need to use the Xcode Tools instead of the Script Editor.

Compilers
: These compilers are based on GCC and provide support for C, C++, Objective-C, Objective-C++, and assembly. Apple's enhancements to GCC for Tiger include support for the G5 (also known as the PowerPC 970) and 64-bit arithmetic, as well as the ability to generate optimized code to run on G5, G4, and G3 systems

Compiler Tools
: These include the Mac OS X Mach-O GNU-based assemblers, Mach-O static link editor, Mach-O dynamic link editor, and Mach-O object file tools, such as *nm*, *otool*, and *otool64*.

Documentation
: There is extensive documentation for Xcode, available in both HTML and PDF formats. The Xcode documentation can be found in */Developer/ADC Reference Library*. These documents are also available online from the Apple Developer Connection (ADC) web site (*http://developer.apple.com*).

You can access the documentation for GCC after you've installed Xcode by opening */Developer/ADC Reference Library/documentation/DeveloperTools/gcc-4.0/gcc/index.html*.

Debugger
: The Apple debugger is based on GNU *gdb*.

Miscellaneous Tools
: These include traditional development tools, such as *make* (both GNU, which is the default, and BSD) and GNU *libtool*, graphical and command-line performance tools, Xcode for WebObjects, parsing tools (such as *lex*, *flex*, *yacc*, and *bison*), standard Unix source code management tools (such as *CVS* and *RCS*), and an extensive set of Java development tools. There's also a frontend to GCC, *distcc*, which uses Bonjour to distribute builds of C, C++, Objective-C, or Objective-C++ code across computers on a network.

Xcode
: Formerly known as Xcode is an IDE for Mac OS X that supports Cocoa and Carbon programming with C, C++, Objective-C, and Java. (Xcode was known as Project Builder in pre-Panther releases of Mac OS X.)

Interface Builder
: This is a graphical user interface (GUI) editor for Cocoa and Carbon applications.

Header Doc 8
: This is a set of command-line tools for including structured comments in source code and header files, which are later used to create HTML and XML output. A set of manpage generation tools is also included. Header Doc's two main Perl scripts are *headerdoc2html* and *gatherheaderdoc*. Kyle Hammond's Cocoa frontend to Header Doc is available at *http://www.isd.net/dsl03002/CocoasProgramming.html*. See */Developer/ADC Reference Library/documentation/DevelopTools/Conceptual/HeaderDoc/index.html* for details.

We won't address the complete Mac OS X development suite in this chapter. Instead, we'll focus on the command-line development tools and how they differ from the implementations on other Unix platforms.

Java programmers will find that the Mac OS X command-line Java tools (see "Java Development Tools" in Appendix B) behave as they do under Unix and Linux. Another resource for Java developers is *Mac OS X for Java Geeks* (O'Reilly).

Perl programmers coming from previous Macintosh systems will find that Mac OS X does not use MacPerl (*http://www.macperl.com*), but instead uses the standard Unix build of the core Perl distribution (*http://www.perl.org*). For additional information on using Perl under Mac OS X, see Chapter 19.

Compiler Differences

GCC is supported on a wide range of platforms, and it is the default compiler on Mac OS X. There are, however, some important differences between the version of GCC that ships with Mac OS X and those found on other Unix systems.

One difference that experienced GCC users may notice, particularly if they have extensive experience with mathematical and scientific programming, is that the Xcode Tools do not include FORTRAN. However, both Fink (*http://fink.sourceforge.net*) and DarwinPorts (*http://darwinports.opendarwin.org*) include *g77*, the GNU FORTRAN '77 compiler. (For information on using Fink and DarwinPorts, see Chapters 13 and 14, respectively.) Also, the Darwin archive includes the source code for *g77*, which you can use to compile FORTRAN code. Additionally, two open source FORTRAN 95 projects are available for Mac OS X, the GNU FORTRAN 95, or *gfortran*, which is a compiler frontend to GCC 4.0 (*http://gcc.gnu.org/fortran*) and the *g95* project (*http://g95.sourceforge.net*). *g95* can be installed on Mac OS X with the binaries provided on its home site or with Fink. At the time of this writing, gfortran for GCC 4 is listed among Fink's unsupported packages.

Mac OS X's C compiler contains a number of Mac-specific features that have not been folded into the main GCC distribution. (It is up to the Free Software Foundation (FSF) to accept and merge Apple's patches.) For information on how Apple's compiler differs from the GNU version, see the *README.Apple* file in the Darwin CVS archive's *gcc4* subdirectory.

As of this writing, Apple's *cc* compiler is based on GCC 4.0. However, GCC 3.3 is also available as */usr/bin/gcc-3.3*. By default, invoking *cc* or *gcc* invokes GCC 4.0; both */usr/bin/cc* and */usr/bin/gcc* are symbolic links to */usr/bin/gcc-4.0*. You can change the default GCC to GCC 3.3 by running the command *gcc_select 3.3*. Similarly, you can change it back to GCC 4.0 with *gcc_select 4.0*. The *gcc_select* command (used with one of the options 3.3 or 4.0) changes the symbolic links */usr/bin/cc* and */usr/bin/gcc* to point to the desired version of *gcc*. Since files in */usr/bin* are changed by this command, you must execute it with *sudo*.

You can see the current settings by running *gcc_select* with no arguments:

```
$ gcc_select
Current default compiler:
gcc version 4.0.0 20041026 (Apple Computer, Inc. build 4039)
```

The Mac OS X Compiler Release Notes (*/Developer/ADC Reference Library/Documentation/releasenotes*) should be consulted for details on the most currently known problems, issues, and features.

Perhaps the most important improvement in GCC 4.0 is the incorporation of Tree Single Static Assignment (SSA) optimization rather than Register Transfer Language, used in older versions of GCC. SSA was available in some earlier versions, but was experimental and had to be switched on by special compiler flags, for example, *-fssa*. Although we haven't tested them thoroughly, according to the Apple's Xcode2 web site (*http://www.apple.com/macosx/features/xcode*), the incorporation of Tree SSA has improved the following optimizations:

- Scalar replacement of aggregates
- Constant propagation
- Value range propagation
- Partial redundancy elimination
- Load and store motion
- Strength reduction
- Dead store elimination
- Dead and unreachable code elimination
- Auto-vectorization to take advantage of the Velocity Engine
- Loop interchange
- Tail recursion by accumulation

See *http://gcc.gnu.org/projects/tree-ssa* for more details on SSA.

Additional improvements in GCC 4.0 include a more efficient C++ parser and a dynamic C++ standard library, *libstdc++*; in pre-Tiger releases of Mac OS X you could only statically link it. There's also support for 128-bit *long double* floating-point types and 64-bit computing.

Compiling Unix Source Code

Many of the differences between Mac OS X and other versions of Unix become apparent when you try to build Unix-based software on Mac OS X. Most open source Unix software uses GNU *autoconf* or a similar facility, which generates a *configure* script that performs a number of tests of the system—especially of the installed Xcode Tools—and finishes by constructing one or more makefiles. After the *configure* script has done its job, you run the *make* command to first compile, and, if all goes well, install the resulting binaries.

Most tarballs include a *configure* script, so you do not need to generate it yourself. However, if you retrieve *autoconf*-managed source code from a CVS archive, you will have to run *autoconf.sh* manually to generate the *configure* file.

In most cases, it's pretty easy to compile a Unix application on Mac OS X. After unpacking the tarball and changing to the top-level source code directory, just issue the following three commands to compile the application:

```
./configure
make
make install
```

Mac OS X web browsers are configured to unpack compressed archives. So, if you click on a link to a tarball, you may find that it gets downloaded to your Desktop and extracted there. If you'd prefer to manage the download and extraction process yourself, Control-click (or right-click) on the link so you can specify a download location.

The following sections deal with issues involved in successfully performing these steps. Determining how to improvise within that three-step procedure reveals some of the differences between Mac OS X and other Unix systems.

The First Line of Defense

Most tarballs include the following files in the top-level directory:

README
: This is an introduction to the application and source code. You'll often find copyright information in this document, notes about bug fixes or improvements made to different versions, and pointers to web sites, FAQs, and mailing lists.

INSTALL
: This document contains step-by-step installation instructions.

PORT or PORTING
: If present, one of these documents will include tips for porting the application to another Unix platform.

These files contain useful information that may help you get the application running on Mac OS X.

Host Type

One of the first difficulties you may encounter when running a *configure* script is that the script aborts with an error message stating that the host system cannot be determined.

Strictly speaking, the *host type* refers to the system on which software will run, and the *build type* refers to the system on which the software is being built. It is possible to build software on one system to run on another system, but to do so requires a cross-compiler. We will not concern ourselves with cross-compiler issues. Thus, for our discussion, both the host type and the build (and target) types are the same: `powerpc-apple-darwin`*`VERSION`*, where the *`VERSION`* denotes the particular version of Darwin. In fact, a *configure* script detects Mac OS X by the host/build type named *Darwin,* since Darwin is the actual operating system underlying Mac OS X. This can be verified by issuing the *uname -v* command, which tells you that you're running a Darwin kernel, the kernel version, and when it was last built.

Many *configure* scripts are designed to determine the host system, since the resulting makefiles differ depending on the type of system for which the software is built. The *configure* script is designed to be used with two files related to the host type, usually residing in the same directory as the *configure* script. These files are *config.guess*, which is used to help guess the host type; and *config.sub*, which is used to validate the host type and to put it into a canonical form (such as *CPUTYPE-MANUFACTURER-OS*, as in `powerpc-apple-darwin8.0.0`).

Although Mac OS X and Darwin have been around for a while now, you may still run across source code distributions that contain older *config.** files that don't work with Mac OS X. You can find out if these files support Darwin by running the *./configure* script. If the script complains about an unknown host type, you know that you have a set of *config.** files that don't support Darwin.

In that case, you can replace the *config.guess* and *config.sub* files with the Apple-supplied, like-named versions residing in */usr/share/automake-1.6*. These replacement files originate from the FSF and include the code necessary to configure a source tree for Mac OS X. To copy these files into the source directory, which contains the *configure* script, simply issue the following commands from within the sources directory:

```
cp /usr/share/automake-1.6/config.sub .
cp /usr/share/automake-1.6/config.guess .
```

Macros

You can use a number of predefined macros to detect Apple systems and Mac OS X in particular. For example, `__APPLE__` is a macro that is defined on every Apple *gcc*-based Mac OS X system, and `__MACH__` is one of several macros specific to Mac OS X. Table 11-1 lists the predefined macros available on Mac OS X

Table 11-1. Mac OS X C macros

Macro	When defined
__OBJC__	When the compiler is compiling Objective-C .m files or Objective-C++ *.M* files. (To override the file extension, use *-ObjC* or *-ObjC++*.)
__ASSEMBLER__	When the compiler is compiling *.s* files.
__NATURAL_ALIGNMENT__	When compiling for systems that use natural alignment, such as *powerpc*.
__STRICT_BSD__	If, and only if, the *-bsd* flag is specified as an argument to the compiler.
__MACH__	When compiling for systems that support Mach system calls.
__APPLE__	When compiling for any Apple system. Defined on Mac OS X systems running Apple's variant of the GNU C compiler and third-party compilers.
__APPLE_CC__	When compiling for any Apple system. Integer value that corresponds to the (Apple) version of the compiler
__VEC__	When AltiVec support was enabled with the *-maltivec* flag.

Table 11-1. Mac OS X C macros (continued)

Macro	When defined
`__APPLE_VEC__`	When AltiVec support was enabled with the *-mpim-altivec* flag.
`__LP64__`	Defined on 64-bit systems such as the G5. This macro can be used to conditionally compile 64-bit code

Do not rely on the presence of the `__APPLE__` macro to determine which compiler features or libraries are supported. Instead, we suggest using a package like GNU *autoconf* to tell you which features the target operating system supports. This approach makes it more likely that your applications can compile out-of-the-box (or with little effort) on operating systems to which you don't have access.

Supported Languages

When using the *cc* command, which supports more than one language, the language is determined by either the filename suffix or by explicitly specifying the language using the *-x* option. Table 11-2 lists some of the more commonly used filename suffixes and *-x* arguments supported by Apple's version of GCC.

Table 11-2. File suffixes recognized by cc

File suffix	Language	–x argument
.c	C source code to be preprocessed and compiled	`c`
.C, .cc, .cxx, .cpp	C++ source code to be preprocessed and compiled	`c++`
.h	C header that should neither be compiled nor linked	`c-header`
.i	C source code that should be compiled but not preprocessed	`cpp-output`
.ii	Objective-C++ or C++ source code that should be compiled but not preprocessed	`c++-cpp-output`
.m	Objective-C source code	`objective-c`
.M, .mm	Mixed Objective-C++ and Objective-C source code	`objective-c++`
.s	Assembler source that should be assembled but not preprocessed	`assembler`
.S	Assembler source to be preprocessed and assembled	`assembler-with-cpp`

Although the HFS+ filesystem is case-insensitive, the *cc* compile driver recognizes the uppercase C in a source file. For example, *cc foo.C* invokes *cc*'s C++ compiler because the file extension is an uppercase C, which denotes a C++ source file. (To *cc*, it's just a command-line argument.) So, even though HFS+ will find the same file whether you type *cc foo.c* or *cc foo.C*, what you enter on the command line makes all the difference in the world, particularly to *cc*.

Preprocessing

When you invoke *cc* without options, it initiates a sequence of four basic operations, or stages: preprocessing, compilation, assembly, and linking. In a multifile program, the first three stages are performed on each individual source code file, creating an object code file for each source code file. The final linking stage combines all the object codes that were created by the first three stages, along with user-specified object code that may have been compiled earlier into a single executable image file.

Frameworks

In Mac OS X, a framework is a type of bundle that is named with a *framework* extension. Before discussing the framework type of bundle, let's first briefly describe the notion of a bundle. A bundle is an important software packaging model in Mac OS X consisting of a directory that stores resources related to a given software package, or resources used by many software packages. Bundles, for example, can contain image files, headers, shared libraries, and executables. In addition to frameworks, there are at least two other types of bundles used in Mac OS X; applications (named with the *.app* extension), and loadable bundles including plug-ins (which are usually named with the *.bundle* extension).

- An *application bundle* contains everything an application needs to run: executables, images, etc. You can actually see these in the Finder if you Control-click on an application's icon, and select Show Package Contents.
- A *framework bundle*, on the other hand, is one that contains a dynamic shared library along with its resources, including header files, images, and documentation.
- A *loadable bundle* contains executables and associated resources, which are loaded into running applications; these include plug-ins, and kernel extensions.

The application and plug-in type bundles are built and organized so that the top level directory is named *Contents*. That is, the directory *Contents/* contains the entire bundle, including any file needed by the bundle. Take for example, Safari. If you Control-click on the Safari application in the Finder and select Show Package Contents, the *Contents/* directory will be revealed in the Finder. To see what's in the *Contents/* directory, quickly hit ⌘-3 to switch the Finder to Column View, and then hit the C key on your keyboard (this highlights the Contents folder). You will see the typical contents of an application bundle, including:

- The required XML property list file named *Info.plist*, which contains information about the bundle's configuration
- A folder named *MacOS/*, which contains the executable
- A folder named *Resources/* that contains, among other resources, image files
- Files named *version.plist* and *PkgInfo*

Applications can also contain application-specific frameworks, that is, frameworks that are not used by any other application or plug-in.

Framework structure

Frameworks are critical in Mac OS X. Cocoa, the toolkit for user interface development, consists of the Foundation and Application Kit (or AppKit) frameworks for Objective-C and Java. Frameworks use a *versioned* bundle structure, which allows multiple versions of the same information; for example, framework code and header files. They are structured in either one of the following ways:

- Symbolic links are used to point to the latest version. This allows for multiple versions of the framework to be present.
- In the Framework bundle structure, the top level directory is named *Resources*. The actual *Resources/* directory need not be located at the top level of the bundle; it may be located deeper inside of the bundle. In this case, a symbolic link pointing to the *Resources/* directory is located at the top level.

In either case, an *Info.plist* file describing the framework's configuration must be included in the *Resources/* directory. (Chapter 12 discusses how to create frameworks and loadable bundles. This chapter only describes how to use the frameworks.)

Before discussing how to use frameworks, let's look at the different kinds of frameworks. A *private framework* is one that resides in a directory named *PrivateFrameworks*, and whose implementation details are not exposed. Specifically, private frameworks reside in one of the following locations.

- *~/Library/PrivateFrameworks*
- */Library/PrivateFrameworks*
- */System/Library/PrivateFrameworks*

An *application-specific framework* can be placed within the given application's package. For example, consider the private framework, *Graphite.framework*, which is located in */System/Library/PrivateFrameworks*. This private framework consists of a directory named *Graphite.framework/*, which, aside from symbolic links and subdirectories, contains the Graphite executable and files named *Info.plist* and *version.plist*. No implementation details are revealed.

A *public framework*, on the other hand, is one whose API can be ascertained, for example, by viewing its header files. Public frameworks reside in appropriate directories named *Frameworks/*. For example, the OpenGL framework resides in */System/Library/Frameworks*. This public framework consists of the directory */System/Library/Frameworks/OpenGL.framework*, which contains (among other things) a subdirectory named *Headers*. Implementation details can be ascertained by examining the header files.

Precisely where a public framework resides depends on its purpose, and where it is placed. When you build an application, you can program the path of the framework. Later, when the application is run, the dynamic link editor looks for the framework in the path that was programmed into the application. If a framework cannot be found, the following locations are searched in the order shown:

~/Library/Frameworks
: This is the location for frameworks used by a single user.

/Library/Frameworks
: Third-party applications that are intended for use by all users on a system should have its frameworks installed in this directory.

/Network/Library/Frameworks
: Third-party applications that are intended for use by all users across a local area network (LAN) should have its frameworks installed in this directory.

/System/Library/Frameworks
: The shared libraries in these frameworks provided by Apple, for example, in the Application Kit (or AppKit), are to be used by all applications on the system.

There are three types of frameworks in */System/Library/Frameworks*:

Simple public framework
: Apple defines a *simple framework* as one which is neither a subframework nor an umbrella framework, and has placed in this category only those frameworks that have been used in older versions of Mac OS X. One such example is AppKit, which is located in */System/Library/Frameworks/AppKit.framework* and can be examined in the Finder.

Subframework

A subframework is public, but has a restriction in that you cannot link directly against it. Its API is exposed, however, through its header files, and subframeworks reside in umbrella frameworks. To use a subframework, you must link against the umbrella framework in which it resides.

Umbrella framework

This type of framework includes other umbrella frameworks and subframeworks. The exact composition of an umbrella's subframeworks is an implementation detail which is subject to change over time. The developer need not be concerned with such changes, since it is only necessary to link against the umbrella framework and include only the umbrella framework's header file. One advantage to this approach is that not only can definitions be moved from one header file of a framework to another, but in the case of umbrella frameworks, the definition of a function can even be moved to another framework if that framework is included in the umbrella framework.

To better understand the difference between simple and umbrella frameworks, compare the composition of the simple */System/Library/Frameworks/AppKit.framework* with the umbrella framework */System/Library/Frameworks/CoreServices.framework*. The umbrella framework contains several other frameworks, namely, *CarbonCore*, *CFNetwork*, *Metadata*, *OSSerrvices*, *SearchKit*, and *WebServicesCore*. The simple framework neither contains subframeworks, nor is it a subframework contained within an umbrella framework.

Including a framework in your application

When including application-specific frameworks, you must let the preprocessor know where to search for framework header files. You can do this with the *-F* option, which is also accepted by the linker. For example:

```
-F directoryname
```

instructs the preprocessor to search the directory `directoryname` for framework header files. The search begins in `directoryname` and, if necessary, continues in the standard framework directories in the order listed earlier.

The *-F* option is necessary only when building application-specific frameworks.

To include a framework object header, use `#include` in the following format:

```
#include <framework/filename.h>
```

Here, *framework* is the name of the framework without the extension, and *filename*.h is the source for the header file. If your code is in Objective-C, the #import preprocessor directive may be used in place of #include. The only difference beyond that is that #import makes sure the same file is not included more than once.

The *-F* option is accepted by the preprocessor and the linker, and is used in either case to specify directories in which to search for framework header files. (This is similar to the *-I* option, which specifies directories to search for *.h* files.) By default, the linker searches the standard directories, */Local/Library/Frameworks* and */System/Library/Frameworks*, for frameworks. The directory search order can be modified with *-F* options. For example:

```
cc -F dir1 -F dir2 -no-cpp-precomp myprog.c
```

results in *dir1* being searched first, followed by *dir2*, followed by the standard framework directories. While the *-F* flag is needed only when building application specific frameworks, the *-framework* is always needed to link against a framework. Specifically, inclusion of this flag results in a search for the specified framework named when linking. Example 11-1 shows "Hello, World" in Objective-C. Notice that it includes the AppKit framework.

Example 11-1. Saying hello from Objective-C

```
#include <Appkit/AppKit.h>

int main(int argc, const char *argv[])
{
  NSLog(@"Hello, World\n");
  return 0;
}
```

Save Example 11-1 as *hello.m*. To compile it, use *-framework* to pass in the framework name:

```
cc -framework AppKit -o hello hello.m
```

The *-framework* flag is accepted only by the linker and is used to name a framework.

Compiler flags of particular interest in Mac OS X are related to the peculiarities of building shared code, for example, the compiler flag *–dynamiclib*, which is used to build Mach-O *dylibs*. For more details, see Chapter 12.

Compiler Flags

You can see the *gcc* manpage for an extensive list of compiler flags. In particular, the *gcc* manpage describes many PowerPC-specific flags, as well as Darwin-specific flags. Table 11-3 describes a few common Mac OS X GCC compiler flags that are specific to Mac OS X. These flags should be used when porting Unix-based software to Mac OS X. We've also included a few flags that enable various Tree-SSA-based optimizations. These are the flags that begin with *–ftree*.

Table 11-3. Selected Mac OS X GCC compiler flags

Flag	Effect
-no-cpp-precomp	Turns off the Mac OS X preprocessor in favor of the GNU preprocessor.
-ObjC, -ObjC++	Specifies *objective-c* and *objective-c++*, respectively. Also passes the *-ObjC* flag to *ld*.
-faltivec	Enables AltiVec language extension. Provided for compibility for earlier versions of GCC.
-maltivec	Enables AltiVec language extension.
-mpim-altivec	Enables AltiVec language extension as defined in the Motorola AltiVec Technology Programming Interface Manual (PIM). This option is similar in effect to *-maltivec*, but there are some differences. For example, *-mpim-altivec* disables inlining of functions containing AltiVec instructions as well as inline vectorization of *memset* and *memcopy*.
-mabi-altivec	Adds AltiVec ABI extensions to the current ABI.
-mnoabi-altivec	Disables AltiVec ABI extensions for the current ABI.
-mnopim-altivec	Disables the effect of *-mpim-altivec*.
-mno-altivec-long-deprecated	Disables the warning of the deprecated *long* keyword in AltiVec data types.
-mnoaltivec	Disables AltiVec language extension.
-arch ppc970 *-arch pp64*	Compile for the PowerPC 970 (aka G5) processor, and assemble only 64-bit instructions.
-mcpu=970 *-mcpu=G5*	Enables the use of G5-specific instructions.
-force_cpusubtype_ALL	This will force a runtime check to determine which CPU is present and will allow code to run on the G3, G4, or G5, regardless of which CPU was used to compile the code. Exercise caution if you use this and G5-specific features at the same time.
-mpowerpc64	When used in combination with *-mcpu=970, -mtune=970*, and *-force_cpusubtype_ALL*, the G5's support for native 64-bit long-long is enabled.
-mpowerpc-gpopt	Use the hardware based floating-point square function on the G5. (Use with *-mcpu=970, -mtune=970*, and *-mpowerpc64*.
-ftree-pre	Partial redundancy elimination on trees.
-ftree-fre	Full redundancy elimination on trees.
-ftree-ccp	Sparse conditional constant propagation on trees.

Table 11-3. Selected Mac OS X GCC compiler flags (continued)

Flag	Effect
-ftree-ch	Loop header copying on trees. Enabled by default with *-O*, but not with *-Os*.
-ftree-dce	Dead code elimination on trees.
-ftree-dominator-opts	
-ftree-elim-checks	Elimination of checks based on scalar.
-ftree-loop-optimize	Loop optimization on trees.
-ftree-loop-linear	Linear loop transformations on trees to improve cache performance and allow additional loop optimizations.
-ftree-lim	Loop invariant motion on trees.
-ftree-sra	Scalar replacements of aggregates.
-ftree-copyrename	Copy renaming on trees.
-ftree-ter	Temporary expression replacement during SSA to normal phase.
-ftree-lrs	Live range splitting during SSA to normal phase.
-ftree-vectorize	Loop vectorization on trees. This enables *-fstrict-aliasing*, by default.
-fstrict-aliasing	Apply the strictest aliasing rules.
-fasm-blocks	Allow blocks and functions of assembly code in C or C+ source code.
-fconstant-cfstrings	Automatic creation CoreFoundation-type constant. (See the *gcc* manpage for details.)
-fpascal-strings	Allow the use of Pascal-style strings.
-fweak-coalesced	Weakly coalesced definitions are ignored by the linker in favor of one ordinary definition.
-findirect-virtual-calls	Use the vtable to call virtual functions, rather than making direct calls.
-fapple-kext	Make kernel extensions loadable by Darwin kernels. Use in combination with *-fno-exceptions* and *-static*.
-fcoalesce-templates	Coalesce instantiated templates.
-fobjc-exceptions	Support structured exception handling in Objective-C. (See the *gcc* manpage for more details.)
-fzero-link	Instructs *dyld* to load the object file at runtime.
-Wpragma-once	Issue a warning about `#pragma` use only once if necessary.
-Wextra-tokens	Issue a warning if preprocessor directives end with extra tokens.
-Wnewline-eof	Issue a warning if a file ends without a newline character.
-Wno-altivec-long-deprecated	Don't issue a warning about the keyword 'long' used in an AltiVec data type declaration.
-Wmost	Same effect as *-Wall -Wno-parentheses*.
-Wno-long-double	Don't issue a warning if the long-double type is used.

Table 11-3. Selected Mac OS X GCC compiler flags (continued)

Flag	Effect
-fast	Optimize for PPC7450 and G5. The *-fast* flag optimizes for G5, by default. This flag can be used to optimize for PPC7450 by adding the flag *-mcpu=7450*. To build shared libraries with *-fast*, include the *-fPIC* flag.
-static	Inhibits linking with shared libraries provided that all of your libraries have also been compiled with *-static*.
-shared	Not supported on Mac OS X.
-dynamiclibs	Used to build Mach-O dylibs (see Chapter 12).
-mdynamic-no-pic	Compiled code will itself not be relocatable, but will have external references that are relocatable.
-mlong-branch	Calls that use a 32-bit destination address are compiled.
-all_load	All members of static archive libraries will be loaded. (See the *ld* manpage for more information.)
-arch_errors_fatal	Files that have the wrong architecture will result in fatal errors.
-bind_at_load	Bind all undefined references when the file is loaded.
-bundle	Results in Mach-o bundle format. (See the *ld* manpage for more information.)
-bundle_loader executable	The `executable` that will load the output file being linked. (See the *ld* manpage for more information.)
-fnon-lvalue-assign	Allow cast and conditionals to be used as lvalues. Although this is on by default in Apple's GCC 4.0, a deprecation warning will be issued whenever an lvalue cast or lvalue conditional is encountered as such lvalues will not be allowed in future versions of Apple's GCC.
-fno-non-lvalue-assign	Disallow lvalue cast and lvalue conditionals.
-msoft-float	Enable software floating-point emulation rather than using the floating-point register set. This emulation is not performed on Mac OS X since the required libraries are not included. On Mac OS X this flag prevents floating-point registers from copying data from one memory location to another.
-Os	Optimize for size. On Apple PowerPC, this disables string instructions. To enable string instructions, use *-mstring*.

Architectural Issues

There are a few architectural issues to be aware of when developing or porting software on Mac OS X. In particular, vectorization, pointer size, endianness, and inline assembly code tend to be the most common issues developers run into.

AltiVec

The Velocity Engine, Apple's name for Motorola 128-bit AltiVec vector processor that allows up to 16 operations in a single clock cycle, is supported on both G4 and G5 processors by the Mac OS X GCC implementation. The Velocity Engine, which executes operations currently with existing integer and floating-point units, can result in significant performance gains, especially for highly parallel operations. The compiler flag *–maltivec* can be specified to compile code engineered to use the AltiVec instruction set. Inclusion of this command-line option to *cc* defines the preprocessor symbol `__VEC__`. (See Table 11-3 for more AltiVec-related compiler flags.)

64-bit Computing

On a 32-bit system, such as Mac OS X running on the G3 or G4, C pointers are 32 bits (4 bytes). On a 64-bit system, such as Mac OS X running on the G5, they are 64 bits (8 bytes). As long as your code does not rely on any assumptions about pointer size, it should be 64-bit clean. For example, on a 32-bit system, the following program prints "4", and on a 64-bit system, it prints "8":

```
#include <stdio.h>
int main( )
{
  printf("%d\n", sizeof(void *));
  return 0;
}
```

Some 64-bit operating systems, such as Solaris 8 on Ultra hardware (sun4u) and Mac OS X Tiger on G5 hardware, have a 64-bit kernel space, but support both 32- and 64-bit mode applications, depending on how they are compiled. On a G5 system, the pointer size is 64-bits. Other data types are mapped onto the 64-bit data type. For example, single precision floats, which are 32-bit, are converted to double precision floats when they are loaded into registers. In the registers, single precision instructions operate on these single precision floats stored as doubles performing the required operations on the data. The results, however, are rounded to single precision 32-bit. Apple has provided several technical documents containing information and advice on optimizing code to take advantage of the 64-bit G5 architecture:

- 64-Bit Transition Guide at *file:///Developer/ADC Reference Library/documentation/Darwin/Conceptual/64bitPorting/index.html*
- Developing 64-Bit Applications at *http://developer.apple.com/macosx/tiger/64bit.html*

- TN2086: Tuning for G5: A Practical Guide at *http://developer.apple.com/technotes/tn/tn2086.html*
- TN2087: PowerPC G5 Performance Primer at *http://developer.apple.com/technotes/tn/tn2087.html*

Additional information can be found at *http://developer.apple.com/hardware/ve/g5.html*. These documents describe in detail the issues involved in tuning code for the G5. We note here only a few issues.

The architecture of the G5 allows for much greater performance relative to the G4. This performance potential is partly due to the fact that the G5 allows 200 instructions in core, compared to only 30 for the G4. Moreover, the G5 has 16 pipeline stages, 2 load/store units, and 2 floating points units, compared to 7 pipeline stages, 1 load/store unit, and 1 floating points unit on the G4. The L1 cacheline size is also 128 bytes on the G5, compared to 32 bytes on the G4. Additionally the processor and memory bandwidth is much greater on the G5, relative to the G4. The technical notes mentioned earlier in this section have additional information on hardware differences.

One important implication of the greater number of pipeline stages on the G5 relative to the G4 is that instruction latencies are greater on the G5. You can often gain significant improvements in performance by using performance tools to identify loops that account for a large percentage of computation time. Once identified, you can either manually unroll these loops, or use the *–funroll-loops* compiler flag. The compiler flag *–mtune-970* can also be useful in this situation, as it schedules code more efficiently for the G5. The *–fast* compiler flag sets these options (among others) automatically.

To better take advantage of the longer cacheline size in L1 cache on the G5, algorithms should be designed for greater data locality, and use contiguous memory accesses when possible. For example, arrays in C store entries rowwise. To ensure contiguous memory accesses, design your code so that it accesses array elements row-by-row. The G5 has four hardware prefetchers, which (if accesses to memory are contiguous) are triggered automatically to help reduce cache misses. Performance tools, such as the CHUD suite (see Chapter 12), can help you optimize code by profiling computation and memory usage—some of them even make suggestions on how to improve performance.

While the G5 running Mac OS X Panther provided a fine computing platform, Mac OS X Tiger, which allows applications to access a 64-bit address space, opens up a new realm of computational capabilities. Since Tiger supports 64-bit arithmetic instructions on PowerPC architectures, even if your code is compiled in 32-bit mode, your code will not necessarily run more efficiently when compiled in 64-bit mode. It should be noted that, even on a G3 system, 32-bit applications have a 128-bit long-double data type, and a 64-bit long-long data type.

To compile 64-bit code using GCC, be sure to use the GCC 4.0, and specify the *ppc64* architecture with *-arch ppc64*. The *-arch ppc* compiler flag together with *-arch ppc64* produces a "fat" binary, that is, one that can be run on either 32-bit or 64-bit systems. When a fat binary is run on a 64-bit system, it runs as a 64-bit executable. On the other hand, when the same fat binary is run on a 32-bit system, it runs as a 32-bit executable. Specifying the *-arch ppc* compiler flag alone produces a 32-bit executable. Since 32-bit is the default, it is unnecessary to specify this flag alone, Additionally, the *–Wconversion* compiler flag may be useful when converting 32-bit code to 64-bit code. The `__LP64__` and `__ppc__` macros can be used to conditionally compile 64-bit code. At the time of this writing, only C and C++ can be compiled in 64-bit mode. Following is a list of things to bare in mind when engaging in 64-bit computing on Tiger.

- Tiger follows the LP64 64-bit data model, also used by SUN and SGI: ints are 32-bit, while longs, long-longs, and pointers are 64-bit.
- In 64-bit code, ints cannot hold pointers.
- Use of a cast between a 64-bit type and a 32-bit type can destroy data.
- In Tiger, only non-GUI applications can be compiled as 64-bit. You can, however, use a 32-bit GUI to launch and control the a 64-bit application.
- Compiling an application as 64-bit produces a 64-bit version of the Mach-O binary format, used in Mac OS X. You can determine if a program was compiled as 64-bit, 32-bit, or flat using the *file* command.
- 64-bit applications may use only 64-bit frameworks, while 32-bit applications may use only 32-bit frameworks.
- Tiger ships with only two 64-bit frameworks: System and Xcelerate.

Endian-ness

CPU architectures are designed to treat the bytes of words in memory as being arranged in big- or little-endian order. Big-endian ordering has the most significant byte in the lowest address, while little-endian has the most significant byte at the highest byte address.

The PowerPC is *bi-endian*, meaning that the CPU is instructed at boot time to order memory as either big- or little-endian. In practice, bi-endian CPUs run exclusively as big- or little-endian. In general, Intel architectures are little-endian, while most, but not all, Unix/RISC machines are big-endian. Table 11-4 summarizes the endian-ness of various CPU architectures and operating systems. As shown in Table 11-4, Mac OS X is big-endian.

Table 11-4. Endian-ness of some operating systems

CPU type	Operating system	Endian-ness
Dec Alpha	Digital Unix	little-endian
Dec Alpha	VMS	little-endian
Hewlett Packard PA-RISC	HP-UX	big-endian
IBM RS/6000	AIX	big-endian
Intel x86	Windows	little-endian
Intel x86	Linux	little-endian
Intel x86	Solaris x86	little-endian
Motorola PowerPC	Mac OS X	big-endian
Motorola PowerPC	Linux	big-endian
SGI R4000 and up	IRIX	big-endian
Sun SPARC	Solaris	big-endian

Inline Assembly

As far as inline assembly code is concerned—if you have any—it will have to be rewritten. Heaven help you if you have to port a whole Just-In-Time (JIT) compiler! For information on the assembler and PowerPC machine language, see the Mac OS X Assembler Guide (*/Developer/ADC Reference Library/documentation/DeveloperTools/Reference/Assembler/index.html*).

X11-based Applications and Libraries

Fink and DarwinPorts (covered in Chapters 13 and 14, respectively) can be used to install many X11-based applications, such as the GNU Image Manipulation Program (GIMP), *xfig/transfig*, ImageMagick, *nedit*, and more. Since Fink understands dependencies, installing some of these applications causes Fink to first install several other packages. For example, since the text editor *nedit* depends on Motif libraries, Fink will first install *lesstif*. (This also gives you the Motif window manager, *mwm*.) Similarly, when you install the GIMP via Fink, you will also install the packages for GNOME, GTK+, and *glib*.

You can also use Fink to install libraries directly. For example:

```
$ fink install qt
```

installs the X11-based Qt libraries; DarwinPorts can be used in a similar manner.

Building X11-based Applications and Libraries

If you cannot find binaries for X11-based applications or prefer to build the applications yourself, many tools are available to do so. When you install the Xcode Tools, make sure you install the optional *X11SDK*, which contains development tools and header files for building X11-based applications. If you didn't install *X11SDK* when you first installed Xcode, you can still install it from the Xcode folder on the Mac OS X Install DVD.

The process of building software usually begins with generating one or more *makefiles* customized to your system. For X11 applications, there are two popular methods for generating makefiles:

- One method is to use a *configure* script, as described earlier in this chapter.
- The other popular method for generating makefiles involves using the *xmkmf* script, which is a frontend to the *imake* utility. *xmkmf* invokes *imake*, which creates the makefile for you. To do this, *imake* looks for a template file called *Imakefile.*

With *imake*-driven source releases, you'll find *Imakefile* in the top-level source directory after you download and unpack a source tarball. After reading the *README* or *INSTALL* files, examine the *Imakefile* to see if you need to change anything. Then the next step is usually to issue the command:

```
$ xmkmf -a
```

When invoked with the *–a* option, *xmkmf* reads *imake*-related files in */usr/X11R6/lib/X11/config* and performs the following tasks recursively, beginning in the top-level directory and then in the subdirectories, if there are any:

```
$ make Makefiles
$ make includes
$ make depend
```

The next steps are usually *make, make test* (or *make check*), and *make install.*

To illustrate this method of building software, consider the script in Example 11-2, which downloads and builds an X11-based game.

Example 11-2. Downloading and building an X11-based game

```
# Download the source tarball
curl -O ftp://ftp.x.org/contrib/games/xtic1.12.tar.gz

# Unpack the tarball
gnutar xvfz xtic1.12.tar.gz

# Change to the top-level build directory
cd xtic1.12/

# Generate the Makefile
xmkmf -a

# Build everything (some X11 apps use 'make World')
make

# Have fun!
./src/xtic
```

AquaTerm

The X Window System is useful to Unix developers and users, since many Unix-based software packages depend on the X11 libraries. An interesting project that sometimes eliminates the need for X windows is the BSD-licensed AquaTerm application, developed by Per Persson (*http://aquaterm.sourceforge.net*). AquaTerm is a Cocoa application that can display vector graphics in an X11-like fashion. It does not replace X11, but it is useful for applications that generate plots and graphs.

The output graphics formats that AquaTerm supports are PDF and EPS. Applications communicate with AquaTerm through an adapter that acts as an intermediary between your old application's API and AquaTerm's API.

At the time of this writing, AquaTerm has adapters for *gnuplot* and *PGPLOT*, as well as example adapters in C, FORTRAN, and Objective-C. For example, assuming that you have installed both X11SDK and AquaTerm, you can build *gnuplot* (*http://www.gnuplot.info*) so graphics can be displayed either in X windows or in AquaTerm windows.

See AquaTerm's web site for extensive documentation, including the latest program developments, examples, mailing lists and other helpful resources.

Xgrid

Xgrid is an application used to create a loosely coupled cluster of Macs that can be used to run an application in parallel. That is, in a manner such that the computational work of an application is partitioned into subtasks and the subtasks are distributed and executed simultaneously across machines in the cluster. The phrase *distributed computing* is often used to describe the situation. Applications that can benefit from distributed computing are those whose computations can be partitioned into relatively large independent tasks, each running on a different processor and requiring little communication with each other. An application in which the same computation is performed on independent chunks of data falls into this category. Such applications are often called *embarrassingly parallel*. The classic examples of embarrassingly parallel applications include Monte Carlo simulation, Mandelbrot set computation, and low level image processing. Creating a distributed cluster can be complicated, and Xgrid is designed to make this task easy.

Conceptually, Xgrid has three components: a client, a controller, and an agent. From the user perspective, the client submits a job to the controller, the controller partitions the job into independent tasks and sends these tasks to available agents in the cluster, then the agents execute the tasks. When an agent complete its task, the results are sent back to the controller, which collects the results and returns the job to the client after the job has completed.

For a job to run on a cluster, the job must not only be parallelizable, it must also be run without user interaction. For command-line applications, no account on the agent is required, since the job is run as user *nobody*. GUI-based applications, on the other hand, require a user account that must be logged on.

Although the full version of Xgrid, including GUI tools, is available for Tiger Server, a stripped down version of Xgrid is bundled with the desktop version of Tiger. This stripped down version includes a System Preference for enabling the Xgrid agent (System Preferences → Sharing → Services → Xgrid), as well as the *xgridctl* command-line tool for starting the Xgrid controller, and *xgrid*, for submitting jobs to the controller as an Xgrid client.

To start the Xgrid controller daemon, *xgridcontrollerd*, enter the following command:

```
$ sudo xgridctl controller start
```

xgridcontrollerd starts whenever Tiger client boots up, after you enter the following command:

```
$ sudo xgridctl controller on
```

The controller daemon listens for submitted jobs from clients and advertises its presence on a LAN via Bonjour.

It's important to allow TCP traffic through port 4111 in case you're running Tiger's built-in firewall. (See the section on The Mac OS X Firewall in Chapter 16 for details.)

To enable the Xgrid agent, you must configure and enable the Xgrid service in the Sharing preference panel, as shown in Figure 11-1.

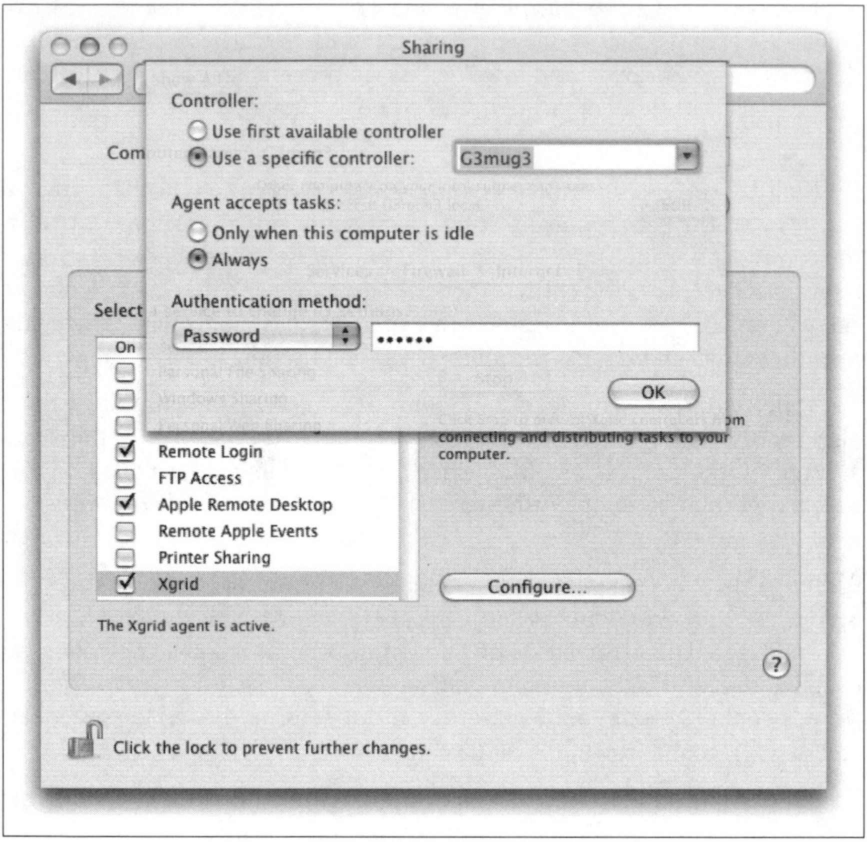

Figure 11-1. Configuring Xgrid Agent in Tiger

Agent configuration involves choosing a controller and either setting the agent to always be available or only when the computer is idle. Since Xgrid supports Bonjour, the hostnames of any controllers on the LAN show up in the drop-down menu of "Use a specific controller." You can also choose the authentication method as one of password, single sign-on (using Kerberos and Directory Services), or none. Xgrid in Tiger supports two-way password authentication between the controller and agents, although currently setting a controller password with *xgridctl* is not supported. In the full version of

Xgrid that ships with Tiger Server, you can use Server Admin to set the Xgrid controller password. If the controller is running on Tiger Server with password authentication, you can supply the controller's password when submitting a job using the *xgrid* command, either with the *–p password* flag or by setting the environment variable:

```
$ export XGRID_CONTROLLER_PASSWORD="good_password"
```

Other Grid Solutions for Mac OS X

Xgrid is Apple's easy to configure and use clustering software, but other more powerful and configurable options are available to turn a cluster of Macs into a high performance computing environment. These include SUN's Grid Engine (*http://gridengine.sunsource.net*), Pooch (*http://www.daugerresearch.com/pooh*), Globus (*http://www.globus.org*), and Condor (*http://www.cs.wisc.edu/condor*).

For problems that can benefit from a tightly coupled algorithmic approach, various ports of Message Passing Interface (MPI) are available for Mac OS X including: MacMPI (used with Pooch), MPICH (*http://www-unix.mcs.anl.gov/mpi/mpich*), and LAM/MPI (*http://www.lam-mpi.org*). See "Introduction to MPI Distributed Programming With Mac OS X" (*http://www.developer.apple.com/hardware/hpc/mpionmacosx.html*) for a fairly detailed overview of MPI on Mac OS X options.

You can obtain more information on Xgrid by visiting the Xgrid web site at *http://www.apple.com/acg/xgrid*, and subscribing to the Apple-maintained Xgrid-users mailing list at *http://www.lists.apple.com/mailman/listinfo/xgrid-users*.

An Xgrid agent for Unix and Linux is available at *http://www.novajo.ca/xgridagent*.

You can submit an Xgrid job from a client with the *xgrid* command:

```
$ xgrid -h hostname -out outdir -p password -job submit command args
```

Here, *hostname* is the IP number or hostname of the machine running the Xgrid controller, *outdir* is the directory in which the results are placed, *password* is the controller's password, and *command args* is a Unix shell command with its arguments.

CHAPTER 12
Libraries, Headers, and Frameworks

This chapter discusses the linking phase of building Unix-based software under Mac OS X, in particular, header files and libraries.

Header Files

There are two types of header files in Mac OS X.

Ordinary header files
: These header files are inserted into source code by a preprocessor prior to compilation. Ordinary header files have a *.h* extension.

Precompiled header files
: These header files have a *.h.gch* extension.

Header files serve four functions:

- They contain C declarations.
- They contain macro definitions.
- They provide for conditional compilation.
- They provide line control when combining multiple source files into a single file that is subsequently compiled.

The mechanism for enabling *POSIX.4* compliance is built into the system header files. The preprocessor variables `_ANSI_SOURCE`, `__STRICT_ANSI__`, and `_POSIX_SOURCE` are supported. Because Mac OS X itself is not *POSIX.4* compliant, you cannot achieve strict *POSIX.4* compliance. Using these mechanisms, however, is best way to approximate *POSIX.4* compliance.

Unix developers will find the ordinary header files familiar, since they follow the BSD convention. The C preprocessor directive #include includes a header file in a C source file. There are essentially three forms of this syntax:

#include <*headername*.h>
: This form is used when the header file is located in the directory */usr/include*.

#include <*directory/headername*.h>
: This form is used when the header file is located in the directory */usr/include/ directory*, where *directory* is a subdirectory of */usr/include*.

#include "*headername*.h"
: This form is used when the header file is located in a user or nonstandard directory. The form should either be in the same directory as the source file you are compiling or in a directory specified by *cc*'s *-Idirectory* switch.

You can use #include, followed by a macro, which, when expanded, must be in one of the aforementioned forms.

As noted in the previous chapter, frameworks in Mac OS X are common when you step outside of the BSD portions of the operating system. To include a framework header file in Objective-C code, use the following format:

```
#import <frameworkname/headerfilename.h>
```

where *frameworkname* is the name of the framework without the extension and *headerfilename* is the name of the header file. For example, the included declaration for a Cocoa application would look like:

```
#import <Cocoa/Cocoa.h>
```

Note that you must use #include rather than #import when including a framework in Carbon code. When preprocessing header files or any preprocessor directives, the following three actions are always taken:

- Comments are replaced by a single space.
- Any backslash line continuation escape symbol is removed, and the line following it is joined with the current line. For example:

  ```
  #def\
  ine \
  NMAX 2000
  ```

  is processed as:

  ```
  #define NMAX 2000
  ```

- Any predefined macro name is replaced with its expression. In Mac OS X, there are both standard ANSI C predefined macros, as well as several predefined macros specific to Mac OS X. For example, `__APPLE_CC__` is replaced by an integer that represents the compiler's version number.

The following rules must be kept in mind:

- The preprocessor does not recognize comments or macros placed between the < and > symbols in an `#include` directive.
- Comments placed within string constants are regarded as part of the string constant and are not recognized as C comments.
- If ANSI trigraph preprocessing is enabled with *cc –trigraph*, you must not use a backslash continuation escape symbol within a trigraph sequence, or the trigraph will not be interpreted correctly. ANSI trigraphs are three-character sequences that represent characters that may not be available on older terminals. For example, ??< translates to {. ANSI trigraphs are a rare occurrence these days.

Precompiled Header Files

Mac OS X's Xcode Tools support and provide extensive documentation on building and using precompiled header files. This section highlights a few of the issues that may be of interest to Unix developers new to Mac OS X when it comes to working with precompiled headers.

Precompiled header files are binary files that have been generated from ordinary C header files and preprocessed and parsed using *cc*. When such a precompiled header is created, both macros and declarations present in the corresponding ordinary header file are sorted, resulting in a faster compile time, a reduced symbol table size, and consequently, faster lookup. Precompiled header files are given a *.h.gch* extension and are produced from ordinary header files that end with a *.h* extension. There is no risk that a precompiled header file will get out of sync with the *.h* file, because the compiler checks the timestamp of the actual header file.

When using precompiled header files, you should not refer to the *.h.gch* version of the name, but rather to the *.h* version in the `#include` directive. If a precompiled version of the header file is available, it is used automatically; otherwise, the real header file (*.h*) is used. So, to include *foo.h.gch*, specify *foo.h*. The fact that *cc* is using a precompiled header is totally hidden from you.

You can create precompiled header files either using the *cc -precomp* or *cc -x c-header -c* compile driver flags. For example, the following command illustrates this process in its simplest, context-independent form:

```
cc -precomp header.h
```

The following command has the same effect:

```
cc -x c-header -c header.h
```

In either case, the resulting precompiled header is named *header.h.gch*. If there is context dependence (for example, some conditional compilation), the *–Dsymbol* flag is used. In this case, the command to build a precompiled header file (with the *FOO* symbol defined) is:

```
cc -precomp -DFOO header.h -o header.h.gch
```

The *–x* switch supplies the language (see "Supported Languages" in Chapter 11):

```
gcc -x c c-header header.h
```

Then, you can compile *main.c* as usual:

```
gcc -o main main.c
```

Example 12-1 shows *header.h*, and Example 12-2 shows *main.c*.

Example 12-1. The header .h file

```
/* header.h: a trivial header file. */

#define x 100
```

Example 12-2. The main .c application

```
/* main.c: a simple program that includes header.h. */

#include "header.h"
#include <stdio.h>

int main( )
{
  printf("%d\n", x);
  return 0;
}
```

There are a few issues to keep in mind when you use a precompiled header file.

- You can include only one precompiled header file in any given compilation.
- Although you can place preprocessor directives before it, no C tokens can be placed before the #include of the precompiled header. For example, if you switch positions of the two #include directives in Example 12-2, the precompiled header, *header.h.gch*, is ignored by the compiler.

- The language of the precompiled header must match the language of the source in which it is included.
- The precompiled header and the current compilation, in which the precompiled header is being included, must be the same. So, for example, you can't include a procompiled header that was produced by GCC 3.3 in a code being compiled with GCC 4.0.

For more details on building and using precompiled header files, read the documentation stored in */Developer/ADC Reference Library/documentation/DeveloperTools/gcc-4.0.0/ gcc/Preccompiled-Headers.html*.

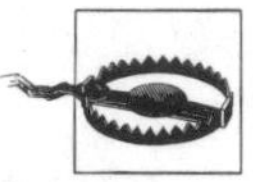

Persistent Front End (PFE) precompilation, needed for C++ and Objective-C++ in pre-Tiger versions of Mac OS X, and *cpp-precomp* are not supported in Tiger.

malloc.h

make may fail to compile some types of Unix software if it cannot find *malloc.h*. Software designed for older Unix systems may expect to find this header file in */usr/include*; however, *malloc.h* is not present in this directory. The set of `malloc()` function prototypes is actually found in *stdlib.h*. For portability, your programs should include *stdlib.h* instead of *malloc.h*. (This is the norm; systems that require *malloc.h* are the rare exception these days.) GNU *autoconf* will detect systems that require *malloc.h* and define the `HAVE_MALLOC_H` macro. If you do not use GNU *autoconf*, you will need to detect this case on your own and set the macro accordingly. You can handle such cases with this code:

```
#include <stdlib.h>
#ifdef HAVE_MALLOC_H
#include <malloc.h>
#endif
```

For a list of libraries that come with Mac OS X, see the "Interesting and Important Libraries" section, later in this chapter.

poll.h

In pre-Tiger versions of Mac OS X, one issue in porting software from a System V platform to a BSD platform such as Mac OS X was the lack of the `poll()` system call function, which provides a mechanism for I/O multiplexing. Panther provided this function through emulation, which made use of its BSD analog `select()`. In Tiger, `poll()` is provided as a native function. The associated header file, */usr/include/poll.h*, is included with Panther as well as Tiger.

wchar.h and iconv.h

Another issue in porting Unix software to pre-Panther versions of Mac OS X was the relatively weak support for wide (i.e., more than 8-bits) character datatypes (e.g., Unicode). Panther and Tiger provide better support for wide character data types by including the GNU *libiconv*, which provides the `iconv( )` function to convert between various text encodings. Additionally, the *wchar_t* type is supported in both Panther and Tiger. The header files *iconv.h* and *wchar.h* are also included. Alternatively, you can use the APIs available in the CoreFoundation's String services, which are described in *CFString.h*.

dlfcn.h

This header file, associated with dl-functions like `dlopen( )`, is included in Tiger. The functions such as `dlopen( )` are actually included in *libSystem*.

alloc.h

Although this header file is not included with Mac OS X, its functionality is provided by *stdlib.h*. If your code makes a specific request to include *alloc.h*, you have several choices. One option is to remove the *#include <alloc.h>* statement in your source code. This may be cumbersome, however, if your include statement appears in many files. Another alternative is to create your own version of *alloc.h*. A sample *alloc.h* is suggested in The Apple Developer Connection's Technical Note TN2071 (*http://developer.apple.com/technotes/tn2002/tn2071.html*).

lcyrpt.h

Although *lcrypt.h* is not included in Mac OS X, its functionality is provided in *unistd.h*.

values.h

The *values.h* file, another header file found on many Unix systems, is not included in Mac OS X. Its functionality, however, is provided by *limits.h*.

The System Library: libSystem

In Darwin, much is built into the system library, */usr/lib/libSystem.dylib*. In particular, the following libraries are included in *libSystem*.

libc

The standard C library. This library contains the functions used by C programmers on all platforms.

libinfo

The NetInfo library.

libkvm

The kernel virtual memory library.

libm

The math library, which contains arithmetic functions.

libpoll

The poll library.

libpthread

The POSIX threads library, which allows multiple tasks to run concurrently within a single program.

librpcsvc

The RPC services library.

libdbm

Database routines.

libdl

The dynamic loader library.

Symbolic links are provided as placeholders for these libraries. For example, *libm.dylib* is a symbolic link in */usr/lib* that points to *libSystem.dylib*. Thus, *-lm* or *–lpthread* do no harm, but are unnecessary. The *-lm* option links to the math library, while *–lpthread* links to the POSIX threads library. Since *libSystem* provides these functions, you don't need to use these options. However, you should use them to make sure your application is portable to other systems. (Since *libm. dylib* and *libpthread.dylib* are symbolic links to *libSystem.dylib*, the extra *-l* options refer to the same library.)

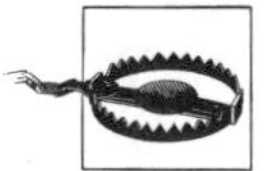

In Mac OS X 10.1 and earlier versions, the *curses* screen library (a set of functions for controlling a terminal display) was part of *libSystem.dylib*. In Mac OS X 10.2, 10.3, and 10.4, the *ncurses* library (*/usr/lib/libncurses.5.4.dylib*) is used in place of *curses*. You may still encounter source code releases that look for curses in *libSystem.dylib*, which results in linking errors. You can work around this problem by adding *-lcurses* to the linker arguments. This is portable to earlier versions of Mac OS X as well, since */usr/lib/libcurses.dylib* is a symlink to *libncurses* in 10.4, 10.3, and 10.2, and to *libSystem* in earlier versions.

Interestingly enough, there is no symbolic link for *libutil*, whose functionality is also provided by *libSystem*. (*libutil* is a library that provides functions related to login, logout, terminal assignment, and logging.) So, if a link fails because of *–lutil*, try taking it out to see if that solves the problem.

libstdc++

In Apple's implementation of GCC prior to GCC 4.0, *libstdc++* was included only as a static library (*libstdc++.a*). In contrast, only the dynamic version of this library, *libstdc++.dyld*, is included in Tiger and Panther (10.3.9). As a consequence, any C++ application compiled with GCC 4.0 won't run on releases of Mac OS X earlier than 10.3.9.

Shared Libraries Versus Loadable Modules

The Executable and Linking Format (ELF), developed by the Unix System Laboratories, is common in the Unix world. On ELF systems, there is no distinction between shared libraries and loadable modules; shared code can be used as a library for dynamic loading. ELF is the default binary format on Linux, Solaris 2.*x*, and SVR4. Since these systems cover a large share of the Unix base, most Unix developers have experience on ELF systems. Thus, it may come as a surprise to experienced Unix developers that shared libraries and loadable modules are not the same on Mac OS X. This is because the binary format used in Mac OS X is *Mach-O*, which is different from ELF.

Mach-O shared libraries have the file type `MH_DYLIB` and the *.dylib* (dynamic library) suffix and can be linked to with static linker flags. So, if you have a shared library named *libcool.dylib*, you can link to this library by specifying the *–lcool* flag. Although shared libraries cannot be loaded dynamically as modules, they can be loaded through the *dyld* API (see the manpage for *dyld*, the dynamic link editor). It is important to point out that shared libraries cannot be unloaded.

Loadable modules, called *bundles* in Mac OS X, have the file type `MH_BUNDLE`. To maintain consistency across platforms, most Unix-based software ports usually produce bundles with a *.so* extension. Although Apple recommends giving bundles a *.bundle* extension, it isn't mandatory.

You need to use special flags with *cc* when compiling a shared library or a bundle on Darwin. One difference between Darwin and many other Unix systems is that no *position-independent code* (PIC) flag is needed, since it is

> **Loading a Bundle**
>
> You cannot link directly against a bundle. Instead, bundles must be dynamically loaded and unloaded by the *dyld* APIs. */usr/lib/libdl.dylib* is provided as a symbolic link to *libSystem.dylib*.
>
> In Panther `dlopen( )`, `dlclose( )`, `dlsym( )`, `dlerror( )` functions were provided interfaces to the dynamic linker using the native *dyld*, `NSModule`, and `NSObjectFileImage` functions. This made porting common Unix source code relatively painless.
>
> In Tiger `dlopen( )`, `dlclose( )`, `dlsym( )`, `dlerror( )` functions are natively part of *dyld*, providing both improved performance and better standards compliance.
>
> Another common porting problem on earlier versions of Mac OS X was the lack of the System V `poll( )` system call function. Panther emulated the `poll( )` function as an interface to the BSD native `select( )` API. In Tiger, `poll( )` is native.

the default for Darwin. Next, since the linker does not allow common symbols, the compiler flag *–fno-common* is required for both shared libraries and bundles. (A common symbol is one that is defined multiple times. You should instead define a symbol once and use C's *extern* keyword to declare it in places where it is needed.)

To build a shared library, use *cc*'s *–dynamiclib* option. Use the *–bundle* option to build a loadable module or bundle.

Building a Shared Library

Suppose you want to create a shared library containing one or more C functions, such as the one shown in Example 12-3.

Example 12-3. A simple C program

```
/*
 * answer.c: The answer to life, the universe, and everything.
 */
int get_answer( )
{
  return 42;
}
```

If you compile the program containing the function into a shared library, you could test it with the program shown in Example 12-4.

Example 12-4. Compiling answer.c into a shared library

```
/*
 * deep_thought.c: Obtain the answer to life, the universe,
 * and everything, and act startled when you actually hear it.
 */
#include <stdio.h>
int main()
{
  int the_answer;
  the_answer = get_answer();
  printf("The answer is... %d\n", the_answer);

  fprintf(stderr, "%d??!!\n", the_answer);
  return 0;
}
```

The *makefile* shown in Example 12-5 compiles and links the library, and then compiles, links, and executes the test program.

Example 12-5. Sample makefile for creating and testing a shared library

```
# Makefile: Create and test a shared library.
#
# Usage: make test
#
CC = cc
LD = cc
CFLAGS = -O -fno-common

all: deep_thought

# Create the shared library.
#
answer.o: answer.c
	$(CC) $(CFLAGS) -c answer.c

libanswer.dylib: answer.o
	$(LD) -dynamiclib  -install_name  libanswer.dylib \
	-o libanswer.dylib answer.o

# Test the shared library with the deep_thought program.
#
deep_thought.o: deep_thought.c
	$(CC) $(CFLAGS) -c deep_thought.c

deep_thought: deep_thought.o libanswer.dylib
	$(LD) -o deep_thought deep_thought.o -L. -lanswer

test: all
	./deep_thought

clean:
	rm -f *.o core deep_thought libanswer.dylib
```

The preceding makefile made use of the *ld* flag *-install_name,* which is the Mach-O analog of *-soname,* used for building shared libraries on ELF systems. The *-install_name* flag is used to specify where the executable, linked against it, should look for the library. The *-install_name* in the makefile shown in Example 12-5 specifies that the *deep_thought* executable is to look for the library *libanswer.dylib* in the same directory as the executable itself. The command *otool* can be used to verify this:

```
$ otool -L deep_thought
deep_thought:
        libanswer.dylib (compatibility version 0.0.0, current version 0.0.0)
        /usr/lib/libmx.A.dylib (compatibility version 1.0.0, current version
92.0.0)
        /usr/lib/libSystem.B.dylib (compaatibility version 1.0.0, current
version
88.0.0)
```

The *-install_name* flag is often used with *@execution_path* to specify a relative pathname of the library. The pathname of the library is relative to the executable. For example, suppose we change the makefile in Example 12-5 by adding an install target:

```
install: libanswer.dylib
    cp libanswer.dylib ../lib/.
```

Then add *install* to the *all* target's dependency list and change the *libanswer* target to the following:

```
libanswer.dylib: answer.o
    $(LD) -dynamiclib -install_name  @execution_path/../lib/libanswer.dylib \
    -o libanswer.dylib answer.o
```

Then the *deep_thought* executable built using this makefile looks for the *libanswer.dylib* in a directory *../lib*. The output from *otool* shows this change:

```
$ otool -L deep_thought
deep_thought:
        @execution_path/../lib/libanswer.dylib (compatibility version 0.0.0,
current version 0.0.0)
        /usr/lib/libmx.A.dylib (compatibility version 1.0.0, current version
92.0.0)
        /usr/lib/libSystem.B.dylib (compatibility version 1.0.0, current
version 88.0.0)
```

The *–install_name* flag is often used with *@execution_path* when building a private framework associated with an application, since private frameworks are located within the application's contents.

Dynamically Loading Libraries

You can turn *answer.o* into a bundle, which can be dynamically loaded using the commands shown in Example 12-6.

Example 12-6. Commands for converting answer.o into a bundle

```
cc -bundle -o libanswer.bundle answer.o
```

You don't need to specify the bundle at link time. Instead, use the *dyld* functions `NSCreateObjectFileImageFromFile` and `NSLinkModule` to load the library. Then, you can use `NSLookupSymbolInModule` and `NSAddressOfSymbol` to access the symbols that the library exports. Example 12-7 loads *libanswer.bundle* and invokes the `get_answer` function. Example 12-7 is similar to Example 12-4, but many lines (shown in bold) have been added.

Example 12-7. Dynamically loading a bundle and invoking a function

```
/*
 * deep_thought_dyld.c: Obtain the answer to life, the universe,
 * and everything, and act startled when you actually hear it.
 */
#include <stdio.h>
#import <mach-o/dyld.h>

int main()
{
  int the_answer;
  int rc;                // Success or failure result value
  NSObjectFileImage img; // Represents the bundle's object file
  NSModule handle;       // Handle to the loaded bundle
  NSSymbol sym;          // Represents a symbol in the bundle

  int (*get_answer) (void);  // Function pointer for get_answer

  /* Get an object file for the bundle. */
  rc = NSCreateObjectFileImageFromFile("libanswer.bundle", &img);
  if (rc != NSObjectFileImageSuccess) {
    fprintf(stderr, "Could not load libanswer.bundle.\n");
    exit(-1);
  }

  /* Get a handle for the bundle. */
  handle = NSLinkModule(img, "libanswer.bundle", FALSE);

  /* Look up the get_answer function. */
  sym = NSLookupSymbolInModule(handle, "_get_answer");
  if (sym == NULL)
  {
    fprintf(stderr, "Could not find symbol: _get_answer.\n");
    exit(-2);
```

Example 12-7. Dynamically loading a bundle and invoking a function (continued)

```
  }

  /* Get the address of the function. */
  get_answer = NSAddressOfSymbol(sym);

  /* Invoke the function and display the answer. */
  the_answer = get_answer( );
  printf("The answer is... %d\n", the_answer);

  fprintf(stderr, "%d??!!\n", the_answer);
  return 0;
}
```

For more information on these functions, see the `NSObjectFileImage`, `NSModule`, and `NSSymbol` manpages. To compile the code in Example 12-7, use the following command:

```
cc -O -fno-common -o deep_thought_dyld deep_thought_dyld.c
```

Two-Level Namespaces

In Mac OS X 10.0, the dynamic linker merged symbols into a single (flat) namespace. So, if you link against two different libraries that both define the same function, the dynamic linker complains because the same symbol was defined in both places. This approach prevented collisions that were known at compile time. However, a lack of conflict at compile time does not guarantee that a future version of the library won't introduce a conflict.

Suppose you linked your application against Version 1 of *libfoo* and Version 1 of *libbar*. At the time you compiled your application, *libfoo* defined a function called `logerror( )`, and *libbar* did not. But when Version 2 of *libbar* came out, it included a function called `logerror( )`. Since the conflict was not known at compile time, your application doesn't expect *libbar* to contain this function. If your application happens to load *libbar* before *libfoo*, it will call *libbar*'s `logerror( )` method, which is not what you want.

So, Mac OS X 10.1 introduced two-level namespaces, which the compiler uses by default. (None of the subsequent releases of Mac OS X, 10.2–10.4, introduced any changes to two-level namespaces.) With this feature, you can link against Version 1 of *libfoo* and *libbar*. The linker creates an application that knows `logerror( )` lives in *libfoo*. So, even if a future version of *libbar* includes a `logerror( )` function, your application will know which `logerror( )` it should use.

If you want to build an application using a flat namespace, use the *–flat_namespace* linker flag. See the *ld* manpage for more details.

Library Versions

Library version numbering is one area where Mac OS X differs from other Unix variants. In particular, the dynamic linker *dyld* checks both major and minor version numbers. Also, the manner in which library names carry the version numbers is different. On ELF systems, shared libraries are named with an extension similar to the following:

```
libname.so.major_version_no.minor_version_no
```

Typically, a symbolic link is created in the library named *libname.so*, which points to the most current version of the library. For example, on an ELF system like Solaris, *libMagick.so.5.0.44* is the name of an actual library. If this is the latest installed version of the library, you can find symbolic links that point to this library in the same directory. These symbolic links are typically created during the installation process.

In this example, both *libMagick.so* and *libMagick.so.5* are symbolic links that point to *libMagick.so.5.0.44*. Older versions of the library may also be present, such as *libMagick.so.5.0.42*. However, although older versions of the library may be present, whenever a newer version is installed, the symbolic links are updated to point to the latest version. This works because when you create a shared library, you need to specify the name of the library to be used when the library is called by a program at runtime.

In general, you should keep older versions of libraries around, just in case an application depends on them. If you are certain there are no dependencies, you can safely remove an older version.

On Mac OS X, the *libMagick* library is named *libMagick.5.0.44.dylib*, and the symbolic links *libMagick.dylib* and *libMagick.5.dylib* point to it. Older versions, such as *libMagick.5.0.42.dylib*, may also be found in the same directory. One difference that is immediately apparent on Mac OS X systems is that the version numbers are placed between the library name and the *.dylib* extension rather than at the end of the filename, as on other Unix systems (e.g., *libMagick.so.5.0.42*).

Another difference on Darwin is that the absolute pathname is specified when the library is installed. Thus, *ldconfig* is not used in Darwin, since paths to linked dynamic shared libraries are included in the executables. On an ELF system, you typically use *ldconfig* or set the `LD_LIBRARY_PATH` variable. In Darwin, use `DYLD_ LIBRARY_PATH` instead of `LD_LIBRARY_PATH` (see the *dyld* manpage for more details).

You can link against a particular version of a library by including the appropriate option for *cc*, such as *-lMagick.5.0.42*. Minor version checking is another way that the Mach-O format differs from ELF. To illustrate this, let's revisit Example 12-4, earlier in this chapter.

Suppose that the library shown in Example 12-4 is continually improved: minor bugs are fixed, minor expanded capabilities are added, and, in time, major new features are introduced. In each of these cases, you'll need to rename the library to reflect the latest version. Assume that the last version of the library is named *libanswer.1.2.5.dylib*. The major version number is *1*, the minor revision is *2*, and the bug-fix (i.e., fully compatible) revision number is *5*. Example 12-8 illustrates how to update this library to release *libanswer.1.2.6.dylib,* which is fully compatible with the release 1.2.5, but contains some bug fixes.

In the *makefile* shown earlier in Example 12-5, replace the following lines:

```
libanswer.dylib: answer.o
        $(LD) -dynamiclib -install_name libanswer.dylib \
        -o libanswer.dylib answer.o
```

with the code shown in Example 12-8.

Example 12-8. Versioning the answer library

```
libanswer.dylib: answer.o
     $(LD) -dynamiclib -install_name libanswer.1.dylib \
           -compatibility_version 1.2 -current_version 1.2.6 \
             -o libanswer.1.2.6.dylib $(OBJS)
      rm -f libanswer.1.dylib  libanswer.1.2.dylib libanswer.dylib
      ln -s libanswer.1.2.6.dylib libanswer.1.2.dylib
      ln -s libanswer.1.2.6.dylib libanswer.1.dylib
      ln -s libanswer.1.2.6.dylib libanswer.dylib'
```

Symbolic links are established to point to the actual library: one link reflects the major revision, one reflects the minor revision, and one simply reflects the name of the library.

The compatibility version number checks that the library used by an executable is compatible with the library that was linked in creating the executable. This is why the phrase *compatibility version* makes sense in this context.

Creating and Linking Static Libraries

The creation of static libraries in Mac OS X is much the same as in Unix variants, with one exception. After installation in the destination directory, *ranlib* must be used to recatalog the newly installed archive libraries (i.e., the *lib*.a* files).

Another issue involving static libraries is the order in which things are listed when libraries are linked. The Darwin link editor loads object files and libraries in the exact order given in the *cc* command. For example, suppose we've created a static archive library named *libmtr.a*. Consider the following attempt to link to this library:

```
$ cc -L. -lmtr -o testlibmtr testlibmtr.o
/usr/bin/ld: Undefined symbols:
_cot
_csc
_sec
```

The rewrite of the command works as follows:

```
$ cc -o testlibmtr testlibmtr.o -L. -lmtr
```

In the first case, the library is placed first and no undefined symbols are encountered, so the library is ignored (there's nothing to be done with it). However, the second attempt is successful, because the object files are placed before the library. For the link editor to realize that it needs to look for undefined symbols (which are defined in the library), it must encounter the object files before the static library.

Creating Frameworks

A shared library can be packaged, along with its associated resources, as a framework. To create a framework you must build and install a shared library in a framework directory. As an example, let's package the *libanswer.dylib* shared library as a versioned framework, using the name *ans*. That is, the framework will be a directory named *ans.framework*, which will contain the shared library file named *ans*. Three basic steps required to build a versioned framework.

1. Create the framework directory hierarchy. If this is the first version of the framework on the system, the bottom level directory will be *A*. This is where the shared library will be installed. If you subsequently install a later version of the shared library, it is installed in directory *B* at the same level of the directory hierarchy as *A*.

   ```
   mkdir -p ans.framework/Versions/A
   ```

2. Build the shared library in the framework Versions directory.

   ```
   cc -dynamiclib -o ans.framework/Versions/A/ans answer.o
   ```

3. Create symbolic links. For the first installation of the shared library (i.e., in *A*), *Current* points to *A*. When a later version of the library is subsequently installed in *B*, the *Current* symbolic link is changed to point to *B*. The older version in *A* can stay on the system in case some application needs the older version. Since the symbolic link *ans.framework/ans*

also points the most recent version of the shared library, it also needs to be updated when the framework is updated.

```
ln -s ans.framework/Versions/A  ans.framework/Versions/Current
ln -s ans.framework/Versions/A/ans  ans.framework/ans
```

The Dynamic Linker dyld: Prebinding, the Pre-Tiger Way

Prior to Mac OS X 10.3.4, whenever you installed an update to the Mac OS X operating system, there was a long phase at the end called *optimization*. What the splash screen called "optimization" was a particular type of optimization, called *prebinding*, which applied only to Mach-O executables. The purpose of prebinding was to speed up launch times of applications.

Launching an Application Built Without Prebinding

Prior to Tiger when an application (or dynamic library) was built without prebinding, *ld* (the static linker) recorded the names of undefined symbols (i.e., the names of symbols that the application must link against). Later, when the application launched, the dynamic linker (*dyld*) had to bind the undefined references from the application to their definitions.

In contrast, if an executable or dynamic library was built with prebinding, the binding essentially occurred at build time. In particular, the library was predefined at a specified address range, a process that otherwise occurred when an application was launched. Rather than mark symbols as undefined, the dynamic linker could use address symbols in a prebound library to reference other application or dynamic library links against it. Additionally, if the prebound library depended on other libraries (a common situation), then the static linker recorded the timestamps of the other libraries. Later, when the prebound library was used, the dynamic linker checked the timestamps of the dependent libraries and checked for the existence of overlapping executable addresses.

If the timestamps didn't match those of the build timestamps, or if there were overlapping executable addresses, the prebinding was broken and normal binding was performed.

Tiger's dyld Renders Prebinding Unnecessary

The trouble with prebinding is that it slows installation time. For Mac OS X 10.3.4, *dyld* was overhauled to improve performance and to better support standards. In Tiger additional improvements were made to *dyld* so that prebinding of applications was made unnecessary. In Tiger, unprebound applications launch as fast as prebound applications. Prebinding in Tiger is deprecated.

Some New Features of dyld

Here are a few of *dyld*'s new features, introduced in Tiger:

- *dyld* runs all initializers as early as possible. Among other things, initializers and statically-linked libraries are run before `main()`.
- *dyld* runs all terminators in reverse order relative to the order in which the corresponding initializers were run. Prior to Tiger, multiple terminators in a linkage unit were run incorrectly, specifically, in the same order as the corresponding initializers.
- `dlopen()`, along with related functions, are now integrated into *dyld*. Panther supported these functions through emulation, while pre-Panther versions of Mac OS X lacked support for these functions altogether.

For more details on *dyld*, see its manpage and */Developer/ADC Reference Library/releasenotes/DeveloperTools/dyld.html*.

Performance Tools and Debugging Tools

The developer tools that ship with Tiger include an impressive array of debugging and tuning tools. These tools are extensively documented at */Developer/ADC Reference Library/documentation/Performance/Conceptual/PerformanceOverview/index.html*. This site includes a more complete list of tools and offers examples to demonstrate the use of these tools. The following short list is intended to give you an idea of what is available.

gdb
: The GNU debugger.

MallocDebug
: Analyzes memory usage.

ObjectAlloc
: Analyzes both memory allocation and deallocation.

heap
: Analyzes memory usage.

leaks
: Lists the addresses and sizes of unreferenced malloc buffers.

malloc_history
: Lists the malloc allocation history of a given process.

vm_stat
: Lists virtual memory statistics.

vmmap
: Displays a virtual memory map in a process, including the attributes of memory regions such as starting addresses, sizes, and permissions.

OpenGL Profiler
: Profiles OpenGL-based applications.

QuartzDebug
: A debugging tool related to the Quartz graphics system.

Sampler
: Performs a statistical analysis of where an application spends its time by providing information such as how often allocation routines, system calls, or other functions are called.

Shark
: Provides instruction-level profiling of execution time of a program, using statistical sampling. Advice on optimization is also provided. (A command-line version, */usr/bin/shark*, is also provided.)

Spin Control
: Monitors programs that become unresponsive and cause the spinning curser.

Activity Monitor
: GUI application, located in */Applications/Utilities*, that displays information on memory and CPU usage for running processes. This application is similar to the command line utility, *top*, which is also included with Tiger.

BigTop
: GUI application, similar to both top and vm_stat, that displays information on memory, CPU, network, and disk usage for running processes.

Thread Viewer
: Profiles individual threads in multithreaded applications.

gprof
: Profiles execution of programs by reporting information such as execution times, and the number of calls for individual functions.

fs_usage
: Displays information on filesystem activity.

sc_usage
: Displays information on system calls and page faults.

otool
: A command-line utility used to display information associated with object files or libraries. Earlier, we used it with the *–L* option, which displays the names and version numbers of the shared libraries used by the given object file. For more details see the *otool* manpage.

top
: Reports dynamically updated statistics on memory and CPU usage for running processes.

c2ph
: Displays information on C-structures in object files.

kdump
: Displays kernel race data.

atos
: Converts to and from symbol names and numeric address of symbols in running programs.

mn
: Displays symbol table for object files.

pagestuff
: Displays information about the logical pages of a Mach-O executable file.

pstruct
: Same as c2ph.

sample
: A command-line tool used to profile a process over a time interval.

CHUD Tools

In addition to the tools listed in the previous section, a set of performance and optimization tools, bundled as the Computer Hardware Understanding Development Tools (CHUD), is available as an option installation with Xcode. You can also download the latest version from *ftp://ftp.apple.com/developer/Tool_Chest/Testing__Debugging/Performance_tools/*.

CHUD tools are used to configure and display the performance monitor counters provided on Apple systems. These performance monitors record events such as cache misses, page faults, and other performance issues. The list provides information on a few of the tools provided with the CHUD collection. For more details see *http://developer.apple.com/tools/performance/*.

MONster
: Provides hardware-related performance measurements and displays the results in a spreadsheet format. (A command-line version, */usr/bin/monster*, is also provided.)

Saturn
: Provides exact (as opposed to statistical) profiling at the function level. For example, it reports how many times a given function is called. Results are represented in graphical format.

CacheBasher
: Analyzes cache performance.

Reggie SE
: Analyzes and modifies CPU and PCI configuration registers.

Skidmarks GT
: Measures processor performance, specifically, integer, floating-point, and vector performance.

amber
: Command-line tool for instruction-level trace of execution threads.

acid
: Command-line tool used to analyze traces provided by Amber.

SimG5
: Command-line tool that simulates the G5 processor. You can use this cycle-accurate simulator to run through a trace file generated by Amber.

SimG4
: Command-line tool that simulates the G4 processor. You can use this cycle-accurate simulator to run through a trace file generated by Amber.

A CHUD framework (*/System/Library/PrivateFrameworks/CHUD.framework*) that enables you to write your own performance tools (among other things) is also provided.

Interesting and Important Libraries

Table 12-1 lists some significant libraries included with Mac OS X, while Table 12-2 lists some significant libraries that *do not* come with Mac OS X—but may be available through Fink (Chapter 13) or DarwinPorts (Chapter 14).

Table 12-1. Important Mac OS X libraries

Library	Description	Headers
libalias	A packet aliasing library for masquerading and network address translation	Not included in Mac OS X; see the *network_cmds* module in the Darwin CVS archive
libBSDPClient	BSDP client library	Not included in Mac OS X
libBSDPServer	BSDP server library	Not included in Mac OS X
libl.a	The *lex* runtime library	Not applicable; lexical analyzers that you generate with *lex* have all the necessary definitions
libMallocDebug	A library for the *MallocDebug* utility (*/Developer/ Applications*)	Not applicable; you don't need to do anything special with your code to use this utility
libSaturn	A library for the *Saturn* utility (*/Developer/ Applications*)	*Saturn.h*
libamber	A library for the *amber* utility	*amber.h*
libbsm	Basic security library	*/usr/include/bsm/libbsm.h*
libedit	Replacement for readline library. *libreadline* is provided as a symbolic link to *llbedlt.*	*histedit.h*
libxslt	XSLT C library, based on the libxml2 XML C developed for the GNOME project	*/usr/include/lib/xslt/xslt.h*
libexslt	Provides extensions to XSLT functions	*/usr/include/lib/exslt/exslt.h*
libfl	Font library	Not included in Mac OS X
libform	Forms library	*form.h*
Libncurses (*libcurses* is available for backward compatibility.)	The new *curses* screen library, a set of functions for controlling a terminal's display screen	*/usr/include/ncurses.h* (*curses.h* is available for backward compatibility)
libicucore	International Components for Unicode library	Not included in Mac OS X
libiodbc, libiodbcinst,	Intrinsic Open Database Connectivity library	*iodbcext.h, iodbcinst.h, iodbcunix.h*
libipsec	IPsec library	*/usr/include/netinet6/ipsec.h*
liblber	lber library	*lber.h*
libltdl	GNU ltdl system independent dlopen wrapper for GNU libtool	*ltdl.h*
libmenu	Menus library	*menu.h*
libmx	Math library with support for long double and complex APIs	*math.h*
libobjc	The library for the GNU Objective-C compiler	*/usr/include/objc/**
libpcap	Packet capture library	*/usr/include/pcap**

Table 12-1. Important Mac OS X libraries (continued)

Library	Description	Headers
libssl and *libcrypto*	An open source toolkit implementing Secure Sockets Layer (SSL) Versions 2 and 3, Transport Layer Security (TLS) Version 1 protocols and a full-strength, general-purpose cryptography library	*/usr/include/openssl/**
libtcl	The Tcl runtime library	*/usr/include/tcl.h*
liby.a	The *yacc* runtime library	Not applicable; parsers that you generate with *yacc* have all the necessary definitions
libz	A general-purpose data-compression library (*Zlib*)	*zlib.h*
libbz2	Compression of files	*bzlib.h*
libpoll	System V *poll(2)* poll library	*poll.h*
libiconv	Character set conversion library	*iconv.h*
libcharset	Character set determination library	*libcharset.h*
libcups	Common Unix Printing System (CUPS)	Not available
libcurl	Command-line tool for file transfer	*/usr/include/curl/**
libgimpprint	Print plug-in, Ghostscript and CUPS driver	Not available
libncurses	Free software emulation of System V *curses*	*ncurses.h*, which is a symbolic link to *curses.h*
libpam	Interface library for the Pluggable Authentication Module (PAM)	*/usr/include/pam/**
libpanel	Panel stack extension for *curses*	*panel.h*
libxml2	XML parsing library, Version 2	*/usr/include/libxml2/**
libruby	Interpreted object-oriented scripting language	*/usr/lib/ruby/1.6/powerpc-darwin7.0/**
libtcl	Tcl scripting language	*tcl.h*
libtk	Graphical companion to Tcl	*tk.h*
libwrap	TCP wrappers; monitors and filters incoming requests for TCP-based services	*tcpd.h*
freetype2	TrueType font rendering library, Version 2	*/usr/X11R6/include/freetype2/**

Table 12-2. Libraries not included with Mac OS X

Fink package	Description	Home page
aalib	ASCII art library	*http://aa-project.sourceforge.net/aalib*
db3	Berkeley DB embedded database	*http://www.sleepycat.com/*
db4	Berkeley DB embedded database	*http://www.sleepycat.com/*

Table 12-2. Libraries not included with Mac OS X (continued)

Fink package	Description	Home page
dtdparser	Java DTD Parser	*http://www.wutka.com/dtdparser.html*
expat	C library for parsing XML	*http://expat.sf.net*
fnlib	Font rendering library for X11	*http://www.enlightenment.org/*
freetype	TrueType font rendering library, Version 1	*http://www.freetype.org/*
gc	General-purpose garbage collection library	*http://www.hpl.hp.com/personal/Hans_Boehm/gc/*
gd	Graphics generation library	*http://www.boutell.com/gd/*
gdal	Translator for raster geospatial data formats	*http://www.remotesensing.org/gdal/*
gdbm	GNU dbm	*http://www.gnu.org*
giflib	GIF image format handling library, LZW-enabled version	*http://prtr-13.ucsc.edu/~badger/software/libungif/*
glib	Low-level library that supports GTK+ and GNOME	*http://www.gtk.org/*
gmp	GNU multiple precision arithmetic library	*http://www.swox.com/gmp/*
gnomelibs	GNOME libraries	*http://www.gnome.org*
gnujaxp	Basic XML processing in Java	*http://www.gnu.org/software/classpathx/jaxp*
gtk	GTK+, the GIMP widget toolkit used by GNOME	*http://www.gtk.org/*
hermes	Optimized pixel format conversion library	*http://www.canlib.org/hermes/*
imlib	General image handling library	*http://www.enlightenment.org/pages/imlib2.html*
libdivxdecore	OpenDivX codec	*http://www.projectmayo.com/projects/detail.php?projectId=4*
libdnet	Networking library	*http://libdnet.sourceforge.net/*
libdockapp	Library that eases the creation of WindowMaker Dock applets	*ftp://shadowmere.student.utwente.nl/pub/WindowMaker/*
libdv	Software decoder for DV format video	*http://www.sourceforge.net/projects/libdv/*
libfame	Fast assembly MPEG encoding library	*http://fame.sourceforge.net/*
libghttp	HTTP client library	*http://www.gnome.org/*
libjconv	Japanese code conversion library	*http://www.kondara.org/libjconv/index.html.en*
libjpeg	JPEG image format handling library	*http://www.ijg.org/*
libmpeg	GIMP MPEG library	*http://www.gimp.org*
libmusicbrainz	Client library for the MusicBrainz CD Index	*http://www.musicbrainz.org*
libnasl	Nessus Attack Scripting Language	*http://www.nessus.org/*

Table 12-2. Libraries not included with Mac OS X (continued)

Fink package	Description	Home page
libnessus	Libraries package for Nessus without SSL support	*http://www.nessus.org/*
libole2	Library for the OLE2 compound file format	*http://www.gnome.org/*
libproplist	Routines for string list handling	*http://www.windowmaker.org/*
libshout	Library for streaming to icecast	*http://developer.icecast.org/libshout/*
libsigc++	Callback system for widget libraries	*http://developer.icecast.org/libshout/*
libstroke	Translates mouse strokes to program commands	*http://www.etla.net/libstroke/*
libtiff	TIFF image format library	*http://www.libtiff.org/*
libungif	GIF image format handling library, LZW-free version	*http://prtr-13.ucsc.edu/~badger/software/ libungif/index.shtml*
libunicode	Low-level Unicode processing library	*http://www.sourceforge.net/projects/libunicode/*
libwww	General-purpose Web API written in C for Unix and Windows	*http://www.w3c.org/Library/Distribution.html*
libxml	XML parsing library	*http://www.gnome.org/*
libxml++	C++ interface to the *libxml2* XML parsing library	*http://sourceforge.net/projects/libxmlplusplus/*
libxpg4	Locale-enabling preload library	*http://www.darwinfo.org/devlist.php3?number=9143*
log4j	Library that helps the programmer output log statements to a variety of output targets	*http://jakarta.apache.org/log4j*
lzo	Real-time data compression library	*http://www.oberhumer.com/opensource/lzo*
neon	HTTP/WebDAV client library with a C API	*http://www.webdav.org/neon/*
netpbm	Graphics manipulation programs and libraries	*http://netpbm.sourceforge.net*
pcre	Perl Compatible Regular Expressions library	*http://www.pcre.org*
pdflib	A library for generating PDFs	*http://www.pdflib.com/pdflib*
pil	The Python Imaging Library; adds image-processing capabilities to Python	*http://www.pythonware/products/pil*
pilot-link	Palm libraries	*http://www.pilot-link.org/*
popt	Library for parsing command-line options	*http://www.gnu.org/directory/popt.html*
pth	Portable library that provides scheduling	*http://www.gnu.org/software/pth/pth.html*
readline	Terminal input library	*http://cnswww.cns.cwru.edu/~chet/readline/ rltop.html*

Table 12-2. Libraries not included with Mac OS X (continued)

Fink package	Description	Home page
slang	Embeddable extension language and console I/O library	*http://space.mit.edu/~davis/slang/*
stlport	ANSI C++ standard library implementation	*http://www.stlport.org/*

The list of available libraries is ever-growing, thanks to an influx of open source ports from FreeBSD and Linux. One of the best ways to keep on top of the latest ports is to install Fink or DarwinPorts (see Chapters 13 and 14, respectively), which lets you install precompiled versions of libraries and applications or install them from source.

Numerical Libraries

Tiger ships with an impressive array of resources used for numerical computing. In addition to support for 64-bit computing, including 64-bit pointers for passing large arrays, and the optimized and extended mathematical libraries, *libm* and *libmx*, many numerical libraries are packaged within the Accelerate umbrella framework. The Accelerate umbrella framework includes libraries shipped with Mac OS X that have been optimized for high performance computing, including a several subframeworks, listed below. The Accelerate framework is located in */System/Library/Frameworks/Accelerate.framework*, and its libraries have been optimized to take advantage of the G5 and the Velocity engine.

vecLib
: Subframework of the Accelerate framework. Includes BLAS, LAPACK, vDSP, vMathLib, vBasicOps, vBigNum, and vForce. It is located in */System/Library/Frameworks/vecLib.framework* (see *http://developer.apple.com/hardware/ve*).

BLAS
: Complete and optimized set (levels 1, 2, and 3) of the basic linear algebra subprograms. (See *http://www.netlib.org/blas/faq.html*.)

LAPACK
: Linear algebra package, written on top of the BLAS library. (See *http://www.netlib.org/lapack/index.html*.) Lapack is designed to run efficiently having most of the actual computations performed by optimized BLAS routines.

vDSP
: Digital signal processing. (See *http://developer.apple.com/hardware/ve/downloads/vDSP.sit.hqx*.)

vBasicOps
: A set of basic arithmetic operations. (See */System/Library/Frameworks/vecLib.framework/Versions/Current/Headers/vBasicOps.h*.)

vBigNum
: A set of basic arithmetic operations on large (128-bit) integers. (See */System/Library/Frameworks/vecLib.framework/Versions/Current/Headers/vBigNum.h*.)

vMathLib
: A set of basic vectorized transcendental functions, optimized for the Velocity engine. (See *http://developer.apple.com/hardware/ve*.)

vForce
: A set of highly optimized elementary functions on many operands. (See */System/Library/Frameworks/vecLib.framework/Versions/Current/Headers/vForce.h*.)

vImage
: Subframework of the Accelerate framework. A set of highly optimized image processing filters. (See */System/Library/Frameworks/vImage.framework/Versions/Current/Headers/vImage.h*.)

To compile code using a subframework of Accelerate you must include the header file with the following line of code.

```
#include <Accelerate/Accelerate.h>
```

For example, you can compile a program named *prog.c*, which makes use of the vecLib framework, as follows.

```
$ gcc -faltivec -framework Accelerate prog.c
```

PART III

Working with Packages

There are a good number of packaging options for software that you compile, as well as software you obtain from third parties. This part of the book covers software packaging on Mac OS X.

Chapters in this part of the book include:

CHAPTER 13

Fink

Fink is essentially a port of the Debian Advanced Package Tool (APT), with some frontends and its own centralized collection site, which stores packaged binaries, source code, and patches needed to build software on Mac OS X. The Fink package manager allows you to install a package, choosing whether to install it from source or a binary package. Consistent with Debian, binary package files are in the *dpkg* format with a *.deb* extension and are managed with the ported Debian tools *dpkg* and *apt-get*.

Fink also provides tools that create a *.deb* package from source. It maintains a database of installed software that identifies packages by the combination of name, version, and revision. Moreover, Fink understands dependencies, uses *rsync* to propagate software updates, supports uninstallation, and makes it easy to see available packages and installed packages. Fink can be used to install over a thousand Unix packages which are freely available and will run on Mac OS X. Fink recognizes and supports Apple's X11 implementation for running X windows applications, but you can also use Fink to install XFree86 if you prefer.

Fink installs itself and all of its packages, with the exception of Xfree86, in a directory named */sw*, thus completely separating it from the main */usr* system directory. If problems occur with Fink-installed packages, you can simply delete the entire */sw* directory tree without affecting your system.

Installing Fink

You can install Fink from binary, from a source tarball, or from source in CVS.

Installing Fink from a Disk Image

The binary installation involves the following steps:

1. Download the binary installer disk image (a *.dmg* file) from *http://fink.sourceforge.net/download*.
2. The disk image should mount automatically and show up in the Finder's Sidebar. If the disk image does not mount after it has downloaded, locate and double-click the *.dmg* file to mount the disk image.
3. Open the mounted disk image and double-click the Fink Installer package inside. At the time of this writing, the name of the Installer package was *Fink 0.7.1 Installer.pkg*.
4. Follow the instructions on the screen.
5. As Fink installs, it will launch the Terminal application and check to see whether you have a *.profile* file in your Home directory. If you don't, Fink will ask you if you want it to create one and add the . */sw/bin/init.sh* line to it. At the prompt, type in a Y and hit Return to create this file. After *.profile* is created, Fink automatically logs you out of the Terminal session; you will need to close the Terminal window with ⌘-W.

After Fink has completed its installation, unmount the disk image and drag the *.dmg* file to the Trash.

The disk image also includes FinkCommander, a graphical frontend to using Fink. For more information, see the "FinkCommander" section, later in this chapter.

Installing Fink from Source

To install the latest release of Fink from source, perform the following steps:

1. Open *http://fink.sourceforge.net/download/srcdist.php* in your browser. After you select the link for the tarball, you must choose a mirror site from which to download the tarball. If your web browser downloads this file to your Desktop, move it to a working directory, such as */tmp*:

```
$ mv ~/Desktop/fink-0.7.1-full.tar.gz /tmp/
```

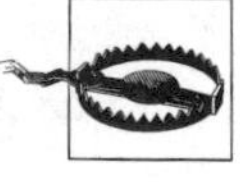

If your browser automatically turned StuffIt loose on it, you may be left with a tar file and a directory. If this is the case, you will have to `mv` the *fink-0.7.1-full.tar* instead of the *.gz* file.

2. Extract the archive:

```
$ gnutar xzf fink-0.7.1-full.tar.gz
```

3. Change into the top-level directory and run the *bootstrap* script:

```
$ cd fink-0.7.1-full
$ ./bootstrap.sh
```

4. Follow the instructions on the screen.

Installing Fink from CVS

You can also install the latest version source of Fink via CVS:

1. Change to a temporary directory (not containing a subdirectory named *fink*). Log into the Fink CVS server. When prompted for a password press, press Return to enter an empty password:

```
$ cd /tmp
$ cvs -d :pserver:anonymous@cvs.sourceforge.net:/cvsroot/fink login
```

2. Download the package descriptions:

```
$ cvs -d :pserver:anonymous@cvs.sourceforge.net:/cvsroot/fink \
  co fink
```

3. Change to the *fink* subdirectory and run the bootstrap script to install and configure Fink:

```
$ cd fink
$ ./bootstrap.sh
```

4. Follow the instructions on the screen.

Fink must be installed and run with superuser privileges whenever you use it to install, uninstall, or update packages. Whether you install and configure Fink from the downloaded tarball or from CVS, the *bootstrap.sh* script will prompt you to configure Fink to be run with *sudo*, *su*, or *root*. If you choose the default *sudo*, you won't have to invoke *fink* explicitly with *sudo*. Instead, you'll automatically be prompted for your administrative password.

Post-Installation Setup

When you install Fink, it should configure your shell initialization files to call either */sw/bin/init.sh* (*sh*, *bash*, and similar shells) or */sw/bin/init.csh* (*csh* or *tcsh*). If not, or if you need to configure Fink for another user, open a Terminal window and run the command */sw/bin/pathsetup.command*. When that's finished, you should close the Terminal window and open a new one to begin using Fink.

Fink can later be updated by entering the commands:

```
fink selfupdate
fink update-all
```

The first command updates Fink itself, including the list and descriptions of available packages, while the second command updates any installed packages. The first time you run *selfupdate*, Fink will prompt you to choose whether to use *rsync* (faster, less bandwidth), CVS, or to "Stick to point releases":

```
$ fink selfupdate
sudo /sw/bin/fink  selfupdate
Password: ********
fink needs you to choose a SelfUpdateMethod.

(1)      rsync
(2)      cvs
(3)      Stick to point releases

Choose an update method [1] 1
I will now run the rsync command to retrieve the latest package
descriptions.
```

The last option means that you'll stay away from the bleeding edge: Fink will be more stable, but you may not get the latest and greatest versions of applications. You can change the *selfupdate* method to CVS by using the command *fink selfupdate-cvs*. You can switch back to using *rsync* with *fink selfupdate-rsync*.

Using Fink

Once Fink has been installed, you can see what packages are available by entering the command *fink list*. You can install a package from source with the following command:

```
$ fink install package
```

The *fink* command is used from the command line to maintain, install, and uninstall packages from source. Table 13-1 lists some examples of its usage.

Table 13-1. Various fink commands

Command	Description
fink apropos foo	Lists packages matching the search keyword, *foo*.
fink build foo	Downloads and builds package *foo*. No installation is performed.
fink checksums	Verifies the integrity of source tarballs.
fink configure	Rerun the configuration process.
fink describe foo	Describes package *foo*.
fink fetch foo	Downloads package *foo*, but doesn't install it.
fink fetch-all	Downloads source files for all available packages.

Table 13-1. Various fink commands (continued)

Command	Description
fink fetch-missing	Like *fetch-all*, but fetches only source code that's not already present.
fink index	Forces a rebuild of the package cache.
fink install foo	Downloads source, then builds and installs package *foo*.
fink list	Lists available packages. "i" is placed next to installed packages. Takes many options. For example, *fink list -i* lists only installed packages. Execute *fink list -help* for a complete set of options.
fink purge foo	Same as *remove* but also removes all configuration files. Use *apt-get remove* instead.
fink rebuild foo	Downloads and rebuilds package *foo*. Installation is performed.
fink reinstall foo	Reinstalls *foo* using *dpkg*.
fink remove foo	Deletes package *foo*, ignoring dependencies. Use *apt-get remove* instead.
fink selfupdate	Updates Fink along with package list. Uses latest officially released fink source. Do this first unless you're updating via CVS.
fink selfupdate-cvs	Updates Fink along with the package list using CVS.
fink selfupdate-rsync	Updates Fink, along with the package list, using *rsync*.
fink update foo	Updates package *foo*.
fink update-all	Updates all installed packages.

FinkCommander

The FinkCommander application provides a graphical user interface for Fink's commands. FinkCommander is distributed with Fink on the Fink installer disk image, but you can also download it directly from the FinkCommander site (*http://finkcommander.sourceforge.net*).

To install FinkCommander, simply drag and drop the application from the disk image into your */Applications* folder (or */Applications/Utilities*, depending on what your preferences are).

You can use FinkCommander's search field, located in the upper-right of the main window, to find packages you are interested in. By default, the menu to the left of the search field is set to search package names. However, you can set it to something else (Description, Category, Maintainer, or Status) before you search. You can also select Binary, Stable, or Unstable to search only binary packages, only packages in the stable branch, or only packages in the unstable branch. Figure 13-1 shows the main window of FinkCommander with a search in progress for packages whose description includes "game."

To install a package with FinkCommander, select it in the main window and select Binary → Install to install a binary package, or Source → Install to

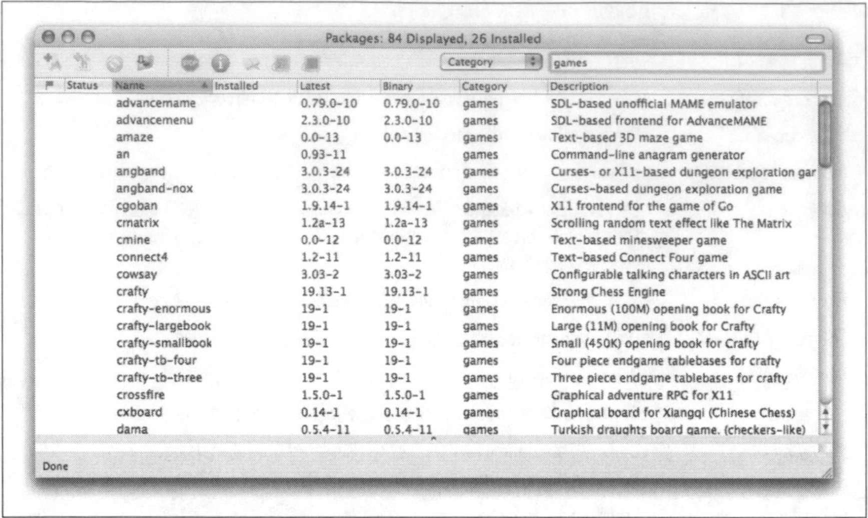

Packages: 84 Displayed, 26 Installed
Category
games
Status Name Installed Latest Binary Category Description
advancemame 0.79.0-10 0.79.0-10 games SDL-based unofficial MAME emulator
advancemenu 2.3.0-10 2.3.0-10 games SDL-based frontend for AdvanceMAME
amaze 0.0-13 0.0-13 games Text-based 3D maze game
an 0.93-11 games Command-line anagram generator
angband 3.0.3-24 3.0.3-24 games Curses- or X11-based dungeon exploration gar
angband-nox 3.0.3-24 3.0.3-24 games Curses-based dungeon exploration game
cgoban 1.9.14-1 1.9.14-1 games X11 frontend for the game of Go
cmatrix 1.2a-13 1.2a-13 games Scrolling random text effect like The Matrix
cmine 0.0-12 0.0-12 games Text-based minesweeper game
connect4 1.2-11 1.2-11 games Text-based Connect Four game
cowsay 3.03-2 3.03-2 games Configurable talking characters in ASCII art
crafty 19.13-1 19.13-1 games Strong Chess Engine
crafty-enormous 19-1 19-1 games Enormous (100M) opening book for Crafty
crafty-largebook 19-1 19-1 games Large (11M) opening book for Crafty
crafty-smallbook 19-1 19-1 games Small (450K) opening book for Crafty
crafty-tb-four 19-1 19-1 games Four piece endgame tablebases for crafty
crafty-tb-three 19-1 19-1 games Three piece endgame tablebases for crafty
crossfire 1.5.0-1 1.5.0-1 games Graphical adventure RPG for X11
cxboard 0.14-1 0.14-1 games Graphical board for Xiangqi (Chinese Chess)
dama 0.5.4-11 0.5.4-11 games Turkish draughts board game. (checkers-like)
Done

Figure 13-1. Searching for packages with FinkCommander

install that package from source. You can remove a package by selecting it in the list and clicking Source → Remove or Binary → Remove.

FinkCommander also lets you run its commands in a Terminal window so you can interact directly with it. Use Source → Run in Terminal → *Command* or Binary → Run in Terminal → *Command* to run the selected command in a new Terminal window, as shown in Figure 13-2.

Installing Binaries

You can download and install binaries via *dselect* (shown in Figure 13-3), a console-based frontend to *dpkg*. To use *dselect*, you must have superuser (or administrator) privileges, so you'll need to run *sudo dselect* in the Terminal. Once *dselect* has started, you can use the following options to maintain, install, and uninstall packages:

[A]ccess
: Chooses the access method to use. Configures the network access method to use.

[U]pdate
: Downloads the list of available packages from the Fink site. This option is equivalent to running *apt-get update*. Table 13-2 lists the *apt-get* and *dpkg* command-line options.

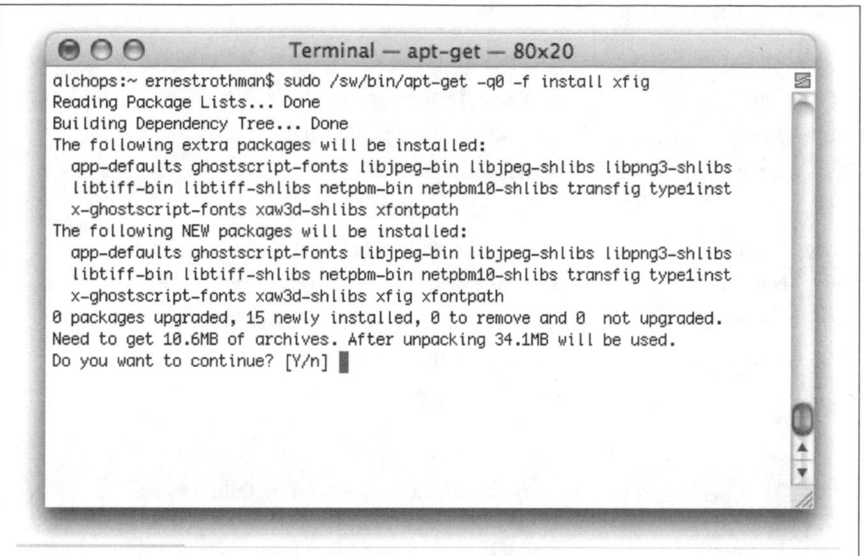

Terminal — apt-get — 80x20
alchops:~ ernestrothman$ sudo /sw/bin/apt-get -q0 -f install xfig
Reading Package Lists... Done
Building Dependency Tree... Done
The following extra packages will be installed:
app-defaults ghostscript-fonts libjpeg-bin libjpeg-shlibs libpng3-shlibs
libtiff-bin libtiff-shlibs netpbm-bin netpbm10-shlibs transfig type1inst
x-ghostscript-fonts xaw3d-shlibs xfontpath
The following NEW packages will be installed:
app-defaults ghostscript-fonts libjpeg-bin libjpeg-shlibs libpng3-shlibs
libtiff-bin libtiff-shlibs netpbm-bin netpbm10-shlibs transfig type1inst
x-ghostscript-fonts xaw3d-shlibs xfig xfontpath
0 packages upgraded, 15 newly installed, 0 to remove and 0 not upgraded.
Need to get 10.6MB of archives. After unpacking 34.1MB will be used.
Do you want to continue? [Y/n]

Figure 13-2. Running the install command in a Terminal window

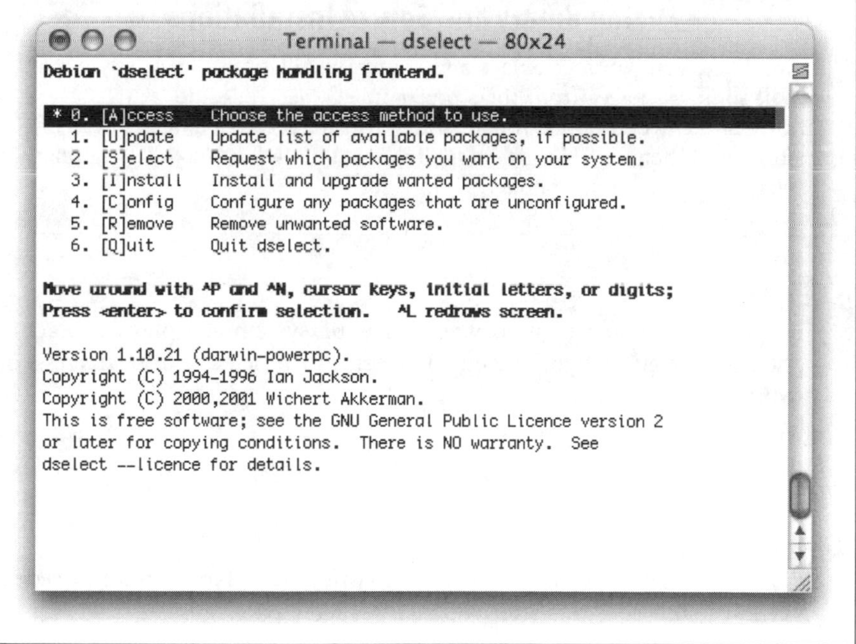

Terminal — dselect — 80x24
Debian `dselect' package handling frontend.
* 0. [A]ccess Choose the access method to use.
1. [U]pdate Update list of available packages, if possible.
2. [S]elect Request which packages you want on your system.
3. [I]nstall Install and upgrade wanted packages.
4. [C]onfig Configure any packages that are unconfigured.
5. [R]emove Remove unwanted software.
6. [Q]uit Quit dselect.
Move around with ^P and ^N, cursor keys, initial letters, or digits;
Press <enter> to confirm selection. ^L redraws screen.
Version 1.10.21 (darwin-powerpc).
Copyright (C) 1994-1996 Ian Jackson.
Copyright (C) 2000,2001 Wichert Akkerman.
This is free software; see the GNU General Public Licence version 2
or later for copying conditions. There is NO warranty. See
dselect --licence for details.

Figure 13-3. The dselect program's main menu

Table 13-2. Some apt-get and dpkg commands

Command	Description
apt-get update	Updates list of available packages. Do this first.
apt-get install foo	Downloads and installs package *foo*.
apt-get remove foo	Deletes package *foo*.
dpkg --list	Lists all installed packages.
dpkg --listfiles foo	Lists all the files from package *foo*.
dpkg --install foo	Installs package *foo*.
dpkg --remove foo	Deletes package *foo*. Leaves configuration files.
dpkg --purge foo	Deletes *foo* and configuration files.
dpkg -S /path/to/file	Tells you which package owns a file.

You must run *[U]pdate* at least once after installing Fink.

Mixing Binary and Source Installations

Using Fink, you can mix binary and source installations. That is, you can install some packages from their precompiled *.deb* files and install others from source. If you do this, you must first use *apt-get* to update the available binaries and then use *fink selfupdate*, followed by *fink update-all*, to update packages installed from source.

[S]elect
: Requests the packages you want on your system. Displays the actual package listing, which is used to select and deselect the packages you want on your system.

[I]nstall
: Installs, upgrades, and configures selected packages. Also removes deselected packages.

[C]onfig
: Configures any packages that are unconfigured. Not actually needed, since [I]nstall does this after you've installed a package.

[R]emove
: Removes unwanted software. Not actually needed, since [I]nstall will do this.

[Q]uit
: Quits *dselect*.

CHAPTER 14
DarwinPorts

The DarwinPorts project (*http://darwinports.opendarwin.org/*), started in 2002 and led by Landon Fuller, Felix Kronlage, Jordan Hubbard, and Kevin Van Vechten, has created a package management system similar to Fink and the FreeBSD ports collection (*http://www.freebsd.org*). It automates the installation of open source Unix- and Aqua-based software on Mac OS X. It is written primarily in Tcl (which is bundled with Mac OS X).

The DP-COCOA project (*http://www.opendarwin.org/projects/dp-cocoa/*), led by Dr. Ernest Prabhakar, provides a Cocoa-based framework for manipulating DarwinPorts. At the time of this writing, there is another graphical user interface called DarwinPorts Manager, which is under active development by the DarwinPorts team.

DarwinPorts provides a way to both install and remove packages from its collection, as well as track package dependencies. This means that if you attempt to install package A, and that package depends on package B, DarwinPorts finds and installs package B first and then goes back to install package A. Similarly, if you attempt to uninstall package B while you have installed another package that depends on package B, DarwinPorts warns you about this dependency and gives you the option to remove other packages that depend on the one you're attempting to remove.

DarwinPorts installs Unix-based packages in */opt/local* by default, ensuring that your Mac OS X-installed system files in */usr* won't be affected. DarwinPorts also allows you to build several Aqua-based applications from source, which are installed in */Applications/DarwinPorts*. Additionally, required libraries are installed in */Library/Tcl/darwinports1.0* (assuming Mac OS X Tiger), and the DarwinPorts infrastructure and descriptions of ported applications reside in a selected user's home directory (for example, *~/darwinports*). If problems occur with DarwinPorts-installed packages, you can delete the entire */opt/local* directory tree without affecting your system. In this case you should also delete the */private/etc/ports* and */Library/Tcl/darwinports1.0* directories to completely remove DarwinPorts.

As you'll see later, you can install either a stable point release of DarwinPorts or a bleeding-edge development version from CVS repository. When you build and install a package with DarwinPorts, it builds the package(s) from source in a special workspace directory called *work*, which you'll find either within the */opt/local/var/db/ports* directory if you've installed a stable point release of DarwinPorts, or in *~/darwinports/dports* directory, if you've installed DarwinPorts from the CVS repository. For example, if you install the *bvi* editor using a point release of DarwinPorts, it is first built in */opt/local/var/db/ports/sources/rsync.rsync.opendarwin.org.dpupdate_dports/editors/bvi/work*. If, on the other hand, you're working with a CVS-development version of DarwinPorts, *bvi* will be built in *~/darwinports/dports/editors/bvi/work*. When you install *bvi*, it is installed in both the *destroot* subdirectory of the *work* directory and in */opt/local* (or whatever you may have defined for *$prefix*) via */usr/bin/install*. A receipt is made for the installation and placed in the */opt/local/var/db/dports/receipts* directory.

As an alternative to installation via */usr/bin/install*, DarwinPorts can produce a *.pkg* (or *.mpkg* to include dependencies) package that can be subsequently installed via the Mac OS X Installer. It can also create an Internet-enabled disk image (*.dmg*) containing a package installer; as well as create packages in the Red Hat Package Manager (RPM) format.

According to the DarwinPorts web site, a GUI-based UnInstaller application is under development. Design of this UnInstaller application will reportedly include the ability to uninstall packages installed by DarwinPorts.

Installing DarwinPorts

You'll find detailed documentation, written by Michael A. Maibaum, on the installation and use of DarwinPorts on the DarwinPorts web site. Although the DarwinPorts site should be checked for the most up-to-date information, a brief description of its installation and usage is provided here.

Before installing DarwinPorts, you must install the Xcode Tools, which as noted in Chapter 7, can be installed from the Mac OS X Install DVD, or downloaded from the Apple Developer Connection web site at *http://developer.apple.com*. Alternatively, on a new Mac, the Xcode Tools installer can be installed from */Applications/Installers/Developer Tools/*. You also need to install X11, which is an optional installation when you install Mac OS X, and the X11 SDK, which is included with Xcode. Installation of DarwinPorts is built around the Concurrent Versioning System (CVS), which is installed with Xcode.

Possible Conflicts Between DarwinPorts and Fink

DarwinPorts and Fink can co-exist on the same system, but if you've already installed Fink (say, in its default location */sw*), there is a chance that the configuration phase (described later) will identify the Fink-installed version of the required software.

For example, if you've installed Tcl/Tk with Fink, DarwinPorts may use the version of Tcl in */sw*, rather than the Mac OS X–bundled Tcl in */usr/bin*. If this happens and you later decide to remove Fink, you'll mess up your DarwinPorts installation.

To avoid this potential problem, you should temporarily remove */sw/bin* from your path (or, if you've added it to your *.bashrc* file, comment out the line `./sw/bin/init.sh`).

To install DarwinPorts, you should be logged in as an administrative user. In the following discussion, assume you're logged in as the administrative user *`ernestrothman`*.

You can install the latest point-release of DarwinPorts either from source or using a binary installer. To install DarwinPorts using the binary installer, download the *.dmg* file from the DarwinPorts web site to your Desktop, double-click this file to mount the disk image, and double-click the *.mpkg* installer in the disk image to install DarwinPorts.

To install DarwinPorts from source, log into Mac OS X as an administrative user and download either the source tarball from the DarwinPorts web site into your home directory.

For example, to install *DarwinPorts-1.0*, enter the following commands:

```
cd
curl
http://darwinports.opendarwin.org/downloads/DarwinPorts-1.0.tar.gz
```

Installing DarwinPorts from CVS

To download DarwinPorts and establish its infrastructure on your system, perform the following steps:

1. Change to your home directory. Log into the OpenDarwin CVS server. When prompted for a password, press Return to supply a blank password:

   ```
   $ cd
   $ cvs -d
   :pserver:anonymous@anoncvs.opendarwin.org:/Volumes/src/cvs/od
   login
   ```

2. Download the package descriptions and DarwinPorts infrastructure:

   ```
   $ cvs -d
   :pserver:anonymous@anoncvs.opendarwin.org:/Volumes/src/cvs/od \
   co -P darwinports
   ```

The directory *~/darwinports/dports* contains the port description files (also known as *Portfiles*), and must be kept even after you've installed DarwinPorts. The location of *dports* is specified in the file */etc/ports/sources.conf*. If you move the *dports* directory, you must change the line *file://~/darwinports/dports* in *dports* to specify the new location.

As an alternative to downloading the DarwinPorts files via the CVS commands above, you can download a nightly tarball (*http://darwinports.opendarwin.org/darwinports-nightly-cvs-snapshot.tar.gz*). To install DarwinPorts from the tarball, download and unpack it in your home directory. This creates the *~/darwinports* directory. You can then proceed as outlined below.

After downloading DarwinPorts, you're now ready to build and install it on your system:

1. Change to the *~/darwinports/base* directory, which is known as the DarwinPorts infrastructure:

   ```
   $ cd darwinports/base
   ```

2. Perform the *configure*, *make*, and *make install* sequence:

   ```
   $ ./configure
   $ make
   $ sudo make install
   ```

   These commands build and install necessary files in */opt/local*, */private/etc/ports*, and */Library/Tcl/darwinports1.0*.

No matter how you installed DarwinPorts, */opt/local/etc/ports/ports/conf* is created with a line pointing to a *dports* directory. If you've installed the latest point release of DarwinPorts, the *dports* directory is specified by */rsync://rsync.opendarwin.org/dpupdate/dports*. If you've installed a CVS-development version of DarwinPorts, a local *dports* directory will be specified as */opt/local/var/db/dports*.

The local *dports* directory contains the ported software descriptions and related *Portfiles*, which are Tcl scripts needed to build and install the ported software. According to documentation on the DarwinPorts site, the *sources.conf* file is used to list the locations of both local and remote port software hierarchies.

Since DarwinPorts software is installed in */opt/local*, you should add */opt/local/bin* to your path. Once you have performed these steps, you'll have a working installation of DarwinPorts. If you want DarwinPorts software to install software in a directory other than */opt/local*, you can edit the file */opt/local/etc/ports/ports.conf* and change the value of prefix from */opt/local* to the directory in which you want packages installed. As an alternative, you could run the *configure* command used in the build of DarwinPorts with the *--prefix* option.

Using DarwinPorts

Once DarwinPorts has been installed, you can see what packages are available with the *port list* command. Since the list is quite long, you may want to pipe this command through the *more* command.

You can also use the *port* command to search for specific packages. For example, the command *port search pine* returns a listing for the *pine* package; the command *port search kde* lists several packages, namely all available packages that contain the string *kde*.

You can install a package from source with the command *sudo port install package*. This command actually performs several steps prior to installing the package on your system. These steps include checking dependencies, downloading the necessary source code including source of dependencies, verifying checksums, configuring packages, building and installing any other required packages, and building the requested package in an intermediate directory called a *destroot*. After these steps have been performed the requested package is installed into an "image repository" directory and "activated." Activation of a port creates hard links to the files in the image repository directory. The port command must be used with *sudo* whenever the directory */opt/local* or */Applications/DarwinPorts* is modified.

For example if you installed *pine-4.58* using the *sudo port install pine* command, *pine* and all its related files are installed into the image repository */opt/local/var/db/dports/software/pine/4.58_1/opt/local/bin*, and then activated through the creation of hard links in the *${prefix}* directory */opt/local/bin*.

The image repository can be revealed via the *port location pine* command. You can subsequently deactivate *pine* by issuing the command *sudo port deactivate pine*, which deletes the hard links in */opt/local/bin* while leaving the *pine* installation in the image repository intact. You can later reactivate *pine* with the *sudo port activate pine* command. The chief advantage of this approach, called *Port Images*, is that it allows you to install multiple versions of a package. With Port Images, you won't need to uninstall one version of a package to make room for another. Instead, you can deactivate one version and activate another version.

This is particularly helpful when you want to test a new version of the software without uninstalling and then reinstalling the older version if you're not happy with the new version.

As mentioned earlier, DarwinPorts automatically checks package dependencies and installs any other required packages. Similarly, if you deactivate a package, you are warned if the package you are deactivating is needed by another installed package.

To uninstall a particular port, use the *port uninstall* command. For example, to uninstall *pine*, enter the command:

```
sudo port uninstall pine
```

To update a particular port, you can enter the following command:

```
sudo port upgrade foo
```

If a new version of *foo* is available, this command will deactivate the currently installed foo port, and install and activate the newer version. This command will also update all of *foo*'s dependencies. If you want to remove the older version of *foo* at the same time, you should enter the following command:

```
sudo port -u upgrade foo
```

You can update all installed ports with the following command:

```
sudo port -a upgrade
```

Creating and Installing Packages in pkg Format

Using DarwinPorts, you can create a *.pkg* package installer using the *port* command with the *package* option, For example, to create a *.pkg* installer for *bvi*, enter the command:

```
port package bvi
```

This downloads the source for *bvi*, builds the application, and creates a double-clickable package installer, named *bvi-1.3.1.pkg*. This package is saved in *~/darwinports/dports/editors/bvi/work*. It's worth noting that this command only creates the package; it does not install the package. To install it (in */opt/local/*), double-click *bvi-1.3.1.pkg* in the Finder, authenticate yourself as an administrative user, and install the package on your system as you would with any other package. When you install a package in this manner, the DarwinPorts database won't list it among its installed packages. For example, if you issue the *port installed* command, this package won't show up in the list. If you enter the command *port clean bvi*, the installer *bvi-1.3.1.pkg* is deleted.

Creating and Installing Packages in RPM Format

If you are planning to create packages in RPM format, the first thing you should do is to install *rpm* (via the *sudo port install rpm* command). Once you have installed *rpm*, you can create RPM packages using the *port* command with the *rpmpackage* option. For example, to create an RPM for *pine*, enter the following command:

```
sudo port rpmpackage pine
```

This command creates the RPM file in *${prefix}/src/apple/RPMS/${arch}*, which in most cases is */opt/local/src/apple/RPMS/ppc*. You can safely use the *sudo port clean pine* command after the RPM is created, since the *port clean* command won't remove the *.rpm* installer.

Before installing RPM packages, however, you need to create */etc/mnttab*, which is the file that keeps track of which RPM packages have been installed. This can be done with:

```
touch /etc/mnttab
```

A summary of the use of the *port* command is provided in Table 14-1.

Table 14-1. Various port commands

Command	Description
`port search` *foo*	Lists packages matching the search keyword, *foo*.
`sudo port install` *foo*	Downloads, builds, and installs package *foo*.
`port destroot` *foo*	Downloads, builds, and installs *foo* into an intermediate destination root, called a "destroot." This is useful for developing and testing new ports.
`sudo port uninstall` *foo*	Deletes package *foo*.
`port installed`	Lists all the installed packages.
`port clean` *foo*	Deletes intermediate files after installation of package *foo*.
`port contents` *foo*	Lists all files installed with package *foo*.
`port deps` *foo*	Lists package *foo*'s dependencies.
`port variants` *foo*	Lists variants of package *foo*.
`port package` *foo*	Build *.pkg* package installer for *foo*. Does not install *foo*.
`port list`	Lists available packages.
`port dmg` *foo*	Build an internet-enabled disk image containing a Mac OS X *.pkg* package installer for *foo*. Does not install *foo*.
`port rpmpackage` *foo*	Build an RPM package for *foo*. Does not install *foo*.
`sudo port activate` *foo*	Activates *foo*. If multiple versions of *foo* are installed, use `port activate` *foo version*.
`sudo port deactivate` *foo*	Activates *foo*. If multiple versions of *foo* are installed, use `port activate` *foo version*.
`port location` *foo*	Displays the location of the image directory in which *foo* is installed.
`port outdated` *foo*	Determine if your installed port *foo* is outdated.
`port outdated`	List all of your outdated ports.
`sudo port upgrade` *foo*	Update *foo* along with its dependencies, while deactivating the currently install *foo*.
`sudo port selfupdate`	Updates DarwinPorts installation, including the infrastructure and the Portfiles.

DarwinPorts Maintenance

How you update your DarwinPorts installation is dependent on how you installed it. If you've installed a stable point release of DarwinPorts, all you need to do is to enter the following command:

```
sudo port selfupdate
```

If, on the other hand, you're working with CVS-development releases of DarwinPorts, and you've maintained your *~/darwinports* directory, you can update your DarwinPorts installation in two steps. The first step is to update the DarwinPorts infrastructure, while the second step is to update your collection of Portfiles, which contain instructions for building ports.

To update your DarwinPorts infrastructure in *~/darwinports*, change to the *~/darwinports/base* directory and enter the following commands:

```
$ cvs -z3 update -dP
$ ./configure
$ make clean && make
$ sudo make install
```

This sequence of commands updates your port command and associated libraries.

To update your Portfiles, change to the *~/darwinports/dports* directory and enter the command:

```
$ cvs -z3 update -dP
```

After this command has completed its work, you should enter the command to build the index of available ports:

```
$ portindex
```

Installing Binaries

The DarwinPorts project provides pre-built binary packages in *.pkg* format that are for use with the Mac OS X Installer. To make use of one of these binary packages, you must first download its installer. Select Go → Connect to Server from the Finder's menu bar, and enter *http://packages.opendarwin.org* to mount the (remote) DarwinPorts binary packages folder as a WebDAV volume on your Desktop. The packages are organized on the WebDAV volume in folders corresponding to the same DarwinPorts categories that you can see at *http://darwinports.opendarwin.org/ports*. To install a binary package, download its *pkg* installer by dragging it to your Desktop, and, once it has been downloaded, double-click the *pkg* file to install.

DPGUI

A Tcl/Tk-based graphical user interface suite of applications, DPGUI is provided by Kevin Walzer and Lori Jareo of WordTech Software (*http://www.wordtech-software.com*). The DPGUI suite consists of two applications,

PortBase and PortView. PortBase, shown in Figure 14-1, is used to install DarwinPorts, update the DarwinPorts infrastructure, and add new or updated port descriptions. The PortView application, shown in Figure 14-2, allows you to manage the installation, updating, and removal of DarwinPorts software ports.

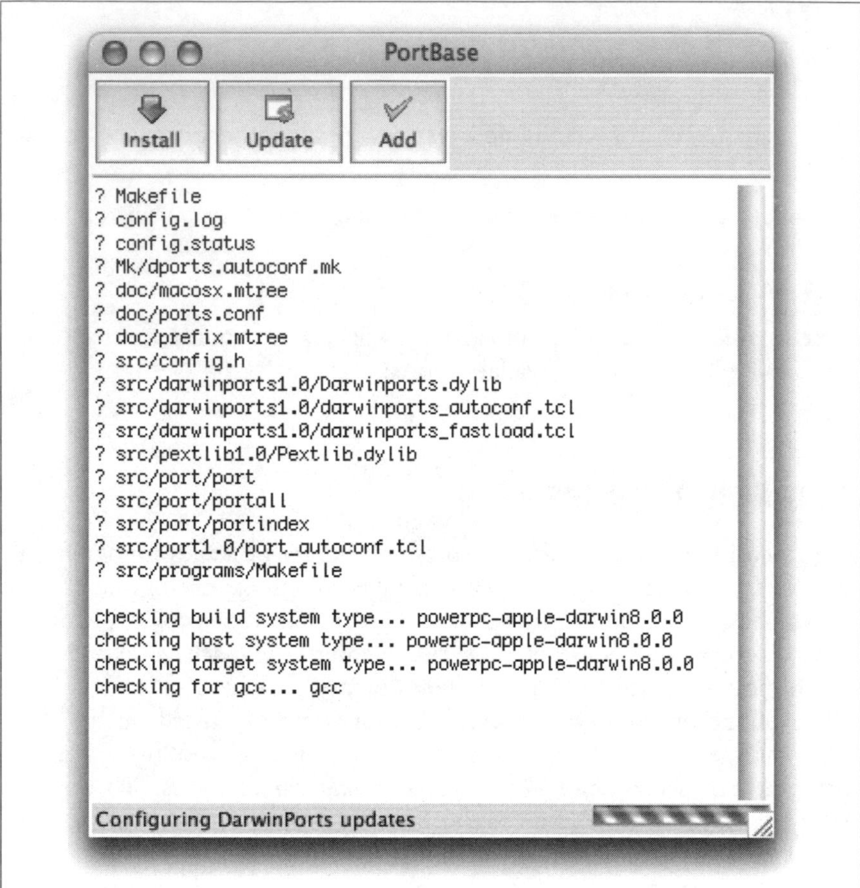

Figure 14-1. PortBase

You can download the DPGUI suite at *http://www.wordtech-software.com/dpgui.html*.

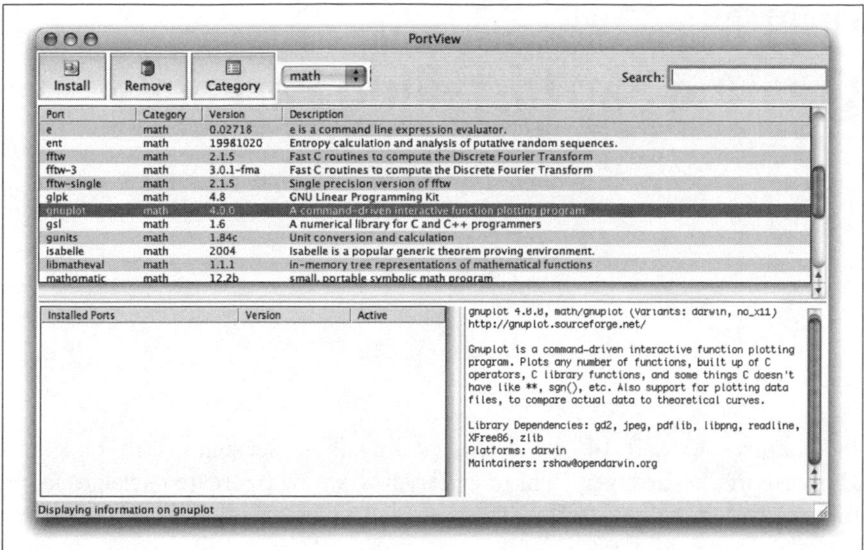

PortView
Install
Remove
Category
math
Search:
Port | Category | Version | Description
e | math | 0.02718 | e is a command line expression evaluator.
ent | math | 19981020 | Entropy calculation and analysis of putative random sequences.
fftw | math | 2.1.5 | Fast C routines to compute the Discrete Fourier Transform
fftw-3 | math | 3.0.1-fma | Fast C routines to compute the Discrete Fourier Transform
fftw-single | math | 2.1.5 | Single precision version of fftw
glpk | math | 4.8 | GNU Linear Programming Kit
gnuplot | math | 4.0.0 | A command-driven interactive function plotting program
gsl | math | 1.6 | A numerical library for C and C++ programmers
gunits | math | 1.84c | Unit conversion and calculation
isabelle | math | 2004 | Isabelle is a popular generic theorem proving environment.
libmatheval | math | 1.1.1 | in-memory tree representations of mathematical functions
mathomatic | math | 12.2b | small, portable symbolic math program
Installed Ports | Version | Active
gnuplot 4.0.0, math/gnuplot (Variants: darwin, no_x11)
http://gnuplot.sourceforge.net/
Gnuplot is a command-driven interactive function plotting program. Plots any number of functions, built up of C operators, C library functions, and some things C doesn't have like **, sgn(), etc. Also support for plotting data files, to compare actual data to theoretical curves.
Library Dependencies: gd2, jpeg, pdflib, libpng, readline, XFree86, zlib
Platforms: darwin
Maintainers: rshaw@opendarwin.org
Displaying information on gnuplot

Figure 14-2. PortView

CHAPTER 15

Creating and Installing Packages

In Chapters 13 and 14, we discussed installing packages with Fink and DarwinPorts, respectively. This chapter shows how to create packages using tools provided with Mac OS X Tiger, as well as with Fink and DarwinPorts.

The following packaging options are supported on Mac OS X by default:

PackageMaker
: Found in */Developer/Applications/Utilities*, PackageMaker can be used to create packages (*.pkg*), which are bundles consisting of all the items that the Mac OS X Installer (*/Applications/Utilities*) needs to perform an installation. PackageMaker can also create metapackages (*.mpkg*), which can be used to install multiple packages at the same time, and distributions, which specify an entire customized installation process involving one or more packages.

  When a metapackage is installed, a "receipt" is placed in the */Library/Receipts* folder. These receipts are named with a *.pkg* extension and appear in the Finder as packages, even though they are not. You cannot use these files to install or update software. Instead, they are used to maintain a record of which packages have been installed on your system. This is how, for example, System Update knows not to install a package (or to update a package) that you've already installed.

gnutar and gzip
: The Unix tape archive tool *gnutar* is used to bundle the directories and resources for distribution. (The *tar* command is provided as a hard link to *gnutar*.) GNU Zip (*gzip*) is used to compress the tar archives to make file sizes as small as possible. Using these tools is generally the simplest way to copy a collection of files from one machine to another.

Mac OS X Tiger supports archiving files and directories in the *.zip* format directly from the Finder by Control-clicking on a file or directory and selecting "Create Archive of ..." from the contextual menu.

Disk Utility
: One of the easiest ways to distribute an application is to use the Disk Utility (*/Applications/Utilities*) to create a disk image. You can use the Disk Utility to create a double-clickable archive, which mounts as a disk image on the user's computer. From there, the user can choose to mount the disk image each time the application is run, copy the application to the hard drive (usually to */Applications*), or burn the image to a CD. Disk Utility has a command-line counterpart, *hdiutil*, which we'll cover in the later section, "Creating a Disk Image from the Command Line."

Each of these tools are discussed separately in the following sections.

Using PackageMaker

Apple's native format for packaging and distributing software is PackageMaker. Packages created with PackageMaker have a *.pkg* extension. When a user double-clicks on a package, the Installer application (*/Applications/Utilities*) is invoked and the installation process begins. These packages are bundles that contain all of the items Installer needs.

You can also use PackageMaker to create *metapackages* for installing multiple packages. Metapackages, or *bundles*, contain meta-information, files, and libraries associated with a given application. Packages can also contain multiple versions of an application; for example, both Mac OS X and Classic versions.

PackageMaker documentation is available in Help Viewer, which is accessible from PackageMaker's Help option in the menu bar.

The basic components of a package are:

- A bill of materials (*.bom*) binary file describing the contents of the package. You can view the contents of a bill of materials with the *lsbom* command. After a package is installed, you can find a copy of this file in */Library/Receipts/packagename/*`Contents/Archive.bom`.
- An information file (*.info*) containing the information entered in the GUI application PackageMaker when the package was created.

- An archive file (*.pax*) containing the complete set of files to be installed by the package (similar to a *tar* archive). The file may be compressed, and have a *.gz* extension.
- A size calculation file (*.sizes*) listing the sizes of the compressed and uncompressed software.
- Resources that the installer uses during the installation, such as *README* files, license agreements, and pre- and post-install scripts. These resources are typically not installed; instead, they are used only during the installation process.

Setting up the Directory

To demonstrate how to create a package, we'll create a short C program and its associated manpage. Example 15-1 shows *hellow.c*, and Example 15-2 shows its manpage, *hellow.1*.

Example 15-1. The Hello, World sample program

```
/*
 * hellow.c - Prints a friendly greeting.
 */

#include <stdio.h>

int main()
{
  printf("Hello, world!\n");
  return 0;
}
```

Example 15-2. The manpage for hellow.c

```
.\" Copyright (c) 2005, O'Reilly Media, Inc.
.\"
.Dd April 15, 2002
.Dt HELLOW 1
.Os Mac OS X
.Sh NAME
.Nm hellow
.Nd Greeting generator
.Sh DESCRIPTION
This command prints a friendly greeting.
```

PackageMaker expects you to set up the files using a directory structure that mirrors your intended installation. So, if you plan to install *hellow* into */usr/bin*, and *hellow.1* into */usr/share/man/man1*, you must create the appropriate subdirectories under your working directory. However, you can use a makefile to create and populate those subdirectories, so to begin with, your *hellow* directory looks like this:

```
$ find hellow
hellow
hellow/hellow.1
hellow/hellow.c
hellow/Makefile
```

Suppose that your *hellow* project resides in *~/src/hellow*. To keep things organized, you can create a subdirectory called *stage* that contains the installation directory. In that case, you'd place the *hellow* binary in *~/src/hellow/stage/bin* and the *hellow.1* manpage in *~/src/hellow/stage/share/man/man1*. The makefile shown in Example 15-3 compiles *hellow.c*, creates the *stage* directory and its subdirectories, and copies the distribution files into those directories when you run the command *make prep*.

Example 15-3. Makefile for hellow

```
hellow:
        cc -o hellow hellow.c

prep: hellow
        mkdir -p -m 755 stage/bin
        mkdir -p -m 755 stage/share/man/man1
        cp hellow stage/bin/
        cp hellow.1 stage/share/man/man1/
```

To get started, you need only *hellow.c*, *hellow.1*, and *Makefile*. When you run the command *make prep*, it compiles the program and copies the files to the appropriate locations in the *stage* directory. After running *make prep*, the *hellow* directory will look like this:

```
$ find hellow
hellow
hellow/hellow
hellow/hellow.1
hellow/hellow.c
hellow/Makefile
hellow/stage
hellow/stage/bin
hellow/stage/bin/hellow
hellow/stage/share
hellow/stage/share/man
hellow/stage/share/man/man1
hellow/stage/share/man/man1/hellow.1
```

The next step is to launch PackageMaker and bundle up the application.

Creating the Package

When you run PackageMaker, you must select one of the following three types of projects.

Single Package Project
: Used to create a package installer for a single package, which can be used as a standalone installer for the package or embedded in a metapackage or distribution.

Metapackage Project
: Used to create a single installer for several packages. Pre-made single packages can be embedded in a metapackage.

Distribution Project
: Used to create a single installer for several packages. This option, which can be used to highly customize the entire installation process, is supported only on Mac OS X 10.4 and higher. Pre-made packages can be added as installation choices by dragging them onto "distribution choices."

Since in the current example a single package is being created, you should choose Single Package Project, and set the options as appropriate for your package. Figures 15-1 through 15-6 show the settings for the *hellow* sample. The options are as follows:

Installer Interface tab
: Contains items that describe the package so the person installing the package can find its name and description (see Figure 15-1):

    Title
    : The title or name of the package.

    Description
    : A description of the package.

    Show Installer Interface Editor
    : Used to customize the installer interface's background image, Introduction blurb, Read Me, and License. This is shown in Figure 15-2.

Contents tab
: Contains information related to file locations and compression (see Figure 15-3):

    Root
    : This option indicates where PackageMaker can find the top-level staging directory.

    Compress Archive
    : You should leave this option enabled, since it makes the package smaller.

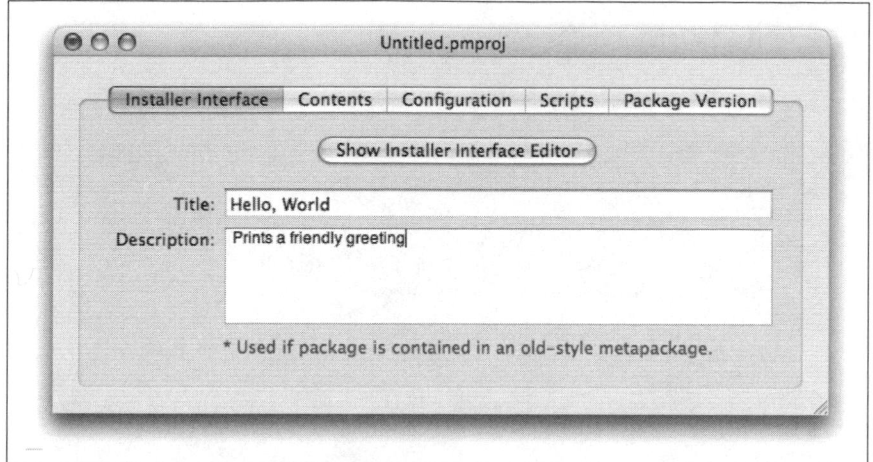

Figure 15-1. PackageMaker's Installer Interface tab.

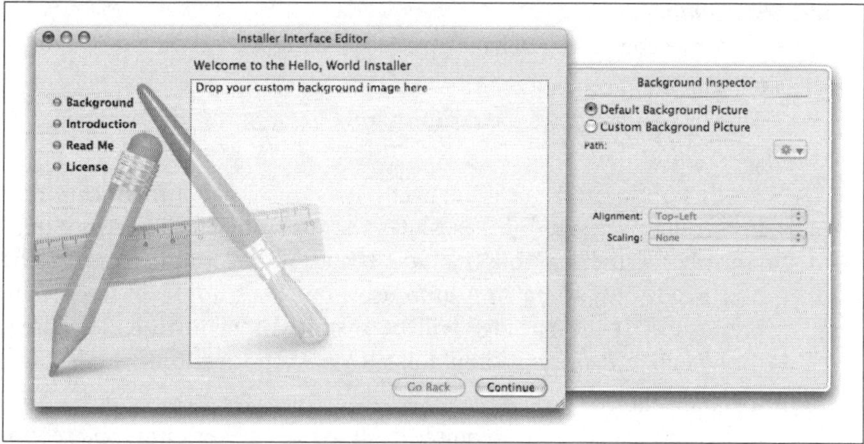

Figure 15-2. PackageMaker's Installer Interface Editor

Remove .DS_Store Files from Archives
: A *.DS_Store* file stores the information used to control how a folder is viewed in the Finder, for example, list or icon view, size of icons, etc.

Preserve Resource Forks
: Traditionally, Mac files consisted of two parts, a data fork and a resource fork. The data fork contains data, while the resource fork contains programming information. For more information about resource forks, see *http://developer.apple.com/documentation/MacOSX/Conceptual/SystemOverview/FileSystem/chapter_8_section_5.html*.

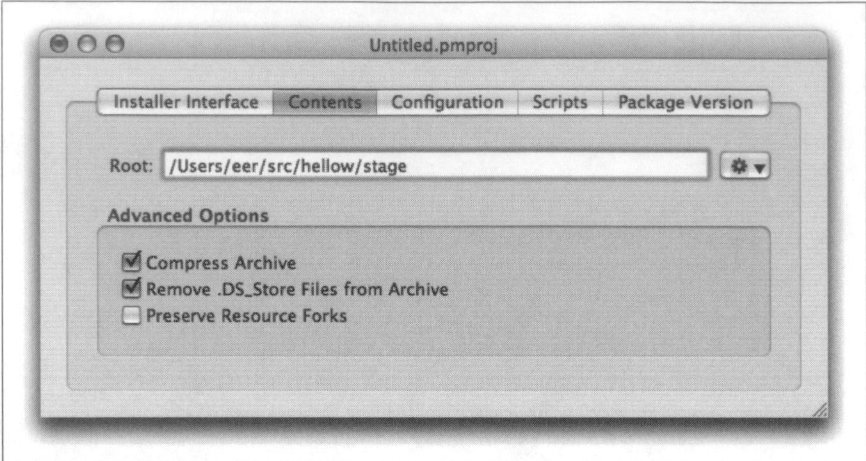

Figure 15-3. PackageMaker's Contents tab

Configuration tab

Specifies miscellaneous package options (see Figure 15-4):

Default Location

This option indicates the default target location for the package.

Authentication

Set this option to Root if the user needs to supply authentication to install the package. (This escalates the user's privileges to *root* temporarily.) Other options include None and Administrator (if the user needs only to be an Admin user, but does not need to escalate privileges). If the package will be installed into a protected directory (such as */usr*), you should use Root Authorization.

Post-Install Action

If this option is set to Required Restart, the system must be rebooted when the installation is finished. Other options include None, Recommended Restart, Required Logout, and Required Shutdown.

Relocatable

This option allows the user to choose an alternate location for the installed files.

Root Volume Only

This option requires that the user install the package on the current root volume (the volume from which Mac OS X was booted).

Follow Symbolic Links

This option causes symbolic links to be followed rather than replaced with actual directories. Prior to Xcode 2.0 and Tiger, PackageMaker's default behavior was not to follow symbolic links, and since there was no interface option to control the handling of symbolic links, it was necessary to edit the Info.plist for a package and set the value for `IFPkgFlagFollowLinks` to Yes.

Overwrite Directory Permissions
: If the installer overwrites an existing file or directory, this option causes it to change the permissions to match what PackageMaker found in the staging area.

Install Fat Binaries
: This option supports multiple architecture binaries.

Allow Revert To Previous Version
: This option allows the user to install an older version of the package over a newer one.

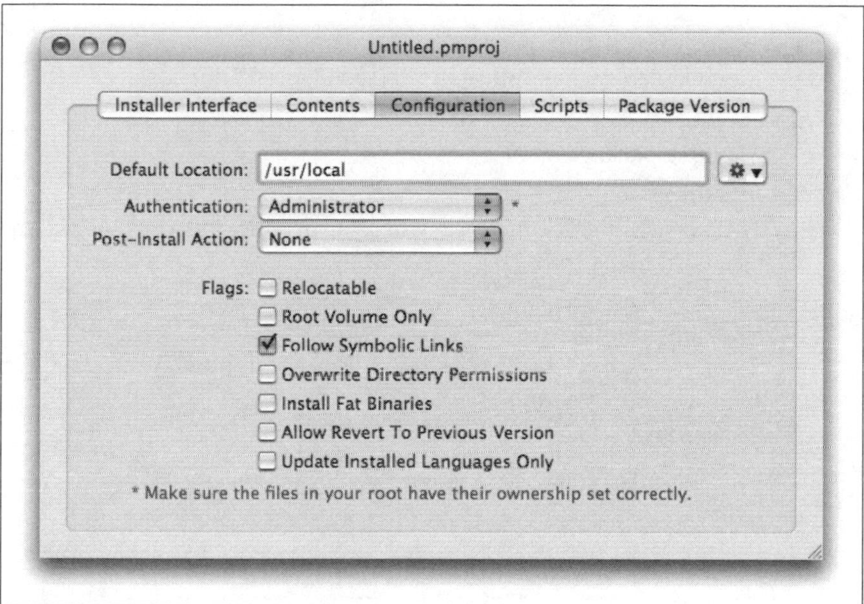

Figure 15-4. PackageMaker's Configuration tab

Scripts tab
: Specifies the location of extra resources (Figure 15-5):

  Extras
  : The optional Extras directory contains scripts and other resources such as *README* files, that are used by the installer but aren't specified in the Installer Interface Editor. See PackageMaker's help for details.

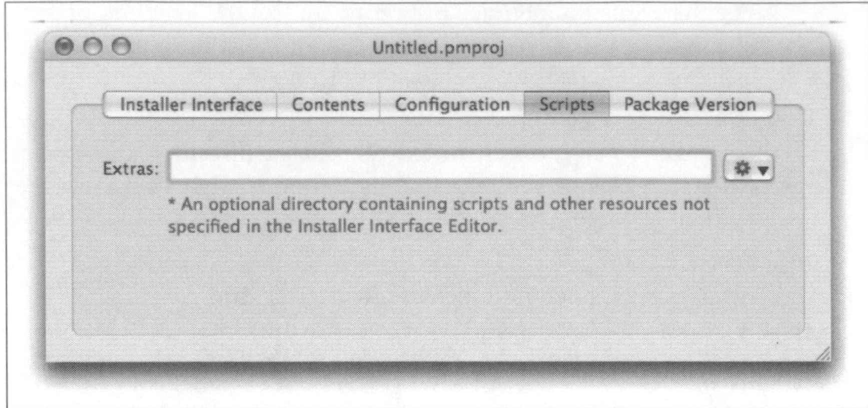

Figure 15-5. PackageMaker's Scripts tab

PackageVersion tab
: Specifies detailed version information (see Figure 15-6):

  Identifier
  : A unique package name.

  Get-Info string
  : The version number to use when inspecting the package in the Finder with Get Info.

  Version:
  : A version number.

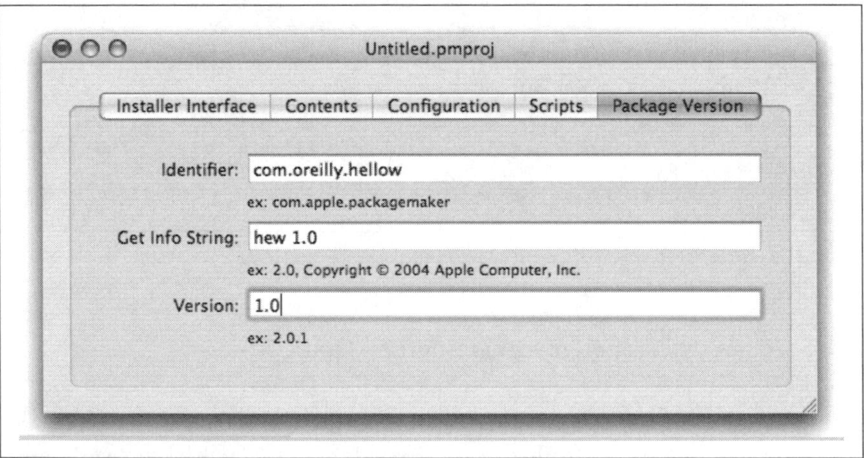

Figure 15-6. PackageMaker's Package Version tab

After you have filled in the package settings, select Project → Build to create the *.pkg* file or select Project → Build and Run to create the *.pkg* file and install the package. After creating the *.pkg* file, to install it, double-click on the file and install as you would any other Mac OS X package. When you quit PackageMaker, you'll be prompted to save the PackageMaker session with its currently filled in values as a *.pmproj* document. If you subsequently double-click your *.pmproj* document, PackageMaker will open with the values that were saved in the *.pmproj* file.

Iceberg is provided by Stepane Sudre as an alternative to PackageMaker. (It is available at *http://s.sudre.free.fr/Software/Iceberg.html*.)

Using GNU tar

The *gnutar* and *gzip* command-line utilities can be used to create *.tar.gz* or *.tgz* tarballs. This type of tarball preserves paths, permissions, symbolic links, as well as authentication and compression. Tools to uncompress the tarball are available for many platforms.

The automated creation of such a tarball can be worked into the same *makefile* that is used to build the software. Preservation of resource forks is tricky, but possible, in this method. For example, the following command preserves Macintosh resource forks (where *foo/* is a directory):

```
$ tar -pczf foo.tgz foo/
```

Every good tarball has a single top-level directory that contains everything else. You should not create tarballs that dump their contents into the current directory. To install software packaged this way, use the following command:

```
$ tar -pxzf foo.tgz
```

This simply unpacks the tarball into the file and directory structure that existed prior to packaging. Basically, it reverses the packing step. This method can be used to simply write files to the appropriate places on the system, such as */usr/local/bin*, */usr/local/lib*, */usr/local/man*, */usr/local/include*, and so on.

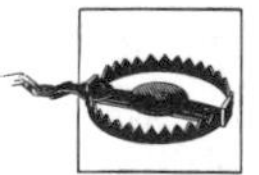

When creating packages, you should keep your package contents out of directories such as */etc*, */usr/bin*, */usr/lib*, */usr/include*, or any top-level directory reserved for the operating system, since you have no way of knowing what a future software update or Mac OS X upgrade will include. For example, the Fink project stays out of Mac OS X's way by keeping most of its files in */sw*. We suggest that you use */usr/local* for the packages that you compile.

This packaging method can also be arranged so that the unpacking is done first in a temporary directory. The user can then run an install script that relocates the package contents to their final destination. This approach is usually preferred, since the *install* script could be designed to do some basic checking of dependencies, the existence of destination directories, the recataloging of libraries, etc. You could also include an *uninstall* script with your distribution.

The disadvantages of the tarball method of distributing software are:

- There is no built-in mechanism for keeping track of which files go where.
- There is no built-in method for uninstalling the software.
- It is difficult to list what software is installed and how the installed files depend on each other or on other libraries.
- There is no checking of dependencies and prerequisite software prior to the installation.

These tasks could be built into *install* and *uninstall* scripts, but there is no inherently uniform, consistent, and coherent method for accomplishing these tasks when multiple software packages are installed in this manner. Fortunately, more sophisticated methods of packaging, distributing, and maintaining software on Unix systems have been devised, such as Red Hat's RPM, Debian's *dpkg*, and Apple's PackageMaker.

Disk Images

Many applications in Mac OS X do not require a special installer. Often, they can be installed by simply dragging the application's folder or icon to a convenient location in the directory structure, usually the */Applications* folder. Applications that are distributed this way are typically packaged as a *disk image*. A disk image is a file that, when double-clicked, creates a virtual volume that is mounted as shown in Figure 15-7.

Inside Applications

Actually, an application *is* a folder with the extension *.app*, which is typically hidden from the user. This folder contains all of the application's resources.

To view the contents of an application bundle, Control-click on the application icon and select Show Package Contents from the pop-up menu; this opens the application's *Contents* folder in the Finder.

You can turn a Java application into a *.app* with the Jar Builder (*/Developer/Applications/Java Tools*). Since Mac OS X comes with Java, you can place your Java application on a disk image, secure in the knowledge that any Mac OS X user can double-click on the application to launch it.

Figure 15-7. A disk image and its mounted volume

Disk images can be created by using Disk Utility (*/Applications/Utilities*) or via the command line (described later). There are two types of disk images. One is a *dual fork* disk image with a *.img* extension, and the other is a *single fork* disk image with a *.dmg* extension. A dual fork disk image requires additional (MacBinary) encoding in order for it to be transferred across networks. The single fork version is preferred for distributing software in Mac OS X, as it requires no additional encoding and, as we shall see later, can be "Internet-enabled."

The Unix command *df* reveals a disk image as a mounted volume that will appear in the */Volumes* directory. When you are done with the mounted volume, unmount it by clicking on the volume (in Figure 15-7, the mounted volume is named Fink 0.7.1 Installer) to select it and choose File → Eject (⌘-E).

You could also Control-click and select Eject Disk from the contextual menu, or drag the mounted volume to the Trash.

Creating a Disk Image with Disk Utility

To create a disk image using Disk Utility, perform the following steps:

1. Launch Disk Utility (*/Applications/Utilities*).
2. Either select File → New → Blank Disk Image or click the New Image icon from the toolbar. Either way, Disk Utility prompts you for a name, location, size (the maximum size is limited by available disk space), encryption options, and format, as shown in Figure 15-8. If you choose to enable encryption, Disk Utility will prompt you for a passphrase.

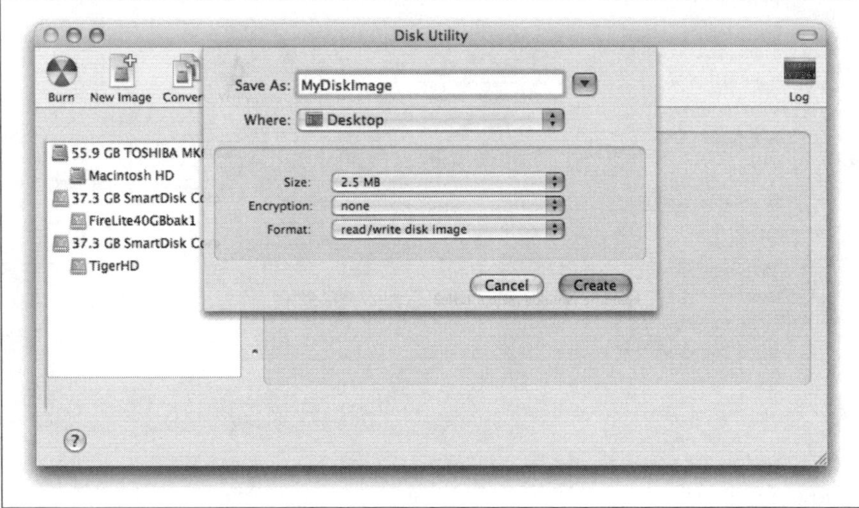

Figure 15-8. Creating a new blank image with Disk Utility

3. Name the new image "MyDiskImage" and choose the Desktop as the location. The new image will be created as *MyDiskImage.dmg* and mounted as *MyDiskImage*. You can change this Volume name to, say "SampleVol," in the Finder.
4. Double-click on the disk icon to open the empty volume in a Finder window, as shown in Figure 15-9.
5. Select File → New Finder Window (or ⌘-N) to open a new Finder window, where you can select the files you want to place in the disk image, as shown in Figure 15-10.
6. To copy the files to the mounted volume, select and then drag the items into the empty *SampleVol* window.

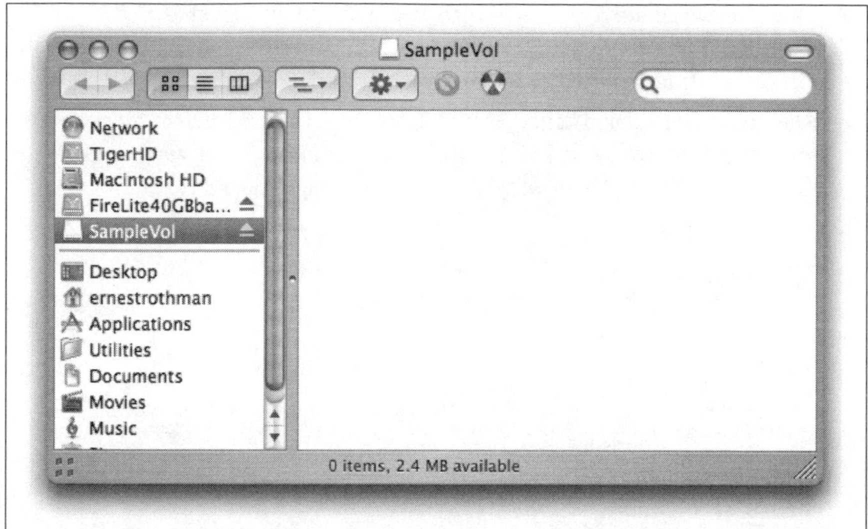

Figure 15-9. A blank disk image, ready to be loaded up with files

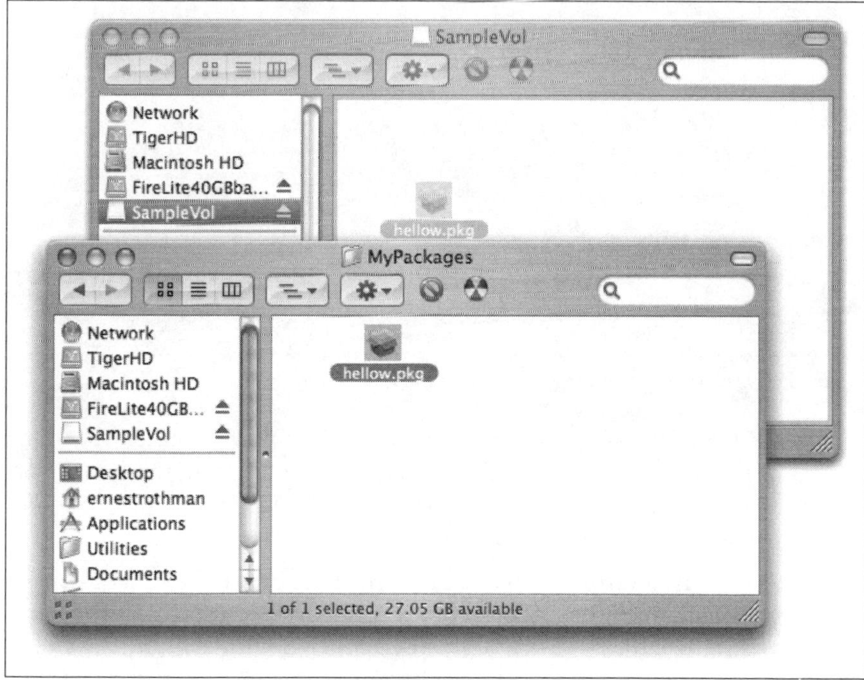

Figure 15-10. Copying the file to the disk image

7. Once you've placed the files into the disk image, eject this disk (⌘-E, click the eject icon next to the *SampleVol* in the left column of the Finder, or drag *SampleVol* to the Trash).

8. Return to the Disk Utility application, highlight *MyDiskImage.dmg* in the left column of Disk Utility, and select Images → Convert, or click the Convert icon from the toolbar, as shown in Figure 15-11.

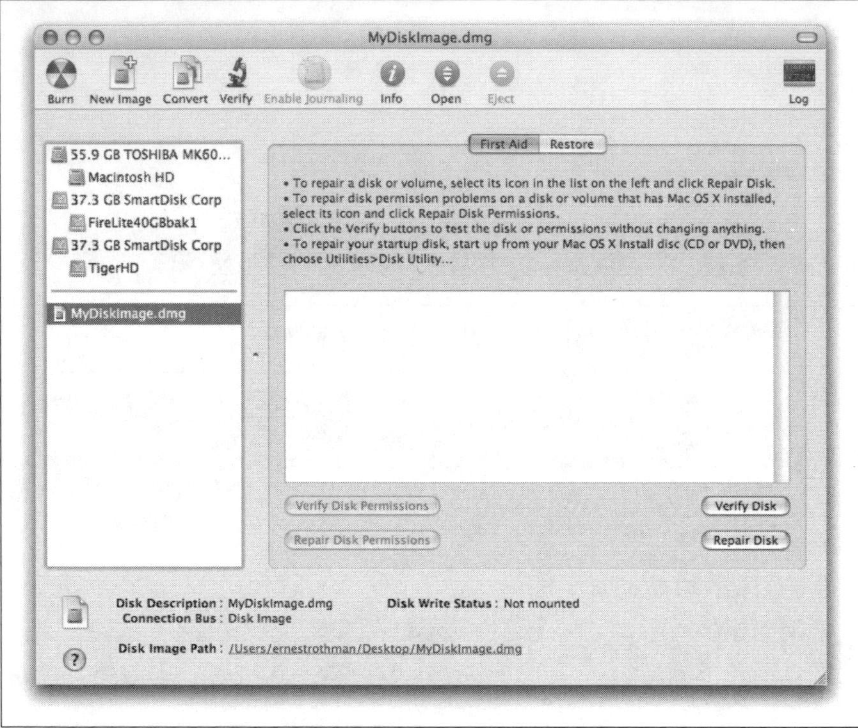

Figure 15-11. Choosing the image to convert in Disk Utility

9. In the Convert Image window, enter either a new name or the same name in the Save As field, and then select read-only from the Image Format pull-down menu, as shown in Figure 15-12. (You can also compress the disk image from this menu.)

10. Click the Save button. If you've given the disk image the same filename as the original image you created, an alert window appears, asking you to confirm whether you want to replace the older file with the new one. Click Replace to finish the process, then quit Disk Utility with ⌘-Q.

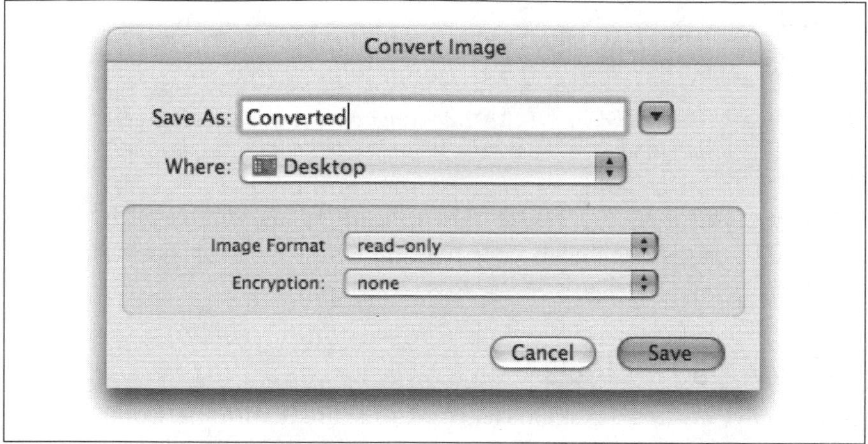

Figure 15-12. Converting an image in Disk Utility

Creating a Disk Image from the Command Line

The following example illustrates how to create a disk image at the command line.

1. Change (*cd*) to the directory where you want to create the disk image:

   ```
   $ cd ~/Documents
   ```

2. Create the disk image of a given size (10 MB in this example) using *hdiutil*:

   ```
   $ hdiutil create -megabytes 10 -fs HFS+ \
       -volname SampleVol Sample.dmg
   ```

3. Mount the image as a volume. Since you named it *SampleVol* when you issued the *hdiutil create* command, it will be mounted as *SampleVol* and will be available in */Volumes/SampleVol*:

   ```
   $ hdiutil mount Sample.dmg
   ```

4. Use the Finder or command-line tools to write to the volume *SampleVol*.

5. When you are done writing to the volume, you can eject it with *hdiutil unmount*:

   ```
   $ hdiutil unmount /Volumes/SampleVol/
   ```

6. Copy the disk image to a compressed, read-only image named *Ready4Dist.dmg*:

   ```
   $ hdiutil convert -format UDZO Sample.dmg -o Ready4Dist.dmg
   ```

The UDZO format option is used to create a UDIF zlib-compressed image. Other formats can be chosen, for example, UDIF *bzip2*, which is available for Mac OS X 10.4+ and can be selected with the UDBZ format option. For a complete list of format options, see the manpage for *hdiutil*.

Whenever you want to mount this volume again, double-click the file *Ready4Dist.dmg* in the finder. Note that the writable disk image *Sample.dmg* is not destroyed in this process.

Distributing Your Image

Once you've created a disk image, you can share it with the world. Put the image up on a web server or FTP server for others to enjoy, share it on your iDisk, or burn it to a CD using Disk Utility (select either select Images → Burn or press ⌘-B).

Internet-enabled disk images

An Internet-enabled disk image is a read-only disk image that cleans up after itself, leaving only the software and no by-products of the download. If you distribute your software as an Internet-enabled disk image, the user just needs to perform these steps:

1. Download the *.dmg* file to the Desktop (i.e., *~/Desktop*) using a web browser.
2. When the download completes, the following sequence of events happens automatically:
    a. The *.dmg* file is mounted.
    b. Its contents are copied to the user's default download folder (e.g., *~/Desktop*).
    c. The disk image is unmounted.
    d. The Internet-enabled flag of the *.dmg* file is set to No.
    e. The *.dmg* file is moved to the Trash.
3. Locate the software and move it to its appropriate location.

The disk image is mounted in a hidden location until its contents are copied to the user's default download folder, which is typically the Desktop folder. If the disk image contains a single file, only this file is copied. On the other hand, if the disk image contains more than one file, a new folder is created in the download folder bearing the root name of the *.dmg* file. Files contained in the disk image are then copied to this folder. For example, if the

Internet-enabled disk image containing multiple files is named *Sample.dmg*, a folder named *Sample* will be created in the download folder and the files contained in the disk image will be copied to the *Sample* folder.

In this scheme, the user does not deal directly with the *.dmg* file (other than initiating the download). This is in contrast to the situation before Internet-enabled disk images were supported, in which the user had to manually unmount the disk image and drag it to the Trash.

To create an Internet-enabled disk image, first create a read-only *.dmg* formatted disk image as described earlier (neither read-write disk images nor older *.img*/*.smi* formats can be Internet-enabled), then set the Internet-enabled flag with the *hdiutil* command:

```
$ hdiutil internet-enable -yes Ready4Dist.dmg
```

If you want to disable the Internet-enabled flag, enter this command:

```
$ hdiutil internet-enable -no Ready4Dist.dmg
```

If you are not sure whether a disk image has its Internet-enabled flag set, the following command reveals this information:

```
$ hdiutil internet-enable -query Ready4Dist.dmg
```

As noted earlier, Internet-enabled disk images are moved to the Trash after they are downloaded and acted upon by Mac OS X. Although their Internet-enabled flags are set to No during the process, you can still rescue *.dmg* files from the Trash in case you want to reinstall the software later.

Creating Fink Packages

You can create your own Fink packages by identifying a source archive and creating a *.info* file in your */sw/fink/dists/local/main/finkinfo* directory.

Creating and Publishing the Tarball

The Fink package system needs a tarball that can be downloaded with the *curl* utility. To illustrate how to create a Fink package, let's use the *hellow-1.0* program (see "Using PackageMaker" earlier in this chapter). In this case, you can use the makefile shown in Example 15-4, which is a little simpler than the one used in Example 15-3.

Example 15-4. Makefile for hellow

```
all:
	cc -o hellow hellow.c
```

Before you proceed, you should create a tarball named *hellow-1.0.tar.gz* with the following contents, and move it to the */Users/Shared/hellow/src* directory:

```
hellow-1.0/
hellow-1.0/hellow.1
hellow-1.0/hellow.c
hellow-1.0/Makefile
```

The *curl* utility can download this file with the following URL: *file:///Users/Shared/hellow/src/hellow-1.0.tar.gz*. (You can host your own files on a public web server or FTP server, or, as in this example, on the local file system with a *file:* URL.)

Creating the .info File

Next, create a *.info* file to tell Fink where to download the package from and how to install it. Fink uses this information to download, extract, and compile the source code, and then to generate and install a Debian package (*.deb* file). This file must be in */sw/fink/dists/local/main/finkinfo*, so you'll need superuser privileges to create it (use the *sudo* utility to temporarily gain these privileges). Example 15-5 shows */sw/fink/dists/local/main/finkinfo/hellow-1.0.info*.

Example 15-5. The hellow-1.0 info file

```
Package: hellow
Version: 1.0
Revision: 1
Source: file:///Users/Shared/hellow/src/%n-%v.tar.gz
Source-MD5: 4ca04528f976641d458f65591da7985c
CompileScript: make
InstallScript: mkdir -p %i/bin
 cp %n %i/bin
 mkdir -p %i/share/man/man1
 cp %n.1 %i/share/man/man1/%n.1
Description: Hello, World program
DescDetail: <<
Prints a friendly greeting to you and your friends.
<<
License: Public Domain
Maintainer: Brian Jepson <bjepson@oreilly.com>
```

The *hellow-1.0.info* file includes several entries, described in the following list. See the Fink Packaging Manual at *http://fink.sourceforge.net/doc/packaging/* for more details.

Package
: The name of the package.

Version
: The package version.

Revision
: The package revision number.

Source
: The URL of the source distribution. You can use percent expansion in the name. (In this example, %n is the name of the package and %v is the package version.) See the Fink Packaging Manual for more percent expansions.

Source-MD5
: The MD5 sum for the file, as calculated by the md5sum binary (*/sw/bin/md5sum*) that comes with Fink. You may need to replace the MD5 sum in the *hellow-1.0.info* file if it's different than what's shown in Example 15-5.

CompileScript
: The command (or commands) needed to compile the source package. The command(s) may span multiple lines, but must begin after the colon.

InstallScript
: The command (or commands) that install the compiled package. The command(s) may span multiple lines, but must begin after the colon.

Description
: A short description of the package.

DescDetail
: A longer description of the package, enclosed with << >>.

License
: The license used by the package. See the Fink Packaging Manual for information on available licenses.

Maintainer
: The name and email address of the maintainer.

Installing the Package

To install *hellow*, use the command *sudo fink install hellow*. This command downloads the source to a working directory, and then extracts, compiles, and packages it, generating the file */sw/fink/dists/local/main/binary-darwin-powerpc/hellow_1.0-1_darwin-powerpc.deb*.

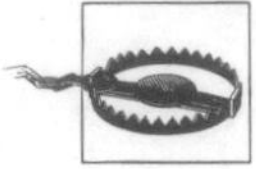

If */sw/etc/fink.conf* has the entry `MirrorOrder: MasterFirst` (the default), it will try to find the *.tar.gz* file on the server designated as `Mirror-master`. Since it is unlikely that *hellow-1.0.tar.gz* is hosted on that server, it will fail, and you'll be presented with several options, including "Retry using original source URL," which means to download the file from the location specified in *hellow-1.0.info*. You could avoid this by changing the `MirrorOrder` to `MasterLast`, but we do not recommend changing the default behavior of Fink, since it could have unpredictable results down the road.

After Fink creates this file, it installs it using *dpkg*. After you've installed *hellow*, you can view its manpage and run the *hellow* command:

```
$ man hellow

HELLOW(1)          BSD General Commands Manual          HELLOW(1)

NAME
     hellow - Greeting generator

DESCRIPTION
     This command prints a friendly greeting.

Mac OS                       April 29, 2005                       Mac OS
$ hellow
Hello, world!
```

This example shows only a portion of Fink's capabilities. For example, Fink can be used to download and apply patches to a source distribution. For more information, see the Fink Packaging Manual (*http://fink.sourceforge.net/doc/packaging/index.php*), which contains detailed instructions on how to build and contribute a *.deb* package to the Fink distribution.

Creating DarwinPorts Packages

As readily as you can create Fink packages, you also can create your own DarwinPorts packages (i.e., ports). To create a port in DarwinPorts, you must first identify a source archive and create a *Portfile* file in the appropriate subdirectory of the dports directory. For example, the Portfile for a game named *foo* would be placed in *~/darwinports/dports/games/foo*, assuming that the DarwinPorts infrastructure has been installed in *~/darwinports*. A Portfile is a actually a TCL script that is similar in purpose to a *.info* file in Fink. The remainder of this chapter is devoted to illustrating the process of creating a DarwinPorts package.

Creating and Publishing the Tarball

The process of creating a package in DarwinPorts begins just as it does when you create a package in Fink. That is, DarwinPorts also needs a tarball that can be downloaded with the *curl* utility. We'll illustrate how to create a DarwinPorts package with the same program, *hellow-1.0,* that we used to illustrate how to create a Fink package earlier in this chapter. As in Fink, you should begin by creating a tarball named *hellow-1.0.tar.gz* with the following contents, and move it to the */Users/Shared/hellow/src* directory:

```
hellow-1.0/
hellow-1.0/hellow.1
hellow-1.0/hellow.c
hellow-1.0/Makefile
```

The *curl* utility can download this file with the following URL: *file:///Users/Shared/hellow/srcs/hellow-1.0.tar.gz*. (As noted in our Fink example earlier, you could also host your own files on a public web server or FTP server. Hosting the tarball on your local system, however, is useful for testing your port.)

Creating the Portfile File

Once the tarball has been placed in *file:///Users/Shared/hellow/src/*, you need to create a file named *Portfile* in *~/darwinports/dports/games/hellow*. The Portfile lists the attributes of the package needed by DarwinPorts, for example, name, version, maintainer(s), where to download the package and how to install it. DarwinPorts uses this information to download, extract, and compile the source code. Information on patchfiles, special configure or compilation flags, and installation or post installation configuration instructions could be included in a Portfile. Example 15-6 shows a Portfile for the *hellow* port.

Example 15-6. The hellow-1.0 Portfile

```
# $ID:  $
PortSystem 1.0
name             hellow
version          1.0
categories       games
maintainers      myemail@mac.com
description      "hello program"
long_description "Classic hello program.  Prints: Hello,\
                  World."
master_sites      file:///Users/Shared/hellow/src
homepage          file:///Users/Shared/hellow
distname          ${portname}-${portversion}
platforms         darwin
```

Example 15-6. The hellow-1.0 Portfile (continued)

```
checksums       md5 4ca04528f976641d458f65591da7985c
configure {}

set instprog    "/usr/bin/install -m 755"
set instman     "/usr/bin/install -m 644"
destroot        {
   system "${instprog} -d ${destroot}${prefix}/bin"
   system "${instprog} -d ${destroot}${prefix}/man/man1"
   system "${instprog} ${worksrcpath}/hellow ${destroot}${prefix}/bin"
   system "${instprog} ${worksrcpath}/*.1 ${destroot}${prefix}/man/man1" }
```

The *Portfile* file includes several items, described in the following list, which includes a few additional items that weren't needed in our simple example. See Michael A. Maibaum's DarwinPorts User Guide (*http://darwinports.opendarwin.org/docs/*), a sample Portfile in *~/darwinports/base/doc/exampleport* and the *portfile* manpage for more details. (You must spell *portfile* in lower case to view the manpage.)

 # $ID: $
: All Portfiles begin with this string, which is a commented out RCS Id tag.

Portsystem 1.0
: The Portsystem version declaration.

name
: The package name.

categories
: Used for organization of packages into categories, e.g., mail, editors, games, etc.

maintainers
: Email addresses of folks maintaining the port.

description
: A short description of the package.

long_description
: A more detailed description of the package.

master_sites
: The URL of the software's source distribution.

homepage
: The URL of the software's web site.

distname
: The name of the distribution, e.g., hellow-1.0.

platform
: Specifies the platform on which the port is to be built.

checksums
: This required command verifies the MD5 checksum.

extract.suffix
: This is used if the source file does not have the default suffix *.tar.gz*.

distfile
: The combination of *name*, *version*, and *extract.suffix*. The default is *${name}-${version}.tar.gz*. This option can be used to override the default if the name of the source file on the server if not in the default form.

depends_lib
: This is used to specify additional libraries or binaries required by the port.

patchfiles
: A list of patch files needed for the package to compile or run. Patch files are placed in a *files/* subdirectory of the directory, which contains the Portfile.

configure{}
: The brackets are left empty if there is no autoconf configure script to run, as in this simple example. If there is a configure script, the argument *-prefix=${prefix}* is passed to it by DarwinPorts. After the *configure{}* line in the above Portfile, there are installation instructions to ensure that the program and its manpage get installed into the correct directory.

The variables *instprog* and *instman* are used to specify exactly which commands are to be used to install the binary and manpage, respectively. The *destroot* key is included to specify exactly what the system should do when the *destroot* option is used with the *port* command.

Building and Installing a Port

Once the *Portfile* file is ready, you can build the port. This involves a sequence of *port* commands, each invoked with the *-v* (verbose) and *-d* (debug) options. To begin this process, you must change to the the directory which contains the *hellow*-related Portfile and verify the MD5 checksum of the tarball:

```
$ ch ~/darwinports/dports/games/hellow
$ port -d -v checksum
```

Since no explicit port name was provided in the preceding command, DarwinPorts obtains, from any Portfile in the current directory, the information that is needed to download and verify the MD5 checksum of the source file. The source tarball file *hellow-1.0.tar.gz* is downloaded into */opt/local/var/db/dports/distfiles/hellow*, and a work directory is created in *~/darwinports/dports/games/hellow*.

Next, extract the source with the following command:

```
$ port -d -v extract
```

This command unpacks *hellow-1.0.tar.gz*, creating the *~/darwinports/dports/games/hellow/work/hellow-1.0* directory. Once the source code has been unpacked, you can build the package with the following command:

```
$ port -d -v build
```

If the build goes well, you can test the installation by first installing the port in the *destroot* directory:

```
$ port -d -v destroot
```

This produces a large number of warning messages, but in the end, if all goes well, both the binary *hellow* and the manpage *hellow.1* will be installed in the *~/darwinports/dports/games/hellow/work/destroot/opt/local* directory. After you've tested the binary and manpage in this *destroot* directory, you can install the *hellow* port system-wide—that is, in */opt/local*. To do this enter the following command:

```
$ sudo port -d -v install
```

This command installs the *hellow* port in */opt/local/var/db/dports/software/hellow/1.0_0/opt/local* and activates it by creating hard links to the installed files in */opt/local*. It also removes the work directory *~/darwinports/dports/games/hellow/work*. You can check that *hellow* has been installed properly by entering the *port installed* command, and by trying to run *hellow* and viewing its manpage. Finally, you should enter the *portindex* command from *~/darwinport/dports* to make your DarwinPorts installation completely aware of the newly installed *hellow* port. Once you've done this, you can uninstall *hellow* as you would uninstall any other port. That is, you could uninstall *hellow* with the following command:

```
$ sudo port uninstall hellow
```

This example shows only a small portion of DarwinPorts' capabilities. For more information, see the sources noted earlier, which contain detailed instructions on how to build and contribute a package to the DarwinPorts distribution.

PART IV

Serving and System Management

This part of the book talks about using Mac OS X as a server, as well as system administration.

Chapters in this part of the book include:

CHAPTER 16
Using Mac OS X as a Server

While most people think of Mac OS X as a client system only, you can also run Mac OS X as a server. If you need Apple's advanced administration tools, you could purchase and use Mac OS X Server (*http://www.apple.com/server/macosx*), but if you're comfortable with the command line, the client version can easily run as a server.

The following services that power the Sharing preference panel are based on the same servers that provide the foundation for everything from private networks to the Internet:

- OpenSSH for remote login
- Samba for Windows file sharing
- Apache for web publishing

However, the System Preferences are limited in what they will let you do. To unleash the full power of Mac OS X as a server, you'll need to install your own administrative tools or edit the configuration files by hand. Once you've unleashed the server lurking inside your Mac, there are many services you can set up. Here are some of the possibilities:

Secure mail server
: If your email provider isn't reliable, or doesn't support the way you want to access your email, you can forward all your email to your personal server and retrieve it from there—whether you're in your home office or on the road.

SSH server
: When you're on the road, there might be some things you want to access back at the home office. Or perhaps you want to help a family member troubleshoot a computer problem while you're on the road.

VNC/Remote Desktop/X11

One step up from a VPN or SSH connection is a remote connection that lets you completely take over the desktop of a computer in your home. This takes remote access and troubleshooting to the next level. For more information, see Chapter 7.

Getting Connected

If you're using a Mac as a production server, then you are probably either co-locating it at your hosting provider's facility or bringing a dedicated line into your home or office. In that case, your Internet Service Provider (ISP) or hosting provider is taking care of all the details: setting up Domain Name System (DNS) records, providing an IP address, and possibly physically hosting your computer in a rack somewhere.

Most hosting providers will take care of setting up entries in the Domain Name System so that you're in the database. However, you will still be responsible for registering the name you want with a domain registrar.

If you're running a Mac at home, you can approximate the same setup, but there are two configuration issues you need to consider:

DNS

If you're using residential broadband, or even the lower tiers of some business-class broadband, your fully-qualified domain name (FQDN) is probably something terrible like *host130.93.41.216.conversent.net*. If you go to your ISP and ask to be set up with a real name, they will either greet you with a blank stare or steer you toward some service that costs hundreds of dollars a month.

IP Address

Again, residential broadband and low-tier business class broadband users suffer, since they are likely to have a dynamic IP address for their service. If you've got this kind of service, your IP address could change as often from every couple of hours to every few days, weeks, or months. In some cases, your IP address may be effectively permanent, but without the guarantee that it will remain static, you never know when you'll have to deal with the hassle. You could ask your ISP for a static IP address, but this may cost extra money, or you may have to move up to a higher tier of service.

Some ISPs, such as Speakeasy, Inc. (*http://www.speakeasy.net/*) offer commercial-class services for well under $100 a month. If you're interested in running services out of your small office or home office (SOHO), check them out.

If you're running a Mac as a server for personal use (for example, remote access via SSH), you can probably get away with plugging into a residential broadband connection and opening a hole in your firewall. However, if you want others to be able to access services such as a web browser, you'll need to solve the DNS and IP address problems. A dynamic DNS service, such as Dynamic Network Services (*http://www.dyndns.org*) can help with this.

Dynamic DNS

Dynamic Network Services, Inc. has been offering dynamic DNS services for many years, and has long been a favorite of dialup and SOHO broadband users who need a permanent domain name even when their IP address is constantly changing. In order for this service to work, you must update the dyndns.org servers every time your IP address changes. The open source DNSUpdate utility (*http://www.dnsupdate.org/*) can detect your public IP address and update the dyndns.org servers with that address, rather than your private address. You must select External Interface when you add a host to DNSUpdate for it to detect and register your public IP address, as shown in Figure 16-1.

That's only half the battle; if your Mac resides behind a firewall router (such as the Apple AirPort Base Station), you'll need to configure it to make your network services visible to the outside world. Otherwise, all incoming traffic will be stopped in its tracks at your firewall. The next section has solutions to this problem.

Serving from Behind a Firewall

If you have a SOHO router (such as the AirPort Base Station) between your Internet connection and your Mac, the router probably has a built-in firewall that protects your Mac from the outside world. Since most access points and routers have a firewall that blocks incoming network traffic, you'll need to open a hole in that firewall for each service you want to use. The list that follows describes our recommendations for exposing a server to the outside world on a SOHO network.

Figure 16-1. Configuring Dynamic DNS with DNSUpdate

Use a wired connection

If you have a wireless access point, such as an AirPort Base Station, that's doing double-duty as your wired Ethernet router, we suggest plugging your Mac server into one of the LAN ports on your access point or one of the LAN ports on an Ethernet switch that's plugged into your access point's LAN port.

Although Wi-Fi speeds typically exceed broadband by quite a lot, actual speeds are often half that of the quoted speed of Wi-Fi networks, and bandwidth is shared among all computers on a given network. So, an 802.11b Wi-Fi network with a raw speed of 11 Mbps is more likely to share 5 to 6 Mbps among machines, and an 802.11g Wi-Fi (AirPort Extreme) network is more likely to have 20 to 25 Mbps available than the 54 Mbps raw speed of the network. This is because Wi-Fi networks have a significant amount of overhead, are susceptible to interference from consumer electronics and microwave ovens, and can experience a sharp drop-off in speeds as the distance between the computer and base station increases.

Be aware of your ISP's Terms of Service

If your ISP does not permit you to run servers on your network, consider asking them whether they have another tier of service that does permit this. As an added bonus, those tiers of service often include one or more static IP addresses. On the downside, they tend to cost quite a bit more than the consumer offerings. ISPs that have restrictive policies in place will often also block certain ports. For example, the Cox cable Internet service that we use does not permit inbound or outbound connections on port 25 (SMTP), nor do they permit inbound connections on port 80 (HTTP). Since these restrictions were implemented around the height of Windows-based worms that used these ports, we believe the restrictions are there primarily to protect against such worms. Prior to that, the only reports we had of Cox actually enforcing their "no servers" rule was in cases where customers were using large amounts of bandwidth.

Although we can't prove that Mac OS X is inherently more secure than Microsoft systems, there are fewer exploits that affect it. If you are diligent about applying security updates, understand the risks and consequences of opening a service (such as a web or IMAP server) to the outside world, and are comfortable monitoring your network for intrusions, you can sleep a little easier while your servers hum away in the night.

Consider non-standard ports
: If your ISP's Terms of Service do not explicitly prohibit running services, but they are still blocking ports to protect against worms, you could choose to run these services on an alternate port that's not blocked. You can do this by either reconfiguring the server, or using your router to handle the redirection.

Open your ports
: One thing a firewall is really good at is keeping traffic out. However, if you want to run a server on your network, you need to selectively let traffic in. This is called *port mapping*, and is described in the next section.

Non-Apple wireless access points may have similar functionality. Look in your access point's documentation for information on port mapping (sometimes referred to as *forwarding*).

Port mapping with an AirPort Base Station

To configure an AirPort Base Station to direct traffic to a Mac that's acting as a server, you should first make sure that the server has a static IP address. By default, an AirPort Base Station will assign addresses in the range of 10.0.1.2

to 10.0.1.200. This will be different if you've specified a different subnet and pool size (in the AirPort Admin Utility, choose Network → Distribute IP addresses → Share a single IP address using DHCP and NAT → Other and set the values as shown in Figure 16-2).

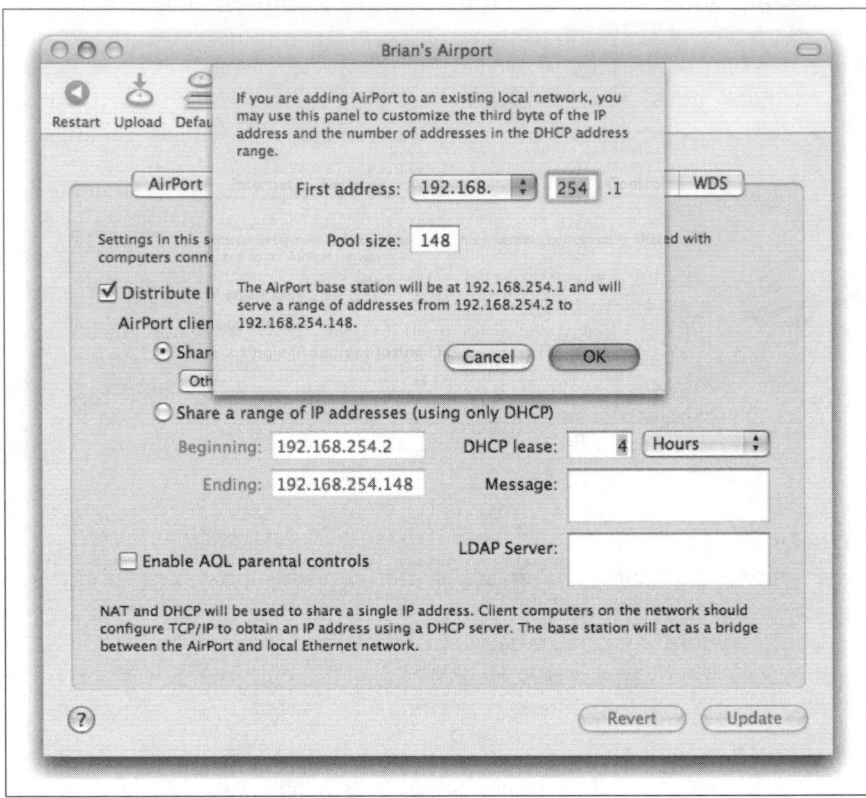

Figure 16-2. Setting subnet and IP address pool size

You must choose your static IP address from outside this pool. If you were using the default AirPort configuration, 10.0.1.201 would be an acceptable choice. If you were using the settings shown in Figure 16-2, then anything over 192.168.254.148 would be OK (we'll use 192.168.254.201 in the next example). Once you have chosen your static IP address, configure your Macintosh server to use this address in Network Preferences. This ensures that your server always has the same IP address, and you can then configure your base station to forward traffic to it.

To configure port mapping, open the AirPort Admin Utility (in */Applications/Utilities*), select your Base Station, and choose Port Mapping. Figure 16-3 shows an AirPort Base Station configured to forward traffic coming in from the outside world on port 22 (ssh) to a machine inside the network with the private address 192.168.254.201 on port 22.

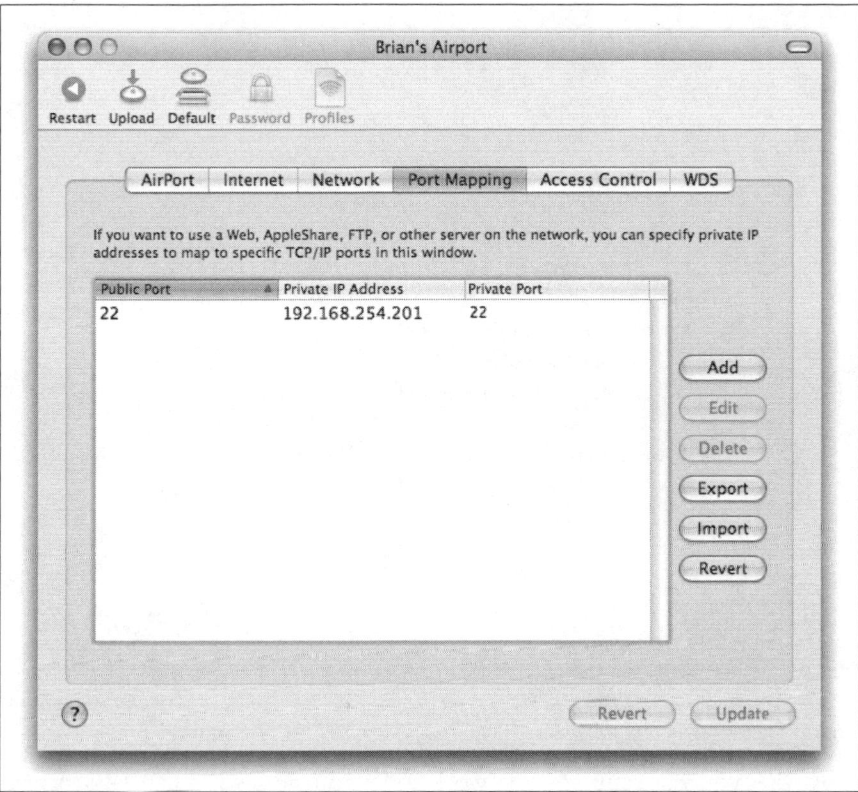

Figure 16-3. Setting up a port mapping with the AirPort Admin Utility

This means that people can ssh to *PUBLIC_IP_ADDRESS* and be directed to the machine at 192.168.254.201 inside the firewall. You can find the value for *PUBLIC_IP_ADDRESS* by selecting the View → Show Summary menu from within the AirPort Admin Utility and looking at the Public (WAN) IP Address, as shown in Figure 16-4.

If you want to open up every port on a given machine, specify the IP address of a *default host* in the AirPort Admin Utility (AirPort → Base Station Options → Enable Default Host). This should be the static IP address of the server on your private network. We do not recommend this because opening every port may expose you to vulnerabilities you're not looking out for. If you've only opened up a select group of services (such as HTTP, SMTP, and SSH), you have a short list of ports to monitor, and therefore, fewer vulnerabilities to worry about.

Figure 16-4. Looking up the public IP address of an AirPort Base Station

Now that you've set up your network so the outside world can talk to your Mac, it's time to configure some services for others to use.

Built-in Services: The Sharing Panel

Mac OS X includes many built-in services that are based on common open source servers such as Samba, Apache, and OpenSSH. Although you can enable and disable these using the Sharing preference panel (System Preferences → Sharing), there's not much configuration you can do there. This section describes each of these services and what you can do to customize them to your liking.

Personal File Sharing

This option controls the AppleTalk Filing Protocol (AFP) service, and corresponds to the `AFPSERVER` entry in */etc/hostconfig* (see Chapter 4 for more information on *hostconfig*). When you enable Personal File Sharing, your Mac shares your Home directory and any mounted volumes (including external drives) with the connected machine.

Windows File Sharing

This option turns on the Samba service, and removes the Disable key in */System/Library/LaunchDaemons/nmbd.plist* (the NetBIOS name server for resolving Windows server names) and */System/Library/LaunchDaemons/smbd.plist* (the server that handles Windows file sharing).

You can add a new share by editing */etc/smb.conf*, and adding an entry. For example, you could share your */Applications* directory with this entry:

```
[Applications]
path = /Applications
read only = yes
```

Next, use the command **`sudo killall -HUP smbd nmbd`** to restart Samba networking with the new configuration file, and without closing any existing connections. Stopping and restarting Windows File Sharing terminates any existing connections. Although Windows clients will usually reconnect to shared resources without complaining, they will get an error if a file transfer is in progress when you interrupt the connection.

Personal Web Sharing

The Apache server is activated when you enable Personal Web Sharing in the Sharing preferences panel (it is disabled by default). This corresponds to the `WEBSERVER` entry in */etc/hostconfig*. Apache's main configuration file is */etc/httpd/httpd.conf*. Individual users' sites are configured with the files that you can find in */etc/httpd/users*. Apache keeps its log files in */var/log/httpd*.

The Apache server that comes with Mac OS X Tiger is based on Apache 1.3.33, and includes several optional modules, which you can enable or disable by uncommenting/commenting the corresponding `LoadModule` and `AddModule` directives in */etc/httpd/httpd.conf*. These modules are described in the following sections.

After you've made any changes to these modules, you should test the changes to the configuration with the command **`sudo apachectl configtest`**, and then have Apache reload its configuration files with **`sudo apachectl graceful`**.

You can browse the source code to Apple's version of Apache, as well as the optional modules, by visiting *http://developer.apple.com/darwin/projects/darwin/*.

dav_module (mod_dav)

This is the WebDAV (Web-based Distributed Authoring and Versioning) module, which lets you export a web site as a filesystem (this is how Apple's iDisk is exported, for example).

If you enable this module with the `LoadModule` and `AddModule` directives as described earlier, you can turn on WebDAV sharing by including the directive `DAV on` within a `<Directory>` or `<Location>` element in *httpd.conf* or one of the user configuration files in */etc/httpd/users*. You will also need to specify the lockfile that *mod_dav* will use. For example, you can enable WebDAV for your web server root by changing *httpd.conf* as shown in **bold**:

```
DAVLockDB /tmp/DAVLock

<Directory />
    Options FollowSymLinks
    DAV on
    AllowOverride None
</Directory>
```

After you make this change and restart Apache, you'll be able to mount your web site with the following command:

```
$ mkdir /mnt
$ mount_webdav http://127.0.0.1/ /mnt
```

See *http://www.webdav.org/mod_dav/install.html* for complete information on configuring this module.

perl_module (mod_perl)

This module embeds the Perl interpreter in each Apache process, letting you run Perl web applications without the overhead of launching a CGI script. *mod_perl* also lets you develop Perl applications that can hook into Apache's responses at various stages. Tiger ships with *mod_perl* 1.29.

After you've enabled *mod_perl* on your server with the `LoadModule` and `AddModule` directives as described earlier, you can get up and running quickly by using the `Apache::Registry` module, which runs most well-behaved Perl CGI scripts under *mod_perl*. You can set up a virtual directory for Perl scripts by adding the following to *httpd.conf* and restarting Apache:

```
Alias /perl/ /Library/WebServer/Perl/
PerlModule Apache::Registry
<Location /perl>
```

```
    SetHandler perl-script
    PerlHandler Apache::Registry
    Options ExecCGI
  </Location>
```

Next, create the directory */Library/WebServer/Perl*, save the following program into that directory in a file called *HelloWorld*, and set that file as executable with chmod:

```
#!/usr/bin/perl -w

use strict;

# workaround for a bug in Mac OS X 10.3
tie *STDOUT, 'Apache';

# run 'perldoc CGI' for more information
use CGI qw(:standard);
print STDOUT header( );
print STDOUT start_html("Sample Script");
print "hello, world";
print end_html( );
```

If you point your browser at *http://localhost/perl/HelloWorld*, you should see a friendly greeting. If not, check */var/log/httpd/error_log* for error messages. You can find complete documentation for *mod_perl* at *http://perl.apache.org/docs/1.0/index.html*.

ssl_module (mod_ssl)

This module allows you to serve documents securely using the HTTPS (TLS/SSL) protocol. To properly configure HTTPS, you need to obtain a server certificate signed by a Certifying Authority (CA). However, after you've enabled *mod_ssl* in *httpd.conf*, you can whip something up pretty quickly for testing using the following steps:

1. Create and change to a working directory for creating and signing your certificates:

   ```
   $ mkdir ~/tmp
   $ cd ~/tmp
   ```

2. Create a new CA. This is an untrusted CA. You'll be able to sign things, but browsers won't trust you implicitly:

   ```
   $ /System/Library/OpenSSL/misc/CA.sh -newca
   CA certificate filename (or enter to create)

   Making CA certificate ...
   Generating a 1024 bit RSA private key
   .....................................++++++
   ..++++++
   writing new private key to './demoCA/private/./cakey.pem'
   ```

```
Enter PEM pass phrase: ********
Verifying - Enter PEM pass phrase: ********
-----
You are about to be asked to enter information that will be incorporated
into your certificate request.
What you are about to enter is what is called a Distinguished Name or a
DN.
There are quite a few fields but you can leave some blank.
For some fields there will be a default value,
If you enter '.', the field will be left blank.
-----
Country Name (2 letter code) [AU]:US
State or Province Name (full name) [Some-State]:Rhode Island
Locality Name (eg, city) []:Providence
Organization Name (eg, company) [Internet Widgits Pty Ltd]:Gold and
Appel Transfers
Organizational Unit Name (eg, section) []:
Common Name (eg, YOUR name) []:Hagbard Celine
Email Address []:hagbard@jepstone.net
```

3. Next, create a certificate request; this generates an unsigned certificate that you'll have to sign as the CA you just created:

```
$ /System/Library/OpenSSL/misc/CA.sh -newreq
Generating a 1024 bit RSA private key
................++++++
..............................................................++++++
writing new private key to 'newreq.pem'
Enter PEM pass phrase: ********
Verifying - Enter PEM pass phrase: ********
-----
You are about to be asked to enter information that will be incorporated
into your certificate request.
What you are about to enter is what is called a Distinguished Name or a
DN.
There are quite a few fields but you can leave some blank.
For some fields there will be a default value,
If you enter '.', the field will be left blank.
-----
Country Name (2 letter code) [AU]:US
State or Province Name (full name) [Some-State]:Rhode Island
Locality Name (eg, city) []:Kingston
Organization Name (eg, company) [Internet Widgits Pty Ltd]:Jepstone
Organizational Unit Name (eg, section) []:
Common Name (eg, YOUR name) []:Brian Jepson
Email Address []:bjepson@jepstone.net

Please enter the following 'extra' attributes
to be sent with your certificate request.
A challenge password []:
An optional company name []:
Request (and private key) is in newreq.pem
```

4. Now, you must sign the key. The passphrase you must enter in this step should be the passphrase you used when you created the CA:

```
$ /System/Library/OpenSSL/misc/CA.sh -sign
Using configuration from /System/Library/OpenSSL/openssl.cnf
Enter pass phrase for ./demoCA/private/cakey.pem:  ********
Check that the request matches the signature
Signature ok
Certificate Details:
        Serial Number: 1 (0x1)
        Validity
            Not Before: Nov 11 19:34:22 2003 GMT
            Not After : Nov 10 19:34:22 2004 GMT
        Subject:
            countryName               = US
            stateOrProvinceName       = Rhode Island
            localityName              = Kingston
            organizationName          = Jepstone
            commonName                = Brian Jepson
            emailAddress              = bjepson@jepstone.net
        X509v3 extensions:
            X509v3 Basic Constraints:
            CA:FALSE
            Netscape Comment:
            OpenSSL Generated Certificate
            X509v3 Subject Key Identifier:
            1C:AA:2E:32:15:28:83:4B:F4:54:F1:97:87:12:11:45:7C:33:47:96
            X509v3 Authority Key Identifier:
            keyid:DC:C0:D7:A5:69:CA:EE:2B:1C:FA:1C:7A:8A:B2:90:F1:EE:
            1E:49:0C
            DirName:/C=US/ST=Rhode Island/L=Providence/O=Gold and Appel
            Transfers/CN=Hagbard Celine/emailAddress=hagbard@jepstone.
            net
            serial:00

Certificate is to be certified until Nov 10 19:34:22 2004 GMT (365 days)
Sign the certificate? [y/n]:y

1 out of 1 certificate requests certified, commit? [y/n]y
[... output truncated ...]
Signed certificate is in newcert.pem
```

At this point, you have two files for use: the signed certificate (*~/tmp/newcert.pem*) and the request file, which also contains the server's private key (*~/tmp/newreq.pem*). The private key is protected by the passphrase you supplied when you generated the request. To configure your server for HTTPS support:

1. Convert the server key so it doesn't require a passphrase to unlock it (you'll need to supply the passphrase you used when you generated the request). This removes the protection of the passphrase, but is fine for

testing. If you don't do this, you'll need to supply a passphrase each time Apache starts up (See *http://www.modssl.org/docs/2.8/ssl_reference.html* for documentation on the SSLPassPhraseDialog, which allows you to send the passphrase to Apache in a variety of ways):

```
$ sudo openssl rsa -in newreq.pem -out serverkey.pem
Enter pass phrase for newreq.pem: ********
writing RSA key********
```

2. Copy these files to a location on your filesystem that's outside of the web server's document tree:

```
$ mkdir /Library/WebServer/SSL
$ cp ~/tmp/serverkey.pem /Library/WebServer/SSL/
$ cp ~/tmp/newcert.pem /Library/WebServer/SSL/
```

3. Enable the `LoadModule` and `AddModule` directives for *mod_ssl*, and add the following lines to *httpd.conf*:

```
<IfModule mod_ssl.c>
  SSLCertificateFile    /Library/WebServer/SSL/newcert.pem
  SSLCertificateKeyFile /Library/WebServer/SSL/serverkey.pem
  SSLEngine on
  Listen 443
</IfModule>
```

4. Stop and restart the web server (it is not enough to use `apachectl graceful` when you install a new certificate):

```
$ sudo apachectl stop
/usr/sbin/apachectl stop: httpd stopped
$ sudo apachectl start
Processing config directory: /private/etc/httpd/users/*.conf
 Processing config file: /private/etc/httpd/users/bjepson.conf
/usr/sbin/apachectl start: httpd started
```

Now, try visiting *https://localhost* in a web browser. You should get a warning that an unknown authority signed the server certificate. It's OK to continue past this point.

For more information about configuring *mod_ssl* for Mac OS X, see *Using mod_ssl* at *http://developer.apple.com/internet/serverside/modssl.html*. The *mod_ssl* FAQ includes information on getting a server certificate that's been signed by a trusted CA: *http://www.modssl.org/docs/2.8/ssl_faq.html#cert-real*.

php4_module (mod_php4)

Enable this module to start serving PHP 4 documents from your Macintosh. After you turn on this module and restart Apache, you can install PHP scripts ending with *.php* into your document directories. For example, save the following script as *hello.php* in */Library/WebServer/Documents*:

```
<html>
<head><title>PHP Demo</title></head>
<body>
<?
  foreach (array("#FF0000", "#00FF00", "#0000FF") as $color) {
    echo "<font color=\"$color\">Hello, World<br /></font>";
  }
?>
</body>
</html>
```

Next, open *http://localhost/hello.php* (use *https://* if you've still got SSL enabled from the previous section) in a web browser; the phrase "Hello, World" should appear in three different colors. If it does not, consult */var/log/httpd/error_log* for messages that might help diagnose what went wrong.

hfs_apple_module (mod_hfs_apple)

This module is enabled by default, and provides compatibility with the HFS+ filesystem's case insensitivity. For more information, see *http://docs.info.apple.com/article.html?artnum=107310.*

bonjour_module (mod_bonjour)

This module is enabled by default. However, *mod_bonjour* does not automatically advertise these user sites. Instead, it only advertises user sites whose *index.html* has been modified.

If you are using PHP as the index document (*~/Sites/index.php*), Apache may not register your site as changed, and thus won't advertise it over Bonjour. For *mod_bonjour* to notice that a file has changed, you must restart Apache (**sudo apachectl restart**) after a page is modified for the first time.

If you want to override the default *mod_bonjour* settings and advertise all user sites on your server, change the relevant section of *httpd.conf*. Here is the default configuration for the *mod_bonjour* section:

```
<IfModule mod_bonjour.c>
    # Only the pages of users who have edited their
    # default home pages will be advertised on Bonjour.
    RegisterUserSite customized-users
    #RegisterUserSite all-users

    # Bonjour advertising for the primary site is off by default.
    #RegisterDefaultSite
</IfModule>
```

To advertise all user sites, comment out the existing RegisterUserSite directive, and uncomment the one that specifies the all-users options, as shown here:

```
<IfModule mod_bonjour.c>
    # Only the pages of users who have edited their
    # default home pages will be advertised on Bonjour.
    #RegisterUserSite customized-users
    RegisterUserSite all-users

    # Bonjour advertising for the primary site is off by default.
    #RegisterDefaultSite
</IfModule>
```

You can also enable Bonjour advertising of the primary site by specifying the RegisterDefaultSite directive. Sites that are advertised on Bonjour appear automatically in Safari's Bonjour bookmark list (Safari → Preferences → Bookmarks → Include Bonjour).

Remote Login

When you turn on Remote Login, the OpenSSH server is enabled. This option removes the Disable key in */System/Library/LaunchDaemons/ssh.plist*. You can configure the OpenSSH server by editing */etc/sshd_config*. For example, you can configure OpenSSH to allow remote users to request X11 forwarding by uncommenting the line:

```
#X11Forwarding yes
```

to:

```
X11Forwarding yes
```

After you make a change to *sshd_config*, restart *xinetd* with **sudo killall -HUP xinetd**.

FTP Access

When you turn on FTP Access in the Sharing preferences panel, the Disable key in */System/Library/LaunchDaemons/ftp.plist* is removed as *launchd* enables the FTP server. Although Mac OS X comes with an FTP server, its capabilities are limited. We suggest bypassing the FTP server that's included with Mac OS X, and installing PureFTPd via Fink (you may need to use the unstable repositories. For more information, see Chapter 13).

To install PureFTPd, issue the command **fink install pure-ftpd** and follow the prompts (if any):

```
$ sudo fink install pure-ftpd
Information about 4787 packages read in 3 seconds.
```

```
The following package will be installed or updated:
 pure-ftpd
```

To switch Mac OS X over to PureFTPd, follow these steps:

1. Make sure that FTP Access is off in System Preferences → Sharing.
2. Backup your existing */System/Library/LaunchDaemons/ftp.plist* file (be sure to add `<key>Disabled</key><true/>` if you decide to back it up to a file in the */System/Library/LaunchDaemons* directory; otherwise, *launchd* may activate both FTP servers) and replace its contents with the following:

    ```
    <?xml version="1.0" encoding="UTF-8"?>
    <!DOCTYPE plist PUBLIC "-//Apple Computer//DTD PLIST 1.0//EN"  "http://
    www.apple.com/DTDs/PropertyList-1.0.dtd">
    <plist version="1.0">
    <dict>
            <key>Disabled</key>
            <true/>
            <key>Label</key>
            <string>org.pureftpd.ftpd</string>
            <key>Program</key>
            <string>/sw/sbin/pure-ftpd</string>
            <key>ProgramArguments</key>
            <array>
                    <string>pure-ftpd</string>
                    <string>-A</string>
                    <string>-lpuredb:/sw/etc/pureftpd.pdb</string>
            </array>
            <key>Sockets</key>
            <dict>
                    <key>Listeners</key>
                    <dict>
                            <key>Bonjour</key>
                            <true/>
                            <key>SockServiceName</key>
                            <string>ftp</string>
                    </dict>
            </dict>
            <key>inetdCompatibility</key>
            <dict>
                    <key>Wait</key>
                    <false/>
            </dict>
    </dict>
    </plist>
    ```

3. Next, use System Preferences → Sharing to restart FTP Sharing.

You'll now need to add users to the PureFTPd password file (*/sw/etc/pureftpd.passwd*). To create a user, use *pure-pw*. Specify an ftp username as well as the uid (`-u`), gid (`-g`), and home directory (`-d`) of a real user to map that ftp user to. You'll be prompted for a password (we suggest you use something different from your login password):

```
# pure-pw useradd bjepson -u 501 -g 501 -d /Users/bjepson/ftpfiles
Password: ********
Enter it again: ********
```

This way, the insecure FTP password can be different from the login password. Note that we used a subdirectory of the user's home directory. Used in conjunction with the -A argument (which chroot's the ftp sessions), this is an acceptable compromise given the insecurity of ftp, which passes usernames and passwords in cleartext.

After you set the user's password, you must create the password database (*pureftpd.pdb*) with pure-pw mkdb.

Now, when you log in, you're trapped in the *ftpfiles* subdirectory. As far as the remote user is concerned, it's the root of the filesystem. This way, even if an attacker obtains your ftp password, they are limited in the damage they can do.

```
$ ftp jepstone.homeunix.net
Trying ::1...
Connected to localhost.
220---------- Welcome to Pure-FTPd ----------
220-Local time is now 17:33. Server port: 21.
220 You will be disconnected after 15 minutes of inactivity.
Name (localhost:bjepson):
331 User bjepson OK. Password required
Password: ********
230-User bjepson has group access to:  80       501
230 OK. Current directory is /
Remote system type is UNIX.
Using binary mode to transfer files.
ftp> ls
229 Extended Passive mode OK (|||65321|)
150 Accepted data connection
226-Options: -l
226 0 matches total
ftp> cd /
250 OK. Current directory is /
ftp> ls
229 Extended Passive mode OK (|||18080|)
150 Accepted data connection
226-Options: -l
226 0 matches total
```

Printer Sharing

When you turn on Printer Sharing, the *cups-lpd* server is enabled. This option toggles the `Disabled` key in */System/Library/LaunchDaemons/printer.plist*. For more information, see "Printer Sharing" in Chapter 6.

Email

Apple has given up on the aging and clunky *sendmail*, and is instead using Postfix, which is easy to configure. (However, Postfix includes a *sendmail*-compatibility wrapper in */usr/sbin/sendmail*.) The following sections describe how to configure Postfix.

Configuring Postfix to Send Email

By default, Mac OS X runs a program called `master`, which monitors the outgoing mail queue, and runs Postfix on the queue as needed. This daemon is controlled by the *launchd* script */System/Library/LaunchDaemons/orgpostfix.master.plist*.

If you want to use Postfix on a standalone server, you must configure two settings in */etc/postfix/main.cf*. The first is the hostname (`myhostname`). This should be a real hostname, something that can be found in a reverse DNS lookup against your IP address. The second is your origin (`myorigin`), which is the domain name from which email appears to originate. This can be the same as your hostname (this is probably the case for small sites). However, if it is not, be sure to specify the correct hostname. For example, here are the settings for a computer named *ip192-168-0-1.ri.ri.cox.net* with all email originating from that machine appearing to come from *username@cox.net*:

```
myhostname = ip192-168-0-1.ri.ri.cox.net
myorigin = cox.net
```

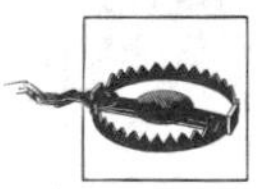

If your ISP's network is configured to block outgoing SMTP to all but their SMTP server, using your ISP's SMTP server as a relay host may be the only way you can configure postfix to deliver mail.

If you don't have a permanent domain name for your Mac OS X server, we suggest configuring Postfix to use a *relay host* (most likely your ISP's SMTP server). To configure Postfix to use a relay, add an entry for `relayhost` in */etc/postfix/main.cf*. For example, we use the following setting:

```
relayhost = smtp-server.oreilly.com
```

Along the same lines, you should configure Postfix to masquerade as the appropriate host using the `myorigin` setting in */etc/postfix/main.cf*. In the case of the previous example, the origin is *oreilly.com* (as in *bjepson@oreilly.com*):

```
myorigin = oreilly.com
```

Configuring Postfix to Receive Email

To enable Postfix to act as a legitimate email destination (that is, mail for *username@yourhost* will go directly to your Macintosh), you must create a startup script that runs the command `postfix start` upon startup, and `postfix stop` upon shutdown. For more details, see "Startup Items" in Chapter 4.

To receive email at your host, you need a Mail Exchange (MX) record pointing to your machine. The MX record is an entry in DNS that identifies the mail server for a particular domain. If your ISP provides you with a static IP address and supports the use of hostnames (this is a given if your Mac is co-located), contact them about setting up the appropriate MX record. If you have residential (or low-end business) broadband, it's very likely that your ISP does not support this, and what's more, they probably block access to port 25 within their network as a security precaution.

If your system can support the use of port 25, you must change the setting for `inet_interfaces` in */etc/postfix/main.cf*. By default, it listens only on 127.0.0.1 (localhost), so you must add the IP address you want it to listen on. For example, we've set up a server behind a firewall, but configured the firewall to forward port 25 to the server (see the "Serving from Behind a Firewall" section earlier in this chapter). The private network address of the server is 192.168.254.104, and because traffic on port 25 is going from the outside world to the private network, we must configure `inet_interfaces` to listen on the 192.168.254.104 interface as well as localhost:

```
inet_interfaces = localhost 192.168.254.104
```

After you make this change, stop and restart Postfix with **`postfix stop`** and **`postfix start`** (it may not be enough to use the command `postfix reload`).

The Mac OS X Firewall

Mac OS X uses FreeBSD's *ipfw2* (IP firewall, version 2) facility to control how incoming and outgoing packets are routed through the system. You use the *ipfw* utility to define a set of rules that controls this. The default rules allow all traffic from any location to come into your computer, using the following *ipfw* rule (65535 is the priority level of the rule, the lowest priority possible):

```
65535 allow ip from any to any
```

To define this rule yourself, you'd issue the following command:

```
# ipfw add 65535 allow ip from any to any
```

Mac OS X uses *ipfw* and several other tools to share your Internet connection and to protect your Macintosh from malicious hackers.

Internet Sharing

When you turn on Internet Sharing (System Preferences → Sharing → Internet), Mac OS X executes */usr/libexec/InternetSharing*, which does quite a bit under the hood. It uses *ifconfig* to configure the interface, *ipfw* and *natd* to handle port redirection, *bootpd* to offer DHCP services to client machines, and *named* to handle DNS lookups. Here is how these are started, along with equivalent invocations you could run as *root*, if you wanted to do this all by hand.

ifconfig

If you're sharing the connection over a port, such as the Ethernet port (*en0* on many systems), it probably has a self-assigned IP address. Internet Sharing sets this to the first host on whatever subnet it is using (the default is 192.168.2.1):

```
# ifconfig en0 192.168.2.1
```

ipfw/natd

Mac OS X adds a firewall rule with a high priority (00010), which diverts any traffic coming into port 8668 on *en1* (the AirPort adapter on many systems):

```
# ipfw add 00010 divert 8668 ip from any to any via en1
```

It also sets the *net.inet.ip.forwarding* sysctl to 1, which enables IP forwarding.

The Network Address Translation Daemon (*natd*) listens on this port. InternetSharing starts it with this command, where *IP_ADDRESS* is the IP address you want to share and *INTERFACE* is the network interface (both the IP address and interface here correspond to "Share your connection from" in the Internet Sharing preference pane). *INTERFACE2* should be the interface you're sharing the connection to:

```
# /usr/sbin/natd -alias_address IP_ADDRESS -interface INTERFACE \
    -use_sockets -same_ports -unregistered_only -dynamic -clamp_mss \
    -enable_natportmap -natportmap_interface INTERFACE2
```

So, if your AirPort adapter (*en1*) was assigned the IP address 192.168.254.150, and you shared that connection to another computer plugged into your Ethernet port (*en0*), *natd* would be invoked like so:

```
# /usr/sbin/natd -alias_address 192.168.254.150 -interface en1 \
  -use_sockets -same_ports -unregistered_only -dynamic -clamp_mss \
  -enable_natportmap -natportmap_interface en0
```

bootpd

This is a combined BOOTP and DHCP server. You can find the DHCP configuration in Directory Services, under */config/dhcp/subnets*. Here is a dump of the settings, which are created when the firewall is started, and deleted when it is stopped:

```
$ nidump -r /config/dhcp /
{
  "name" = ( "dhcp" );
  "bootp_enabled" = ( "" );
  "dhcp_enabled" = ( "en0" );
  "reply_threshold_seconds" = ( "4" );
  "detect_other_dhcp_server" = ( "1" );
  CHILDREN = (
    {
      "name" = ( "subnets" );
      CHILDREN = (
        {
          "name" = ( "192.168.2" );
          "net_address" = ( "192.168.2.0" );
          "net_mask" = ( "255.255.255.0" );
          "dhcp_router" = ( "192.168.2.1" );
          "lease_max" = ( "3600" );
          "client_types" = ( "dhcp" );
          "dhcp_domain_name_server" = ( "192.168.2.1" );
          "net_range" = ( "192.168.2.2", "192.168.2.254" );
          "_creator" = ( "com.apple.nat" );
        }
      )
    }
  )
}
```

To allocate addresses in a different subnet, you'd need to change each occurrence of 192.168.2 to a private subnet that conforms to the rules in RFC 1918 (*ftp://ftp.rfc-editor.org/in-notes/rfc1918.txt*) and load those into Directory Services. Then you'd need to start bootpd with this command:

```
# /usr/libexec/bootpd -P
```

named

This is the BIND (Berkeley Internet Name Domain), which provides DNS services to client machines. When you start Internet Sharing, it creates a configuration file for named in */etc/com.apple.named.conf.proxy* and runs named with that as its configuration file. Here is a trimmed-down version (comments and white space removed) of that file:

```
controls { };
options {
        directory "/var/named";
        listen-on { 192.168.2.1;  };
        forward first;
        forwarders { 192.168.254.1;  };
};
zone "." IN {
        type hint;
        file "named.ca";
};
zone "localhost" IN {
        type master;
        file "localhost.zone";
        allow-update { none; };
};
zone "0.0.127.in-addr.arpa" IN {
        type master;
        file "named.local";
        allow-update { none; };
};
acl can_query {any;};
```

You'd need to create this file and run *named* against it if you wanted to start it by hand. Be sure to change any occurrences of 192.168.2 to the appropriate subnet if you changed the DHCP settings. The `forwarders` setting should be set to the name of your Mac's DNS server. Internet Sharing launches named as:

```
# /usr/sbin/named -c /tmp/com.apple.named.conf.proxy -f
```

For more information, see the respective manpages for these commands, as well as the Advanced Networking section of the *FreeBSD Handbook* (*http://www.freebsd.org/doc/en_US.ISO8859-1/books/handbook/*).

The Mac OS X Firewall

When you enable the firewall (System Preferences → Sharing → Firewall), Mac OS X sets up the following rules to keep traffic from getting into your computer:

```
02000 allow ip from any to any via lo*
02010 deny ip from 127.0.0.0/8 to any in
```

```
02020 deny ip from any to 127.0.0.0/8 in
02030 deny ip from 224.0.0.0/3 to any in
02040 deny tcp from any to 224.0.0.0/3 in
02050 allow tcp from any to any out
02060 allow tcp from any to any established
65535 allow ip from any to any
```

In addition, the firewall sets up rules for any services you have enabled in the Sharing tab, such as this one, which allows SSH connections by explicitly permitting traffic on port 22:

```
02070 allow tcp from any to any dst-port 22 in
```

Tiger introduces some advanced capabilities (press Advanced in the Firewall preference pane to set these, as shown in Figure 16-5).

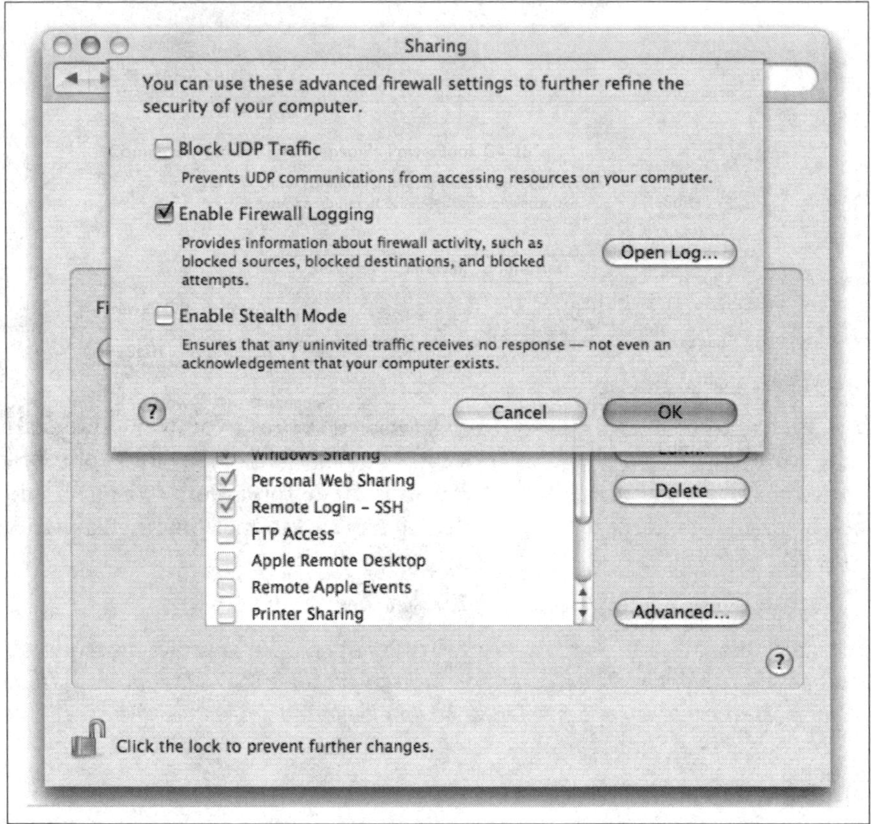

Figure 16-5. Configuring advanced firewall options

Enable Firewall Logging

If you've enabled this in the advanced settings, this rule will also be in effect, which logs anything that's not permitted:

```
12190 deny log tcp from any to any
```

The Mac OS X firewall is configured such that only the protocols you specify are allowed through. So, if something is not checked, it won't be permitted through. Here's what you'd see in the firewall log (*/var/log/ipfw.log*) if you tried to FTP from 192.168.254.150 to a machine (192.168.254.154) whose firewall didn't permit it:

```
Apr  3 15:30:49 brian-jepsons-powerbook-g4-15 ipfw:  12190 Deny TCP
   192.168.254.201:32769 192.168.254.150:21 in via en1
```

Block UDP Traffic

This option puts a number of rules into effect, which blocks UDP (User Datagram Protocol) traffic on all but a few essential ports (noted in the # comments):

```
20310 allow udp from any to any dst-port 53 in   # DNS
20320 allow udp from any to any dst-port 68 in   # bootpc
20321 allow udp from any 67 to me in             # bootps
20322 allow udp from any 5353 to me in           # Bonjour
20340 allow udp from any to any dst-port 137 in  # Samba
20350 allow udp from any to any dst-port 427 in  # SLP
20360 allow udp from any to any dst-port 631 in  # CUPS
20370 allow udp from any to any dst-port 5353 in # Bonjour
22000 allow udp from any to any dst-port 123 in  # network time
30510 allow udp from me to any out keep-state
30520 allow udp from any to any in frag
35000 deny log udp from any to any in
```

Enable Stealth Mode

This option renders your server somewhat invisible by setting the following *sysctls* to 1:

```
net.inet.tcp.blackhole
net.inet.udp.blackhole
net.inet.tcp.log_in_vain
net.inet.udp.log_in_vain
```

This sets both the `blackhole` (don't reply at all to connections; act as if there's not even a server there) and `log_in_vain` (log all those rejections in */var/log/ipfw.log*) options for UDP and TCP traffic. It also sets the following firewall rule to deny ICMP echo requests:

```
20000 deny icmp from any to me in icmptypes 8
```

Add Your Own Rules

You can add your own packet filter rules by clicking the New button on the Firewall tab. You can also add your own firewall rules using the *ipfw* utility, but the Firewall tab remains disabled until you reboot or clear the rules with **sudo ipfw flush**.

For example, you could add a custom firewall rule such as this one, which permits Telnet from only one host (192.168.254.150):

```
# ipfw add 02075 allow tcp from 192.168.254.150 to any dst-port 23 in
```

However, if you navigated to the Firewall preferences pane, you'd get the message shown in Figure 16-6. (You'll also get this message if you're running an application that uses *ipfw* to its own twisted ends, such as Virtual PC.) You can get things back to normal by deleting the rule:

```
# ipfw delete 02075
```

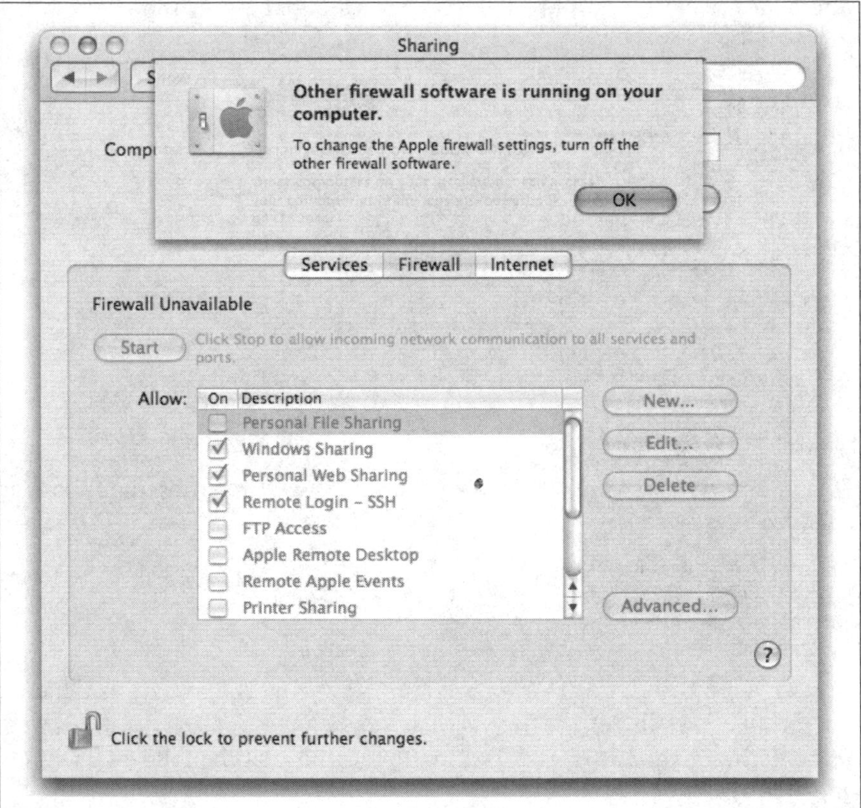

Figure 16-6. You won't be able to make changes until you put things back the way you found them

You may need to quit and restart the System Preferences application before it notices that you've reset the firewall to the default rules. For more information, see the *ipfw* manpage.

CHAPTER 17

System Management Tools

Mac OS X comes with many tools for tweaking and spying on various aspects of your system, including memory, kernel modules, and kernel state variables. Some of these tools come directly from BSD, while others are unique to Mac OS X. Most of the BSD-derived utilities have been filtered through Mach and NeXTSTEP on their way to Mac OS X.

For more details on any of these utilities, see their respective manpages.

Diagnostic Utilities

Mac OS X includes many diagnostic utilities that you can use to monitor your system and investigate problems.

top

The *top* utility displays memory statistics and a list of running processes. It is divided into two regions: the top region contains memory statistics, and the bottom region contains details on each process.

You can specify the number of processes to show by supplying a numeric argument. By default, *top* refreshes its display every second and sorts the list of processes by process ID (PID) in descending order. You can set *top* to sort by CPU utilization with *-u*, and you can specify the refresh delay with the *-s* option. Figure 17-1 shows the output of *top -u 16* (if you wanted to refresh the output every 3 seconds, you could run *top -s3 -u 16*).

Table 17-1 describes the values shown in the top region, and Table 17-2 describes the columns in the bottom region (process information).

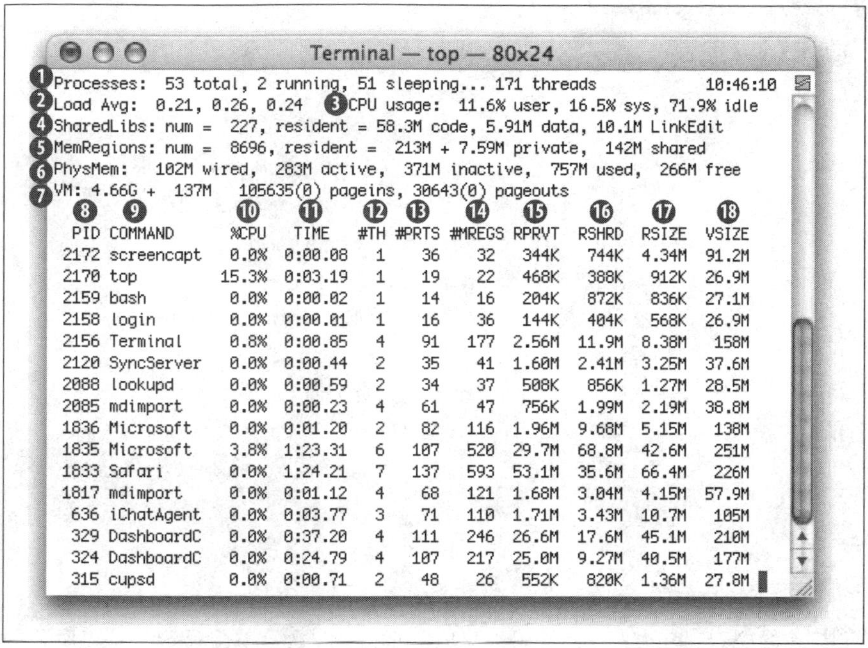

```
Terminal — top — 80x24
Processes:  53 total, 2 running, 51 sleeping... 171 threads            10:46:10
Load Avg:  0.21, 0.26, 0.24   CPU usage:  11.6% user, 16.5% sys, 71.9% idle
SharedLibs: num =  227, resident = 58.3M code, 5.91M data, 10.1M LinkEdit
MemRegions: num =  8696, resident =  213M + 7.59M private,  142M shared
PhysMem:   102M wired,  283M active,  371M inactive,  757M used,  266M free
VM: 4.66G +  137M   105635(0) pageins, 30643(0) pageouts

  PID COMMAND      %CPU   TIME   #TH #PRTS #MREGS RPRVT  RSHRD  RSIZE  VSIZE
 2172 screencapt   0.0%  0:00.08   1    36    32   344K   744K  4.34M  91.2M
 2170 top         15.3%  0:03.19   1    19    22   468K   388K   912K  26.9M
 2159 bash         0.0%  0:00.02   1    14    16   204K   872K   836K  27.1M
 2158 login        0.0%  0:00.01   1    16    36   144K   404K   568K  26.9M
 2156 Terminal     0.8%  0:00.85   4    91   177  2.56M  11.9M  8.38M   158M
 2120 SyncServer   0.0%  0:00.44   2    35    41  1.60M  2.41M  3.25M  37.6M
 2088 lookupd      0.0%  0:00.59   2    34    37   508K   856K  1.27M  28.5M
 2085 mdimport     0.0%  0:00.23   4    61    47   756K  1.99M  2.19M  38.8M
 1836 Microsoft    0.0%  0:01.20   2    82   116  1.96M  9.68M  5.15M   138M
 1835 Microsoft    3.8%  1:23.31   6   107   520  29.7M  68.8M  42.6M   251M
 1833 Safari       0.0%  1:24.21   7   137   593  53.1M  35.6M  66.4M   226M
 1817 mdimport     0.0%  0:01.12   4    68   121  1.68M  3.04M  4.15M  57.9M
  636 iChatAgent   0.0%  0:03.77   3    71   110  1.71M  3.43M  10.7M   105M
  329 DashboardC   0.0%  0:37.20   4   111   246  26.6M  17.6M  45.1M   210M
  324 DashboardC   0.0%  0:24.79   4   107   217  25.0M  9.27M  40.5M   177M
  315 cupsd        0.0%  0:00.71   2    48    26   552K   820K  1.36M  27.8M
```

Figure 17-1. Sample output from top

Table 17-1. Memory information displayed by top

Item number	Item	Description
1	`Processes`	Number of processes and threads. A running process is currently using CPU time, while a sleeping process is not.
2	`Load Avg.`	Average system load (the number of jobs vying for the CPU's attention) over the last 1, 5, and 15 minutes.
3	`CPU usage`	Breakdown of CPU usage, listing time spent in `user` mode, kernel (`sys`) mode, and `idle` time.
4	`SharedLibs`	Number of shared libraries in use, along with their memory utilization.
5	`MemRegions`	Number of Mach virtual memory regions in use, along with memory utilization details.
6	`PhysMem`	Physical memory utilization. Memory that is `wired` cannot be swapped to disk. `active` memory is memory that's currently being used, `inactive` memory is memory that Mac OS X is keeping "on deck" for processes that need it, and `free` memory is memory that's not being used at all.
7	`VM`	Virtual memory statistics, including the total amount of virtual memory allocated (the sum of the `VSIZE` in the process list), as well as paging activity (data paged in and out of physical memory).

Table 17-2. Process information displayed by top

Item number	Item	Description
8	PID	Process ID
9	COMMAND	Program's name
10	%CPU	Percentage of the CPU that the process is using
11	TIME	Total amount of CPU time this process has used
12	#TH	Number of threads in this process
13	#PRTS	Number of Mach ports
14	#MREGS	Number of memory registers
15	RPRVT	Resident private memory
16	RSHRD	Resident shared memory
17	RSIZE	Resident memory
18	VSIZE	Process's total address space, including shared memory

fs_usage

The *fs_usage* utility shows a continuous display of filesystem-related system calls and page faults. You must run *fs_usage* as *root*. By default, it ignores anything originating from *fs_usage*, *Terminal*, *telnetd*, *sshd*, *rlogind*, *tcsh*, *csh*, or *sh*.

Figure 17-2 shows the output of *fs_usage* monitoring the startup of a new *bash* shell, and displaying the following columns:

- Timestamp
- System call
- Filename
- Elapsed time
- Name of the process

latency

latency measures the number of context switches and interrupts, and reports on the resulting delays, updating the display once per second. This utility must be run as *root*. Example 17-1 shows a portion of its output.

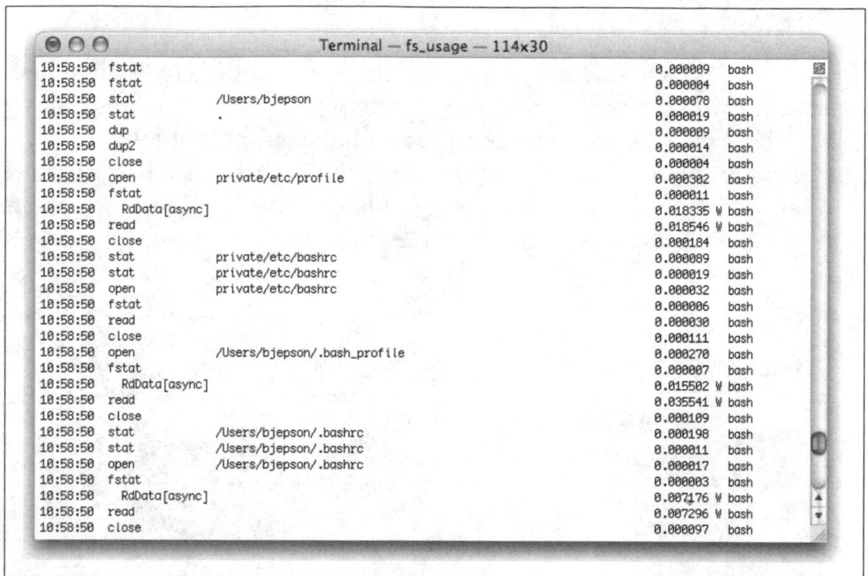

Terminal — fs_usage — 114x30
10:58:50 fstat 0.000009 bash
10:58:50 fstat 0.000004 bash
10:58:50 stat /Users/bjepson 0.000078 bash
10:58:50 stat . 0.000019 bash
10:58:50 dup 0.000009 bash
10:58:50 dup2 0.000014 bash
10:58:50 close 0.000004 bash
10:58:50 open private/etc/profile 0.000302 bash
10:58:50 fstat 0.000011 bash
10:58:50 RdData[async] 0.018335 W bash
10:58:50 read 0.018546 W bash
10:58:50 close 0.000184 bash
10:58:50 stat private/etc/bashrc 0.000089 bash
10:58:50 stat private/etc/bashrc 0.000019 bash
10:58:50 open private/etc/bashrc 0.000032 bash
10:58:50 fstat 0.000006 bash
10:58:50 read 0.000030 bash
10:58:50 close 0.000111 bash
10:58:50 open /Users/bjepson/.bash_profile 0.000270 bash
10:58:50 fstat 0.000007 bash
10:58:50 RdData[async] 0.015502 W bash
10:58:50 read 0.035541 W bash
10:58:50 close 0.000109 bash
10:58:50 stat /Users/bjepson/.bashrc 0.000198 bash
10:58:50 stat /Users/bjepson/.bashrc 0.000011 bash
10:58:50 open /Users/bjepson/.bashrc 0.000017 bash
10:58:50 fstat 0.000003 bash
10:58:50 RdData[async] 0.007176 W bash
10:58:50 read 0.007296 W bash
10:58:50 close 0.000097 bash

Figure 17-2. Monitoring filesystem operations with fs_usage

Example 17-1. Partial output from latency

```
Sat Apr  2 11:07:35                                    0:04:18
                     SCHEDULER     INTERRUPTS
---------------------------------------------
total_samples          209208         336535

delays <  10 usecs     183575         332310
delays <  20 usecs      11999           3197
delays <  30 usecs       2416            836
delays <  40 usecs       1289            158
delays <  50 usecs        624             25
delays <  60 usecs        492              6
delays <  70 usecs        323              2
delays <  80 usecs        329              1
delays <  90 usecs        280              0
delays < 100 usecs        235              0
total  < 100 usecs     201562         336535
```

The SCHEDULER column lists the number of context switches and the INTERRUPTS column lists the number of interrupts.

sc_usage

The *sc_usage* utility samples system calls and page faults, then displays them onscreen. *sc_usage* must be run by *root* or by someone with superuser privileges. The display is updated once per second. You must specify a PID, a command name, or a program to execute with the *-E* switch. For example, to monitor the Finder, use *sudo sc_usage Finder*. Figure 17-3 shows the output of running *sc_usage* on the Finder. Table 17-3 explains *sc_usage*'s output.

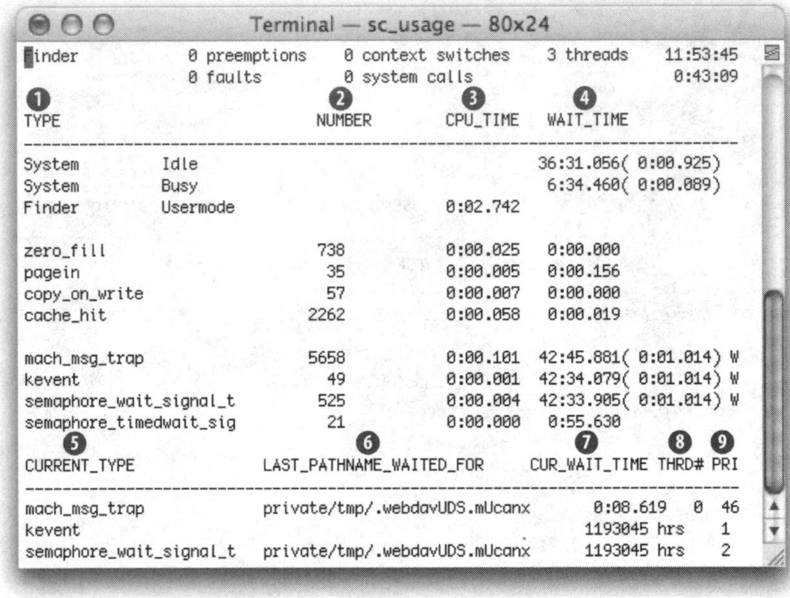

```
Terminal — sc_usage — 80x24
Finder          0 preemptions     0 context switches    3 threads     11:53:45
                0 faults          0 system calls                       0:43:09
❶                               ❷              ❸          ❹
TYPE                           NUMBER         CPU_TIME   WAIT_TIME
-------------------------------------------------------------------------------
System         Idle                                      36:31.056( 0:00.925)
System         Busy                                       6:34.460( 0:00.089)
Finder         Usermode                       0:02.742

zero_fill                         738         0:00.025   0:00.000
pagein                             35         0:00.005   0:00.156
copy_on_write                      57         0:00.007   0:00.000
cache_hit                        2262         0:00.058   0:00.019

mach_msg_trap                    5658         0:00.101  42:45.881( 0:01.014) W
kevent                             49         0:00.001  42:34.079( 0:01.014) W
semaphore_wait_signal_t           525         0:00.004  42:33.905( 0:01.014) W
semaphore_timedwait_sig            21         0:00.000   0:55.630
  ❺                                ❻                       ❼          ❽   ❾
CURRENT_TYPE              LAST_PATHNAME_WAITED_FOR     CUR_WAIT_TIME THRD# PRI
-------------------------------------------------------------------------------
mach_msg_trap             private/tmp/.webdavUDS.mUcanx      0:08.619   0   46
kevent                                                   1193045 hrs       1
semaphore_wait_signal_t   private/tmp/.webdavUDS.mUcanx  1193045 hrs       2
```

Figure 17-3. sc_usage monitoring the Finder

Table 17-3. Information displayed by sc_usage

Item number	Row	Description
1	TYPE	System call type
2	NUMBER	System call count
3	CPU_TIME	Processor time used by the system call
4	WAIT_TIME	Absolute time that the process spent waiting
5	CURRENT_TYPE	Current system call type

Table 17-3. Information displayed by sc_usage (continued)

Item number	Row	Description
6	LAST_PATHNAME_WAITED_FOR	Last file or directory that resulted in a blocked I/O operation during a system call
7	CUR_WAIT_TIME	Cumulative time spent blocked
8	THRD#	Thread ID
9	PRI	Scheduling priority

vm_stat

The *vm_stat* utility displays virtual memory statistics. Unlike implementations of *vm_stat* in other Unix systems, it does not default to continuous display. Instead, it displays accumulated statistics.

To obtain a continuous display, specify an interval argument (in seconds), as in *vm_stat 1*. Figure 17-4 shows the output of *vm_stat* with no arguments.

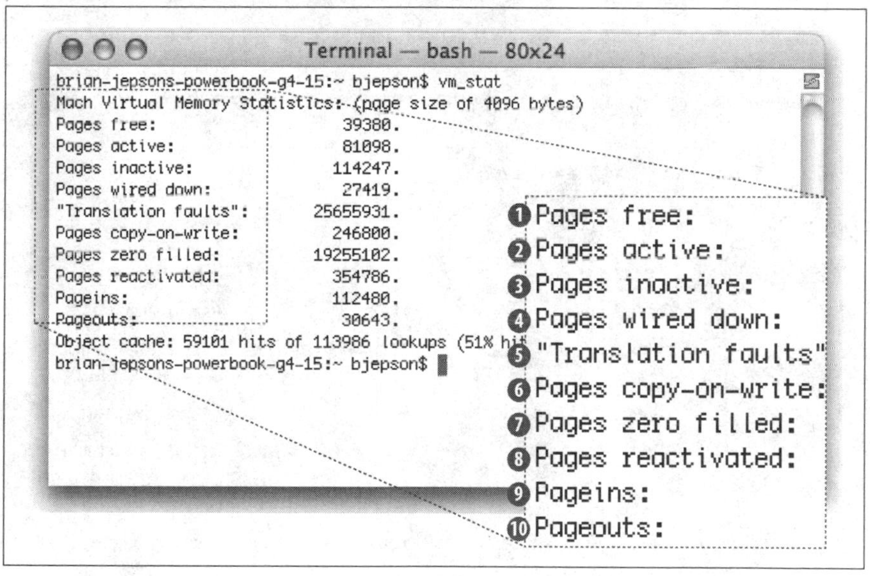

Figure 17-4. vm_stat displaying accumulated statistics

Figure 17-5 shows the output of *vm_stat 1*. Table 17-4 describes the information that *vm_stat* displays (the item numbers correspond to the callouts in both figures).

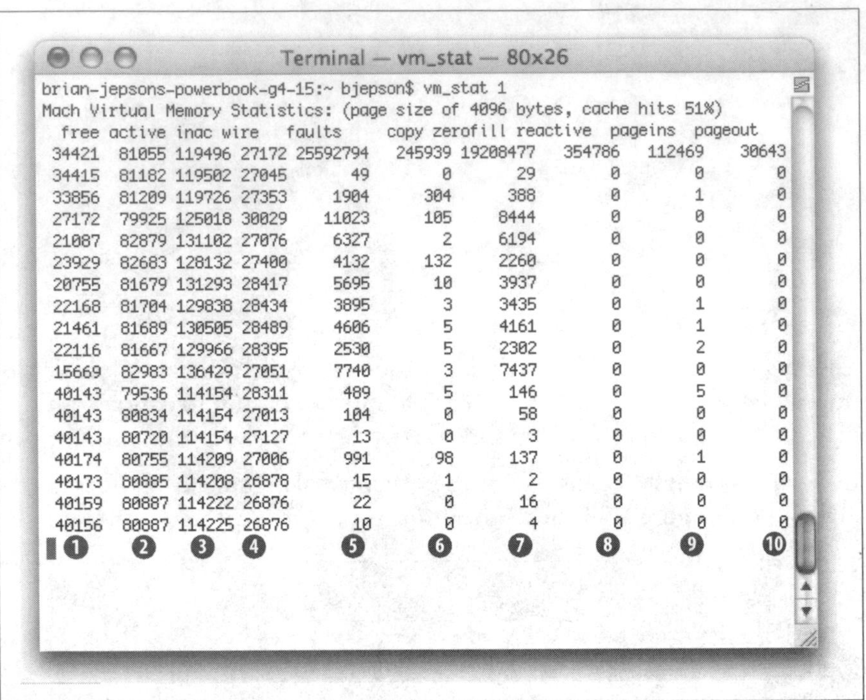

Terminal — vm_stat — 80x26
brian-jepsons-powerbook-g4-15:~ bjepson$ vm_stat 1
Mach Virtual Memory Statistics: (page size of 4096 bytes, cache hits 51%)
free active inac wire faults copy zerofill reactive pageins pageout
34421 81055 119496 27172 25592794 245939 19208477 354786 112469 30643
34415 81182 119502 27045 49 0 29 0 0 0
33856 81209 119726 27353 1904 304 388 0 1 0
27172 79925 125018 30029 11023 105 8444 0 0 0
21087 82879 131102 27076 6327 2 6194 0 0 0
23929 82683 128132 27400 4132 132 2260 0 0 0
20755 81679 131293 28417 5695 10 3937 0 0 0
22168 81704 129838 28434 3895 3 3435 0 1 0
21461 81689 130505 28489 4606 5 4161 0 1 0
22116 81667 129966 28395 2530 5 2302 0 2 0
15669 82983 136429 27051 7740 3 7437 0 0 0
40143 79536 114154 28311 489 5 146 0 5 0
40143 80834 114154 27013 104 0 58 0 0 0
40143 80720 114154 27127 13 0 3 0 0 0
40174 80755 114209 27006 991 98 137 0 1 0
40173 80885 114208 26878 15 1 2 0 0 0
40159 80887 114222 26876 22 0 16 0 0 0
40156 80887 114225 26876 10 0 4 0 0 0
1 2 3 4 5 6 7 8 9 10

Figure 17-5. vm_stat's continuous output

Table 17-4. Information displayed by vm_stat

Item number	Accumulated mode	Continuous mode	Description
1	`Pages free`	`free`	Total free pages
2	`Pages active`	`active`	Total pages in use that can be paged out
3	`Pages inactive`	`inac`	Total inactive pages
4	`Pages wired down`	`wire`	Total pages wired into memory (cannot be paged out)
5	`Translation Faults`	`faults`	Number of times *vm_fault* has been called
6	`Pages copy-on-write`	`copy`	Number of faults that resulted in a page being copied
7	`Pages zero filled`	`zerofill`	Number of pages that have been zero-filled
8	`Pages Reactivated`	`reactive`	Number of pages reclassified from inactive to active

Table 17-4. Information displayed by vm_stat (continued)

Item number	Accumulated mode	Continuous mode	Description
9	`Pageins`	`pagein`	Number of pages moved into physical memory
10	`Pageouts`	`pageout`	Number of pages moved out of physical memory

Kernel Utilities

Mac OS X includes various utilities that interact with the kernel. With these utilities, you can debug a running kernel, load and unload kernel modules or extensions, or set kernel variables.

ddb

The *ddb* utility can debug a running kernel. It is not included with the current version of Mac OS X. If you want to use *ddb*, you can find its source code in the *xnu* (Darwin kernel) source code (*http://www.opensource.apple.com/darwinsource/*).

ktrace

Use *ktrace* to perform kernel tracing (tracing system calls and other operations) on a process. To launch a program and generate a kernel trace (*ktrace.out*, which is not human-readable), use *ktrace command*, as in *ktrace emacs*. Kernel tracing ends when you exit the process or disable tracing with *ktrace -cp* `pid`. You can get human readable output from a *ktrace* file with *kdump -f ktrace.out*.

Kernel Module Utilities

The following list describes utilities for manipulating kernel modules. For more information, see the kernel extension tutorials available at *http://www.opendarwin.org/en/articles/*:

kextload
: Loads an extension bundle. Requires superuser privileges.

kextunload
: Unloads an extension bundle. Requires superuser privileges.

kextstat
: Displays the status of currently loaded kernel extensions. Table 17-5 describes this utility's output. Figure 17-6 shows sample output.

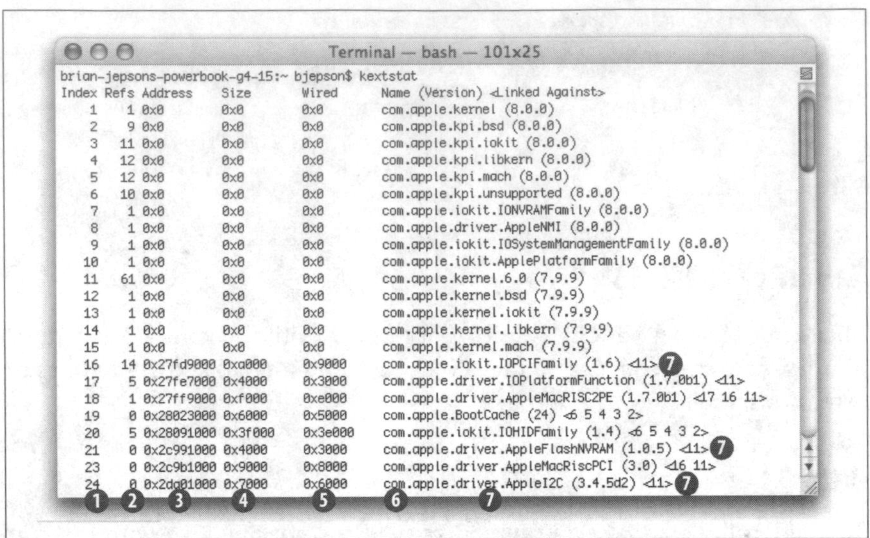

Figure 17-6. Partial output of kextstat

Table 17-5. Information displayed by kextstat

Item number	Column	Description
1	`Index`	Index number of the loaded extension. Extensions are loaded in sequence; gaps in this sequence signify extensions that have been unloaded.
2	`Refs`	Number of references to this extension from other extensions.
3	`Address`	Kernel space address of the extension.
4	`Size`	Amount of kernel memory (in bytes) used by the extension.
5	`Wired`	Amount of *wired* kernel memory (in bytes) used by the extension.
6	`Name (Version)`	Name and version of the extension.
7	`<Linked Against>`	Index of kernel extensions to which this extension refers.

sysctl

sysctl is a standard BSD facility for configuring kernel state variables. Use *sysctl name* to display a variable name, as in *sysctl kern.ostype*. Use *sysctl -a* to display all variables. If you have superuser privileges, you can set a variable with *sysctl -w name=value*.

Table 17-6 lists the *sysctl* variables on Mac OS X. See the *sysctl(3)* manpage for a description of the *sysctl* system call and more detailed information on the kernel state variables.

Table 17-6. sysctl's kernel state variables

Name	Type	Writable	Description
hw.activecpu	`int`	no	The number of CPUs currently active (may be affected by power management settings).
hw.availcpu	`int`	no	Number of available CPUs.
hw.busfrequency	`int`	no	Bus frequency in hertz. Divide by one million for a megahertz figure.
hw.busfrequency_max	`int`	no	Maximum bus frequency in hertz.
hw.busfrequency_min	`int`	no	Minimum bus frequency in hertz.
hw.byteorder	`int`	no	Variable that returns 4321, showing the ordering of four bytes on the PowerPC platform.
hw.cachelinesize	`int`	no	The cache line size in bytes.
hw.cpufrequency	`int`	no	CPU frequency in hertz. Divide by one million for a megahertz figure.
hw.cpufrequency_max	`int`	no	Maximum CPU frequency in hertz.
hw.cpufrequency_min	`int`	no	Minimum CPU frequency in hertz.
hw.cpusubtype	`int`	no	The mach-o subtype of the CPU (see */System/Library/Frameworks/Kernel.framework/Versions/A/Headers/mach/machine.h*).
hw.cputype	`int`	no	The mach-o type of the CPU.
hw.epoch	`int`	no	Variable that indicates whether your hardware is "New World" or "Old World." Old World Macintoshes (pre-G3) have a value of `0`.
hw.l1dcachesize	`int`	no	Level 1 data cache size in bytes.
hw.l1icachesize	`int`	no	Level 1 instruction cache size in bytes.
hw.l2cachesize	`int`	no	Level 2 cache size in bytes.
hw.l2settings	`int`	no	Level 2 cache settings.
hw.l3cachesize	`int`	no	Level 3 cache size in bytes.
hw.l3settings	`int`	no	Level 3 cache settings.
hw.logicalcpu	`int`	no	Number of logical CPUs.
hw.logicalcpu_max	`int`	no	Maximum number of available logical CPUs.
hw.machine	`string`	no	Machine class (*Power Macintosh* on most systems).
hw.memsize	`int`	no	Memory size.
hw.model	`string`	no	Machine model.
hw.ncpu	`int`	no	Number of CPUs.
hw.optional.altivec	`int`	no	Indicates whether AltiVec is enabled.
hw.optional.datastreams	`int`	no	Indicates whether PowerPC data stream instructions are supported by the CPU.

Table 17-6. sysctl's kernel state variables (continued)

Name	Type	Writable	Description
hw.optional.dcba	`int`	no	Indicates whether the PowerPC DCBA instruction is supported by the CPU.
hw.optional.floatingpoint	`int`	no	Indicates whether floating-point operations are supported by the CPU.
hw.optional.graphicsops	`int`	no	Indicates whether graphics operations are supported by the CPU.
hw.optional.stfiwx	`int`	no	Indicates whether the PowerPC STFIWX instruction is supported by the CPU.
hw.pagesize	`int`	no	Software page size in bytes.
hw.physicalcpu	`int`	no	Number of physical CPUs.
hw.physicalcpu_max	`int`	no	Maximum available physical CPUs.
hw.physmem	`int`	no	Physical memory in bytes.
hw.tbfrequency	`int`	no	The base frequency used by Mac OS X for its timing services.
hw.usermem	`int`	no	Non-kernel memory.
hw.vectorunit	`int`	no	Variable that indicates whether you are running on an AltiVec-enabled CPU.
kern.aiomax	`int`	no	Maximum AIO requests.
kern.aioprocmax	`int`	no	Maximum AIO requests per process.
kern.aiothreads	`int`	no	Maximum number of AIO worker threads.
kern.argmax	`int`	no	Maximum number of arguments supported by `exec()`.
kern.boottime	`struct timeval`	no	The time when the system was booted.
kern.clockrate	`struct clockinfo`	no	System clock timings.
kern.coredump	`int`	yes	Determines whether core dumps are enabled.
kern.corefile	`string`	yes	Location of core dump files (%P is replaced with process id).
kern.delayterm	`int`	unknown	Unknown or undocumented.
kern.dummy	`n/a`	n/a	Unused.
kern.hibernatefile	`string`	yes	Unknown or undocumented.
kern.hibernatemode	`int`	yes	Unknown or undocumented.
kern.hostid	`int`	yes	Host identifier.
kern.hostname	`string`	yes	Hostname.
kern.ipc.*	`various`	n/a	Various IPC settings.
kern.job_control	`int`	no	Variable that indicates whether job control is available.
kern.low_pri_delay	`int`	yes	Set/reset throttle delay in milliseconds.

Table 17-6. sysctl's kernel state variables (continued)

Name	Type	Writable	Description
kern.low_pri_window	`int`	yes	Set/reset throttle window in milliseconds.
kern.maxfiles	`int`	yes	Maximum number of open files.
kern.maxfilesperproc	`int`	yes	Maximum number of open files per process.
kern.maxproc	`int`	yes	Maximum number of simultaneous processes.
kern.maxprocperuid	`int`	yes	Maximum number of simultaneous processes per user.
kern.maxvnodes	`int`	yes	Maximum number of vnodes.
kern.netboot	`int`	no	Variable that indicates whether the system booted via NetBoot.
kern.ngroups	`int`	no	Maximum number of supplemental groups.
kern.nisdomainname	`string`	yes	NIS domain name.
kern.osrelease	`string`	no	Operating system release version.
kern.osrevision	`int`	no	Operating system revision.
kern.ostype	`string`	no	Operating system name.
kern.posix.sem.max	`int`	yes	Maximum number of POSIX semaphores.
kern.posix1version	`int`	no	The version of POSIX 1003.1 with which the system attempts to comply.
kern.saved_ids	`int`	no	This is set to `1` if saved set-group and set-user IDs are available.
kern.securelevel	`int`	increment only	The system security level.
kern.shreg_private	`int`	no	Indicates whether shared memory regions can be privatized.
kern.sugid_coredump	`int`	yes	Determines whether SUID and SGID files are allowed to dump core.
kern.sugid_scripts	`int`	yes	Determines whether to permit SUID and SGID scripts.
kern.symfile	`string`	no	The kernel symbol file.
kern.sysv.*	`various`	n/a	System V semaphore settings. See */System/Library/Frameworks/Kernel.framework/Versions/A/Headers/sys/sysctl.h*.
kern.sysv.shmall	`int`	yes	The maximum size of a shared memory segment.
kern.sysv.shmmax	`int`	yes	The maximum number of shared memory pages.
kern.sysv.shmmin	`int`	yes	The maximum number of shared memory segments per process.
kern.sysv.shmmni	`int`	yes	The maximum number of shared memory segments.
kern.sysv.shmseg	`int`	yes	The minimum size of a shared memory segment.

Table 17-6. sysctl's kernel state variables (continued)

Name	Type	Writable	Description
kern.usrstack	`int`	no	Address of USRSTACK.
kern.version	`string`	no	The kernel version string.
net.appletalk.routermix			Unknown or undocumented.
net.inet.*	`various`	n/a	IPv4 settings.
net.inet6.*	`various`	n/a	IPv6 settings.
net.key.*	`various`	n/a	IPSec key management settings.
net.link.ether.inet.*	`various`	n/a	Ethernet settings.
net.local.*	`various`	n/a	Various network settings.
user.bc_base_max	`int`	no	Maximum ibase/obase available in the *bc* calculator.
user.bc_dim_max	`int`	no	Maximum array size available in the *bc* calculator.
user.bc_scale_max	`int`	no	Maximum scale value available in the *bc* calculator.
user.bc_string_max	`int`	no	Maximum string length available in the *bc* calculator.
user.coll_weights_max	`int`	no	Maximum number of weights that can be used with `LC_COLLATE` in the locale definition file.
user.cs_path	`string`	no	Value for `PATH` that can find all the standard utilities.
user.expr_nest_max	`int`	no	Maximum number of expressions you can nest within parentheses using *expr*.
user.line_max	`int`	no	Maximum length in bytes of an input line used with a text-processing utility.
user.posix2_c_bind	`int`	no	Variable that returns `1` if the C development environment supports the POSIX C Language Bindings Option; otherwise, the result will be `0`.
user.posix2_c_dev	`int`	no	Variable that returns `1` if the C development environment supports the POSIX C Language Development Utilities Option; otherwise, the result will be `0`.
user.posix2_char_term	`int`	no	Variable that returns `1` if the systems supports at least one terminal type specified in POSIX 1003.2; otherwise, the result will be `0`.
user.posix2_fort_dev	`int`	no	Variable that returns `1` if the system supports the POSIX FORTRAN Development Utilities Option; otherwise, the result will be `0`.
user.posix2_fort_run	`int`	no	Variable that returns `1` if the system supports the POSIX FORTRAN Runtime Utilities Option; otherwise, the result will be `0`.

Table 17-6. sysctl's kernel state variables (continued)

Name	Type	Writable	Description
user.posix2_localedef	`int`	no	Variable that returns `1` if the system allows you to create locale; otherwise, the result will be `0`.
user.posix2_sw_dev	`int`	no	Variable that returns `1` if the system supports the POSIX Software Development Utilities Option; otherwise, the result will be `0`.
user.posix2_upe	`int`	no	Variable that returns `1` if the system supports the POSIX User Portable Utilities Option; otherwise, the result will be `0`.
user.posix2_version	`int`	no	Variable that returns the POSIX 1003.2 version with which the system attempts to comply.
user.re_dup_max	`int`	no	Maximum repeated occurrences of a regular expression when using interval notation.
user.stream_max	`int`	no	Maximum number of streams a process may have open.
user.tzname_max	`int`	no	Maximum number of types supported for a time zone name.
vfs.*	`various`	n/a	Various VFS settings.
vm.loadavg	`string`	no	Current load average.
vm.swapusage	`string`	no	Current swap file usage.

System Configuration

Although you can perform most system configuration through the System Preferences program, the *scutil* and *defaults* commands let you poke around under the hood. You can get even further under the hood with the *nvram* command (perhaps further than most people would need or want to get).

scutil

Mac OS X stores network configuration in a database called the dynamic store. You can get at this database using *scutil*, the system configuration utility. Before you can do anything, you must connect to the configuration daemon (*configd*) with the *open* command (*close* the session with the close command, and exit *scutil* with *quit*):

```
Chez-Jepstone:~ bjepson$ sudo scutil
Password: ********
> open
```

List the contents (a collection of keys) of the configuration database with the *list* command. The following shows abbreviated output from this command:

```
> list
  subKey [0] = DirectoryService:PID
  subKey [1] = Plugin:IPConfiguration
  subKey [2] = Setup:
  subKey [3] = Setup:/
  subKey [4] = Setup:/Network/Global/IPv4
  subKey [5] = Setup:/Network/HostNames
  subKey [6] = Setup:/Network/Interface/en1/AirPort
  subKey [7] = Setup:/Network/Service/48A67922-40FB-4FE0-B475-DEB8D9B2665C
```

You can show the contents of a key with the show command. The contents of a key are stored as a dictionary (key/value pairs). For example, here are the default proxy settings for built-in Ethernet on Mac OS X (to verify that Service shows a *UserDefinedName of Built-in Ethernet*, you should use *show Setup:/Network/Service/8D89866C-BFF5-4965-8BE8-A55DCDD4169F/Interface*—you will probably need to replace *8D89866C-BFF5-4965-8BE8-A55DCDD4169F* with a value obtained from the list command shown earlier):

```
> show Setup:/Network/Service/8D89866C-BFF5-4965-8BE8-A55DCDD4169F/Proxies
<dictionary> {
  ExcludeSimpleHostnames : 0
  AppleProxyConfigurationSelected : 2
  ProxyAutoDiscoveryEnable : 0
  FTPPassive : 1
}
```

Here are the proxy settings for a Mac OS X machine that's been configured to use a proxy server:

```
> show Setup:/Network/Service/8D89866C-BFF5-4965-8BE8-A55DCDD4169F/Proxies
<dictionary> {
  FTPPassive : 1
  ProxyAutoDiscoveryEnable : 0
  ExcludeSimpleHostnames : 0
  HTTPProxy : 192.168.254.201
  HTTPPort : 80
  AppleProxyConfigurationSelected : 2
  HTTPEnable : 1
}
```

To change an entry, lock the database, initialize an empty dictionary entry with *d.init*, and get the current values of the key you want to change:

```
> lock
> d.init
> get Setup:/Network/Service/8D89866C-BFF5-4965-8BE8-A55DCDD4169F/Proxies
```

Make your changes to the dictionary, then check them with *d.show*:

```
> d.add HTTPPort 8888
> d.add HTTPProxy proxy.nowhere.oreilly.com
> d.show
<dictionary> {
  FTPPassive : 1
  ProxyAutoDiscoveryEnable : 0
  ExcludeSimpleHostnames : 0
  HTTPProxy : proxy.nowhere.oreilly.com
  HTTPPort : 8888
  AppleProxyConfigurationSelected : 2
  HTTPEnable : 1
}
```

Currently, these changes are not kept permanently. To make permanent changes, use the System Preferences → Network user interface.

If you are happy with the dictionary values, set the key (this copies the dictionary into the specified key), unlock the database, and examine the key:

```
> set Setup:/Network/Service/8D89866C-BFF5-4965-8BE8-A55DCDD4169F/Proxies
> unlock
> show Setup:/Network/Service/8D89866C-BFF5-4965-8BE8-A55DCDD4169F/Proxies
<dictionary> {
  FTPPassive : 1
  ProxyAutoDiscoveryEnable : 0
  ExcludeSimpleHostnames : 0
  HTTPProxy : proxy.nowhere.oreilly.com
  HTTPPort : 8888
  AppleProxyConfigurationSelected : 2
  HTTPEnable : 1
}
```

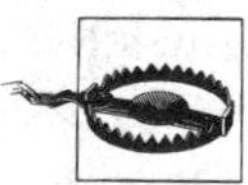

Be careful while the database is locked. If you try to do something seemingly innocuous, such as switching network locations, you could cause the system to behave erratically. It's best to get in and out of the database as quickly as possible.

defaults

When you customize your Mac using the System Preferences, most of those changes and settings are stored in what's known as the *defaults* system. Nearly everything that you've done to make your Mac your own is stored as a *property list* (or *plist*). This property list is, in turn, stored in *~/Library/Preferences*.

Every time you change one of those settings, that particular property list is updated. For the initiated, there is another way to alter the property lists: use the Property List Editor application (*/Developer/Applications/Utilities*) and the other is by using the *defaults* command in the Terminal. Whether you use System Preferences, or the *defaults* command, any changes you make affect the current user.

Using the *defaults* command is not for the foolhardy. If you manage to mangle your settings, the easiest way to correct the problem is to go back to that application's Preferences pane and reset your preferences. In some cases, you can use *defaults delete*, which will be reset to the same defaults when you next log in. Since the *defaults* command affects only the current user, you could also create a user just for testing random *defaults* tips you pick up on the Internet.

Here are some examples of what you can do with the *defaults* command. For more information, see the manpage.

View all of the user defaults on your system

```
$ defaults domains
```

This command prints a listing of all of the *domains* in the user's defaults system. The list you'll see is run together with spaces in between—not quite the prettiest way to view the information.

View the settings for the Dock:

```
$ defaults read com.apple.dock
```

This command reads the settings from the *com.apple.dock.plist* file, found in *~/Library/Preferences*.

Change your Dock's default location to the top of the screen

```
$ defaults write com.apple.dock orientation top
```

This command moves the Dock to the top of the screen underneath the menu bar. After changing this setting, you'll need to logout from the system and then log back in to see the Dock under the menu bar.

nvram

The *nvram* utility modifies Open Firmware variables, which control the boot-time behavior of your Macintosh. To list all Open Firmware variables, use *nvram -p*. The Apple Open Firmware page is *http://bananajr6000.apple.com/*.

To change a variable, you must run *nvram* as *root* or as the superuser. To set a variable, use *variable=value*. For example, to configure Mac OS X to boot verbosely, use *nvram boot-args=-v*. (Booting into Mac OS 9 or earlier will reset this variable.) Table 17-7 lists Open Firmware variables. Some variables use the Open Firmware Device Tree notation (see the technotes available at the Apple Open Firmware page).

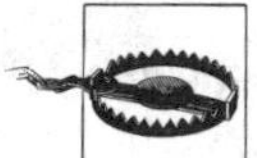

Be careful changing the *nvram* utility, since incorrect settings can turn an iMac G5 into a $2000 doorstop. If you render your computer unbootable, you can reset Open Firmware by zapping the PRAM. To zap the PRAM, hold down Option-⌘-P-R as you start the computer, and then release the keys when you hear a second startup chime. (If your two hands are busy holding down the other buttons and you have trouble reaching the power button, remember that you can press it with your nose.)

Table 17-7. nvram variables

Variable	Description
auto-boot?	The automatic boot settings. If `true` (the default), Open Firmware will automatically boot an operating system. If `false`, the process will stop at the Open Firmware prompt. Be careful using this with Old World (unsupported) machines and third-party graphics adapters, since the display and keyboard may not be initialized until the operating system starts (in which case, you will not have access to Open Firmware).
boot-args	The arguments that are passed to the boot loader.
boot-command	The command that starts the boot process. The default is *mac-boot*, an Open Firmware command that examines the `boot-device` for a Mac OS startup.
boot-device	The device to boot from. The syntax is *`device`*`:`[*`partition`*],*`path`*: *`filename`*, and a common default is `hd:,\\:tbxi`. In the path, `\\` is an abbreviation for */System/Library/CoreServices*, and `tbxi` is the file type of the *BootX* boot loader. (Run */Developer/Tools/GetFileInfo* on *BootX* to see its type.)
boot-file	The name of the boot loader. (This is often blank, since `boot-command` and `boot-device` are usually all that are needed.)
boot-screen	The image to display on the boot screen.
boot-script	A variable that can contain an Open Firmware boot script.
boot-volume	Unknown or undocumented.
console-screen	A variable that specifies the console output device, using an Open Firmware Device Tree name.
default-client- ip	An IP address for diskless booting.
default-gateway- ip	A gateway address for diskless booting.
default-mac- address?	Unknown or undocumented.
default-router- ip	A router address for diskless booting.
default-server- ip	An IP address for diskless booting.
default-subnet- mask	A default subnet mask for diskless booting.
diag-device	A private variable; not usable for security reasons.

Table 17-7. nvram variables (continued)

Variable	Description
diag-file	A private variable; not usable for security reasons.
diag-switch?	A private variable; not usable for security reasons.
fcode-debug?	A variable that determines whether the Open Firmware Forth interpreter will display extra debugging information.
input-device	The input device to use for the Open Firmware console.
input-device-1	A secondary input device (so you can have a screen and serial console at the same time). Use *scca* for the first serial port.
little-endian?	The CPU endianness. If `true`, initializes the PowerPC chip as little endian. The default is `false`.
load-base	A private variable; not usable for security reasons.
mouse-device	The mouse device using an Open Firmware Device Tree name.
nvramrc	A sequence of commands to execute at boot time (if *use-nvramc?* is set to `true`).
oem-banner	A custom banner to display at boot time.
oem-banner?	The `oem` banner settings. Set to `true` to enable the `oem` banner. The default is `false`.
oem-logo	A 64-by-64 bit array containing a custom black-and-white logo to display at boot time. This should be specified in hex.
oem-logo?	The `oem` logo settings. Set to `true` to enable the `oem` logo. The default is `false`.
output-device	The device to use as the system console. The default is `screen`.
output-device-1	A secondary output device (so you can have everything go to both the screen and a serial console). Use *scca* for the first serial port.
pci-probe-mask	A private variable; not usable for security reasons.
ram-size	The amount of RAM currently installed. For example, 256 MB is shown as `0x10000000`.
real-base	The starting physical address that is available to Open Firmware.
real-mode?	The address translation settings. If `true`, Open Firmware will use real-mode address translation. Otherwise, it uses virtual-mode address translation.
real-size	The size of the physical address space available to Open Firmware.
screen-#columns	The number of columns for the system console.
screen-#rows	The number of rows for the system console.
scroll-lock	Set by page checking output words to prevent Open Firmware text from scrolling off the top of the screen.
selftest-#megs	The number of MB of RAM to test at boot time. The default is `0`.
use-generic?	The device node naming settings. Specifies whether to use generic device node names such as "screen," as opposed to Apple hardware code names.
use-nvramrc?	The command settings. If this is `true`, Open Firmware uses the commands in *nvramrc* at boot time.

Table 17-7. nvram variables (continued)

Variable	Description
virt-base	The starting virtual address that is available to Open Firmware.
virt-size	The size of the virtual address space available to Open Firmware.

Third-Party Applications

Although you can perform system administration through the utilities supplied with Mac OS X, several third-party applications provide convenient frontends to these utilities:

Cocktail
: Kristofer Szymanski's Cocktail (*http://www.macosxcocktail.com/*) is a shareware application that provides a GUI frontend to a wide range of system administrative tasks and interface configurations.

GeekTool
: Tynsoe.org offers the free GeekTool (*http://projects.tynsoe.org/en/geektool/*), which can redirect the output of system logs, Unix commands, and dynamically generated images to the desktop.

MacJanitor
: Brian Hill's MacJanitor (*http://personalpages.tds.net/~brian_hill/macjanitor.html*) is a freeware application that does one thing and does it well: it runs the periodic jobs that are scheduled to run in the wee hours of the night by default (see "Scheduling Tasks" in Chapter 4).

TinkerTool System
: Marcel Bresink's TinkerTool System (*http://www.bresink.com/osx/TinkerToolSys.html*) is a shareware application that can do many things, including run the periodic jobs mentioned earlier, manage log files, and tune the network configuration.

CHAPTER 18

Free Databases

Although there are some great binary distributions for open source databases such as MySQL and PostgreSQL, both build out of the box on Mac OS X. This chapter describes how to install them from source and get them set up so you can start playing with them. Fink is a good first stop for MySQL or PostgreSQL, since you can use it to install a binary build or compile from source.

You can also get MySQL as a binary package from MySQL AB (*http://www.mysql.com*), as well as Server Logistics (*http://www.serverlogistics.com/*). Server Logistics offers a selection of open source packages, one of which is Complete MySQL (*http://www.serverlogistics.com/mysql.php*), which includes the MySQL server, a System Preferences pane for MySQL, ODBC/JDBC drivers, and documentation.

Another database worth considering is already installed on Mac OS X Tiger systems. SQLite, which is one of the key components of Tiger's Core Data Framework, is a self-contained embeddable SQL engine that's in the public domain. Since it's already there, and it's the simplest of the three, we'll look at SQLite first.

SQLite

SQLite is a public domain embeddable database that's implemented as a C library. In Mac OS X, it's also one of several backends used by the Core Data framework, which also uses XML and binary formats for storing persistent data.

Where to Find SQLite

You can find documentation, source code, and other SQLite resources at *http://www.sqlite.org*. However, Mac OS X Tiger includes SQLite 3 already installed. You'll find the header and library in the usual places (*/usr/include/sqlite3.h* and */usr/lib/libsqlite3.dylib*), and the command-line interface in */usr/bin/sqlite3*. Mac OS X Tiger also includes a Tcl (*/usr/lib/sqlite3/libtclsqlite3.dylib*) and PHP (*/usr/lib/php/DB/sqlite.php*) interface, and interfaces are available for many other languages.

Using SQLite

To use SQLite, simply start *sqlite3* with the name of a database file. If the file doesn't exist, it will be created. You can use standard SQL statements to create, modify, and query data tables. There are a number of non-SQL commands that start with a dot, such as the indispensable *.help* and *.quit*.

```
$ sqlite3 mydata.db
SQLite version 3.1.3
Enter ".help" for instructions
sqlite> CREATE TABLE foo (bar CHAR(10));
sqlite> INSERT INTO foo VALUES('Hello');
sqlite> INSERT INTO foo VALUES('World');
sqlite> SELECT * FROM foo;
Hello
World
sqlite> .quit
```

You can also issue SQL commands in one-liners from the shell prompt:

```
$ sqlite3 mydata.db 'SELECT * FROM foo;'
Hello
World
```

MySQL

To get the source distribution of MySQL, download the latest tarball from *http://dev.mysql.com/downloads/*.

At the time of this writing, we weren't able to get the most recent production version (4.1.*x*) of MySQL to compile out of the box on Mac OS X Tiger. We were able to get an earlier version (4.0.24) working, but we had to use the GCC 3.3 compiler. You can use the command `gcc_select 3.3` to specify the GCC 3.3 compiler or use this command under *sh* or *bash* to tell *configure* to use GCC 3.3:

```
CC=gcc-3.3 CXX=g++-3.3 ./configure \
  --prefix=/usr/local/mysql
```

Compiling MySQL

To compile MySQL from source:

1. Extract the tarball:

```
$ cd ~/src
$ tar xvfz ~/Desktop/mysql-4.0.24.tar.gz
```

2. Change to the top-level directory that *tar* created and run the *configure* script. We suggest specifying a prefix of */usr/local/mysql* so it stays out the way of any other binaries you have in */usr/local*.

```
$ cd mysql-4.0.24/
$ ./configure --prefix=/usr/local/mysql
```

3. Next, type *make* to compile MySQL. Go get a few cups of coffee (compiling could take 20 minutes or more).

Installing MySQL

If the compilation succeeded, you're ready to install MySQL. If it didn't succeed, you should first search the MySQL mailing list archives (*http://lists.mysql.com*) to see if anyone has reported the same problem you experienced, and whether a fix is available (otherwise, you should submit a bug report). If you're having a lot of trouble here, you may want to install one of the binary packages. If everything went OK, you can now install MySQL:

1. Run *make install* as root:

```
$ sudo make install
```

2. Install the default configuration file and databases:

```
$ sudo cp support-files/my-medium.cnf /etc/my.cnf
$ cd /usr/local/mysql
$ sudo ./bin/mysql_install_db --user=mysql
```

3. Set permissions on the MySQL directories:

```
$ sudo chown -R root  /usr/local/mysql
$ sudo chown -R mysql /usr/local/mysql/var
$ sudo chgrp -R mysql /usr/local/mysql
```

4. Now you're ready to install a startup script for MySQL. See "Startup Items" in Chapter 4 for a sample MySQL startup script. After you've created the startup script, start MySQL:

```
$ sudo SystemStarter start MySQL
```

Configuring MySQL

Next, you need to configure MySQL. At a minimum, set the root user's password and create a user and a working database for that user. Before using MySQL, add the following line to your *.bash_profile* and start a new Terminal window to pick up the settings:

```
export PATH=$PATH:/usr/local/mysql/bin
```

To set the root password and create a new user:

1. Use *mysqladmin* to set a password for the root user (qualified as *root@localhost* and just plain old *root*). When you enter the second line, there will be a root password in place, so you need to use *-p*, and you'll be prompted for the password you created on the first line:

   ```
   $ mysqladmin -u root password 'password'
   $ mysqladmin -u root -p -h localhost password 'password'
   Enter password: ********
   ```

2. Create a database for your user (you'll be prompted for the *mysql* root user's password):

   ```
   $ mysqladmin  -u root -p create dbname
   Enter password: ********
   ```

3. Log into the *mysql* shell as root, and grant full control over that database to your user, qualified both as *user@localhost* as well as the username alone (the -> prompt indicates that you pressed return without completing the command, and the *mysql* shell is waiting for more input):

   ```
   $ mysql -u root -p
   Enter password: ********
   Welcome to the MySQL monitor.  Commands end with ; or \g.
   Your MySQL connection id is 12 to server version: 4.0.16-log

   Type 'help;' or '\h' for help. Type '\c' to clear the buffer.

   mysql> GRANT ALL PRIVILEGES ON dbname.* TO username@localhost
       -> IDENTIFIED BY 'password';
   Query OK, 0 rows affected (0.08 sec)

   mysql> GRANT ALL PRIVILEGES ON dbname.* TO username
       -> IDENTIFIED BY 'password';
   Query OK, 0 rows affected (0.00 sec)
   ```

```
mysql> quit
Bye
```

Using MySQL

You should be able to log in to MySQL as the user defined in the previous section, and do whatever you want within your database:

```
$ mysql -u username -p dbname
Enter password: ********
Welcome to the MySQL monitor.  Commands end with ; or \g.
```

```
Your MySQL connection id is 16 to server version: 4.0.16-log

Type 'help;' or '\h' for help. Type '\c' to clear the buffer.

mysql> CREATE TABLE foo (bar CHAR(10));
Query OK, 0 rows affected (0.06 sec)

mysql> INSERT INTO foo VALUES('Hello');
Query OK, 1 row affected (0.00 sec)

mysql> INSERT INTO foo VALUES('World');
Query OK, 1 row affected (0.01 sec)

mysql> SELECT * FROM foo;
+-------+
| bar   |
+-------+
| Hello |
| World |
+-------+
2 rows in set (0.00 sec)

mysql> quit
Bye
```

PostgreSQL

To get the source distribution of PostgreSQL, download the latest tarball from *http://www.postgresql.org/download*. At the time of this writing, the latest release was 8.0.1, so we downloaded *postgresql-8.0.1.tar.bz2*.

Compiling PostgreSQL

Before installing PostgreSQL, you must install readline (*http://www.gnu.org/directory/readline.html*). This program enables support for command-line editing and history in the PostgreSQL shell (*psql*). Use *fink install readline* to install it, if you have Fink installed. To compile PostgreSQL from source:

1. Extract the tarball:

   ```
   $ cd ~/src
   $ tar xvfj ~/Desktop/postgresql-8.0.1.tar.bz2
   ```

2. Change to the top-level directory of the tar and run the *configure* script. We suggest specifying a prefix of */usr/local/pgsql* so it stays out the way of any other binaries you have in */usr/local*.

   ```
   $ cd postgresql-8.0.1/
   $ ./configure --prefix=/usr/local/pgsql \
   >   --with-includes=/sw/include --with-libs=/sw/lib
   ```

3. Next, type *make* to compile PostgreSQL. Go take a walk around the block while you wait (compiling could take 20 minutes or more).

Installing PostgreSQL

If everything went OK, you're ready to install. If it didn't go OK, check the PostgreSQL mail list archives (*http://www.postgresql.org/lists.html*) to see if anyone has reported the same problem you experienced and whether a fix is available (otherwise, you should submit a bug report).

1. Run *make install* as root:

```
$ sudo make install
```

2. Create the *postgres* group and user (this is the PostgreSQL superuser). Be sure to choose an unused group ID and user ID:

```
$ sudo niload group . <<EOF
> postgres:*:1001:
> EOF
$ sudo niload passwd . <<EOF
> postgres:*:1001:1001::0:0:PostgreSQL:/usr/local/pgsql:/bin/bash
> EOF
```

3. Create the data subdirectory and make sure that the *postgres* user is the owner of that directory:

```
$ sudo mkdir /usr/local/pgsql/data
$ sudo chown postgres /usr/local/pgsql/data
```

4. Use *sudo* to get a shell as the *postgres* user (supply your own password at this prompt):

```
$ sudo -u postgres -s
Password: ********
postgres$
```

5. Run the following commands to initialize the PostgreSQL installation:

```
$ /usr/local/pgsql/bin/initdb -D /usr/local/pgsql/data
```

6. You can now log out of the *postgres* user's shell.

Adding the Startup Item

Now you're ready to create a startup script for PostgreSQL (see "Startup Items" in Chapter 4). First, create the script shown in Example 18-1, save it as */Library/StartupItems/PostgreSQL/PostgreSQL*, and mark it as an executable.

Example 18-1. Startup script for PostgreSQL

```
#!/bin/sh

# Source common setup, including hostconfig.
#
```

Example 18-1. Startup script for PostgreSQL (continued)

```
. /etc/rc.common

StartService( )
{
    # Don't start unless PostgreSQL is enabled in /etc/hostconfig
    if [ "${PGSQL:=-NO-}" = "-YES-" ]; then
        ConsoleMessage "Starting PostgreSQL"
        sudo -u postgres /usr/local/pgsql/bin/pg_ctl  \
          -D /usr/local/pgsql/data \
          -l /usr/local/pgsql/data/logfile start
    fi
}

StopService( )
{
    ConsoleMessage "Stopping PostgreSQL"
    su postgres -c \
      "/usr/local/pgsql/bin/pg_ctl -D /usr/local/pgsql/data stop"
}

RestartService( )
{
    # Don't restart unless PostgreSQL is enabled in /etc/hostconfig
    if [ "${PGSQL:=-NO-}" = "-YES-" ]; then
        ConsoleMessage "Restarting PostgreSQL"
        StopService
        StartService
    else
        StopService
    fi
}

RunService "$1"
```

Next, create the following file as */Library/StartupItems/PostgreSQL/StartupParameters.plist*:

```
{
  Description     = "PostgreSQL";
  Provides        = ("PostgreSQL");
  Requires        = ("Network");
  OrderPreference = "Late";
}
```

Then, add the following line to */etc/hostconfig*:

```
PGSQL=-YES-
```

Now PostgreSQL will start automatically when you reboot the system. If you want, you can start PostgreSQL right away with:

```
$ sudo SystemStarter start PostgreSQL
```

Configuring PostgreSQL

Before you proceed, you should add the following line to the *.bash_profile* and start a new Terminal window to pick up the settings (you should also add this to the *postgres* user's *.bash_profile*):

```
export PATH=$PATH:/usr/local/pgsql/bin
```

By default, PostgreSQL comes with weak permissions; any local user can connect to the database without authentication. Before changing anything, you must start a shell as the *postgres* user with *sudo* and stay in this shell until the end of this section:

```
$ sudo -u postgres -s
Password: ********
postgres$
```

To start locking things down and to set up a non-privileged user:

1. Create the *postgres* user's home database

   ```
   $ createdb
   ```

2. Set a password for the PostgreSQL superuser:

   ```
   postgres$ psql -U postgres -c \
   >    "alter user postgres with password 'password';"
   ```

3. Under the default permissions, any local user can impersonate another user. So, even though you've set a password, it's not doing any good! You should edit */usr/local/pgsql/data/pg_hba.conf* to require MD5 passwords, give the *postgres* user control over all databases, and change the configuration so users have total control over databases that have the same name as their username. To do this, change *pg_hba.conf* to read:

   ```
   # TYPE DATABASE USER     IP-ADDR   IP-MASK                                 METHOD
   local  all      postgres                                                      md5
   local  sameuser all                                                           md5
   host   all      postgres 127.0.0.1 255.255.255.255                            md5
   host   sameuser all      127.0.0.1 255.255.255.255                            md5
   host   all      postgres ::1 ffff:ffff:ffff:ffff:ffff:ffff:ffff:ffff md5
   host   sameuser all      ::1 ffff:ffff:ffff:ffff:ffff:ffff:ffff:ffff md5
   ```

4. Once you've made this change, reload the configuration with *pg_ctl* (from here on in, you'll be prompted for a password when you run *psql* as the *postgres* user):

   ```
   postgres$ pg_ctl -D /usr/local/pgsql/data reload
   ```

5. Now you're ready to add a normal user. Use the *psql* command to create the user and a database. Because the username and database name are the same, that user will be granted access to the database:

   ```
   postgres$ psql -U postgres -c "create database username;"
   Password: ********
   CREATE DATABASE
   ```

```
postgres$ psql -U postgres -c \
>   "create user username with password 'password';"
Password: ********
CREATE USER
```

To give more than one user access to a database, create a group with the same name as the database (for example, *create group databasename*), and create users with the *create user* command as shown in step 5. Finally, add each user to the group with this command:

```
alter group databasename add user username
```

Using PostgreSQL

After configuring PostgreSQL's security and setting up an unprivileged user, you can log in as that user and play around with the database:

```
$ psql -U username
Password: ********
Welcome to psql 7.4, the PostgreSQL interactive terminal.

Type:  \copyright for distribution terms
       \h for help with SQL commands
       \? for help on internal slash commands
       \g or terminate with semicolon to execute query
       \q to quit

username=> CREATE TABLE foo (bar CHAR(10));
CREATE TABLE
username=> INSERT INTO foo VALUES('Hello');
INSERT 17148 1
username=> INSERT INTO foo VALUES('World');
INSERT 17149 1
username=> SELECT * FROM foo;
    bar
------------
 Hello
 World
(2 rows)

username-> \q
```

For more information on building and using PostgreSQL, see *Practical PostgreSQL* by John C. Worsley and Joshua D. Drake (O'Reilly). *Practical PostgreSQL* covers installing, using, administrating, and programming PostgreSQL.

PHP and Perl

On Mac OS X Panther, MySQL support is built in to PHP. If you want PostgreSQL support, you must reinstall PHP from source.

You can install general database support in Perl by installing the DBI module with the *cpan* utility. After that, you can install the DBD::mysql module for MySQL-specific support, and DBD::Pg for PostgreSQL-specific support. Because there are some steps to these installations that the *cpan* utility can't handle, you should download the latest builds of these modules from *http://www.cpan.org/modules/by-module/DBD/* and install them manually. Be sure to check the *README* files, since some aspects of the configuration may have changed.

The DBD:mysql module requires a database in which to perform its tests. You can use the database and username/password that you set up earlier in "Configuring MySQL." To install DBD::mysql, you must first generate the *Makefile*, compile the code, test it, and then install the module if the test run is successful. For example:

```
$ perl Makefile.PL --testdb=dbname --testuser=username \
>  --testpassword=password
$ make
$ make test
$ sudo make install
```

As with DBD::mysql, the DBD::Pg module needs a directory to perform its tests. If you'd like, you can use the database, username, and password that you set up earlier when configuring PostgreSQL.

You must first generate the *Makefile*, compile the code, set up environment variables that specify the database, username, and password, and then run the tests. If the tests run successfully, you can install DBD::Pg:

```
$ perl Makefile.PL
$ make
$ export DBI_DSN=dbi:Pg:dbname=username
$ export DBI_USER=username
$ export DBI_PASS=password
$ make test
$ sudo make install
```

CHAPTER 19

Perl and Python

As far as Perl and Python are concerned, Mac OS X is just another Unix. But there are some niceties and some quirks that make things a little different from the developer's perspective. In particular, much of Mac OS X's non-Unix APIs, such as Carbon and Cocoa, are accessible through extension modules in both languages.

We suggest limiting your customization of the Perl and Python that came with Mac OS X, since they are both fair game for modification during an upgrade or patch. You could either end up modifying something that the system depends on, or you could end up with a partially broken installation the next time Software Update performs a big Mac OS X update.

It's fine to install whatever modules you want, but if you choose to install a customized or newer version of either Perl or Python, install them in */usr/local* so they don't interfere with the ones in */usr*. Check the documentation (*INSTALL* or *README* files) that came along with the source code for any information specific to Mac OS X, and instructions for specifying an alternate installation prefix.

Perl for Mac OS X Geeks

The following sections list a few of the extras that come with Mac OS X. You can find these in */System/Library/Perl/Extras*, which is among the paths that the bundled version of Perl searches for modules.

Mac::Carbon

This module comes by way of MacPerl (*http://www.macperl.org*), a distribution of Perl for Mac OS 9 and earlier. Mac::Carbon (which is included with Mac OS X) gives Perl programmers access to the Carbon APIs. Its test suite is great; make sure you have your speaker volume turned up when you run it. One of the many modules included with Mac::Carbon is MacPerl; here's an example that pops up a dialog box and asks a question:

```
#!/usr/bin/perl -w

use strict;
use MacPerl qw(:all);

my $die_in_the_vacuum_of_space = 0;
my $answer = MacPerl::Ask("Tell me how good you thought my poem was.");
if ($answer =~
    /counterpoint the surrealism of the underlying metaphor/i) {
  $die_in_the_vacuum_of_space = 1;
}
print $die_in_the_vacuum_of_space, "\n";
```

For more information, you can access the Mac::Carbon documentation with `perldoc Mac::Carbon`.

PerlObjCBridge.pm

This module gives you a way to call into the Objective-C runtime on Mac OS X. Given an Objective-C call of the form:

```
Type x = [Class method1:arg1 method2:arg2];
```

you can use the equivalent Perl code:

```
$x = Class->method1_method2_($arg1, $arg2);
```

You could also create an `NSString` and display it with the following script:

```
#!/usr/bin/perl -w

use strict;
use Foundation; # import Foundation objects

my $string = NSString->stringWithCString_("Hello, World");
print $string, "\n";      # prints NSCFString=SCALAR(0x858398)
print $string->cString() , "\n"; # prints Hello, World
```

You can read the documentation for this module with `perldoc PerlObjCBridge`.

Mac::Glue

This module lets you invoke Apple Events from Perl. To use it with an application, you'll need to create a layer of glue between this module with the *gluemac* utility, which is installed along with Mac::Glue. For example, to create the glue for the Terminal application, do the following:

```
$ sudo /System/Library/Perl/Extras/bin/gluemac \
    /Applications/Utilities/Terminal.app/
Password: ********
What is the glue name? [Terminal]:
Created and installed App glue for Terminal.app, v1.5 (Terminal)
```

This also creates documentation for the module. To read it, use `perldoc Mac::Glue::glues::`*`appname`*, as in `perldoc Mac::Glue::glues::Terminal`.

Before you use Mac::Glue, be sure to run (as root) both the *gluedialect* and *gluescriptadds* scripts in */System/Library/Perl/Extras/bin*. These scripts create supporting files and OSA bindings for Mac::Glue.

Here's a short example that uses the Terminal glue to open a telnet session to the Weather Underground:

```
#!/usr/bin/perl -w

use strict;
use Mac::Glue;
my $terminal = new Mac::Glue 'Terminal';
$terminal->geturl("telnet://rainmaker.wunderground.com");
```

You can read the documentation for this module with `perldoc Mac::Glue`.

Python for Mac OS X Geeks

The following sections list a few of the Python extras that are available for or come with Mac OS X.

Carbon

As with Perl, you can access Carbon APIs from within Python. You can find a list of Carbon APIs with `pydoc Carbon`; short-named modules (such as CF) are usually the API you're interested in. The corresponding long-named module (such as CoreFoundation) will be the constants you need for the API. You can read documentation for a specific module with `pydoc Carbon.MODULE`, as in `pydoc Carbon.CF`.

Python also includes a number of other modules (have a look in */System/Library/Frameworks/Python.framework/Versions/2.3/lib/python2.3/platmac*), including EasyDialogs, which you can use to produce a Python version of the Perl example we showed earlier:

```
#!/usr/bin/pythonw

import EasyDialogs
import re

die_in_the_vacuum_of_space = 0
answer = \
  EasyDialogs.AskString("Tell me how good you thought my poem was.", "")
s = "counterpoint the surrealism of the underlying metaphor"
if re.compile(s).search(answer):
  die_in_the_vacuum_of_space = 1
print die_in_the_vacuum_of_space
```

Apple Events

Appscript (*http://freespace.virgin.net/hamish.sanderson/appscript.html*) is a bridge between Python and Apple Events that lets you write Python scripts in a very AppleScript-eqsue fashion. For example, consider the following snippet of AppleScript:

```
tell app "Finder" to get name of every folder of home
```

Using Appscript, you could write this as the following Python script:

```
#!/usr/bin/pythonw

from appscript import *
app('Finder').home.folders.name.get( )
```

At the time of this writing, we could not get Appscript to work under Tiger. We suggest that you check the Appscript home page and grab the latest version.

PyObjC

PyObjC (*http://pyobjc.sourceforge.net/doc/intro.php*) is a bridge between Python and Objective-C, and includes access to Cocoa frameworks, support for Xcode, and extensive documentation and examples. To install PyObjC, you can either download an installer from its web site, or grab the source code and run the command `sudo python setup.py bdist_mpkg --open`, which builds a metapackage and launches the Mac OS X installer on it.

Here's a very simple example that creates an NSString and prints it out:

```
#!/usr/bin/python

from Foundation import *
import objc

string = NSString.stringWithCString_("Hello, World")
print string # prints Hello, World
```

Once you've got PyObjC installed, check out the documentation in */Developer/Python/PyObjC/Documentation* and see the examples in */Developer/Python/PyObjC/Examples*.

PART V
Appendixes

These appendixes include miscellaneous reference information.

APPENDIX A
Mac OS X GUI Primer

If you're a Unix Geek who's new to Mac OS X, some of the terminology may not be that obvious. Although you know what most things do, you probably haven't connected them with their street names. This short appendix gets you up to speed with what everything's called, and provides some details on what each of them does.

Figure A-1 shows Mac OS X's desktop. Each numbered item is explained in the following list:

1. Legend has it that the Apple menu almost didn't survive the transition from the classic Macintosh operating system into Mac OS X, but that the cries of the faithful kept it there. This menu leads to more information about your Mac, quick access to Dock, Network, and System Preferences, as well as recently-opened documents and options for sleeping, restarting, and shutting down the system.
2. The menu bar is where the frontmost application's menus appear. Unlike Windows and Linux desktops like GNOME and KDE whose menus are attached to individual windows, Mac OS X's menu bar changes appearance and function based on which application is in the foreground.
3. Some parts of the operating system, including Bluetooth networking, AirPort, and your battery, install a menu extra in the rightmost side of the menu bar. Use these to check the status of these items and click the menu extra for a menu that lets you adjust things. Command-drag to rearrange your menu extras, or Command-drag an item off of the menu bar to consign it to oblivion (to bring it back, you'll need to poke around System Preferences to find the appropriate option). Notice that the username appears to the right if you have more than one user on the

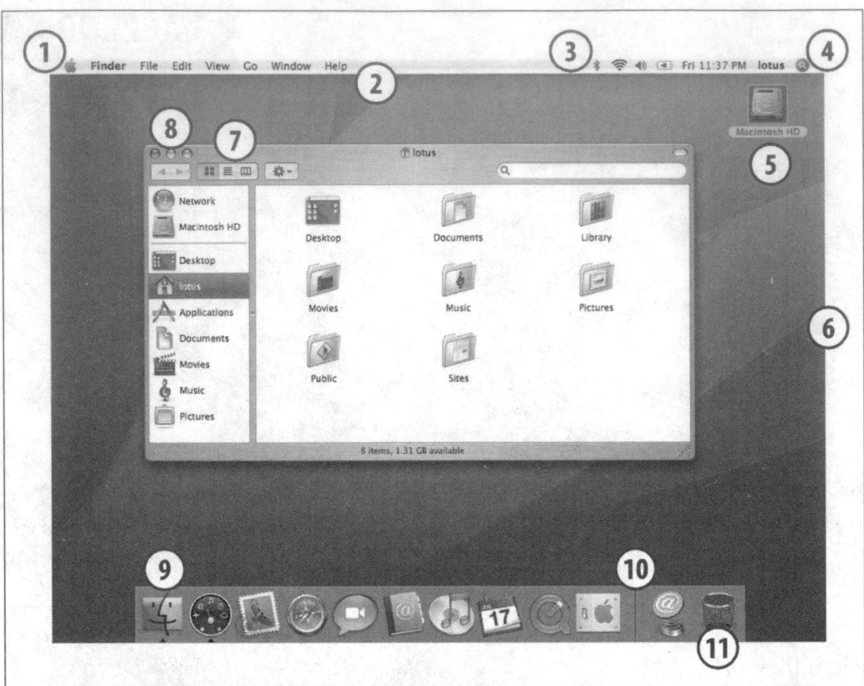

Figure A-1. The Mac OS X desktop

system and if you've enabled Fast User Switching (System Preferences → Accounts → Login Options). Click the name to login as another user while keeping your session active.

4. To the far right of the menu bar, Spotlight awaits your moment of need. For more information, see Chapter 2.
5. By default, all mounted volumes appear on the Desktop. You can unmount a volume by dragging it to the Trash (located at the far right edge of the Dock), or you can hide all of them by selecting Finder → Preferences → General → Show these items on the Desktop.
6. The Finder is your view on the filesystem. On the Finder's left edge is the Sidebar, which includes mounted volumes as well as a list of commonly-used directories. You can drag and drop items into this list.
7. The Finder has three views: Icon view (⌘-1), List view (⌘-2), and Column view (⌘-3). Use this widget to select which of the three views to use on a given window, or use the keyboard shortcuts to quickly switch views without using the mouse.

8. All windows have three buttons in the upper-left corner:
   - The red button closes windows
   - The yellow button minimizes windows to the right edge of the Dock
   - The green button zooms windows, expanding or reducing their size depending on their previous state.
9. The Dock contains the applications you need to use the most. The leftmost icon is always the Finder, followed by Dashboard, a new addition for Tiger. You can rearrange the others as you see fit, and drag new items onto the Dock. To remove an icon from the Dock, simply drag it off toward the Desktop and the icon disappears in a poof of smoke.
10. Drag the Dock separator up and down to resize the Dock. Control-click (or right-click) on it to adjust the Dock's options.
11. The right side of the Dock contains documents and the Trash. Drag files to the Trash to delete them, drag volumes to the Trash to unmount or eject them (in the case of optical or floppy disks), and Control-click (or right-click) the Trash when you want to empty it. You can add documents or directories to the right side by dragging them there.

The Finder's application menu also contains an option for Empty Trash, as well as the Secure Empty Trash option, which when selected, overwrites files in the Trash so many times that they're impossible to recover.

Empty Trash also has the Shift-⌘-Delete keyboard shortcut, while Secure Empty Trash has none. If you find yourself using Secure Empty Trash enough, you can add a keyboard shortcut for it in System Preferences → Keyboard & Mouse → Keyboard Shortcuts.

Click the Dashboard icon in the Dock (or press F12) to bring up Dashboard, an alternate universe that lurks under your Mac. In Dashboard, you'll find a set of "Widgets" that provide you with quick access to information such as time and date, weather, and a calculator. Dashboard, shown in Figure A-2, is explained in the following list:

1. The Calculator widget is one of four widgets visible on the screen right now. If you hover the mouse over a widget and a little *i* appears in the lower-right corner, you can click it to customize that widget.
2. This disclosure button shows and hides the list of additional widgets. When this list is active, a circled *x* appears in the upper-left corner of your current widgets; click this *x* to remove the widget.

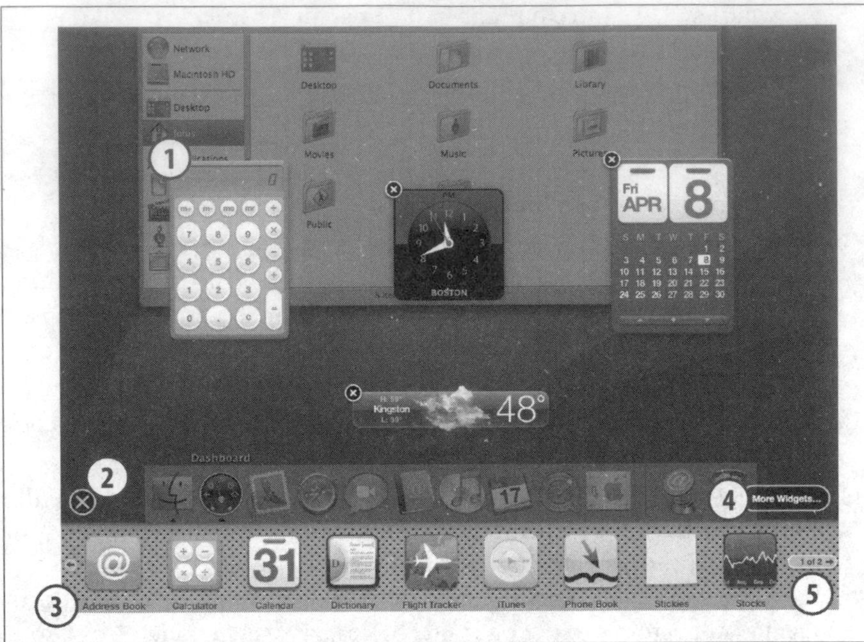

Figure A-2. Mac OS X Tiger's Dashboard

3. Choose a widget from this list and it immediately appears on the Dashboard.
4. There are more widgets available online (see *http://www.apple.com/macosx/dashboard*); click this button to open your browser up to Apple's list of additional Dashboard widgets.
5. If you've installed more widgets than can appear onscreen, click here to see them.

Dashboard lets you keep frequently-accessed information at your fingertips without cluttering up your Desktop. If there's a widget you want that doesn't already exist, all you need is a little JavaScript and HTML skill to build it. For more information on how to create your own Dashboard widgets, see *http://developer.apple.com/macosx/tiger/dashboard.html*.

APPENDIX B

Mac OS X's Unix Development Tools

The version of Unix that you'll encounter in Mac OS X's Terminal is similar to other versions you have seen, but dissimilar in some fundamental and often surprising ways. Although most tools are in their usual place, some are not on the system, while others are not where you would typically expect to find them on other Unix systems.

The lists shown in this Appendix contain a sampling of the Unix commands developers will find on Mac OS X. It is, by no means, a complete list of the Unix utilities found on your system. Because there are so many commands, they are organized into several categories. If you are an experienced Unix user, many of these commands will be familiar to you, but we've referenced them here so you can quickly determine whether a command you need is available. Unless otherwise specified, all of the tools in the following lists can be found in */usr/bin* or */usr/libexec*. Some tools are available with the standard distribution of Mac OS X, but others are available only after installing the Xcode Tools. (See Chapter 11 for more information about the Xcode Tools).

Standard Unix Development Tools

The following commands are development tools commonly found on most Unix and Linux systems:

bison
: *yacc*-compatible parser generator.

bsdmake
: BSD make program. Use this if you have any BSD makefiles.

cvs
: High-level revision control system that sits on top of RCS.

distcc

Frontend that distributes gcc builds across a network.

flex, flex++

A tool that generates lexical analyzers. See *lex & yacc* (O'Reilly).

cc, gcc

Apple's customized version of *gcc*, the GNU C compiler.

gdb

Source-level debugger.

gnumake, make

Automate the steps necessary to compile a source code package. GNU and BSD make are included. See *Managing Projects with make* (O'Reilly).

lex

Generates lexical analyzers. See *lex & yacc* (O'Reilly).

rcs

Manages file revisions.

Apple's Command-Line Developer Tools

The following are some of the utilities that are installed along with the Xcode Tools package. Most of them are found in */Developer/Tools* unless otherwise specified. Xcode depends on some of these tools; some of them have their roots in Macintosh Programmer's Workshop (MPW), which is Apple's old development environment.

agvtool

Acts as a versioning tool for Xcode projects.

BuildStrings

Creates resource string definitions.

CpMac

Serves as an alternative to *cp*; preserves resource forks when copying. As of Mac OS X Tiger, *cp* also preserves resource forks, so this is only included for compatibility with older scripts.

cvs-unwrap

Extracts a *tar* file created by *cvs-wrap*.

cvs-wrap

Combines a directory into a single *tar* file.

cvswrappers
Checks an entire directory into CVS as a binary file.

DeRez
Displays the contents of a resource fork.

GetFileInfo
Displays extended information about a file, including creator code and file type.

/usr/bin/leaks
Searches a process for memory leaks.

MergePef
Merges code fragments from one file into another.

MvMac
Serves as an alternative to *mv*; preserves resource forks when copying. As of Mac OS X Tiger, *mv* also preserves resource forks, so this is only included for compatibility with older scripts.

/usr/bin/opendiff
Graphical diff utility.

/usr/bin/otool, /usr/bin/otool64
Displays parts of object files and libraries in a friendly format.

packagemaker
Command line version of PackageMaker.app (see Chapter 15).

pbhelpindexer
Creates an index of Apple's API documentation for Xcode.

pbprojectdump
Used by Xcode's FileMerge feature to produce more readable diffs between file versions.

PPCExplain
Provides verbose descriptions of PowerPC assembler mnemonics.

ResMerger
Merges resource manager resource files. Xcode's build system compiles *.r* files into *.rsrc* files using *Rez*, and if needed, Xcode merges multiple files using *ResMerger*.

Rez
Compiles resource files.

RezWack
Embeds resource and data forks in a file.

/usr/bin/sdp
Converts a scripting definition file into another format.

SetFile
  Sets HFS+ file attributes.

SplitForks
  Splits the resource fork, moving it from a dual-forked file into a file named *._pathname*.

uninstall-devtools.pl
  Uninstalls Xcode and the rest of the developer tools.

UnRezWack
  Removes resource and data forks from a file.

WSMakeStubs
  Generates web service stubs from a WSDL file.

Macintosh Tools

The following tools work with Macintosh files, disks, applications, and the Mac's clipboard:

bless
  Makes a system folder bootable.

diskutil
  Manipulates disks and volumes.

ditto
  Copies directories, and optionally includes resource forks for copied files.

hdiutil
  Manipulates disk images.

installer
  Installs packages; command-line tool.

lsbom
  Lists the contents of a Bill of Materials (BOM) file, such as those deposited under */Library/Receipts*.

open
  Opens a file or directory. See "The open Command" in Chapter 1.

pbcopy
  Copies standard input to the clipboard.

pbpaste
  Sends the contents of the clipboard to standard output.

pstopdf
  Convert EPS and PS files to PDF format.

screencapture
  Takes a screenshot of a window or the screen.

sips
  Scriptable image processing system for altering image files.

Java Development Tools

Use the following tools to develop, debug, and run Java applications:

appletviewer
  Java applet viewer.

jar
  Java archive tool.

java
  Java Virtual Machine.

javac
  Java compiler.

javadoc
  Java documentation generator.

javah
  Generates C and header files for JNI programming.

javap
  Disassembles class files and inspects member signatures.

jdb
  Java Debugger.

jikes
  Fast open source Java compiler (installed as part of the Developer Tools package).

Text Editing and Processing

Use the following tools to edit, convert, and otherwise manipulate text:

awk
  Pattern-matching language for textual database files.

cut
  Tool that selects columns for display.

emacs
  GNU Emacs.

ex
: Line editor underlying *vi*.

fmt
: Produces roughly uniform line length.

groff
: Document formatting system that can render *troff* typesetting macros to PostScript, HTML, and other formats.

join
: Merges different columns into a database.

nano
: Simple text editor that's a clone of the pico editor.

paste
: Merges columns or switches their order.

pico
: Symbolic link to *nano*.

sed
: Stream editor.

texi2html
: Converts Texinfo to HTML.

tr
: Command that substitutes or deletes characters.

vim
: Visual text editor.

Scripting and Shell Programming

The following commands include shells and programs useful in shell scripts:

bash
: Bourne Again shell (default).

csh
: C shell.

echo
: Repeats command-line arguments on standard output.

expr
: Performs arithmetic and comparisons.

ksh
: The Korn shell.

line
: Reads a line of input.

lockfile
: Makes sure that a file is accessed by only one script at a time.

perl
: Practical Extraction and Report Language, Version 5.8.6.

php
: PHP scripting language Version 4.3.10, used for web development.

printf
: Formats and prints command-line arguments.

python
: Python scripting language, Version 2.3.5.

ruby
: Ruby scripting language, Version 1.8.2.

sh
: Standard Unix shell.

sleep
: Causes a pause during processing.

tclsh
: Tool Command Language (Tcl) shell, Version 8.4.

tcsh
: Tenex C shell.

test
: Command that tests a condition.

xargs
: Command that reads arguments from standard input and passes them to a command.

zsh
: Enhanced Unix shell.

Working with Files and Directories

Use the following tools to compare, copy, and examine files:

cat
: Concatenates and displays files.

cd
: Changes directory.

chflags
: Changes file flags.

chmod
: Changes access modes on files.

cmp
: Compares two files, byte-by-byte.

comm
: Compares two sorted files.

cp
: Copies files.

diff
: Compares two files, line-by-line.

diff3
: Compares three files.

file
: Determines a file's type.

head
: Shows the first few lines of a file.

less
: Serves as an enhanced alternative to *more*.

ln
: Creates symbolic or hard links.

Symbolic and hard links are not the same as Carbon aliases that you create in the Finder (File → Make Alias, or ⌘-L). Unix programs cannot follow Carbon aliases, but all Mac OS X applications (Carbon, Cocoa, Classic, and Unix) can follow symbolic or hard links.

ls
: Lists files or directories.

mkdir
: Makes a new directory.

more
: Displays files one screen at a time.

mv
: Moves or renames files or directories.

patch
: Merges a set of changes into a file.

pwd
: Prints the working directory.

rcp
: Insecurely copies a file to or from a remote machine. Use *scp* instead.

rm
: Removes files.

rmdir
: Removes directories.

scp
: Secures alternative to *rcp*.

sdiff
: Compares two files, side-by-side and line-by-line.

split
: Splits files evenly.

tail
: Shows the last few lines of a file.

vis
: Displays nonprinting characters in a readable form.

unvis
: Restores the output of *vis* to its original form.

wc
: Counts lines, words, and characters.

zcmp
: Compares two compressed files, byte-by-byte.

zdiff
: Compare two compressed files, line-by-line.

File Compression and Storage

The following tools can be used to compress, decompress, and archive files:

bzip2
: Compresses files.

bzip2recover
: Recovers data from corrupted *bzip2*-compressed files.

bzcat
: Displays contents of compressed files.

bunzip2
: Uncompresses a files that was compressed with *bzip2*.

compress
: Compresses files to free up space (use *gzip* instead).

cpio
: Copies archives in or out.

gnutar
: GNU version of *tar*; available only if you have installed the Developer Tools package.

gunzip
: Uncompresses a file that was compressed with *gzip*.

gzcat
: Displays contents of compressed files.

gzip
: Compresses a file with Lempel-Ziv encoding.

tar
: Tape archive tool. GNU *tar* has more features and fewer limitations.

uncompress
: Expands compressed (*.Z*) files.

zcat
: Displays contents of compressed files.

Searching and Sorting

You can use the following tools to search and sort files:

egrep
: Extended version of *grep*.

fgrep
: Searches files for literal words.

find
: Searches the system for filenames.

grep
: Searches files for text patterns.

locate
: Faster version of *find*; however, it depends on a database that is periodically updated by the weekly periodic job. If the database is out of date, *find* is more accurate.

sort
: Sorts a file (use *-n* for numeric sorting and *-u* to eliminate duplicates).

strings
: Searches binary files for text patterns.

uniq
: Reports or filters duplicate lines in a file.

unzip
: Extracts files from a Zip archive.

zgrep
: Searches compressed files for text patterns.

zip
: Creates a Zip archive.

Miscellaneous Tools

The following tools assist you with performing such tasks as searching online documentation, switching user IDs, and controlling how programs run:

apropos
: Locates commands by keyword.

clear
: Clears the screen.

dc
: Serves as a reverse-polish arbitrary precision calculator.

man
: Gets information on a command.

nice
: Changes a job's priority.

nohup
: Keeps a job running even if you log out.

passwd
: Changes your password.

script
: Produces a transcript of your login session.

su
: Allows you to become the superuser. Since the *root* account is disabled by default, you should use *sudo* instead.

sudo
: Executes a command as another user. This tool is usually used to temporarily gain superuser privileges.

Index

Symbols

Numbers

A

We'd like to hear your suggestions for improving our indexes. Send email to *index@oreilly.com*.

B

C

D

E

F

H

I

J

K

L

M

N

O

P

Q

R

S

T

U

V

W

X

Y

Z

About the Author

Brian Jepson is an O'Reilly editor, programmer, coauthor of all editions of *Mac OS X for Unix Geeks,* and coauthor with Dave Taylor on the Jaguar and Panther editions of *Learning Unix for Mac OS X* (O'Reilly). He's also a volunteer system administrator and all-around geek for AS220, a nonprofit arts center in Providence, Rhode Island. AS220 gives Rhode Island artists uncensored and unjuried forums for their work. These forums include galleries, performance space, and publications. Brian sees to it that technology, especially free software, supports that mission.

Ernest e. Rothman is an associate professor of mathematics and chair of the Mathematical Sciences Department at Salve Regina University (SRU) in Rhode Island. Like Brian, Ernie has coauthored every edition of *Mac OS X for Unix Geeks*. He holds a Ph.D. in Applied Mathematics from Brown University and held positions at the Cornell Theory Center in Ithaca, New York, before coming to SRU. His academic interests are in scientific computing, computational science, and applied mathematics education. As a longtime Unix aficionado, Ernie has enjoyed tinkering with Mac OS X since the day it was first released. You can keep abreast of his latest activities at *http://homepage.mac.com/samchops*.

Colophon

Our look is the result of reader comments, our own experimentation, and feedback from distribution channels. Distinctive covers complement our distinctive approach to technical topics, breathing personality and life into potentially dry subjects.

The animal on the cover of *Mac OS X Tiger for Unix Geeks* is a Siberian tiger. The Siberian tiger is the largest member of the cat family, including lions. A male averages 7 to 9 feet in length, and it usually weighs about 500 pounds. A female weighs slightly less, averaging about 300 pounds. This animal is native to Siberia and parts of China. Its fur color ranges from yellow to orange, with black stripes, although a few white tigers with black stripes have been spotted. The fur is long and thick, to help the animal survive its native cold climates. An interesting fact about tiger stripes is the pattern of each tiger's stripes is unique to that tiger. Therefore, stripes are a useful tool for identifying different tigers.

The Siberian tiger is endangered. Although there are about 1,000 living in captivity, only about 200 to 300 live in the wild. This is partly due to industrial encroachment on its natural habitat, limiting the tiger's hunting resources. Poaching is also a serious problem; in some areas of the world, tiger parts are thought to have great medicinal value, so these parts bring great financial gain to sellers.

Mary Brady was the production editor for *Mac OS X Tiger for Unix Geeks*. Katherine T. Pinard proofread the book. Genevieve d'Entremont and Mary Anne Weeks Mayo provided quality control. Lydia Onofrei provided production assistance. Ellen Troutman-Zaig wrote the index.

Ellie Volckhausen designed the cover of this book, based on a series design by Edie Freedman. The cover image is an original illustration created by Susan Hart. Karen Montgomery produced the cover layout with Adobe InDesign CS using Adobe's ITC Garamond font.

David Futato designed the interior layout. This book was converted by Keith Fahlgren to FrameMaker 5.5.6 with a format conversion tool created by Erik Ray, Jason McIntosh, Neil Walls, and Mike Sierra that uses Perl and XML technologies. The text font is Linotype Birka; the heading font is Adobe Myriad Condensed; and the code font is LucasFont's TheSans Mono Condensed. The illustrations that appear in the book were produced by Robert Romano, Jessamyn Read, and Lesley Borash using Macromedia FreeHand MX and Adobe Photoshop CS. The tip and warning icons were drawn by Christopher Bing. This colophon was written by Mary Brady.

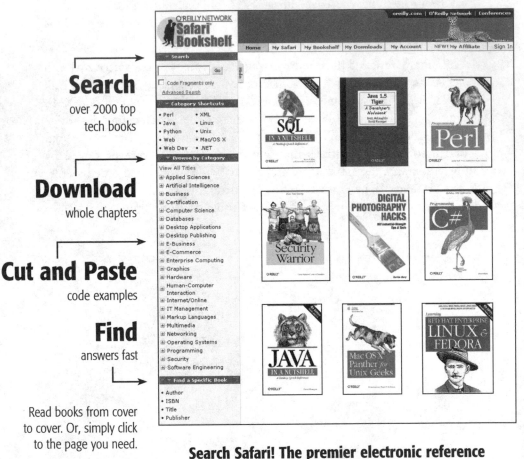

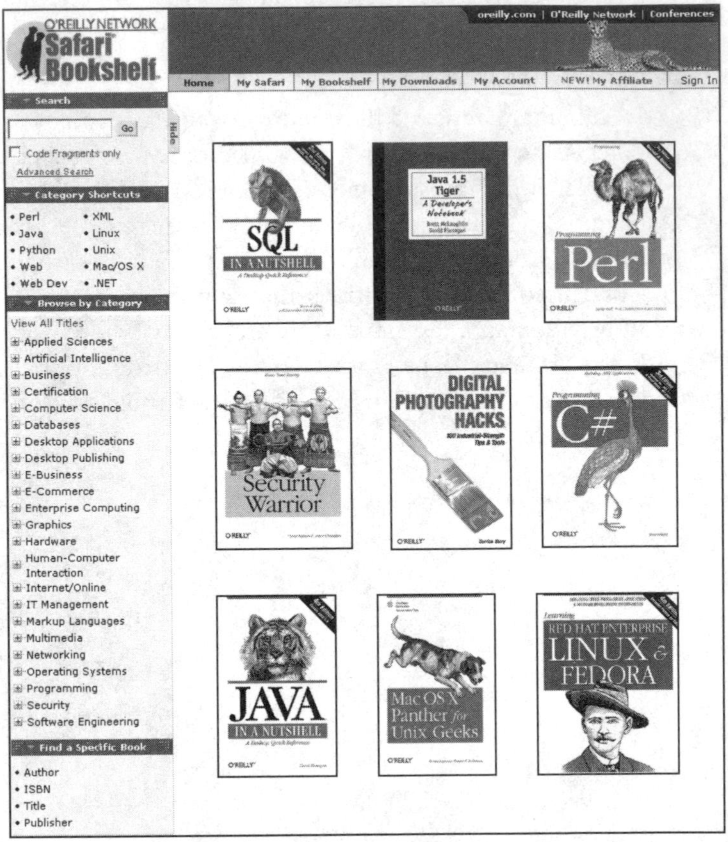